BY RACHEL L. SWARNS

American Tapestry:
The Story of the Black, White, and
Multiracial Ancestors of Michelle Obama

Unseen:
Unpublished Black History from the
New York Times Photo Archives

THE
272

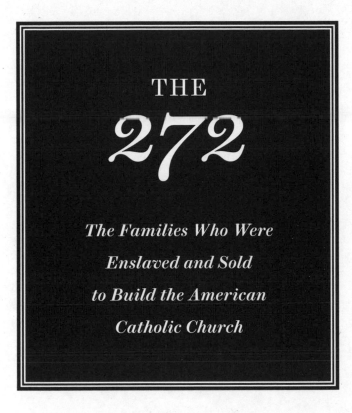

THE
272

The Families Who Were
Enslaved and Sold
to Build the American
Catholic Church

Rachel L. Swarns

RANDOM HOUSE
NEW YORK

For my parents

Contents

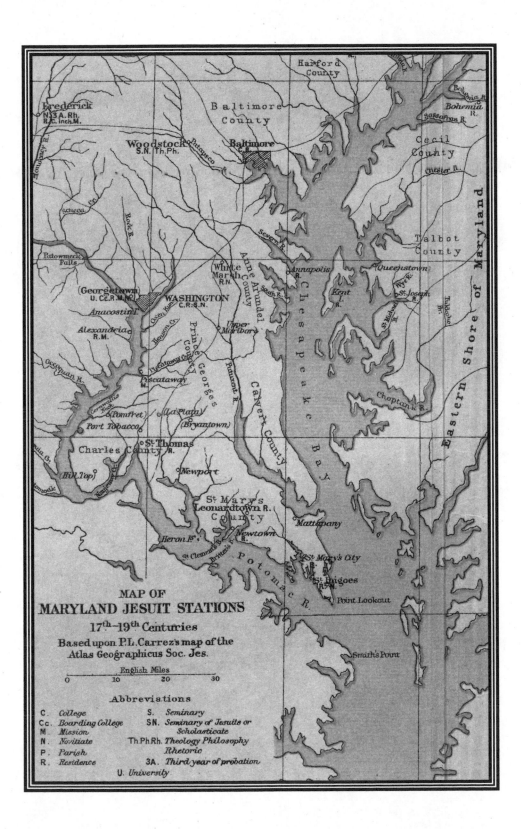

MAP OF
MARYLAND JESUIT STATIONS
17th–19th Centuries
Based upon P.L.Carrez's map of the
Atlas Geographicus Soc. Jes.

English Miles
0   10   20   30

Abbreviations

C.   College
Cc. Boarding College
M.   Mission
N.   Novitiate
P.   Parish
R.   Residence
U.   University

S.   Seminary
SN. Seminary of Jesuits or
       Scholasticate
Th.Ph.Rh. Theology Philosophy
       Rhetoric
3A. Third year of probation

Prologue

JEREMY ALEXANDER WAS SITTING IN HIS OFFICE WHEN HIS cell phone rang. It was 2016, the Wednesday before Thanksgiving. He was looking forward to heading home for the long weekend with his family, but he had been eagerly awaiting this call.

The woman on the line was someone who had connected with him on Ancestry, the genealogy website. Jeremy had submitted a DNA sample to Ancestry a few years earlier, hoping to find out more about his family's origins. He'd been born and raised in Chicago, but, like most African Americans, his family had roots in the South.

The caller's name was Melissa Kemp, and she was from Maryland. She had emailed him a few weeks earlier because she believed that they had a common ancestor, an enslaved woman who had been born in Maryland and sold to Louisiana. He was astonished. Could that be true?

"No way," he told her. "My family is all down south. There was never any discussion about a Maryland connection whatsoever."

They walked through what they knew about their forebears, untangling the branches of their family tree. Melissa thought the link might be a woman named Anna Mahoney Jones. Her own direct ancestor was an enslaved woman named Louisa Mahoney Mason. Louisa and Anna were sisters torn apart by a slave sale in 1838. Melissa asked if he had heard about the story in *The New York Times* earlier that year that had described the sale: 272 men, women, and children had been sold by the nation's most prominent Jesuit priests to save Georgetown University, the nation's first Catholic institution of higher learning. Some of those people, she told him, were probably his ancestors.

Jeremy was dumbfounded. Did he know about Georgetown? "Are you sitting down?" he asked her. At that very moment, he told her, he was at his desk in an office at Georgetown University, where he was an executive assistant in the college's office of technology commercialization. And Melissa was telling him that the Catholic priests who had founded the university—his employer—had owned and sold his ancestors. "I was completely in shock," he said. "Blown away."

THE STORY OF the sale that shattered the Mahoney family became national news in April 2016, when an article that I wrote—"272 Slaves Were Sold to Save Georgetown. What Does It Owe Their Descendants?"—appeared on the front page of *The New York Times*.

I had stumbled onto the story a few months earlier, when a colleague at the *Times* forwarded me an email from Richard J. Cellini, the chief executive officer of a technology company and an alumnus of Georgetown. Richard had become interested in the sale when students at Georgetown had organized a demonstration and a sit-in during the fall of 2015. The students were troubled that the names of the sales' main architects had been memorialized on two campus buildings. Georgetown's administration, which had several months earlier established a working group to find ways to acknowledge and make amends for its roots in slavery, had already been considering a name change and agreed to remove the names.

Jesuit scholars and historians of slavery were familiar with Catholic slaveholding. But public memory of that history had largely faded in the United States. As Richard followed the news of the protests from his home in Cambridge, Massachusetts, he began to wonder why so little was known about the #GU272, the group of enslaved people memorialized in a hashtag coined by the protesting students.

Richard was a well-to-do white lawyer and a practicing Catholic who had never spent much time considering slavery or racial injustice. But he found himself unable to stop thinking about the enslaved people who had been sold to save his alma mater, people whose names had languished in Georgetown's archives for decades. When he reached out to Professor John Glavin, a member of Georgetown's working group, to get more information about the people who had been sold, he was told that almost all of them had perished in Louisiana, leaving no descendants. Nearly three hundred had been sent south, and nearly every one of them had died? University officials say that no one in the university's leadership or in the working group's leadership believed that version of events. Richard didn't believe it either. It seemed completely implausible.

Within two weeks, he had set up an independent nonprofit, the Georgetown Memory Project, hired eight genealogists, and raised more than $10,000 from fellow alumni to finance their research. By the time my story ran, his team, led by the genealogist Judy Riffel, not only had determined that more than two hundred people had survived the voyage from Maryland to Louisiana but had identified a handful of living descendants.

"This is not a disembodied group of people who are nameless and faceless," Richard said. "These are real people with real names and real descendants."

My article was accompanied by a short companion piece, which invited readers to contact us if they believed they had a personal connection to the sale. More than a million people read the stories, including Melissa Kemp, Louisa Mahoney's great-great-great-great-granddaughter. And scores of those readers—who had lived for decades with holes in their family histories—reached out to us, saying that the articles had finally given them some vital information. But it also left them with agonizing, unanswered questions about their ancestors and the Church they loved.

Today, the Catholic Church is the largest religious denomination in the United States, with more than 60 million members, more than nineteen thousand parishes, and enormous influence in the nation's political, cultural, educational, and religious life. Americans often view it as a northern institution that has welcomed, educated, and nurtured waves of newcomers from Europe and Latin America. But there is a darker history both for the Church and for our country: For more than a century, the American Catholic Church relied on the buying, selling, and enslavement of Black people to lay its foundations, support its clergy, and drive its expansion. Without the enslaved, the Catholic Church in the United States, as we know it today, would not exist.

The priests in Maryland, who relied on the proceeds derived from slave labor and slavery, built the nation's first Catholic college, the first archdiocese, and the first Catholic cathedral and helped establish two of the earliest Catholic monasteries. Even the clergymen who established the first Catholic seminary operated a plantation and relied on enslaved laborers. The priests prayed for the salvation of the souls of the people they held captive, even as they sold their bodies. The 1838 slave sale that tore the Mahoney sisters apart helped save Georgetown from bankruptcy and helped stabilize the Jesuits in Maryland, aiding them as they established and supported new schools and colleges in the North that would educate generations of immigrants and their children and grandchildren.

Yet enslaved Black men, women, and children remain invisible in the origin story traditionally told about the emergence of Catholicism in the United States. Their stories are rarely recounted at Mass, in Sunday school, or in Catholic primary schools and colleges. Their joys and struggles, their determination to resist slavery, and their resilience in the face of it had long been mostly disregarded, if not forgotten, by the very institutions they were forced to serve. I have spent the better part of a decade poring over eighteenth- and nineteenth-century letters, tattered receipts, fraying ledger books, wills, and property records scattered in archives, courthouses, and historical societies trying to unearth and piece together their stories.

Along the way, I learned about Jeremy's and Melissa's ancestors, Anna and Louisa, the Mahoney sisters, who traced their lineage back to the 1600s, when the Jesuits and the family's matriarch, a free Black woman named Ann Joice, first arrived in Maryland. This book follows the family's trail from one generation to the next, starting with Ann Joice's arrival in the New World and moving on to her descendants, some of whom found their way to freedom while the rest lived with the agonizing knowledge that they might never enjoy liberty.

Often, though, the trail grows cold. The sisters' footsteps have faded over the course of centuries. Like other slaveholders, the Jesuits typically deprived the enslaved of the tools they'd need to write their stories. Denied literacy by priests who deemed them unworthy of an education, the Mahoney sisters, like millions of other enslaved people, were effectively silenced. As a result, there are questions about their lives that I cannot answer, personal experiences that I cannot depict. Sometimes, as I studied the spidery script of the Jesuits' handwritten letters, the sisters and their ancestors seemed like ghosts passing through this world, leaving barely a trace.

But some of the Mahoneys found a way to confound the priests and to preserve at least a portion of their history. They could not read or write, but they could speak. The elders passed their story on to their children, who passed it on to their children, who passed it on to their children, and on down, keeping elements of the saga alive, in some branches of the family, well into the twenty-first century.

The arc of the Mahoney family's experience—from their seventeenth-century enslavement, first by Catholic gentry and then, decades later, by Catholic priests, to their twenty-first-century negotiations with both the Church and Georgetown over reparations—tells the singularly American story of a country, and an institution, built on forced labor and its halting efforts to grapple with what some have described as our nation's original sin.

Their story also offers us a rare and layered portrait of an enslaved family, an enduring saga that helps illuminate the experiences of the millions of enslaved families whose stories remain untold. Both of the Mahoney sisters knew that the slave traders were coming for them that fall of 1838, but only one managed to escape. They would never see each other again. To understand their anguish and their fierce determination to survive, we need to understand their family's story. And to do that, we need to go back to the beginning.

THE
272

Arrivals

THE PRIESTS SAILING ON BOARD THE SHIP THAT CARRIED the first English settlers to Maryland feared they might not make it at all. The sea itself turned against them.

The ship, the *Ark,* was a modern marvel, four hundred tons of wood and iron. But it shuddered and keeled on its voyage as howling winds tore its mainsail and raging waters dislodged its rudder and swept the deck. There were some 140 souls on board: men and women, noblemen and indentured servants, Protestants and Catholics, adventurers and priests, all clinging to the vessel tossed by the raging sea.

Father Andrew White had envisioned the journey to Maryland as a divine mission to bring Christianity to a new world. But on that night, he feared that mission would end before it began, with the ship engulfed by the ocean.

So he prayed. He called to the heavens, describing the *Ark's* sacred mission, and promised to dedicate his life to bringing Catholicism to the native people. "I had scarcely ended," he marveled, when the winds began to subside and the ocean began to calm, sparing the ship.

The *Ark* stopped at Barbados, Guadeloupe, and Virginia. Then,

in March 1634, the ship sailed up the Potomac River and anchored
at a small island in Maryland that the priests named St. Clement's.
Disembarking, the voyagers found a land of oak and walnut groves,
verdant meadows, and flocks of herons that swooped and soared
over the shimmering waters. The men carved a rough cross from a
tree and fell to their knees as the Jesuit priest officiated at the first
Catholic Mass in the British colonies in America. "We erected it as
a trophy to Christ the Savior," wrote Father White, describing the
cross, "with great emotion of soul."

They had been sent to Maryland under the auspices of Cecil
Calvert, Lord Baltimore, a prominent English Catholic, who had
received permission from the king of England to establish a new
territory. English Catholics, viewed as disloyal to the monarchy because of their suspected allegiance to the pope, faced a raft of harsh
restrictions at home. They could be fined, imprisoned, deported,
even executed for practicing their faith. The new colony would be
a place where they could worship freely, a place where gentlemen
farmers and fortune hunters could acquire vast tracts of land, where
impoverished white women could work in households of the
wealthy and impoverished white men could work the fields and
then save to buy plots of their own.

Lord Baltimore would allocate more than twenty thousand acres
of the colony's land to the early Jesuits. In order to work the land,
they planned to rely on indentured servants—Father White brought
somewhere between twenty and forty-four with him on that first
voyage—and initially focused their evangelizing on the people indigenous to the region, the Piscataway. "We had not come thither
for the purpose of war, but for the sake of benevolence, that we
might imbue a rude race with the precepts of civilization, and open
up a way to heaven," wrote Father White with the characteristic
condescension common among Europeans at the time.

Nobody knew whether Catholicism would thrive or wither in
the fledgling colony in those early years, but the first reports weren't
promising. Four of the first fourteen priests to settle in Maryland

returned to England within a year. Four died of yellow fever. Three died in Virginia. One was killed in an accidental shooting. And two, including Father White himself, were shipped back home in chains when a Protestant uprising toppled Maryland's Catholic governor.

Still, White's fellow Jesuits continued to spread the faith, seeking converts among the native people, Protestant settlers, and newcomers who kept coming to the colonies hungry for opportunity and undeterred by the political tumult, hardship, and uncertainty they found there. Among them was Ann Joice, who arrived on a ship that pulled in to the wharf sometime around 1676. She was a teenager, and she had waited for weeks on the sea crossing to feel this new land under her feet. She would tell the people she met that she had been born in the tropics, in a slave society, and that she had ended up in England sometime in the mid-1600s. There, she told them, she had signed on as an indentured servant to Charles Calvert, the son of Cecil Calvert. The Calverts had regained control of the colony from the Protestants, and Charles had become Maryland's new proprietor.

The passing centuries have swept away much of her story. Her kinfolk no longer remember the name of the mother who bore her, the village that nurtured her childhood, or how she found her way to Europe. But they do know that she stepped off that ship dreaming of a new life. Black people, who first arrived as captives in the British colonies in 1619, were not always assumed to be slaves. And in the early decades following the Jesuits' arrival, Maryland had become a place where they could wrest some autonomy from employers and enslavers and savor a measure of independence and freedom.

Black people accounted for a tiny fraction of the population at the time—less than 1 percent in the 1660s and 1670s—and most of them, like Ann, had been born in the Caribbean or had spent time there or elsewhere in the Americas. Historians have described them as the charter generations, the first generations of Black people to establish roots in the British territory in the Chesapeake. Many spoke English, practiced Christianity, knew how to navigate life in the European colonies, and worked side by side with white laborers.

George Alsop, a white indentured servant who worked in Maryland, painted a rosy portrait of life there, one that might have appealed to a young Black woman dreaming of a better life for herself. He described fair-minded masters who allowed servants to rest indoors during sweltering summers and required little outdoor work during bitter winters. He pointed out that indentured servants who successfully completed their four- or five-year terms of service could become landowners in their own right, describing laws that required such servants to receive "Fifty Acres of Land, Corn to serve him a whole year, three Sutes of Apparel, with things necessary to them, and Tools to work with all" once their contracts ended. Such indentured servants would become "Masters and Mistresses" themselves, he wrote.

And if Ann had asked, the Catholics who arrived in Maryland with the first bands of English settlers might have offered, as proof, the story of a mixed-race man who had accompanied them, a man known as "Mathias Sousa, a Molato." De Sousa served the Jesuits for several years as an indentured servant and then set out on his own. Living as a free man, he entered into contracts, testified in court, led a trading expedition, and even joined free white men at a gathering of the General Assembly, the colony's legislative body, where he may have voted.

But de Sousa himself might have told Ann a different story. Hardship had cut his time as a free man agonizingly short. By 1641, he had fallen into debt and was forced back into indentured servitude. He might also have warned Ann of the threat to Black men and women in British America, which had only grown since his own arrival. In 1641, Massachusetts became the first British colony to recognize slavery as a legal institution. Connecticut followed in 1650. In 1662, Virginia's General Assembly passed a law that ensured that the children of an enslaved woman would also be slaves.

By 1664, Maryland had passed its own law, declaring that "all Negroes or other [slaves] already within [the colony] And all Negroes and other [slaves] to bee hereafter imported" would henceforth be considered slaves for life, as would their children. The situation on the ground was more complex. Some Black people—likely a small and rapidly shrinking number—continued to work as indentured servants, and some even took their employers to court to defend their rights. With Calvert, Lord Baltimore, himself as her patron, Ann may have felt confident that her work contract would be honored. But she lived in a time when blackness and slavery were quickly becoming synonymous.

Charles Calvert lived in a grand manor on a plantation in St. Mary's County known as Mattapany, near the mouth of the Patuxent River. Ann became a familiar figure in his home, tending to the kitchen and the table of the most prominent family in the colony even as she tended her own dreams. Some of the old-timers said that she was of mixed race, while others described her as "jet black." She was "a pretty woman," one recalled, born into "an East India family" who worked as either a cook or a maid. Ann told her children and grandchildren that the arrangement was meant to be temporary. Once she completed her term of indenture with Lord Baltimore, the Calverts would go their way and she would go hers.

In 1684, Calvert sailed home to England. He planned to return to Maryland, but in the meantime, he sent Ann to the home of his powerful cousin Colonel Henry Darnall, a wealthy Catholic who served as the colony's deputy governor, where she could complete her contracted service. Ann went, bearing her indenture papers and the promise from Calvert himself.

But the colony had dramatically curtailed the rights of Black people. Baptism or conversion to Christianity, once grounds for making a claim for freedom, no longer had any bearing on an enslaved person's status. White men were increasingly relying on enslaved workers, and some—including Colonel Darnall—viewed Black people's few remaining work contracts with contempt.

Ann's new home was in Prince George's County, at the Woodyard, Colonel Darnall's vast tobacco plantation. Darnall wore a cloth suit trimmed with gold, owned several wigs, and imported bricks from England to build his large brick mansion. A devout Catholic, he sent his sons to Jesuit schools in Europe and, as anti-Catholic sentiment in the colony mounted, kept a secret set of rooms in his home where his family could worship without fear of persecution. He owned more than thirty thousand acres of land, and he relied on enslaved laborers—more than a hundred in all—to keep it running.

Even as Ann worked there, alongside Black men, women, and children who knew they would never be free, she clung to Lord Baltimore's promise. And when she had completed her service, she went to Darnall and presented him with her contract.

Darnall had other plans.* On his plantation, Black people served for life, and he had no intention of letting Ann Joice go. As she later told her grandson, Darnall seized her indenture papers, the only tangible evidence of her free status, and set them on fire.

It was a shattering loss. No one knows whether Ann Joice raged or wailed or singed her fingers as she frantically tried to gather the burning scraps. But Darnall's next move suggests that she protested, as he shipped her away from his plantation, handing her over to another white man who would teach her what happened to Black people who forgot their place.

The man forced Ann into a dank kitchen cellar, imprisoning her underground so that she spent the passing seconds, hours, weeks, and months in the darkness. Her grandson, who would later recount this story in court, did not describe the details of her ordeal. He did not say whether she screamed, pounded her fists against the walls, or wept in the silence.

---

*Ann Joice was not the only one to accuse Darnall of violating the terms of her indenture. Darnall was sued by two Black people who accused him of disregarding their work contracts and forcing them into slavery. Ross Kimmel, "Blacks Before the Law in Colonial Maryland," MA thesis, University of Maryland, 1974, Maryland State Archives, https://msa.maryland.gov/msa/speccol/sc5300/sc5348/html/chap4.html.

. . .

BY THE LATE seventeenth century, Maryland had embraced the expansion of slavery, tying blackness to perpetual servitude. Prominent Catholics did so with the endorsement of Catholic leaders in Rome, who sanctioned the buying and selling of human beings who were, increasingly, of African descent. Some Catholics would cite St. Paul, who in Philippians urges Christ's followers to become slaves of God, just as Christ had done. In Ephesians, he offers Christians guidance on how to embody this principle within their relationships, including within the master-slave relationship. "Slaves, be obedient to your human masters with fear and trembling, in sincerity of heart, as to Christ," he advised. Many Catholics saw these passages as proof that slavery was ordained by God himself.

Other defenders of slavery pointed to early Catholic leaders such as St. Augustine,* who had noted that Christ "did not make men free from being slaves." At the time, men, women, and children of any race or tribe could find themselves in bondage. But to use this passage as justification was to ignore that slavery had become increasingly racialized as Europeans pressed into Africa and the Americas, seizing territory and enslaving the people of color they encountered.

Religion and conquest would go hand in hand, and at first, Church leaders frowned on the enslavement of Christians, regardless of whether they were African converts or Europeans. In 1435, Pope Eugene IV condemned the enslavement of the peoples of the Canary Islands since many of them had converted—or seemed likely to convert—to Christianity. "Some of these people were already baptized," he wrote, noting with concern that some had been subjected "to perpetual slavery." He ordered that they be restored to "their earlier liberty."

In a series of papal bulls, Pope Nicholas V made it clear that

---

* The preeminent theologian who served from A.D. 396 to 430 as bishop of Hippo in what is now Algeria.

nonbelievers were fair game. In 1452, the pope explicitly gave the king of Portugal the right to "invade, search out, capture, vanquish, and subdue all Saracens (Muslims) and pagans whatsoever . . . [and] to reduce their persons to perpetual slavery, and to apply and appropriate to himself and his successors the kingdoms, dukedoms, counties, principalities, dominions, possessions, and goods, and to convert them to his and their use and profit."

It would not be long before Spain, hungry for territory, gold, and labor of its own, followed suit. In 1493, just one year after Christopher Columbus landed in Hispaniola, the Spanish monarchs successfully pressed Pope Alexander VI for a similar dispensation, this time in the American "Indies." Thousands of Native Americans died in battles against the Spaniards. European diseases and harsh labor conditions killed many more. Those who survived were enslaved. But by the early sixteenth century, some priests would advocate for indigenous people in the Americas to be freed and replaced with Africans.

Father Bartolomé de las Casas, who arrived on the Caribbean island of Hispaniola in 1502, was greatly affected by the suffering of the enslaved indigenous people. He returned to Spain and in 1516 argued that Africans should replace Native Americans in the plantations and gold mines of the Americas. The shift, he said, would spare indigenous people from forced labor while increasing the profits of the Spanish Empire. The priest's ideas took root, lending credence to the racist idea that Africans, viewed as strong and beastly and thus more suited to a life of labor and subservience, should serve as enslaved laborers in the Americas. European powers used the Church's logic as a justification for their conquests in Africa and their increasingly lucrative trade in Black bodies.

In 1537, Pope Paul III condemned the notion that "Indians . . . should be treated as dumb brutes created for our service, pretending that they are incapable of receiving the Catholic Faith." On the contrary, he continued, "the Indians are truly men and that they are not only capable of understanding the Catholic Faith but, according to our information, they desire exceedingly to receive it." Thus, he wrote, indigenous people in the Americas were "by no means to be deprived of their liberty or the possession of their property." On the question of freedom and liberty for Africans, however, the Church's supreme leader remained silent. The Church's silence served as a sanction, and the clamor for Black enslaved workers grew. The "entire population . . . of Espanola, San Juan and even Cuba are demanding that they should have negroes to mine gold" and labor in the fields, Bishop Sebastián Ramírez de Fuenleal wrote.

Las Casas would come to publicly regret the role he had played in promoting the African slave trade. His subsequent readings about the exploitation of Africans left him convinced that the purchase, sale, and enslavement of Black people were little more than a "horror." But his change of heart had little impact.

The Jesuit order of priests, formally known as the Society of Jesus, was established by Ignatius of Loyola in 1540, just as slavery was expanding its reach. It would become the first Catholic order to embrace teaching as a key ministry, and it opened schools and sent priests around the globe. Its members would also defend, and participate in, the enslavement of Africans and their descendants. "It seems that nothing should be changed," argued Baltasar Barreira, an influential Jesuit who traveled to Africa and dismissed concerns about the legitimacy of the African slave trade in 1606.

Five years after the Jesuits arrived in Maryland, Rome once again condemned the enslavement of indigenous people. There was no criticism, however, of the brutal and bustling trade in Africans and the enslavement of growing numbers of Black people in the Americas. It would not take long for Catholics in Maryland to embrace the trade. European servants had become increasingly scarce, and the colony soon shifted from an indentured to an enslaved workforce.

Ann Joice spent five or six months as a prisoner in that basement, according to her grandson. When she finally emerged into the daylight, her transformation was complete. She was returned to Darnall and to the Woodyard plantation not as an indentured servant but as a slave.

As the years passed, Ann cooked for the Darnalls. White men were drawn to her, and, powerless to reject their advances, she became a mother, giving birth to several mixed-race children. One white woman, who remembered Ann in her later years, would describe her as "an elderly mulatto woman," who never "had any pretensions to freedom." Though that woman, who was a child when she met Ann, may have gotten that impression as she watched the enslaved woman bustle around the kitchen, Ann never forgot what she had lost. Somewhere along the way, she made a decision. She was enslaved, but she would not stay silent. She decided to tell her descendants and anyone else who would listen how the Catholic gentry of Maryland had stolen her freedom. Darnall had stripped her of everything. She would have no wealth, no land, and no savings to leave her family, but she still had her story. She would share it with her children and grandchildren, and they would pass it on from one generation to the next. *Our liberty was stolen. We should be free people.* That story would be her legacy.

A Church's Captives

OVER THE NEXT FEW DECADES, SLAVERY'S ROOTS DEEPENED and spread throughout British America. By the early 1700s, enslaved Black people accounted for between two-thirds and three-quarters of Maryland's workforce. And prosperous gentlemen farmers weren't the only Catholics adopting the system of forced labor.

In 1717, Father William Hunter, a prominent Jesuit priest, gave Bretton's Neck, a sprawling Maryland plantation controlled by his order, to a new owner. Along with the hogs and milk cows, candlesticks and chalices, he handed over fifteen Black men, women, and children. Hunter described the four men, four women, four boys, and three girls by name in the itemized list of his possessions: Will, Jack, Kitt, Peter, Mary, Teresa, Clare, Peggy, Jack, Clemm, Tomm, James, Betty, Cath, and Susan. The handwritten deed recording that transfer is the oldest known record of Jesuit slaveholding in Maryland.*

Mounting hostility toward Catholics in Maryland helped propel

---

* It is important to note that Catholics were far from the only religious denomination to embrace slavery. Protestants—including Quakers for a time—argued that Christianity and slavery were compatible.

the shift to a reliance on slave labor, particularly among the wealthy Catholics—gentry and priests—who dominated the rural economy. Having removed the Calverts from power, the colony's Protestant English leaders passed a series of discriminatory laws that targeted the Catholic minority, including a tax on the importation of "all Irish Papist Servants imported into the Province." Indentured servants could no longer be counted on as a reliable labor source.

The servant tax touched off fears that the Protestant Assembly might decide to confiscate the Jesuits' properties. So the priests transferred Church property, which they held under their own names, to Catholic laymen, who would serve as caretakers until the danger had passed. Within six years, once the threat of expropriation had passed, the property at Bretton's Neck formally passed back into Father Hunter's hands.

The threat of expropriation was only one of the many challenges Catholics faced. Maryland's Protestant leaders barred local Catholics from voting, holding public office, or serving on juries. Catholics were forced to practice their religion privately, and many chafed at the restrictions that forced them out of the political sphere. But they still belonged to the colony's social and economic elite, and the new laws did not prevent them from prospering. By the 1750s, half of the colony's wealthiest men were Catholic, even though Catholics accounted for only about 10 percent of the population.

Families such as the Carrolls, the Darnalls, the Diggeses, and the Bennetts amassed vast plantations worked by enslaved laborers. Ann Joice's children and grandchildren found themselves passed from one generation of Darnalls to the next, from one Catholic family to another. Precisely how Ann Joice's descendants ended up in the hands of the Jesuits remains unclear. But wealthy Catholics in Maryland were tightly knit, bound together by their shared faith, family ties, intermarriage, business partnerships, and Protestant discrimination. They didn't hesitate to support the priests with bequests of land and human property.

That was the case with James Carroll, a merchant, landowner, and slave trader who came from a devout Catholic family. Two of his nephews became Jesuit priests, as did his second cousin, once removed, who would become the first Catholic bishop in the new United States. So it was not surprising that in 1728, when Carroll wrote his will, he bequeathed more than a thousand acres of land in Anne Arundel and Prince George's counties to the Jesuit superior, George Thorold. The Jesuits also inherited his human property, who would become the nucleus of the slave community on a large Jesuit plantation in Prince George's County known as White Marsh.

Six years later, on a blank page in his almanac, Father Arnold Livers provided further details of the Jesuits' expanding slaveholdings. He listed twenty-seven enslaved people at Newtown plantation and twenty at St. Inigoes plantation, both in St. Mary's County. Ann Joice's descendants would find themselves enslaved at both White Marsh and St. Inigoes. It is likely that they, too, passed from prosperous Catholics to the priests who ministered to them.

But inheritance was not the only means of acquiring Black people. In 1756, the Jesuits purchased "a Negro man called Tom" for the Bohemia plantation in Cecil County. Five years later, the Jesuits at Bohemia paid cash for "a Negro-man named Charles."

By the mid-1700s, the Jesuit order had become one of the largest enslavers in Maryland. In an accounting sent to their leaders in London in 1765, the priests reported that they owned eight plantations with a total of 12,677 acres, 192 slaves, and a total income of £696 for the year. The plantations and enslaved workers sustained the Jesuits and their mission as they ministered to their scattered flock. The priests, the report said, typically spent two Sundays a month at their home plantations and the rest of the month tended to the spiritual needs of the ten thousand Catholics they served in Maryland and rural Pennsylvania, riding on horseback "as far sometimes as 20 or 30 miles" to say Mass, hear confessions, and offer the sacraments.

The Jesuits also felt responsible for the spiritual needs of their

Black captives. In 1749, Father George Hunter wrote that the "greater glory of God" required that all enslaved people be recognized as "members of Jesus Christ, redeemed by his precious blood." The Jesuits believed that the enslaved had souls that needed to be tended, and they often baptized and married enslaved people, emphasizing the sanctity of family bonds. They often required them to attend Mass and policed their behavior, chastising and at times punishing those who refused to embrace or abide by Catholic mores. The implicit contradiction in tending to the souls of people they'd designated as assets to be bought and sold rarely seemed to trouble the Jesuits, who seemed focused on surviving in a land that was often hostile to them.

For their part, enslaved men and women negotiated the religious demands of their Catholic enslavers in different ways. Some refused to accept the religion that the white men forced on them. Others, noting similarities between their own West African religious traditions and those of the Catholic faith, embraced a synthesis. In West African traditions, the religious constellation included a supreme being as well as lesser deities and ancestral spirits, who seemed akin to the Catholic saints, the Virgin Mary, and Jesus Christ, who interceded on behalf of mortals.

For some, Catholicism struck a deep chord, offering solace and a sense of community. Of the roughly twenty enslaved people at St. Inigoes between 1767 and 1769, fourteen were counted as members of the Catholic congregation. Whether they embraced the faith or joined for more pragmatic reasons remains unknown. But they surely found that they could use conversion, or the facade of conversion, and displays of public piety to improve their status and their circumstances. They knew that the priests were willing to impose harsh penalties on those who dared to flout Catholicism's moral code. When one priest discovered that enslaved parents on his plantation had engaged in marital infidelity, he sold their children as punishment.

· · ·

BY THE MID-1700S, Darnall's Woodyard plantation—and at least one of Ann Joice's descendants—had ended up in the hands of Stephen West, Jr., a wealthy Anglican merchant. West owned several stores, which sold household furnishings, furniture, tools, and jewelry. He also owned several ships, which he used to export tobacco and import goods from the West Indies.

West entertained on the estate, but he also manufactured cloth there—cotton, linen, and wool—and he invented a newfangled machine for spinning cotton that turned twenty-two spindles at once. To get the work done, the work in the fields as well as on the looms, he relied on slave laborers, including Tom Crane, one of Ann Joice's mixed-race descendants. Tom's brother Jack Wood may have worked at the Woodyard, too, perhaps hired out to West by another family.

Ann Joice was dead by then. But the brothers never forgot the stories she had passed on. They carried themselves with confidence and pride when they walked the plantation, and white people noticed.

"They thought themselves above the level of Common Slaves," recalled Peter Knight, a white man who knew them. Knight said that it was because they knew they "would have been free" if Darnall hadn't burned the contract that documented Ann Joice's indentured servitude. White people commented on the brothers' strength and physical prowess. One man described the brothers as "the strongest men he ever knew to come from one woman." Among the enslaved at the Woodyard, the two men were imposing figures. Tom was so fair skinned that he looked like a white man, and he and his brother made it clear that they would not be treated like human property.

In June 1770, the two brothers and another enslaved man were walking through the woods with one of West's overseers, a man named William Ellson, when tensions began to boil. Precisely what happened between the men remains in dispute. But a newspaper would later report that Ellson had "threatened to chastise" them for an unnamed offense. The men had refused to tolerate such treatment, the newspaper reported, and had beaten the overseer sense-less with a club.

The news of what happened next appeared in *The Maryland Gazette,* which described the attack as "a most horrid" event. "Supposing him dead, they carried him some distance and covered him with leaves," the newspaper reported, "but soon discovered that he had crept out of the place where they had put him." The *Gazette* reported that the white man had begged for his life, to no avail: Jack had cut his throat with a broadax, leaving him mortally wounded. The authorities arrested and indicted all three—Jack, Tom, and the third man, described only by his first name, Davy—on charges of premeditated murder.

On June 14, 1770, the enslaved men stood in court, accused of "being moved and seduced by the instigation of the Devil." Jack was charged with killing the overseer, while the others were accused of helping him. The newspaper didn't report the enslaved men's account of what happened in the woods, but all three men initially declared themselves innocent of the crime.

As time passed, though, that changed. Jack later confessed "frequently and willingly" to killing Ellson, court records show. Tom and Davy maintained their innocence, but another Black man, a witness in the case, described them as "aiders and abettors," testifying that they had tried to help conceal the crime.

What Jack and Tom said in court, how they described what happened that day, and how they defended themselves against the accusations remains unknown. Did the overseer attack the enslaved men in the woods? Was Jack coerced into confessing to the crime? Was the witness who had pointed the finger at Tom and Davy credible? A detailed transcript of the proceedings has yet to emerge, so these critical questions remain unanswered.

But there is no doubt that the killing of an overseer by slaves was the kind of crime that inspired outrage and fear in white communities. A panel of white jurors was called to hear the case. They listened to the evidence and rendered their decision that same month, finding all three of the enslaved men guilty of murder. The devastating news spread across Woodyard and the other plantations where Ann Joice's enslaved descendants lived and labored. But they were powerless to stop the horrifying spectacle about to unfold.

Among whites, there was little doubt about the appropriate sentence. The men had killed a white man and threatened to upend the social order of a community and a country reliant on the subservience of Black people. On July 2, 1770, the court issued the death warrants.

Two days later, Jack and Tom faced their punishment. A court official cut off their right hands. Then they were hanged. When their lifeless bodies were finally lowered to the ground, officials cut off their heads and quartered their bodies. Then, according to the court's orders, the bloody body parts of Wood, Crane, and Davy were displayed "in the most public places in this county."

Ann Joice's descendants would not regain the free status she had by rights conferred on them through violence. But they knew what they had lost, and they never stopped passing on the story of their stolen liberty.

IN 1773, POPE Clement XIV ordered the suppression of the Jesuit order, which by then was running more than eight hundred universities, seminaries, and secondary schools around the world. The move came in response to mounting opposition from a range of critics in Europe, including Catholic monarchs and statesmen who feared that the Jesuits' allegiance to the pope and the influence they wielded as the primary educators of Europe's nobility made them a dangerous and subversive force. The suppression order left the priests in Maryland "headless," as one scholar described them, cut off from their Jesuit leadership in Europe. Formally subject to a bishop in London, they became determined to chart their own course. Three years later, the rumble of war would shift the ground under their feet again.

Most Catholics supported the Revolutionary War. They saw opportunity in the vision and idealism expressed by men determined to build a country free from British rule. The country the revolutionaries envisioned might finally offer the kind of freedom and equality that had so far been denied them in colonial America. Charles Carroll of Carrollton, known as the wealthiest man in the colonies, became the only Roman Catholic to sign the Declaration of Independence. His cousin Father John Carroll accompanied Benjamin Franklin and others on a journey to Canada to try to persuade French Canadians to join their cause.

Their mission failed. But the American victory gave Father Carroll and other Catholics cause to celebrate as they watched the new nation embrace religious freedoms once unimaginable. Carroll marveled that "the fullest & largest system of toleration is adopted in almost all the American states: publick protection & encouragement are extended alike to all denominations & R[oman] C[atholics] are members of Congress, assemblies & hold civil & military posts as well as others."

The Catholic Church could finally dream openly about expansion. The first priority would be to establish new institutions, a college and a seminary, that would nurture a new generation of priests and extend the Church's influence in the new republic. "The object nearest my heart," Father Carroll wrote in 1783, "is to establish a college on this continent for the education of youth, which might at the same time be a Seminary for future Clergymen."

That same year, Carroll successfully pressed for a full meeting of the clergy, held at the White Marsh plantation, to discuss his plans. He viewed the plantations and enslaved workers, which had already financed the livelihoods of a generation of priests, as a critical funding stream for the Church as it began to grow and extend its influence.

The priests who gathered at White Marsh, in a series of meetings that took place over the next year and a half, would create a new organization, the Representative [or Select] Body of the Clergy.

The group, made up of six elected leaders, would oversee the plantations and the distribution of the income they produced. The priests decided that they would continue to control the land, property, and enslaved people they had amassed over the past century until and unless the Jesuit order was restored.

But even as Carroll began laying the groundwork for the new college, the former Jesuits' plantations and large slaveholdings, the foundation of the Church and its projects, began attracting criticism.

Father Patrick Smyth, an Irish priest who had spent time in Maryland, assailed the former Jesuits and their slaveholding in a pamphlet that circulated in Europe in 1788, just as Carroll was trying to raise funds from friends and supporters there. Smyth portrayed Carroll and the others as wealthy lords who prospered on their plantations, indifferent to the struggles of the Catholic faithful. "Are they obliged to live, like the apostles, by the work of their hands?" he asked. "No, they have a prodigious number of negroes, and these sooty rogues will not work, unless they be goaded, and whipped, and almost flayed alive. O God of Heaven!" he exclaimed. "Are your very ministers become taskmasters? They who should cherish the hapless African in their bosoms and share the sad burdens of his afflictions?"

Father Carroll dismissed the charges as baseless, countering that the clergy "treat their negroes with great mildness and are attentive to guard them from the evils of hunger and nakedness." He also emphasized the priests' efforts to nurture the spiritual lives of their slaves. "Besides the advantage of this humane treatment," he said of the enslaved, "they are instructed incessantly in their duties of Christianity and their morals watched, I may say, with fatherly solicitude."

But in Maryland, it was already clear that the financial needs of Carroll and the ex-Jesuits trumped any paternal feelings they might have had toward the people they held in bondage. By the time Smyth published his attack, the Select Body of the Clergy had proposed renting out slaves to help retire the plantations' debts. But the priests were interested in something far beyond maintaining what they had.

In January 1789, just four months before George Washington was inaugurated president of the United States, Carroll secured the deed to an acre of land atop a hill overlooking the village of Georgetown. There he meant to establish his academy, the nation's first Catholic institution of higher learning. He would describe the college as his greatest work. "I think I am rendering to Religion the greatest service, that will ever be in my power."

The priests had hoped to raise money for the college in Europe, but given Smyth's allegations against them, Catholic leaders in Rome had decided, at least for a time, against funding Carroll's new academy. "Amongst other difficulties, which we shall have to overcome in the undertaking of the academy, pecuniary resources will be a great one," Carroll wrote. ". . . The first expense of erecting proper buildings and securing the salaries for the Masters will be very great."

Carroll, who would become the nation's first Catholic bishop that same year, started a fundraising campaign "applied to the finishing of the Academy at Georgetown," but he knew that the lion's share of the financing for the new college would have to come from the priests' plantations and the labor of their enslaved workers.

At a meeting with Carroll at the White Marsh plantation, the priests gave their treasurer the authority to direct "all savings" from the general fund to the new college. Then they turned their attention to the Black men, women, and children they held captive, focusing not on their physical or spiritual needs but on how their labor and the sales of their bodies could be used to cover the mission's expenses. The priest who recorded the White Marsh discussion conveyed no emotion or moral anguish in describing the need to cull the stock of surplus—"supernumerary"—human beings. "That there being great danger of our Estates suffering from keeping supernumerary slaves, it is advisable & necessary to dispose of such as may be judged a burthen [burden]," he wrote.

The clergy directed the managers of the plantations to "determine on each plantation or settlement what is a sufficient number of slaves for the use & service of the said plantation, & that they be empowered, & are thereby directed to sell to the best advantage all that shall exceed that number." The managers were told to conduct a similar inventory every three years and "to dispose of them in the above manner."

In addition to paying off plantation debt and covering the cost of any needed repairs, the profits generated from the sale of human property were intended to flow into the province's general fund, which was funding the new academy. Even the salary of the academy's new president, who was yet to be chosen, was to be paid out of the income generated by one of the estates.

Fourteen months after the White Marsh meeting, enslaved people living on the Bohemia plantation began to vanish. Nell and her son, Perry, were sold for $4 in July 1790. That same month, the priest who ran the plantation received about £22 in partial payment for the sale of an enslaved woman named Esther. Sarah and Jerry, described as "a Negro girl" and "a negro boy" in the plantation's financial records, disappeared in January 1791, sold for £50. By March 1792, four more people were gone, handed over in exchange for a horse, blacksmith tools, and £112.

The flurry of sales initiated by the priests in the 1790s would ultimately tear more than two dozen enslaved people from their homes on the Bohemia estate. If the priests felt any angst over their departure, they seemed willing to live with it. By 1792, the priests, who had established a civil corporation—the Corporation of Roman Catholic Clergymen—to control and manage their properties, were turning to the plantations once again. They had decided to allocate any profits generated by the estates over the next three years to cover the costs of building a hall, a "study-place" and dormitories at Georgetown. By 1793, the enslaved people at Bohe-

mia had fallen under the control of the priests in charge of the nation's first Catholic seminary, St. Mary's, which opened its doors in
Baltimore in 1791, the same year that Georgetown received its first
students. George Washington would visit Georgetown's campus
himself several years later, and two of his grandnephews would join
the student body. The bishop's grand projects were finally taking
shape.

Carroll, whose own annual pension would be covered by the
profits from the plantations, had invited the Sulpicians, an order of
French priests, to open and run the new seminary. The Sulpicians
were given control of the Bohemia plantation and any "profit aris-
ing from the Bohemia estate." The French priests took stock and
over the next four years sold at least eleven people (men, women,
and children). The handwritten notations describing the sales are
spare. There are no surnames, no physical descriptions. And there
is no description of the terror that must have engulfed the plantation as people began to disappear one by one. In one instance, a
mother and her infant were sold to one buyer, while her four-year-
old daughter was sold to another.

The Church frowned on splitting up families and separating
spouses, and there is evidence that some of the priests took this into
account in managing their estates. But at Bohemia, financial necessity trumped both religious convention and the lives of the families
who supported the seminary. It was a harbinger of what was to
come.

The former Jesuits took note of what was happening at Bohemia
and at a meeting of the Corporation of Roman Catholic Clergymen in August 1795, they decided to admonish the Sulpicians. But
they weren't being reprimanded for selling Black people or breaking up families but for failing to hand over the profits.

The Black people at Bohemia—some forty-three in all—resisted
that harsh treatment. At least one woman ran away. Others refused
to follow orders, leading the overseer for the Sulpicians to grumble
about what he described as "the lack of docility and the very bad

behavior of the negroes who work there." The enslaved, the over-seer complained, were frustrating efforts to operate the plantation "on a sound financial basis." It was a sign of the times. White people were not the only ones inspired by the ideals of liberty and equality newly enshrined in the Declaration of Independence and the new Constitution.

Freedom Fever

FOR GENERATIONS, THE PRIESTS SPOKE OF THE BEAUTY OF St. Inigoes, the Jesuit plantation near the banks of the Potomac River in southern Maryland. Towering pine trees flanked the church and its soaring steeple, while tangles of sweet honeysuckle, flowering dogwoods, aromatic sassafras, and cedars adorned the two-thousand-acre estate. Larks and robins filled the mornings with their melodies, and perch, shad, and rockfish shimmered in the rushing waters. Visiting Jesuits stopped to marvel at the plantation's glorious sunsets that set the trees ablaze in "scarlets, reds, greens and yellows" during the waning days of summer.

In the late 1790s, a Joice descendant named Harry Mahoney worked the plantation's fields of golden wheat and leafy tobacco. Some of the priests who knew him called him "Big Harry" and his shoe size, 10.5, was recorded. Another priest described him as sickly, recalling the time tuberculosis had ravaged his body. In the decades to come, he would be remembered as a man with a sweet tooth and a taste for whiskey and as a leader among the enslaved. Most consistently, though, the priests described him as a loyal, faithful servant descended from a long line of faithful servants. They had forgotten, or did not know of, his family's long history of contesting their enslavement.

Harry watched the changing seasons, the migration of the geese, the priests who came and went. But while the Jesuits savored the sights, sounds, and profits of the estate, he and many of the other enslaved laborers at St. Inigoes listened for something else: the rumblings of resistance. All across the state, freedom fever was spreading. Even on the plantations that supported the priests and Georgetown, some Black people had begun to arm themselves, not with weapons but with lawsuits.

Emboldened by the egalitarian ideology of the Revolutionary War, hundreds of enslaved Black men and women had begun to fight for their freedom in Maryland's courts. Many argued that they were descendants of freeborn women and should never have been enslaved in the first place. And they swayed some white judges and juries who found the contradictions between the soaring language in the Declaration of Independence and the harsh realities of slavery increasingly difficult to reconcile.

On the White Marsh plantation, in 1791, enslaved members of the Queen family made that argument when they sued Father John Ashton for their freedom. Ashton, one of the founders of Georgetown College, enlisted some of the state's most prominent lawyers to handle his case. But the Queen family still triumphed in court and promptly celebrated by abandoning the estate and their lives of servitude. Harry Mahoney's kinsmen Charles and Patrick Mahoney were also owned by Father Ashton. They petitioned for their freedom that same year, declaring that they, too, had the right to live as free people because the freedom of their matriarch, Ann Joice, had been stolen. A legal victory on that basis would have meant freedom for the entire Mahoney clan.

Harry knew the story, passed down through the generations, that his family had been cheated out of its freedom by powerful Catholics. All of the Mahoneys, who were scattered across several Maryland plantations, knew it, and the hunger for reclaiming their liberty burned within them. The Mahoneys were mixed race with fair complexions, and light skin was often accompanied by privileged status. But when Harry chose a bride, he picked a recent arrival,

Anna, a dark-skinned woman born in Africa. The woman was an orphan who was treated badly on the plantation, and Harry felt sorry for her, one of his daughters would tell a priest decades later. But Harry also knew that Anna had something he did not: She had tasted freedom in her lifetime.

The couple slips into and out of the records collected by the priests over the years, surfacing at tax time, when the priest in charge of the plantation tallied the number of enslaved people he owned, and disappearing afterward. But others who lived at St. Inigoes later on have provided hints of what life was like for the Mahoneys. In the spring they would walk out of the slave quarters and see the peach orchards, with their sweet fruit ripening, and the apple orchards, with the fruit still to come. They would pass the brick barn and the cow house, where the cattle lowed and jostled. The manor house, where the priests lived, faced due south, near the weaver's home and the house where the plantation's meat was stored. The enslaved laborers tended the wheat and corn that they worked for the priests and the small vegetable gardens that they grew for themselves. In the same year that Harry's relatives filed their lawsuit against Father Ashton, Harry and his wife had their first child. It looked as though his generation might finally shake off its shackles and abandon the plantations, and his child might be born free.

News of the verdict finally arrived in October 1797. The jury hearing the Mahoneys' case left the waters muddied, finding neither for the Mahoneys nor for Ashton. The jurors declared that if the court should be of the "opinion that the Petitioner's entitled to Freedom then the Jurors aforesaid find the Issue in this Cause for the Petitioner."

Though the court agreed to a request for a retrial by Father Ashton's lawyers, the verdict was apparently good enough for the Mahoneys. In December, Charles and Patrick Mahoney left the White Marsh plantation where they had been enslaved. Father Ashton posted a notice in *The Maryland Gazette* in January 1798, asking for help in hunting them down. "They pretend that they are set free by the verdict in the last general court, but were ordered by the court to return home till a point of law should be settled related to their case," he wrote. "This they refuse to do."

Ashton said that the two men were "well known" in Annapolis and in the forests of Prince George's County surrounding White Marsh. He warned any sympathizers among the newspaper's readers against "harbouring or employing them."

At the time, the Maryland Abolition Society counted among its members dozens of white artisans, merchants, and tradesmen who might offer assistance to enslaved runaways. And the number of free Blacks in the state had swelled dramatically. In the decade between 1790 and 1800, the number of free Blacks in Maryland more than doubled, jumping from 8,043 to 19,587. This substantial community of color assisted and offered safe haven to fugitives. Ashton, perhaps mindful that his warning to sympathizers might not have its intended effect, also offered an $8 reward for the capture of the fugitive Mahoneys. But it was of no avail.

Patrick and Charles weren't the only Mahoneys who found their way to freedom. Another relative, an enslaved carpenter named Robert Mahoney, had managed to buy first his own freedom and then that of his wife and youngest daughter. Both Robert and his daughter, who had moved to Philadelphia, returned to visit Harry, both of them willing to take a perilous journey that required evading the white men who patrolled the fields and towns, hunting for Black people who might be runaways. Even free Black people ran the risk of being kidnapped and sold into slavery. Harry learned from them about faraway places in the north, unimaginable places, where more Black people were free. Harry would pass Robert's story down to his children, who would pass it down to their children and share it with the white priests who knew them. As they awaited a resolution in the court case, he and other members of the Mahoney clan hoped that they would soon experience that freedom firsthand.

In 1799, a second jury found in favor of the Mahoneys, finding that Charles Mahoney was a free man. That decision, too, was appealed, but the Mahoneys felt confident that the lower court's decision would be upheld. One of the Mahoneys enslaved by Charles Carroll, who was a distant relative of Father Ashton, told him that the family's lawyers "had obtained such proof as must put their right to freedom on a new tryal out of all doubt."

This time, though, Ashton's lawyer presented two new witnesses who claimed that Ann Joice had never been an indentured servant and had never been free. She was, instead, "a Guinea negro," who had been purchased from a slave ship that traveled from England to Maryland. Neither witness could provide proof to corroborate his claim. And the steward's logbook, which allegedly contained a detailed account of the happenings on the ship that had carried Ann Joice to Maryland, was no longer available to be scrutinized. "The rats got at it," the witness explained, "and [it] is not now in existence."

Despite the lack of evidence, the jurors found the new witnesses persuasive, and they came back with a damning verdict. "The said Charles Mahoney is not a free man," they determined and ordered him to "return to the service of the said John Ashton there to remain." It was a decisive victory for Father Ashton, for the Jesuits, and for prominent Catholic slaveholders such as Charles Carroll. None of them would be forced to relinquish their human property for the foreseeable future.

Ashton then made an unexpected move: He decided to bring his bitter feud with the Mahoney brothers to an end by freeing them. It was a remarkable turn of events, leading one historian who has studied the case to wonder whether the Mahoneys paid the beleaguered priest to resolve the matter once and for all. In any case, in 1803, Ashton began signing the necessary legal papers to free the siblings, freeing Patrick Mahoney in December 1803; Charles, who had been living in Anne Arundel County, five months later; and their brother Daniel the following year.

Harry may have celebrated when he learned that his kinsmen had been set free. But he also had to confront an unbearable truth. After the Jesuits prevailed in court, he knew that he and the rest of his family might be forced to spend the rest of their lives in slavery.

As the flurry of manumissions inspired by the fervor of the Revolutionary War faded and unfavorable legal decisions made it harder for the enslaved to win their freedom through the courts, fear began to replace hope among the enslaved people on the Catholic plantations. Once again, Black people were reminded that the Catholic clergymen who owned them viewed them as chattel. As the fledgling Church expanded, the former Jesuits had no compunction about shipping them from one estate to another.

In describing slave sales, some priests emphasized the efforts they made to keep enslaved families together, suggesting that they only sold slaves deemed disruptive or unruly, at least until the late 1830s. But their own records show otherwise. As hard times befell Georgetown College, all the enslaved people at St. Inigoes, including the Mahoneys, knew they had to tread carefully.

Enrollment at Georgetown College had plummeted. Economic woes in the capital, along with a shortage of qualified faculty and the implementation of strict rules and moral codes that made the school less appealing to non-Catholics, were all contributing to the college's decline. "The College," the trustees wrote, "is not supplied sufficiently with capable Masters, to raise its credit & estimation in the eye of the public: few students are sent to it, & consequently declines in reputation, & in the means of subsistence & improvement."

To compensate, the Corporation of Roman Catholic Clergymen, the body established to manage the vast plantations, had given Georgetown's president direct control of the Bohemia plantation to ensure that more income and produce would flow into the college. Proceeds from the White Marsh plantation funded the salary of Georgetown's professor of philosophy and the costs of his students. But it would not be enough, and they decided to dispose of some human assets. The corporation told the plantation managers that they could "dispose of unruly slaves, or to sell, or exchange them in cases of intermarriage, & other apparent causes" as long as the managers received approval from their superiors and informed the corporation at the next meeting. Not long after Father Ashton freed Patrick Mahoney, the priests sold an enslaved man at St. Inigoes for $320, a transaction neatly recorded in one of the Jesuits' accounting ledgers: "Sale of Nigroe Frank from St. Inigoes." Another laborer at St. Inigoes, an enslaved man named Matt, decided to make a run for it. But he was captured in February 1804, the month after Frank was sold.

That spring, fear descended on the enslaved community at St. Inigoes, which now consisted of forty-one people, most of them children. Many of the older men and women suffered from injuries or illnesses accumulated over a lifetime of servitude. Charles, fifty-one, had a broken arm. Will, sixty-three, was described as "a cripple." Tom, sixty-seven, was blind in one eye. Dorothy, forty-nine, was described as bedridden "for life," while Cate, sixty-two, was "always sick & helpless." Even Harry and his wife, Anna, struggled with health problems that summer: He had tuberculosis, and she suffered from dropsy, the swelling caused by excess fluid in the body that typically affects the legs and feet. They had three children, two girls, who were twelve and six, and one boy, who was ten. Could they keep the family together? With the Jesuits looking to slave sales to raise money, no one could be sure.

In 1805, the Jesuit order was partially restored in the United States when it affiliated with that of Russia, the one branch of the order that had survived the Church's suppression of the Jesuits. But the financial situation of the American priests remained precarious. As selling only disruptive or rebellious people did not bring in enough cash, the priests turned their attention to anyone deemed "superfluous." ("The sale of a few unnecessary negroes" would help cover some of the estates' expenses, Bishop John Carroll wrote in 1805.)

In 1806, St. Inigoes began sending cash in annual installments to support the college. But the college continued to flounder, and Bishop Carroll began to think it should be closed. "Disagreeable as this truth is," he wrote in February 1807, "we cannot shut it out of our minds."

The Jesuits weren't the only people struggling through hard times. And they weren't the only ones turning to slave sales to raise money. Overfarming of tobacco, the cash crop that had powered the eighteenth-century economy in the Chesapeake, had exhausted the land. Word was spreading about the cheap land and abundant, fertile soil in the Deep South and the territories out west, and farmers all across Maryland and Virginia were setting out to claim it.

White men began sharing stories about the prospects in places such as Georgia, Tennessee, and Louisiana and talking about new crops such as cotton and sugar. There were fortunes to be made by ambitious men, particularly those with a supply of free labor. Between 1804 and 1808, the demand for enslaved workers soared. In New Orleans, the average price of a slave increased by nearly a third, from less than $500 to more than $600.

In the past, a slave sale in Maryland might mean one local farmer selling an enslaved person to another farmer. A family broken apart might then find some comfort in knowing that their loved ones had been shipped to a nearby county. Increasingly, though, slaves were sold to white men who marched or shipped them hundreds of miles away. Charles Ball, an enslaved man who worked on a plantation in Calvert County, Maryland, would never forget the moment when he was sold and shipped down south. "This man came up to me, and, seizing me by the collar, shook me violently, saying I was his property and must go with him to Georgia," related Ball, who described the way he had then been surrounded and bound in the presence of twenty white men, making escape impossible. "At the sound of these words, the thoughts of my wife and children rushed across my mind, and my heart died away within me. I saw and knew that my case was hopeless, and that resistance was vain."

Decades later, Ball could still remember the feel of the iron collar that was padlocked around his neck and the cries of the enslaved man who was chained beside him. He was handcuffed and shackled to more than two dozen other men and marched to Georgia. "I asked if I could not be allowed to go to see my wife and children, or if this could not be permitted, if they might not have leave to come to see me," he said, "but was told that I would be able to get another wife in Georgia."

In the first decade of the 1800s, nearly 22,000 people were sold to plantation owners in Tennessee, up from 6,645 in the 1790s. Between 1800 and 1809, as Harry, Anna, and the other Jesuit slaves at St. Inigoes contended with the terror of being sold, 11,231 enslaved people were forcibly moved south to Georgia—up from 6,095 in the previous decade. Word of such sales to the Deep South spread through enslaved communities across Maryland.

There are no existing accounts of how the people on the plantations faced the ever-growing threat. It is unclear whether word trickled back to St. Inigoes and whether Harry and Anna lay awake at night, whispering to each other as their children slept, fearful of what the morning might bring. What is known is that by the spring of 1809, when the couple had five children—three boys and two girls between the ages of one and eighteen—and Anna was pregnant with her sixth, danger was imminent.

We don't know how the Jesuits finally decided who would stay on the farms and who would be marketed and shipped away. Did the overseer watch the laborers at work and pass on the names of the men and women who powered through the sweltering heat and those who faltered? Did they look carefully for signs of discontent, for people who challenged the priests, for people who longed too openly for freedom or who belonged to families, such as the Mahoneys, with long histories of resistance?

At St. Inigoes, sometime in 1809 or 1810, the priests decided to sell eleven people, including a thirty-four-year-old man named Peter and his entire family, "constituting of eight persons young and old." Watt, who appears to have been about eighteen, and an elderly couple, husband and wife, were also sold. The priests received $212 for Watt, $350 for the elderly couple, and $1,300 for Peter and his family, which was paid partly with cash—$636—and partly in kind. The Jesuits at St. Inigoes received another enslaved family valued at about $700 in exchange for Peter's.

Witnesses to slave sales described the anguish that typically engulfed the enslaved families and communities that were torn apart. William Green, a Maryland man who remained enslaved while many of his relatives went free, never forgot the day that his older brother was sold and forced into a chain gang of more than a hundred people who were "driven off to the far South to toil and die upon a sugar or cotton plantation." "Think dear reader for one moment," Green wrote later, "how you would feel if a brother or sister were taken from before your eyes and chained with a heavy iron chain, and driven off where you would never hear from them again. Would not your blood boil within you? I hastened to bid my brother good-bye, but was scarcely permitted to say even that to him, and I have never heard a word from him from that day to this."

The precious bonds of family and community were agonizingly fragile, easily ruptured when a slaveholder died or fell upon hard times. One day, Peter and his family and the others had belonged to the enslaved community at St. Inigoes that had filled the slave quarters with laughter and song. Then they were gone.

By 1810, Harry and Anna had welcomed their sixth child, Daniel, who carried the name of one of the freed Mahoney relatives. Harry had learned that the law favored his white enslavers. Running away was no solution, not for a couple with three children under the age of four. Harry had to come up with some other strategy to ensure that his growing family would remain safe and intact.

He was nearly forty years old. If he had hopes of freedom, if he raged inside at the white priests who held him and his family captive, he buried those feelings deep inside. In an effort that was likely to make his family more secure, he made a name for himself among the priests as a steady, reliable Black man, a servant who knew his place. He became known not as a dissenter or an agitator but as the Jesuit planters' right-hand man, a man who could be trusted to keep his own people in line. He became the plantation foreman.

A New Generation

THOMAS MULLEDY STRODE INTO GEORGETOWN COLLEGE FOR the first time in the fall of 1813. By the time he took his seat in class, the walls had been plastered and glass had finally replaced the wooden boards that had covered the windows.

He was nineteen, older than most of the other students, and the gregarious, brash young man left an indelible impression on his classmates and professors. He was handsome and hot-tempered, with black, curly hair and hazel gray eyes, and he quickly became known as a young man who would not hesitate to use his fists. He was hungry for opportunity and determined to use his considerable intellect to climb far beyond his rural upbringing in Virginia.

It was no surprise that an ambitious young man drawn to the priesthood had found his way to the clergymen at Georgetown College. Using the cash raised by slave labor on plantations, the former Jesuits had already established the nation's first archdiocese, in Baltimore, and helped to finance St. Mary's Seminary. They had helped establish two of the earliest Catholic communities of religious women, the Carmelites of Baltimore and the Georgetown Visitation sisters. (The nuns would enslave and sell Black people as well.) But the school's pleasant new facade barely masked the truth:

The college, and the mission, was in crisis. The priests had opened a new school in 1808, the New York Literary Institution, which was siphoning off students and resources from Georgetown. By 1813, the mission's leaders, desperate to revive their flagship institution, had given Georgetown's president complete control over St. Inigoes and all of the enslaved people who lived there. Still, it was not enough. Georgetown's deficit stood at $3,000 a year, even with the income streaming in from the St. Inigoes and St. Thomas Manor plantations. It was clear that the Jesuits could not support two schools while simultaneously reviving their religious order in the United States.

Carroll, now an archbishop, could not contain his disillusionment about the state of the college he had created, lamenting that the college had "sunk to the lowest degree of discredit." Father Giovanni Grassi, an Italian-born priest who would become the college's next president, described the demoralizing sensation of becoming "a sorrowful spectator of the miserable state of this college," with its debts and sinking reputation.

It could hardly have been a less auspicious time to begin a college career. War had broken out between the United States and Great Britain as the young republic, bristling at its former colonizer's efforts to interfere with its international trade, moved to reassert its independence. Within a year, students would see the streets of their city occupied by British soldiers. But for Mulledy, a young man just beginning his studies, Georgetown was a place of promise. He had grown up in Romney, a small village in western Virginia, and knew all too well the hardships of life on a farm. His father, an Irish immigrant, had settled there in what is now Hampshire County, West Virginia, and had tried his hand at several occupations, serving as a surveyor, a coroner, a merchant, a farmer, and a deputy sheriff. By 1810, three years before Mulledy entered Georgetown, his father owned four enslaved people, which gave the family some social standing. But he would still struggle economically for decades. (Many years later, Mulledy's sister, Mary, would write to her brother, complaining that their father was talking about "raising cattle and making a fortune[,] yet he is doing worse than nothing on the farm[.] [S]everal hogs died from poverty[.] [H]e did not even try to get corn.")

There were few economic opportunities for young, ambitious men in his secluded village. Mulledy taught school for a time at an academy, which was built with rough, unhewn stones and had an "uncouth" exterior. When it became clear that the Catholic immigrant's son would have to leave his hometown to find a path forward, Georgetown was a natural choice. Mulledy appears to have paid his own way through college, as did his younger brother, Samuel, who joined him at Georgetown, though coming up with the cash was not easy. (One year, Samuel gave the college two horses in lieu of cash for tuition.)

Mulledy brought his raw determination to succeed to the classroom, and his fiery temperament became well known on campus. As the war between England and the United States intensified, Grassi, who had become Georgetown's president in 1812, reassured parents and the public that the business of the college would continue as usual. But by August 1814, it was clear that the fighting would soon engulf the nation's capital. "The people are mobilized for war," Grassi wrote in his diary on August 22.

Two days later, British soldiers marched through the streets of Washington. Mulledy joined the students streaming out of the college to see the troops. One of the British soldiers saw Mulledy and taunted him, calling him "old" and "ugly." Mulledy was "a short youth at the time," observers recalled, but he did not hesitate. He confronted the soldier, telling him to take off his coat if he wanted to exchange insults, and warning "I will thrash you" until the soldier backed down.

By nightfall, the British troops had torched both the Capitol Building and the home of the US president. The War and Treasury buildings soon followed, leaving the night sky ablaze. Grassi watched the raging flames from the top story of one of the college buildings.

Some residents fled to the countryside, but Mulledy and the other students stayed put as the priests hid the sacred items used for Mass. In the end, the British did not march on Georgetown but withdrew to their ships and sailed for Baltimore, and classes started on time, as scheduled, five days later. Unscathed by the war, the college went on to flourish under Grassi's leadership.

Grassi had reduced student tuition from $220 a year to $125 a year, hoping to boost the number of day students and boarders who could attend. (The college covered the costs of students inclined to enter the priesthood.) And he had persuaded the Jesuit leadership to close its school in New York City and send its talented faculty (along with "an elegant set of maps" and six students) to Georgetown.

The new faculty, drawn from the defunct New York academy, helped bolster the school's academic offerings. Grassi's decision to reduce tuition led to a surge in enrollment that wiped out the school's debts. More than a hundred students attended Georgetown during the 1815–1816 academic year—107 in all, the highest number ever enrolled in the college. Grassi boosted the profile of the school in other ways as well, hobnobbing with members of Congress and prominent men in Washington and inviting them to visit the school atop the hill in Georgetown. Soon the school, which increasingly attracted Protestants as well as Catholics, was drawing students from New York, Pennsylvania, South Carolina, Louisiana, and beyond, in addition to the children of Washington's elite. Representative Henry Clay of Kentucky, the speaker of the House of Representatives, and Mayor James Blake of Washington, DC, both sent their sons there. Those connections helped, particularly when Grassi successfully applied for a federal charter that would allow the college to award degrees for the first time. "Mr. Grassi," Archbishop Carroll wrote in the fall of that year of 1815, ". . . continually adds celebrity and reputation to the character of his college."

All of that had a profound impact on Mulledy. The country boy grew comfortable mingling with the sophisticated, wealthy students around him and thrived in the intellectually stimulating environment. Grassi, who was a mathematician and astronomer, had opened a museum on campus that drew students and members of the public to gaze at the stars through his telescope. He created a model of the solar system and had his students describe it to an audience that included members of Congress. He even launched a gas-filled balloon from the campus grounds with the help of a fellow mathematician.

Mulledy watched and learned as Grassi enhanced the college's facilities—overseeing the construction of new rooms for boarding students—and wooed official Washington to help burnish the college's reputation. More than a decade later, when Mulledy became Georgetown's president, he would employ similar strategies. His experience at the college under Grassi's leadership persuaded him to take a pivotal step, one that would have far-reaching implications for both the church and the plantations: In 1815, he decided to join the Jesuit order, which had been fully restored in the United States a year earlier.

Mulledy left Georgetown and took the winding country roads to the White Marsh estate in Prince George's County, Maryland, home of the Jesuit seminary. There, in the heart of one of the country's largest Jesuit plantations, attended to by enslaved laborers, he and the other seminarians would deepen their understanding of theology. The young men studied under the tutelage of Father Anthony Kohlmann, a bespectacled, charismatic Jesuit who as vicar general of New York had started the construction of the first Catholic cathedral in the city—which would be only the second in the United States—and had founded the New York Literary Institution in New York City, the school that for a time had drawn faculty and financial resources from Georgetown. Kohlmann had moved to Maryland after the Literary Institution was shut down, taking charge of the seminary in 1815. But the time he spent ministering to Irish, German, and French immigrants in New York City had electrified him, prompting him to reevaluate the Jesuits' long-

standing commitment to the plantations and their mission in rural
Maryland.

Kohlmann believed that the Church's future lay in the young nation's rapidly growing urban centers, such as New York, Philadelphia, and Baltimore. He wanted the Jesuits to "take possession" of
those cities, establishing a network of schools across the Northeast
that would expand the order's reach and influence. To accomplish
that, he made a bold proposal: The Church should sell its plantations and the enslaved people whose work had financed the Jesuits'
mission since the early 1700s. The money raised from such a sale,
he argued, would enable the Jesuits to achieve his vision.

The Jesuit leadership had, in fact, recently embraced the idea of
divesting itself of "the greatest part of the blacks on the different
plantations," at least on paper. Under the plan, which was debated
in 1813 and adopted a year later, the men, women, and children
enslaved on Jesuit plantations across Maryland would be sold for "a
term of years after which they should be entitled to their freedom,"
and the profits from the mass sale would be vested in "some safe
fund," for the benefit of the plantations and for other purposes. The
reasoning behind the decision remains unclear. The priests may
have been weary of the financial drain they were experiencing hiring lawyers to challenge the lawsuits filed by enslaved men and
women such as the Mahoneys. Though Georgetown was doing
better, the need to come up with cash during the economic downturn that had accompanied the War of 1812 may have also played a
role. Archbishop Carroll also happened to be facing criticism from
overseas. Two Irish priests who had spent time in Philadelphia had
complained to Rome, accusing Carroll and the Maryland Jesuits of
trafficking in slaves, though there is no evidence that Rome formally responded. The news of a mass emancipation might have cast
Carroll in a kinder light. After all, the plan, if implemented, would
amount to one of the largest manumissions in the nation.

Some Jesuits remained deeply attached to the Church's rural
roots and opposed the plan, which so far had not been carried out.

But Kohlmann remained an avid proponent of a mass sale that would finance a Jesuit expansion, and his ideas resonated deeply with Mulledy and several of the other young seminarians at White Marsh. Under his direction, Mulledy and the other young men donned traditional Jesuit cassocks and studied in the mornings and evenings. They prayed together, attended Mass together, and fished, swam, shot with bows and arrows, and played ball on the expansive plantation. They even traveled to St. Inigoes, where Harry Mahoney was caring for his growing family.

In his correspondence, Kohlmann stressed the importance of providing "good and sufficient clothing" for the Black people who labored at White Marsh, and at least one seminarian noted that he treated them with affection. But Kohlmann's primary message remained the same: The plantations were poorly run, their surpluses mismanaged. The future of the Catholic Church lay in the cities, not in the countryside. Mulledy took it all in as he observed the enslaved communities on the Jesuit estates and bonded with the young seminarians who would become his partners in systematically dismantling them.

Among them was another young Virginian, William McSherry. Like Mulledy, McSherry was the son of an Irish immigrant who had turned to slaveholding in the new world. But McSherry's family was far more prosperous. His wealthy father, a fashionable man who favored lace ruffles and silver buckles, owned a large estate and enslaved dozens of people. McSherry stood over six feet tall, while Mulledy was about five foot eight and was better known for his genial manner than his intellect. Even as they treated the enslaved like chattel, many older priests had paternalistic views of the people they held in bondage, describing them as children in need of care and spiritual guidance. But Mulledy and McSherry would dispense with such notions. They saw the Black men and women they had met on the plantations as commodities that could be used to expand the growing reach of the Jesuits, who by early 1817 had already donated land valued at $40,000—about $870,000 in today's dollars—for the completion of the Basilica of the National Shrine of the Assumption of the Blessed Virgin Mary in Baltimore, which would be celebrated as the first Roman Catholic cathedral in the nation.

By the summer of 1817, Mulledy was back at Georgetown. Grassi had returned to Rome, and Georgetown's new administrator had ordered Mulledy to take up teaching along with his religious studies. The unexpected assignment was supposed to be temporary. But in September of that year, Kohlmann became president of the college and ordered Mulledy to stay on. Mulledy, who had entered Georgetown only four years earlier, now found himself in the ranks of the faculty as the college's professor of poetry. Within weeks, the young professor was forced to demonstrate his mettle.

After supper one evening, a group of students armed with rocks, knives, and clubs attacked an unpopular faculty member who was responsible for maintaining order and discipline at the college. The young men jumped over tables and chairs in the study hall as they charged the hapless instructor. Mulledy, the athletic seminarian, leapt into the fray. The instructor targeted by the attack would later say that Mulledy's "fearless action and skill contributed most in strangling the conspiracy at its birth and in discovering and expelling [from the melee] those most responsible."

Kohlmann promoted Mulledy, putting him in charge of student discipline at Georgetown. In Rome, senior Jesuits began to view Mulledy as one of a handful of promising young men destined for leadership in the order's US mission. In 1819, Mulledy's name ended up on a short list of seminarians selected to travel to Italy to advance their studies. Mulledy, who wrote poems in his spare time, had demonstrated a keen intellect in addition to his physical prowess. He was frank, sometimes brutally so, and funny, earning the admiration of his peers and his students. But even as his star rose among the Jesuit leadership overseas, some Jesuits at home were quietly expressing doubts about his temperament and suitability for the priesthood.

In a letter written just two months before Mulledy was scheduled to depart for Rome, a senior Jesuit lamented the "want of
religious spirit & solid piety" that was "very evident" among certain
individuals. He pointed specifically at Mulledy, noting that Mulledy's "conduct" made it doubtful that he would be admitted to the
Jesuit order. "It is to be lamented, that men, that might be of im-
measurable utility, should thus blighte [sic] the hopes conceived of
them," the priest wrote. "Every remedy, that patience & prudence
can apply, must be used to correct and save them."

The letter does not describe the troubling "conduct" that
Mulledy had engaged in. But it likely referred to what one historian described as his "lack of religious discipline," his failure to follow rules that required Jesuits to meditate daily and examine their
consciences twice daily and barred them from activities that might
prove tempting to the flesh, such as going out unaccompanied and
receiving visitors, especially females, in their private quarters.

Mulledy apparently rebelled against those rules, even as he excelled in his religious studies. He was known to be reckless and to
drink heavily. Even Kohlmann, who had groomed and promoted
him, viewed him as rash and hotheaded, "subject to very strong
passions of pride and anger and having vacillated" over whether he
truly wanted to become a priest. Jesuit leaders wrestled with the
conundrum. What should be done?

The dearth of talented and able-bodied Jesuits, what one priest
described as the "present scarcity of men" at Georgetown College
and in the leadership pipeline, seems to have persuaded doubtful
Jesuits to give Mulledy a chance. Sending him to study in Rome,
one Jesuit leader wrote, might be "a final experiment to save him."

On the morning of June 6, 1820, Mulledy set out on a steamboat
that sailed from Georgetown to the port city of Alexandria, Virginia. At Alexandria, he stood on the wharf alongside McSherry
and four other seminarians, serenaded by a band of students and
cheered on by the president of Georgetown College and a group of
faculty members. Among them was Kohlmann, who had in the

end offered qualified praise for the young man. ("At present," he wrote, "I conceive him to be as firm in his vocation as ever.")

Mulledy was twenty-five years old, and he was being celebrated that day, along with the others, as one of the most promising young seminarians of his generation.

The men boarded the schooner *America,* which would carry them to Cádiz, Spain, the first stop on their voyage. "A fair breeze soon hurried us from the sight of land," one of the young men recalled. Mulledy and his companions sailed through days of torrential rains and clear nights with moonlit skies, past the lush Azores to the bustling port at Gibraltar. They ogled the passing ships as well as a shoal of dolphins and a flying fish, and endured stretches of seasickness and boredom.

By September, Mulledy and the others had arrived at the Roman College. "They are all well, in good health and in good spirits," reported Grassi, who received them in Rome, adding wryly that the young men were "quite sick of water" after the long sea journey. Kohlmann hailed them as the "First Fruits of the American Mission . . . the objects of our great hopes."

But all the praise in the world could not dispel the loneliness Mulledy felt as an American in a bustling, unfamiliar European city. He turned to poetry, describing in verse his longing for home.

> Oh! am I thus forced to depart
> From the home where I learnt to be free!
> 'Tis true! but I leave thee my heart,
> And my thoughts shall be fixed upon thee!

Eight years would pass before he set foot on US soil again.

Back at home, there was no doubt that Georgetown and the Jesuits of the Maryland mission desperately needed a new cadre of faculty and leaders. The college and the mission, which had flourished under Grassi's leadership, were again floundering. The United States had been hit hard by an economic recession, later known as the Panic of 1819, and the republic was reeling. Banks failed, and property values plunged in New York, Pennsylvania, and Virginia. The prices of agricultural goods dropped by half. Poverty spread across the country, from the eastern seaboard to towns out west.

James Neil, a Jesuit scholastic who returned to New York from Rome in 1820, the same year that Mulledy departed for Europe, described his astonishment at the depth of the economic devastation. He found the country "in the greatest misery. Many persons whom I left here with 70 or 80,000 dollars capital are now beggars & lodged in the poor house."

Georgetown, which had enjoyed an economic and intellectual renaissance in the eighteen-teens, was once more in crisis, as was the Jesuit mission itself. Hard times had befallen the enslaved people, who were still laboring on the plantations to keep the Jesuits afloat. "Our affairs wear an alarming appearance," warned Adam Marshall, the Jesuit official in charge of finances, in the summer of 1820, "a heavy and empty treasury: immense tracts of land, resembling rather an Indian hunting ground than lands inhabited by men acquainted with the arts of civilized life."

Father Grassi had been succeeded by a series of ineffectual presidents, including Kohlmann, who was accused of erratic leadership and excessive spending. (Grassi himself was accused of absconding with money from the mission, a charge that he denied.) Enrollment plunged from 108 in 1817 to 61 in 1820. The professors who had formed the core of Georgetown's well-regarded faculty left. So dire was the situation that the Jesuit priest tapped to succeed Kohlmann in 1820 described the college as having "one foot in the grave of disgrace and the other beginning to sink."

Father Peter Kenney, sent from Ireland to assess the state of the troubled Maryland mission, found the Jesuits bedeviled by infighting, weakened by the "arguments and disputes that suddenly arose among our men." The priests seemed to battle over everything. Foreign-born priests challenged the curriculum, pushing for a traditional focus on Latin and Greek grammar, befitting men destined

for the priesthood, while the "natives" called for a broader education built on Latin and Greek literature, mathematics, and science.
And still they argued about the Jesuit mission and where and
whether Georgetown and the plantations fit into it. Some Jesuits,
such as Kohlmann, argued that the estates should be sold and the
profits used to build schools in major cities around the country.
Others viewed the plantations as the very heart of their mission.

In Rome, Kenney delivered a sober assessment of the situation in
the United States, outlining what he described as "the most
wretched state of the mission that has existed for some 200 years."
He ticked off a litany of problems, describing a deeply divided,
fractious organization led by elderly priests and served, on the one
hand, by foreign priests who did not know the English language
and, on the other, American priests who tended toward secular
vices. Mulledy and others would blame the enslaved for the mission's financial troubles, describing them as a burdensome, unsustainable expense. The truth was, as Kenney pointed out, that
financial mismanagement among the Jesuits themselves was ram-
pant. "There is not any where a regular & uniform system of keeping the books," he had written earlier that year, explaining that "he
could not exactly learn the actual state of each farm, but every
where, almost, complaints of bad management, unprofitable contracts, useless & expensive experiments & speculations."

Between 1820 and 1824, the sale of land, stock, and enslaved
people brought more than $30,000—about $894,000 in today's
dollars—into the Maryland mission's coffers. (The Jesuits even
mortgaged the White Marsh plantation to raise cash.) Yet the mission's debts continued to balloon, leading one Jesuit scholar to suggest that corruption, in addition to mismanagement, was to blame.
Thomas Hughes, a Jesuit who wrote a multivolume history of the
Jesuits in Maryland, described Marshall, the priest in charge of the
mission's finances at the time, as akin to a "common embezzler."

By the fall of 1827, Georgetown had barely a score of boarding
students and only about sixty students altogether, taught by a fac-

ulty that had been decidedly lackluster for years. "Instead of a Constellation of Fathers, supporting a College, which might lead millions to Catholicity," one priest wrote, "we have a few unfledged boys, capable only of taking charge of the lowest classes."

It didn't help that the two most recent presidents of the college had been foreign-born priests who struggled with English. Their appointments had outraged many of the American-born Jesuits and puzzled outsiders, who were reluctant to send their sons to a school headed by men who struggled to speak the country's language.

Meanwhile, in Rome, Mulledy, who had immersed himself in literature and science, had completed his studies and been ordained in 1825 along with McSherry and four others. He had successfully overcome the reservations about his lack of piety as a young man. But in Rome, too, he rubbed some people the wrong way. He became known in some quarters as an uncouth, arrogant American with a fiery temper. He was a big man with a "bull-like voice," and he often spoke his mind, dispensing with niceties. "Savage," declared the Dutch Jesuit Jan Roothaan, who would become the superior general of the Jesuits worldwide. But even some of Mulledy's critics saw his potential. His defenders described him as charming, pious, zealous, and a passionate supporter of the Jesuits and their mission.

Soon it was time for Mulledy and his cohort of American Jesuits to return home. The Maryland Jesuits were so strapped for cash, though, that it took until 1828 for them to come up with enough money to cover the cost of the travel. The voyage took 171 days on board a ship buffeted by such rough waves that the Jesuits feared they might not survive. It was not until December of that year that Mulledy, McSherry, and the others finally stepped off a ship in Philadelphia after nearly a decade overseas. By January, those promising young Jesuits had assumed some of the most important positions at the beleaguered college.

In the fall of 1829, at the start of the academic year, a notice appeared on the front page of the evening edition of the *United States'*

Telegraph. It was September 22. A new president, Andrew Jackson, sat in the White House. And a new president, Thomas Mulledy, had just taken over at Georgetown.

Mulledy, now thirty-five, had wasted no time. "The College is situated on the Northern bank of the Potomac, and commands a full view of Georgetown, Washington, the Potomac, and a great part of the District of Columbia," read the notice. Students would have the opportunity to witness the workings of the new republic's governmental institutions, strolling from campus to Congress and the Supreme Court for unparalleled views of the nation's most powerful men at work. In the classroom, the pupils would study English and French grammar, calligraphy, and arithmetic and then move on to more advanced classes with a reading list that included Cicero, Ovid, Virgil, and Homer. (Music, drawing, and dancing would be taught, too, but at an extra charge.)

As for the student body itself, the college would admit only literate boys and young men with "good moral character," Mulledy said, and all would be required to have two suits for daily wear, and for public occasions, a blue cloth coat and pantaloons with a black velvet waistcoat in winter and white pantaloons with a black silk waistcoat in summer. Students from all religious denominations were welcome. The notice prominently included his name and title, "Rev. Thomas F. Mulledy, president," and directed all inquiries to be addressed to the "President of the College."

But anyone who knew Mulledy recognized that his vision extended far beyond the college campus. He wanted to do more than revitalize Georgetown; he wanted to build a network of Jesuit colleges. The dream of his mentor, Father Kohlmann, had become his own. And there was only one way to finance that dream. Four months after he assumed the presidency of Georgetown, he wrote a letter to the Jesuit leadership in Rome.

Something must be done, he said, about the enslaved people on the plantations.

The Promise

IN THE CRAMPED SLAVE QUARTERS AT ST. INIGOES, BABY Louisa began to distinguish the voices and footsteps of her parents and to recognize the smiles of her older sister. Louisa was only a year or two younger than Anny, and the affection between the two girls would bloom and deepen.

Harry and Anna Mahoney nurtured them, the youngest members of their sprawling, tight-knit family, some eight children in all. But on a plantation, the singsong lullabies of enslaved parents were often laced with fear. Louisa was born into slavery around 1813, around the time Mulledy entered Georgetown as a student, and she would soon learn that she and her siblings belonged to the priests, not to their parents. Harry and Anna's love, on its own, would not be enough to keep their children safe.

So they taught the girls what they knew. Louisa and Anny would learn about their ancestors and kinfolk and their family's long fight for freedom. They would learn how to carry themselves among the priests who viewed them as property. And when war with the British came to Maryland, the Mahoneys would learn that joy and opportunity sometimes flowered in the rockiest of soils and that even the enslaved could resist and struggle to expand the boundaries of their circumscribed lives.

. . .

IN APRIL 1813, a year before the British occupied the US Capitol, their warships streamed into Chesapeake Bay and headed for St. Mary's Peninsula, where the enslaved labored on the St. Inigoes plantation.

Panicked, the clergy living on the estate scrambled to move precious foodstuffs and supplies to safety, to neighbors whose modest homes might not be targeted. Joseph Mobberly, the religious brother responsible for overseeing the enslaved community, raced across the plantation, shouting orders as Black workers loaded ox-carts and corralled cattle. The priests had already rushed their novices, who had been studying on the plantation, back to Georgetown. Now the enslaved workers rushed the oxcarts to the homes of neighboring farmers, where they unloaded precious provisions—dried beef, herring, codfish, flour, sugar, whiskey, port, and candles—into cellars for safekeeping.

It was only the beginning. For more than a year, as Louisa learned to crawl and toddle, the British continued their incursions, sending soldiers across the peninsula and then withdrawing to their ships in the face of attacks from local farmers, who organized a civilian militia. The enemy seized St. George's Island, which belonged to the priests, landing thousands of troops at Point Lookout in the southernmost corner of the county. Americans huddled in their homes while the British plundered plantations, seizing cattle, horses, bridles, bedding, silverware, even teacups.

"They have burnt every house," wrote Father Francis Neale, a priest who lived at St. Inigoes plantation and described the "great devastation" he had witnessed on St. George's Island in November 1813 after the British had withdrawn. The soldiers had also cut down trees—oaks, pines, and hickories—and taken the wood for timber.

The priest had no doubt that the enemy would return. The only question was when. It was a question that weighed on everyone at St. Inigoes, including the enslaved community, which numbered about forty people in all. "The enemy is nearer to us than we are to you," continued Neale in his letter to Father Grassi, who was in charge of the Maryland mission as well as Georgetown College. Neale described his frantic plans to ship the estate's cattle to Georgetown and the St. Thomas Manor plantation as soon as possible. "In twelve hours they may be with us again and we are without defense."

Fear engulfed the estate's inhabitants, including Harry and Anna and their children. The enslaved people in St. Mary's County witnessed it all: houses aflame, planters scrambling to save their livestock and their homes, British troops bursting onto plantations and capturing and imprisoning white men of fighting age and "robbing even the women and children of their clothes," one witness wrote.

But as apprehension spread through the slave quarters in St. Mary's County, so did a sense of exhilaration and opportunity. Many enslaved men and women ran, seeking shelter and freedom behind enemy lines. On April 2, 1814, the British made it official and issued a proclamation intended to devastate Maryland's plantation economy. "This is therefore to Give Notice, that all those who may be disposed to emigrate from the United States will, with their Families, be received on board of His Majesty's Ships or Vessels of War, or at the Military Posts that may be established," the proclamation read. Enslaved people, it said, "will have their choice of either entering into His Majesty's Sea or Land Forces, or of being sent as FREE settlers to the British Possessions in North America or the West Indies, where they will meet with all due encouragement."

Freedom—which had seemed like an impossible dream to many Black people—was finally within reach. All across the county, enslaved men and women asked themselves the agonizing question: Should they run? On some plantations, where white men were compelled to join civilian militias and could not closely supervise their estates, the answer was clear. Hundreds ran. But in other places, people were forced to make wrenching calculations. Harry and Anna had their young daughters to consider, along with their older children. Could they all get away without attracting attention? Would Louisa's cries wake the overseer or the priests? A single misstep could imperil them all. They knew that runaways could expect to be whipped or sold.

They deliberated as the Jesuits sold yet another Black family to settle a debt and as the war flared on the shores of St. Mary's County. The enslaved men and women at St. Inigoes were working in the wheat fields in the summer of 1814 when word came that the British, who had withdrawn their troops, were mounting yet another invasion. The enemy was edging closer.

But it was around that time that the head priest at St. Inigoes strode into church and delivered a sermon that electrified the community. Before a crowd of white farmers and enslaved churchgoers, Father Maximilian Rantzau, a German-born priest, spoke his mind, assailing the enslavers sitting before him. "It was on the duty of Masters towards their servants," wrote Father Neale, who counted slaveholders among his kinfolk and reported on the sermon with dismay. "It has given much allarm." He described the sermon as "ill-timed," given the constant threat of invasion from the British and, undoubtedly, the fears among planters that they would lose their enslaved laborers to the enemy. Some white churchgoers walked out in protest, "filled with indignation," he wrote. The enslaved people, on the other hand, cheered as the German priest spoke, upsetting the white men and women "on seeing the conduct & exultation of the servants," Neale continued. "Mr. Rantzau [ought] to have said these things either in private, or in the absence of the slaves," he wrote disapprovingly.

But it was too late to silence the outspoken priest. Whether Harry and Anna crowded into the church that day along with the other enslaved men and women remains unknown, but Neale made it clear that news of the radical homily had spread widely. Did the German priest's sermon convince them that their prospects were better in bondage on a plantation supervised by a relatively forward-thinking master? Or was running with so many young children too risky to contemplate seriously? What is clear is that as enslaved people in St. Mary's County calculated the odds of escape, Louisa's and Anny's parents decided to stay put—or at least to bide their time.

Decades later, Louisa would tell her children about the time when the British had finally marched on the plantation. Her father saw the brig sailing toward St. Inigoes from the mouth of the Patuxent River and the soldiers disembarking on the bank of the plantation's garden. Harry wanted to get his wife and children to safety. But he was the plantation's foreman. So first he ran to the manor house. He grabbed the priests' money bag and raced outside to gather his family and all of the enslaved girls on the plantation, leading them into the relative safety of the deep woods. They were gone by the time a British soldier burst into the manor house where the priests lived, bearing a saber and accompanied by four other men. The soldiers rummaged through the chapel there, tearing through the priests' vestments, stripping the altar, and seizing the tabernacle, the sacred hosts, the holy oils, and a picture of St. Francis Xavier.

"Great God, what were my feelings!" wrote Brother Mobberly, who had recently been reassigned to St. Inigoes.

Mobberley managed to recover the tabernacle, a chalice, and several of the vestments. But the soldiers refused to part with the booty they had seized: blankets, feather beds, silver spoons, curtains, candlesticks, silverware, shoes, tea, and medicines. The men also carted off clothing, food, whiskey, and an enslaved woman and two of her children before withdrawing to their ship, leaving Father Rantzau huddled in his room, dazed and disoriented.

"We are in deep distress," Mobberly wrote to Father Grassi, pleading for help. "I wish to receive immediate instructions how to act. We may hourly expect another attack."

The clock was ticking. No one knew when the soldiers would return. Father Rantzau remained in the house while Mobberly and the rest of the enslaved people fled into the forest.

"I took two wagon loads of articles that were under my care, and deposited them in a ruinous hut in a forest about 5 miles distant, placing there a family of faithful servants"—the Mahoneys—"to guard them," Mobberly wrote.

Harry and a team of enslaved carpenters raced to repair several dilapidated huts—"old cabbins neither fit for man or beast," Mobberly reported—so they would have some place to stay. For days, Harry and the other men stood guard over the wagons, the cattle, the hogs, and the food in a drenching rain as Louisa and Anna huddled with their mother and siblings in the wretched cabins. Everyone was on edge, bracing for another British attack. But Harry had already started thinking beyond the hardships of the moment. He worried about the months to come, about the winter, about the cold and the shortage of food. He had his children to consider. They had no vegetable gardens in the woods. They could not work the fields. Without grass, the cattle would starve. His family and the rest of the enslaved community would go hungry. He discussed his concerns with Mobberly, telling him that they needed to start planning now. "We must then purchase corn—for we have not more than enough to last us until the next harvest—this is Harry's opinion," Mobberly wrote to Grassi. "It has been a bad crop year . . . and I very much doubt whether this county can afford bread enough for its inhabitants next year if the war continues."

Mobberly urged Grassi to send Harry, his family, and the rest of the enslaved people, along with the plantation's wagons and ox-carts, to safety at the White Marsh plantation, some sixty miles away, where they would have secure housing and food. He believed that the St. Inigoes plantation should be broken up and sold, he said, leaving only a priest with a handful of elderly servants on the estate. What other options did they have? "We can scarcely sleep in our beds, by day we cannot work—constant alarms—always on the watch—while we keep guard in front, we know not at what moment the Enemy may appear in our rear & surprise our Blacks," he wrote, describing his own "distress and misery." "A sale on this farm ought to take place," he concluded.

But Father Rantzau, the German priest in charge of the plantation, disagreed. He refused to abandon the manor house, despite the threat of another British incursion, and continued to travel to meet with his congregants and to say Mass. He urged Mobberly to put aside his worries, joking that the loss of so many of their possessions might mean an opportunity to acquire new ones. He said they should hang on and "continue the farm as it was before." Mobberly, he said, was "too anxious."

Rantzau turned out to be right. The United States and Great Britain signed a treaty in December 1814, bringing the war to an end. The soldiers returned some of what they had taken during the raid, but not everything. Mobberly would estimate that the church's losses totaled $1,800, and Father Rantzau reported a loss of his own: "They carried off my bag containing several thousand dollars."

But when Harry emerged from the woods with his family, he brought the German priest some good news: He told Rantzau that he had saved the money bag and guided the enslaved girls on the plantation to safety, ensuring that they would not be captured by the British. "I led them two miles away to the top of the hill in the woods," Harry said. "There, I buried the money."

Filled with gratitude, the priests vowed that they would never forget his valor and loyalty. To reward him, Louisa later told her children, they had made a pledge to him that her family would cling to for decades: They promised that he would never be sold.

There is no record of Harry's emotions when he heard those words, no account of the reaction of his wife and children when he told them they were safe. The priests had decided to sell off nearly all of their enslaved people. But Harry and his wife and children no longer had to worry. They would not be sold.

Rantzau had accurately predicted that St. Inigoes could survive the war. But Harry was right, too, when he predicted that hard times still lay ahead. Despite his urgings, the clergymen were unable to get enough food to the enslaved families as winter set in. In March 1815, a new priest, Father John Henry, arrived at St. Inigoes with food and cattle and found that they were desperately needed. "It appears that they are well deprived of everything at St. Inigo's, and that my sheep, hogs, cattle, meat, house and kitchen furniture are very welcome," he wrote that month. "There is not a single sheep there, no oxen, no pigs, no butter, and that made me send down a pretty large pot of it."

War, hunger, and hardship marked Louisa's and Anny's earliest years. But the girls also learned from their elders how to carve out space for themselves and the people they loved and to savor moments of joy and laughter. The enslaved families they knew tended their own gardens, which were filled with sweet potatoes, cabbages, and cotton. They raised chickens and sold oysters, eggs, and cabbages to passing sailors and others to earn some cash of their own. In good years, women sometimes saved enough to purchase a hat or a dress for Sunday church services, delighting in the rare opportunity to set aside the rough, worn workaday shifts provided by the priests. Black worshippers relished the sense of community they found in the estate's church, even though they were typically segregated from whites, and they often decorated their homes with religious images or "holy prints."

Their meat and produce supplemented the cornmeal and pork that Mobberly and his overseers parceled out each week to the families, but hunger was still an all-too-frequent companion in slave quarters that were so overcrowded that one priest would describe the enslaved as being "hived" in their homes.

Still, the girls had their parents, their siblings, and their community. And they had each other. Everyone knew them: Anny and Louisa, Louisa and Anny, the youngest of the Mahoney girls. They became so close that as adults they would name their firstborn daughters after each other. And as they grew, they would immerse themselves in the vibrant social life on the estate.

Enslaved children on plantations around the country shot marbles made of clay, waded in cool streams and brooks, and gathered wild berries that stained their fingers and mouths with sweet, sticky juice. Girls in particular enjoyed ring games, holding hands and singing while their friends clapped in the middle of the circle. They listened to older people tell riddles and stories about the creatures that inhabited the woods, about their ancestors, and about the white people who held them in captivity.

At St. Inigoes, Anny and Louisa learned to walk, run, and play on an estate filled with farm animals of all sorts: horses, sheep, cows, hogs, turkeys, and ducks. They could explore woods filled with towering pines, red maples, and white oaks and foxes, hares, minks, and raccoons. They could chase wild geese and swans on the banks of St. Mary's River and marvel at the porpoises that spouted glistening plumes of water high into the air. As they grew older, they could stare at the billowy clouds and dream about far-away places, such as Philadelphia, where their cousins lived free.

Reality inevitably intruded on their dreams. Rain and cold found their way into their dilapidated hut. Hunger gnawed at them. Their parents and the other grown-ups in the slave quarters woke every morning to do forced labor in the tobacco and wheat fields and in the manor house.

Because Harry's courage had endeared him and his family to the Jesuits, his family was spared the harsh labor of the fields. The few surviving sacramental records from the county also show that he and his wife had at least one of their children baptized, and at least two of their daughters would be known for their piety and signs of religious devotion that often won favor from the priests. But Louisa and Anny were still enslaved, and their childhoods were marked by struggle and the agonizing awareness that the people around them could be bought and sold at any time.

"[WE] WERE SURPRISED and mortified to learn that in direct contradiction to the humane decision of the Corporation, sales of Negroes for life have been made and are making from the estate of the White-Marsh," Archbishop Carroll wrote to a fellow priest in October 1815.

Carroll wasn't the only Catholic priest raising questions about the legitimacy of slave sales. Around the same time, a Belgian priest in Kentucky reached out to Rome. "What judgement must one make," he asked, "about the selling of slaves. . . . What if they are sold to heretics, or at a public auction?" The Holy See's Office of Propaganda forwarded the question to the Holy Office, which responded, "This is not allowed." That response, which was directed to the Belgian priest, not to the faithful as a whole, did not change the Church's official position. The Catholic Church continued to maintain its silence on the larger question of slaveholding, and priests continued their practice of buying and selling people.

Carroll's concerns about the sales at White Marsh did not mean that he felt any hesitation about the buying and selling of Black people. In the same letter in which he described the unauthorized sales of human property, he matter-of-factly discussed the authorized sale of enslaved people from Deer Park, another plantation. "You have received the price of the Blacks, which belonged to that estate," he wrote, explaining that the profits would help cover the cost of relocating and resettling a new priest on the plantation.

Other Black families were moved from one Jesuit plantation to another, uprooted from their communities by priests who relocated people as they worked to boost the mission's profits. Louisa and Anny would soon learn from their elders that a Black child's value was not measured by her infectious laugh or her curiosity but by her utility. Mobberly, the Jesuit brother responsible for overseeing the enslaved community, boasted that St. Inigoes produced and shipped $1,850 of produce annually to Georgetown under his watch. He made his attitude crystal clear: It was labor that counted.

The changing of the guard, the regular rotation of priests to new assignments, only enhanced Mobberly's power. Rantzau, the priest who had chided white planters for failing in their duties toward the enslaved, had acknowledged the humanity of the people his order held in bondage. But now he was gone, and in his absence, Mobberly began pressing his superiors to execute their plans for a mass sell-off of the enslaved.

Mobberly knew the families on the plantation. He had seen Harry's leadership in action during the war and had relied on his counsel. He knew that Anny, Louisa, and the other children had huddled in the dilapidated hut in the woods while Harry stood guard over the plantation's provisions. He knew, too, that the Jesuits had promised Harry that he and his family would never be sold But none of that changed his mind.

"We are in the dark as long as we keep slaves," he wrote to Father Grassi, reminding him that the slaves were children of God. "We have their souls to answer for." But he was no abolitionist; he was thinking about dollars and cents. He had tallied up the estate's expenditures—the cost of bread, meat, linens, shoes, medicine, and other expenses for the enslaved people on the plantation—and concluded that hiring white tenant farmers would save the church $334.46 a year. The enslaved people were also becoming increasingly difficult to manage, he complained. "I know the resolve made by the Board concerning slaves, & the sooner that resolution is executed, the better it will be," he said.

Mobberly was voicing what would become a familiar refrain among some Jesuits, that the Black people owned by the priests were draining the mission's coffers, even though the Maryland mission continued to rely on their labor and the sale of their bodies to expand the Church mission, to cover expenses, and to pay down debt. Slaveholders all across the Chesapeake were struggling, but the Black men and women who labored on the plantations were not to blame. Earnings from the sale of tobacco, the region's staple crop, had slumped after the war. Meanwhile, two years of drought had resulted in severe shortages of corn, leaving planters all across St. Mary's County with "apprehensions of the gloomiest kind," one observer wrote.

Mobberly's complaints provided a useful cover for a problem that compounded those struggles, one that few Jesuits wanted to publicly acknowledge or to tackle head-on: the wasteful spending and mismanagement of funds by priests and Jesuit leaders. But in 1816, a priest who had served as the treasurer for the Maryland mission spoke up. In a strikingly frank letter, Father Robert Fenwick warned that the income drawn from the plantations was being squandered at the expense of the enslaved people who were producing it. "We should not be in such pitifull povity [*sic*] at present," he wrote to Father Grassi from White Marsh, "particularly when it proceads [*sic*] from our bad econimy [*sic*]." Fenwick, who had overseen the order's finances, described the hardships experienced by the enslaved people on the plantations as "most disguisting," particularly "after having gone through my hands so much money . . . when I was there."

Fenwick had witnessed the impact of the mismanagement firsthand. White Marsh needed money to buy clover seed and plaster to enrich the estate's depleted soil, to build new stables and hire men to dig ditches, and to help clear the meadows, improvements that should have been made "some years past." And the enslaved families lacked food and adequate clothing, conditions that Fenwick described as "an injustice." "Many of them are in very great kneed [*sic*] of blankets," he continued, "which by right they ought to have had last winter." He believed that the Jesuits were failing to meet the needs of the very people laboring to provide the goods and income necessary to support the church and the college. "We are indetted [*sic*] to them," he wrote.

But his was a lonely voice. At St. Inigoes, Mobberly viewed the people who planted, cultivated, and harvested the produce with disgust. In his diary, he repeated the common myths and slanders whites used to justify their sense of racial superiority: Black people were cannibals, who had "been accustomed in their own Country to feast upon roasted Infants [saying that] a pickaninny (a roasted infant) was the sweetest morsel they have ever tasted!"

"Vices the most notorious seem to be the portion of this unhappy race," he continued in another diary entry, "idleness, treachery, revenge, cruelty, impudence, stealing, lying, profanity, debauchery, nastiness and intemperance are said to have extinguished the principle of natural law."

Mobberly, like many other men of his day, used the Bible to justify slavery, and he described America's system of bondage as essential, saying it sustained Black people who would otherwise find themselves in abject poverty. "Where slavery exists, beggars are rarely found," he wrote. "We must therefore conclude that slavery is not only lawful, reasonable and good, but that it is also necessary."

By 1817, a new priest had arrived at St. Inigoes. His name was Joseph Carbery. Carbery had attended Georgetown, yet another man of faith shaped by the college's Jesuit pipeline. He tended to the needs of local Catholics, while also focusing on repairing the aging church, painting and plastering the house of worship, and building an altar and brick confessional.

Carbery would become known as a champion of the enslaved and a sharp critic of the Jesuit leadership's treatment of the people it owned. But for the first few years of his tenure at St. Inigoes, Mobberly still managed the day-to-day operations of the plantation. Mobberly hired the overseers. Mobberly decided how much food and clothing was distributed to the members of the enslaved community and determined the jobs they were forced to do. In his diary, he suggested that the "rod"—floggings, whippings, and other forms of harsh treatment—was necessary to ensure that Black people would follow orders and improve their productivity.

That same year, Mobberly received news that St. Inigoes would receive an infusion of new people. Father Ashton, who had been sued by the Mahoneys and had managed White Marsh for decades before being ousted by his fellow Jesuits, had died. Father Grassi decided that the eleven enslaved people he had owned would go to St. Inigoes: two men; two women, including one who was described as "sickly"; three teenagers; and four children. (Those men, women, and children were valued at $3,675 as part of the assessment of Ashton's estate.) They soon found that they were joining an enslaved community at odds with the man in charge.

As foreman, Louisa's father was the Black man charged with enforcing Mobberly's rules. But records suggest that Harry and the other enslaved men and women on the plantation found ways to resist the priests' rule.

In his diary, Mobberly described how Black people rebelled against harsh masters who "corrected" their behavior with a whipping: They would spread the word, damaging the man's reputation. His geese, chickens, and pigs would begin to disappear. Plantation tools would turn up broken. His horse might be borrowed in the middle of the night and ridden to the point of collapse. At St. Inigoes, enslaved families raised chickens and, in defiance of Mobberly's orders, harvested oysters on weekends and holidays.

Mobberly went through five overseers between 1816 and 1820 as he struggled to find a white man who could wield enough authority to keep the St. Inigoes enslaved community in line. He chafed at what he described as the constant insubordination that he and other white slaveholders had to endure. "Some years ago Blacks were more easily kept in due subordination, and were more patient under the rod of correction than they are now because then discipline flourished, but now it is going to decay," he complained.

Discontent also simmered among the free Black people who labored at St. Inigoes. Among those Black workers was Stephen Barnes, who was paid for digging ditches on the estate. A man described simply as "Old Free Abraham" did the dirty, grueling job of breaking flax. Dick and Gabe worked in timber, sawing planks of wood. "Free Charles & Stephen," who may well have been brothers, also chopped wood. (Charles was also occasionally mentioned by his full name, Charles Barnes.) The plantation was prone to being flooded by the St. Mary's River, so Mobberly often needed help to build and expand the ditches that kept water from flooding the fields. They were familiar figures on the plantation, and the Barnes family, in particular, would grow close to the Mahoneys. Many enslaved people in Maryland had free people in their families, just as the Mahoneys did. The courts had provided a pathway to freedom for some, while others had purchased their freedom or been manumitted by their owners. And although the Barnes brothers earned money for their labor and Harry and his family did not, enslaved and free blacks often shared common aspirations and worked hand in hand to press for better treatment.

In Maryland, free Blacks routinely faced discrimination from whites, who denied them the right to vote, the right to work in certain occupations, and the right to attend certain schools. And they were often treated by whites with contempt. Father Joseph Zwinge, the Jesuit treasurer who would write about the plantations many decades later, described the free blacks at St. Inigoes dismissively as stragglers who could barely eke out a living. "These free negroes were generally very poor and were worse off than slaves," he wrote, describing what he had learned from the plantation ledgers, former slaves, and parishioners in St. Inigoes.

Like Harry and his family, many free Blacks, such as the Barnes men, dreamed of resisting, of toppling the regime that marginalized them. Free in name but restricted by the laws and practices of the white people around them, they had learned how to navigate white-dominated society. But in the spring of 1817, Stephen and Charles Barnes decided that quiet resistance was not enough.

They met outside a local tavern on April 7, 1817, the Monday after Easter. It was a half hour before sunset, and the Barnes men joined about two hundred others, some enslaved, some free. The *New York Evening Post* reported that a brawl had broken out and several white people had tried to "command the peace." That was when they realized that it was not just an ordinary bar fight. "Suddenly," the writer recounted, "as if by preconcert, [the Blacks] turned upon the whites, and drove them off the lot, with outrageous violence."

The Black men called out to one another to fall into ranks, telling each other that this "was their time, if they meant to be free," the newspaper reported. The men then stoned the whites in their midst and beat them with sticks. When a constable tried to intervene, they attacked him, hurling stones, sticks, and fence rails until he and the other white men fled on foot into a neighboring house.

The crowd chased the constable down, following him to the house and bursting inside. When they realized that he had managed to escape, they ransacked the home. Then bullets flew into the crowd, fired from a nearby house. The Black men surrounded the house, destroyed the door and the windows, and warned the white people inside that that they would "set fire to it, and burn every soul in it alive" if they fired their weapons again.

Word of the insurrection spread among the terrified white community, heightening long-simmering fears that Black people might be preparing to massacre the families who controlled their lives. Black people—more than six thousand of them, slave and free—had outnumbered whites in St. Mary's for nearly two decades. By 1810, they accounted for about 52 percent of the population. Fears that enslaved and free people of color might join forces to overthrow the white hierarchy had long fueled nightmares all across the South. But on that night, no one was killed. The Black men scattered, disappearing into the night. If they had hoped to overthrow the white slaveholders, they had failed.

The following morning, the white men of St. Mary's County organized foot patrols to search the surrounding forests for the men who had organized and participated in the riot. For days, the fugitives stayed on the run, eluding capture, but in the end, more than a dozen were apprehended.

Some were whipped and sent back to their enslavers. At least five enslaved men were arrested on charges of insurrection. At least four free Black men were arrested and charged, including three members of the Barnes family, Stephen, Jere, and Charles. Officials described Charles as "a free negro not having the fear of God before his Eyes but being moved and seduced thereto by the instigation of the Devil." He and the other men had dared to step beyond the bounds of their circumscribed lives, to challenge white authority, and county officials wanted to make sure they paid dearly for it.

On May 12, 1817, five enslaved men found guilty of insurrection were sentenced to death by hanging. The following month, the governor of Maryland commuted the death sentences, news that came as an enormous relief to the prisoners, their families, and their supporters in the Black community. Instead, the governor decided that the punishment would be what most enslaved people in Maryland feared most: They would be sold to the Deep South.

"I do hereby order and direct that the Sheriff of the said County shall on or before the first day of August next cause the said Negroes Harry Jack Abraham Joe and John to be transported to the Apelousas there to be sold as Slave for life for the benefit of the State of Maryland," Governor Charles Carnan Ridgely wrote in his order.

Word had spread about the backbreaking work in the cotton and sugarcane fields of the Deep South and about the brutal treatment that the enslaved endured there. Southern enslavers had developed a harsh new labor system, different from the one commonly employed in the Chesapeake. Enslaved people were under constant surveillance, forced to work at a furious, unrelenting pace, and subject to extreme and unpredictable violence, all of which were designed to extract the highest possible levels of productivity from them. The new system helped usher in a boom in cotton production at a terrible cost. Malnourished workers died young. A quarter of the enslaved babies born perished before their first birthdays. Survivors grew familiar with whippings that left the body bloody as a price for slowing or stumbling as they worked.

"The sugar and cotton plantations . . . we knew all about them," said Lewis Hayden, an enslaved man recalling his childhood in the 1810s. "When a friend was carried off, why, it was the same as death."

The men who were spared from sale faced punishment in Maryland. "Many [of the accused] were flogged," the Washington, DC, *Daily National Intelligencer* reported, "and suffered to return to their homes." What happened to Charles Barnes remains unknown. But Stephen Barnes was sentenced to ten years in prison. He died in the state penitentiary.

Mobberly's ledger book suggests that life on the St. Inigoes plantation went on as usual after the uprising, at least for the priests. In

November, the estate shipped 100 bushels of turnips, 60 bushels of potatoes, and 20 bushels of corn to Georgetown College.

By the spring of 1818, the anxiety in the white community had eased so much that the archbishop of Baltimore paid a visit to St. Inigoes, where he dined with Father Carbery and officiated at a religious ceremony for eighty-one people. The archbishop, who spent several days on the plantation, praised the estate's church, which Carbery had painstakingly restored, as "handsome and clean" and noted "the great piety" of the congregation.

The respectful reception that the archbishop received on the estate masked the tension building over Mobberly's unfair treatment. The failed insurrection made it clear that a violent overthrow was unlikely to succeed. But in the slave quarters where Louisa was now about five years old, people agreed that something needed to be done.

THE FOLLOWING YEAR, in September 1819, Father Peter Kenney, Rome's emissary, arrived in New York, charged with, among other things, investigating the situation on the plantations. In February 1820, the priest set out for the estates, stopping at St. Thomas Manor in Charles County and Newtown and St. Inigoes in St. Mary's County.

When he arrived at St. Inigoes, the enslaved people on the plantation knew the time to speak their minds had finally come. They understood that challenging a white man, any white man, was perilous. Mobberly had already shown that he would not hesitate to treat those who challenged him harshly. For years the Black people at St. Inigoes had relied on a strategy of quiet resistance, keenly aware that Mobberly might flog them or try to persuade his superiors to sell them and their children. But they took their chances and laid out for Kenney a devastating portrait of life on the estate under Mobberly.

They told him about their mistreatment and poor living conditions. The Jesuits provided a one-story, one-room wooden hut for each family, which under the best of circumstances "presented a nice appearance to the eye," one priest said, but the dwellings had deteriorated to such an extent that even a senior Jesuit would describe the housing provided to the enslaved as "very bad." Their concerns left a deep impression on the Irish priest. "They are furious against Mobberly nor can it be hoped, that he can do good by remaining with them," he wrote in April of that year. "Indeed, there have been instances of undue treatment, even allowing for exaggerations."

During his visits to the Jesuit plantations, Kenney learned that the enslaved sometimes received inadequate food—"In some places they have only had one pound & a quarter of meat: often this has not been sound"—and harsh treatment. He discovered that pregnant women were being whipped and that some women were even whipped inside the priests' homes. This particular kind of punishment, he wrote, "should not be inflicted on any female in the house, where the priest lives. (Sometimes they have been tied up in the priests own parlor, which is very indecorous.)"

Such treatment had given the enslaved "cause to complain," he wrote. The Jesuits, Kenney said, governed the plantations with "arbitrary regulation," with different rules on different farms, rules that "frequently changed" when a new manager took over.

He told the Jesuit leaders in Maryland that they needed to change their ways. He urged them to provide enough food for their enslaved people, to determine whether they were allowed to raise their own chickens and hogs, and to agree among themselves whether the laborers should have afternoons off on Saturdays so that uniformity would prevail from one plantation to the next.

He also addressed complaints raised by some priests who had expressed outrage that some of the Black people they owned refused to embrace the Catholic faith and its rules and requirements. In response, Kenney said the enslaved must be sent to church on Ash Wednesday and Good Friday and that the priests must find a way "to promote morality and the frequentation of the sacraments."

That the Jesuits often engaged in high-minded discussions about the morality of the enslaved even while they were willing to buy and sell their fellow human beings was not lost on the enslaved people on the plantations. Some Black men and women apparently flouted Catholic mores by engaging in amorous interludes "in the very threshold of the sanctuary," Kenney continued disapprovingly. "The scandal is enormous," he wrote.

Even though Kenney was willing to listen to the enslaved men and women on the plantations and to press the Jesuits to improve their living conditions, he wasn't primarily interested in their general welfare. His priority was the health of the Catholic mission, and he believed that all the enslaved on the plantations should be sold, whether or not it tore families apart.

Finding a way to replace the slaves on the plantations, he said, "either by employing whites, or letting out their lands to reputable tenants, or any other way in which it can be effected without injury to the property" would "relieve this mission of an immense burthen & a painful responsibility & the whole Society of the odium which is thrown on it . . ."

But the American Jesuits were determined to hold on to their human property. In August 1820, they formally rescinded their earlier plan to free the Black people they held captive after selling them to buyers who could use their labor for a term of several years. The plan had never been carried out and was deemed "prejudicial" to the interests of the Maryland mission, which still counted on the income and produce from the plantations.

Back in Rome later that year, Kenney laid out his findings for the Jesuit leadership. He did not mince words when he outlined the problems on the Maryland plantations. The enslaved "complain continually about us," he wrote in October 1820—with some good reason, he pointed out, noting that the slaves "live in such a destitute manner that they create a scandal for Catholics."

Father Adam Marshall, who soon took over the administration of the Jesuit mission in Maryland, reported his own grim findings in a letter to his superior in Rome four months later, describing plantations "in a very wretched condition, very poorly provided with the necessities for cultivation, their buildings insufficient & in ruins, particularly those which accommodate the slaves which are almost universally unfit for human beings to live in."

A few months after the Black community at St. Inigoes stood up to Mobberly by voicing their complaints to Kenney, Mobberly was ousted from the estate. He would never supervise a plantation again. It was a hard-won victory for the enslaved people who had suffered under his rule for nearly a decade.

His removal propelled a new man to power at St. Inigoes. Father Carbery, the priest who had arrived just four years earlier to tend to the congregation, was selected to take over the day-to-day management of the plantation and the enslaved community. The priest, who came from a well-known family in St. Mary's County, had been watching Mobberly and familiarizing himself with the operations of the estate.

Carbery would develop a view of Black initiative and capacity that differed sharply from that of the other white men of his generation. He saw a way for Black people and white people to work together to improve productivity and the lives of the enslaved on the plantation.

6

A College on the Rise

WHEN THOMAS MULLEDY, FRESH FROM HIS YEARS IN ROME, assumed Georgetown's presidency in 1829, his presence was felt almost immediately. Within months of his arrival, the number of boarding students jumped from twenty to sixty. "The College increases," he reported proudly in a letter to Father Roothaan, now the head of the Jesuits worldwide, in January 1830. The new students included the adopted son of the nation's president, Andrew Jackson, as well as the son of the secretary of state.

But there were other issues on Mulledy's mind as he wrote to Roothaan that winter. "As is my duty, I write to you, to inform you of the affairs in this world," he said. He was only four months into his presidency, but he was determined to attack what he viewed as one of the biggest problems facing the Jesuits in the United States: their reliance on the plantation economy and enslaved labor. "Would it not be better to sell these farms and to invest the money in banks?" he asked. He said that the proceeds from the sale of the goods produced on the estates were used mostly to maintain the enslaved workers who produced them and were "badly spent by the Fathers who are their handlers."

And as for the captive men, women, and children, Mulledy

ticked off a number of complaints, describing them as amoral, chronically unhappy, and difficult to manage. "Are the reasons for the misbehavior of these slaves not so numerous that it is almost impossible to make them good Christians or faithful servants?" he asked. "Are our slaves not proverbially the most wicked in the whole country? Are they not difficult to govern? Does American mania for emancipation (now so general) not render them discontented?"

Mulledy suggested selling them all, at least for a term of several years, after which they might be freed, revisiting the plan that the Jesuits had adopted and rescinded years earlier. Otherwise, he warned, they might be obliged to sell them for good, which would force families to be separated. "And is this not an odious thing in America?"

Mulledy was calling for nothing less than the dismantling of the plantation system that had supported the Jesuits for more than a century. He was not alone. His compatriots, the men who had studied with him in Rome, agreed. The new generation of American-born Jesuit leaders—Mulledy and McSherry—had returned from Italy with a new vision. (Father James Ryder, who had been born in Ireland, shared their views.) All three were first- or second-generation Irish Americans who dreamed of transforming Georgetown from a small, chronically understaffed college into the flagship of a network of Jesuit institutions of higher education across the northeastern United States.

For a white man looking to profit from slave sales, it could hardly have been a better time. Cotton production in the Deep South was booming, fueling the demand for enslaved workers and sending their prices skyrocketing. Between 1830 and 1835, the price of Black men in New Orleans nearly doubled. The number of enslaved men and women forcibly relocated to southern cotton and cane states was soaring.

But Mulledy's plans outraged and scandalized some of the older priests and some of the foreign-born priests, who viewed the plantations as part and parcel of the Jesuit tradition in the United States. They were horrified by the notion of selling the enslaved people they believed they were responsible for caring for. They also chafed at Mulledy's leadership style, objecting to his brusque and impulsive manner, his refusal to tolerate opposition, and what some viewed as his neglect of religious discipline among the college's students.

With the gulf between the American-born and European-born priests widening, Father Kenney, who had been sent by Rome to set things right in the troubled American mission nearly a decade earlier, was dispatched to the United States once again. As before, he carried the title of special visitor, but this time, he was also appointed the superior of the Maryland mission, in charge of overseeing the fractious Jesuits and charged not only with determining whether the plantations were financially viable but whether the conditions on the estates had deteriorated to such an extent that the enslaved men and women there were forced to live like animals. Should the Jesuits feel financially and morally compelled to sell off the plantations and slaves "and use the revenue for other things"? Roothaan wondered.

"He tells me, that he is aware, that a great variety of opinions exist on the subject & therefore that I should be careful to scrutinize every pro & con, that can be offered on the matter," wrote Kenney, describing the mission that Roothaan had entrusted to him.

Kenney departed Liverpool for the United States in September 1830, just as Georgetown was resuming classes for the fall. Mulledy, who was beginning his second year as Georgetown's president, had turned to the newspapers once again to help promote the college, reminding readers of the *United States' Telegraph* that classes would start on September 15 and that "no charge is made for tuition," noting that the Jesuits had "appropriated for the support of its Professors the annual income of its estates." Mulledy may have sharply questioned the value of the plantations, but the college still counted on the income the estates produced.

Kenney was impressed with what he found. "By the grace of God," he wrote on January 10, 1831, "everything is going so well that I have found little to change." He described Mulledy as "an active rector—he gives satisfaction to the members of the house and strongly upholds discipline both among the boarders and the religious, and is highly regarded by outsiders." Kenney remained keenly aware of Mulledy's shortcomings, his "extremely impetuous enthusiasm and excessive patriotism," but said the new college president was working on these defects and striving to serve God as he rehabilitated the college.

He was also impressed by the college's impressive surge in enrollment; by that fall, the number of boarding students had jumped again, from 60 to 102. And Mulledy had begun expanding the campus facilities, creating a new library, a new museum, and a new chapel. He had done so while maintaining fiscal discipline, noted Kenney, who pointed out that the college's debts had been markedly reduced.

"Nothing escapes his hands," wrote a fellow Jesuit of Mulledy in the spring of 1831. "The college is flourishing."

Mulledy wanted the college to expand even more and to charge tuition to raise additional funds. Kenney agreed to support the call to charge tuition. (The plan was approved by Rome in 1833 for day students only; Mulledy used the change as an opportunity to increase the fees of all students.) And he increasingly favored Mulledy's position on the plantations, despite opposition from priests who advocated for the enslaved.

"The greatest threat we can do to them," wrote Father Fidèle de Grivel to Roothaan that year, "is to tell them: I will sell you."

Grivel, a French priest who had been originally assigned to advise Father Kenney, objected to the proposed mass sale for different reasons. He argued that it would be impossible to find enough white farmers to cultivate the land and difficult to find a buyer who would be willing to pay what the enslaved workforce was worth. Plus, he said, the Jesuits would likely squander the profits, all the while losing their influence and standing in a society dominated by wealthy slaveholders.

And what, he asked, would become of the enslaved?

He depicted some enslaved workers as lazy but dismissed some of the myths and stereotypes white people often held about Black people. Using the paternalistic language common to the priests at the time, he protested that they were devout, faithful Catholics, "The negroes here do not have any bad smell, whatever a bunch of travelers write about it, etc," he wrote. "They are almost all married (or widowed): one does not hear any talk of adultery, nor other disorders, and I believe that their morals are better than those of the white Americans, [and] even more so (than those) of Europeans (in certain countries)." He said that the priests remained sharply divided over the question even as Mulledy and his allies pressed "to sell [everything] and place our money in the bank." He warned that Father Kenney, who was supposed to weigh in on the matter, was already firmly situated in Mulledy's camp.

In fact, Kenney visited the Bohemia plantation shortly after his return to the United States, tallying up the number of enslaved people—nine in total, including three children—and reporting disapprovingly on what he viewed as their poor work ethic, lack of religious piety, and flagrant disregard for the plantation's rules. One man had married without the permission of the priests in charge of the plantation, he complained. Another had opened a saloon in his home, selling whiskey to Black people at Bohemia and nearby plantations. Others traveled to Delaware, without seeking permission, to buy and sell goods at a local market.

"Not one has been to the Sacraments for 12 yrs except an old woman: seldom is one seen at mass on Sundays," he wrote. "All swear & curse: 2 are drunk 10 or 12 times in the year . . . they hold it to be no sin to take either from the farm or house, what they may want or wish to have in either diet, drink or clothing."

The enslaved people even left the plantation, without approval, for their own purposes. "Two of the men are married to slaves in other farms, & are frequently away without leave even for the whole night," he complained, adding that "even the young female goes out at night."

Kenney did not outline a plan right then to address what he clearly viewed as a plantation run amok. But Grivel was right in his suspicions. So far, Mulledy and his supporters had been unable to persuade Rome to sell off all the nearly three hundred Jesuit slaves. (Roothaan had decided against a mass sale even before Kenney had completed his assessment of the estate's viability.)

But Kenney, who had begun prodding the Jesuits to divest themselves of their enslaved labor force back in the 1820s, seemed determined to move forward, even if it meant selling one handful of human beings at a time. The Irish priest had demonstrated that he could be sympathetic to the enslaved, as he was with the men and women of St. Inigoes, but he still believed the Maryland Jesuits would be better off without them. By documenting what he described as sinful and immoral behavior among the Black people at Bohemia, he was laying the groundwork for their removal.

He was soon talking openly about his plan to sell the enslaved people. "I regret that the sale of the wicked slaves at Bohemia" has "been so long delayed," he wrote to Mulledy in December in a letter that suggested that some of the brothers working at the plantation might have felt uneasy about the plan.

Within weeks, the sales had begun. Kenney described them matter-of-factly in his handwritten notes, amid his description of the accounting of the bushels of wheat that had been harvested and sold. "Sale of boy Jery & little Mary," he wrote.

Women were sold. Men were sold. The children were sold, too, including one boy who was shipped away from the plantation on his own, without parents or relatives.

"Sould the little Boy Jerry to Alfred B. Thomas for $150," read one notation in a Jesuit ledger that documented Kenney's sale in January 1832.

"Sould Jacob to Jacob Caulk for 9 years and six months for $250 after that Term of years he is to be free," read another.

On February 2, Phillis, fifty-four, and Mary, the nine-year-old girl, appeared in the records as having been sold for $80.50. Three days later, the Jesuits recorded the sale of David Mackey, who had been sold for $150. The enslaved people were sold mostly to white tenant farmers and neighbors on nearby farms. (Two of the enslaved women on the Bohemia plantation were shipped to St. Joseph's, another Jesuit farm.) When it was all over, only one of the original Bohemia slaves remained, "a boy" named Bill.

That summer, Kenney celebrated the Fourth of July at Georgetown with Mulledy before returning to Bohemia. Students fired the cannon on campus from early morning through nightfall while the American flag fluttered atop the college. Kenney and the other guests listened to a reading from the Declaration of Independence and sat down for a dinner punctuated by "many patriotic toasts" and songs. Kenney looked around campus and was pleased with what he saw.

Mulledy had embarked on an ambitious expansion project at Georgetown. He had already built a four-story brick infirmary. But he wanted to do even more. He dreamed of a large building that would provide spaces for students and faculty in which to meet, dine, study, and pray. Grivel heard about it and wrote to a fellow priest in London, describing Mulledy's plan to build "a large building, cellar, banquet, two stories above & a large garret 120 feet long & 30 broad To join the new & old College."

Mulledy's advisers felt inclined to support him. In a short time, he had transformed the college into a high-profile institution that enjoyed the support of powerful men and prominent families in the nation's capital. President Andrew Jackson declared "that he did not know a more honest and disciplined college in America than Georgetown," one priest reported.

But once again, the money question weighed heavily on everyone. The surging enrollment had helped to reduce the college's debts to about $2,000. But the "large building" would greatly increase that debt and the pressure to sell enslaved people. One senior Jesuit, the mission's treasurer, voiced those concerns, fearing that Mulledy's ambitions would outpace the college's funds.

Kenney had reservations, too, at least initially. "I need not say, that I feel greatly inclined to sanction the immediate erection of the new building," he wrote, "but it is necessary to proceed with caution, when there is question of $12,000, tho it may be a very reasonable sum for the value to be obtained."

Mulledy found a way. A seminarian, who had yet to take his final vows, offered a $12,000 loan at 6 percent annual interest. "Began foundation of new building," Mulledy wrote in his diary.

Several days after the Fourth of July festivities, Kenney was back in Bohemia, praising the "indefatigable" Mulledy and the "flourishing" college, pointing to its 130 full-time boarders and its new infirmary and noting that workers had just broken ground on the four-story addition that would include a chapel, a refectory, and a study hall.

Kenney was also pleased with what he found on the Bohemia plantation. He reported to Mulledy that the brother in charge of managing the estate "looks much better than he did last year." "He attributes much of his renewed health to the peace, which the absence of his wicked slaves allows him to enjoy," he said.

That brother may well have treasured that peace of mind. But among the scores of enslaved people on the rest of the Jesuit plantations, word had spread about the possibility of a mass sale and with it a mounting sense of dread.

By that summer of 1832, many of the enslaved people in St. Mary's County, where the Mahoneys lived, were begging for information. Father Peter Havermans, who was working at the Newtown plantation, also situated in St. Mary's County, described his feelings of helplessness as he fielded their desperate questions. Would they be sold? When would they be sold? The priest had no answers.

"There is only one thing that makes me here gloomy and that is the present situation of our servants," he wrote to a fellow priest that July. "They all have heard that they are sold, or are to be sold, and that they are to be carried out of the state." The mood, he said, was grim.

Love and Peril

GLISTENING WATERWAYS CRISSCROSSED ST. MARY'S COUNTY, drawing young men to the twisting creeks and rivers and the vast, shimmering expanse of the Chesapeake Bay. Some became fishermen or oystermen. Others turned to the shipbuilding trade.

Arnold Jones worked on the boats that carried people and produce on schooners and steamers, pilot boats and ferries. He was an enslaved man, but he had learned the ways of the mariners who navigated the inlets and shoals. He lived near the St. Inigoes estate and had become a sailor in his own right, a Black man so skilled in his trade that he had become one of the most valuable possessions of the white man who had enslaved him.

Arnold was nearly thirty and worldly, a voyager who knew the big cities of Baltimore and Washington, DC, and one day, he caught Anny Mahoney's eye. She was about eighteen or nineteen and sheltered, having spent her entire life on the St. Inigoes plantation.

Some Jesuit priests tried to control the romantic lives of the Black people they owned, weighing in on the suitability of potential partners, even forbidding marriages in some instances. But Anna had good reason to believe that Father Carbery would bless her union. He saw Black people in a different light.

When Carbery mingled with the enslaved at St. Inigoes, he didn't see lazy, childlike, or defiant people; he saw people with initiative and drive who longed for the freedom to control their own lives. His fellow priests had long complained that the enslaved neglected the fields for their own gardens and slipped away without permission to sell their produce to earn money for themselves. But where other Jesuits saw problems, Carbery saw possibilities. And around the time Arnold and Anny started courting, he had decided to find a way to harness the creative energy of the people on the plantation.

Back in the 1820s, Kenney had urged the Maryland Jesuits to consider shifting their farming model from one that relied on enslaved laborers to one that relied on white tenant farmers. Carbery wondered instead if there was a way to transform the Black laborers at St. Inigoes into tenant farmers. What if he gave the Black men and women on the plantation the freedom to plant and sell a portion of everything they grew?

It would be an experiment, one that would transform the relationship between the priest and the people he owned. It would certainly be viewed with skepticism by some in the Jesuit leadership, not to mention the estate's white neighbors, who might fear that the unorthodox arrangement would only undermine their authority and encourage defiance and willfulness among the enslaved on other plantations.

But Carbery, who had a seat on the board of the Corporation of Roman Catholic Clergymen, which controlled the Jesuit plantations, had some influence of his own. He believed in the character and the capacity of the Black people at St. Inigoes, and he believed that this new way of working would result in greater productivity. Whether he sought approval from the Jesuit senior leadership remains unknown. But we do know that he put his plan into motion.

He divided the plantation into five or six farms. He decided to farm the first with about forty enslaved workers. He rented out the second to a white tenant farmer, who would pay $300 a year in rent. Then he divided the remaining parts among any Black families that could pay him a dollar and a quarter per acre each year. The families could farm the land as they pleased, giving a portion of the produce from each harvest to him and selling the rest. Meanwhile, he promised to make any necessary repairs to the houses, stables, and barns.

Kenney arrived at St. Inigoes in the summer of 1832. He had last set foot on the plantation more than a decade earlier, and he was astonished by its transformation. "I am much delighted to see the total change in the house for the better," he wrote in his journal, describing the manor house as "well furnished & abundantly supplied with every thing that is necessary to exercise hospitality with neatness, comfort and generosity." "What a difference from its standing in 1820!" he marveled. "It does not owe a single cent! It was then very heavy in debt."

Carbery's radical methods were clearly bearing fruit. Under his watch, the plantation was productive, and the enslaved at St. Inigoes enjoyed a degree of independence rare in a slaveholding society.

Some traveled long distances on their own, visiting relatives on neighboring farms. In at least one instance, Carbery allowed an enslaved man to abandon St. Inigoes altogether. ("I had no objections to Lewis leaving this place, as he never liked to live in the country," the priest wrote to a fellow priest at Georgetown, urging him to hire the enslaved man as a blacksmith.)

The priest became known as a white man who recognized the humanity of Black people. He expressed admiration for the craftsmanship of an enslaved man who built a windmill on the estate. "He had no instructions from anyone," he wrote. "She is well built and appears to answer well." And he praised Black Catholics—the Mahoneys among them—and proudly described those who converted to the faith. "Most all the Blacks have imbraced the Catholic faith," he reported years later, "& are good & edifying."

When William Gaston, Georgetown's first student, who would

become a US congressman and a prominent justice on North Carolina's Supreme Court, decided to free an enslaved young man he owned, he turned to Carbery. Gaston, who would go on to affirm that free Blacks could be state citizens, wanted to be sure that the young man received vocational training in preparation for freedom. He trusted that Carbery would provide it. "I place my boy Augustus under the charge of the Revd. Joseph Carbury, to receive moral and religious instruction, to be taught an useful trade, and, when qualified to make fit use of his freedom to be emancipated," he wrote. (Carbery kept his word and freed the man in 1830.)

Carbery came from a prominent family with deep roots in St. Mary's County—his brother served as mayor of Washington, DC—and counted slaveholders among his kinsmen, which may have provided him some insulation from criticism. But Thomas Hughes, the twentieth-century chronicler of the early Catholic Church in the United States, viewed Carbery with disdain. In Hughes's eyes, Carbery was "an ignoramus" who could barely read, a country bumpkin compared to the sophisticated and worldly European Jesuits, who were steeped in the order's traditions. But Carbery earned the respect of his contemporaries, despite what some may have described as his eccentric views on issues of race. He was known among the Jesuits as a skilled farmer, which was no small matter to the Jesuits, whose plantations were so often poorly run.

In the 1820s, Kenney had even considered putting Carbery in charge of the finances of the entire Jesuit mission in Maryland, though Carbery was not highly positioned in the Jesuit hierarchy. The dearth of qualified priests made him an attractive candidate. "Many speak in favor of Mr. Carbery, who tho at first might not carry the authority which the place would require, yet his good conduct would increase it," Kenney wrote, "he would certainly be active & industrious, he would improve with experience."

Instead, Carbery was elected a member of the Select Body of the Clergy and became a trustee of the powerful Corporation of Roman Catholic Clergymen, which gave him a seat at the table in the decision-making about the Jesuits' plantations and enslaved workforce. Still, he remained known as a modest man whose homespun humor endeared him to people. He collected jokes in his diary, writing down his favorites, all rooted in the agricultural life he knew so well. ("When is a fowl's neck like a bell? When it's rung for dinner." "Why is the sun like a good loaf? Because it's light when it rises." "I wonder, said a woman of humor, why my husband & I quarrel so often, for we agree uniformly on one grand point: He wishes to be master, & so do I.")

He loved horses and brewed homemade remedies when they fell ill. "Take of Wallnut tree bark, red oak bark, sassafras roots, spicewood twigs, young pine tops, the running briar, each as much as you can grasp in both hands, boiled in four gallons of water to two, then add a pint of soft sope," he wrote, describing his treatment for horse ailments.

Black people described Carbery as a gentle man, and he became particularly close to the Mahoney family, honoring the promise the Jesuits had made in recognition of Harry's courage during the War of 1812. No one in the family had been sold, and he spared them from having to do field work. The Mahoney women cooked and cleaned at the manor house, with its grand parlor and high ceilings, while the Mahoney men cared for the horses and helped Carbery and the other resident priests and their visitors.

As for Anny, she and Arnold received permission to marry and were blessed with two children in the early 1830s. Anny named her firstborn Arnold, after his father. She named her baby girl, born sometime around 1832, after her beloved sister Louisa.

The infants joined an enslaved community of about ninety people, according to Carbery's handwritten list. The population of enslaved people had grown by nearly a third. The number of young children had nearly doubled, while some of the elderly had vanished from the list altogether, capturing the cycles of birth and death on the estate. Anny's parents, Harry and Anna, were elders now and still in good health.

Anny knew, as she tended her growing family, as did Louisa, that they enjoyed a rare degree of privilege. And Anny had married a man who had grown accustomed to charting his own course, traveling far beyond the watchful eye of his enslaver.

That was why the news in November 1833 must have come as such a blow. That month, some looked to the sky and saw what they believed to be a fearful omen. On November 13, in the hours before dawn, the dark skies overlooking the plantation exploded in a shower of stars. Thousands of fiery meteors blazed through the night in what one witness described as "the most grand and alarming spectacle which ever beamed upon the eye of man." The stars fell in torrents, like cascades of raindrops during a deluge or snowflakes during a blizzard, and the heavens thundered. "To the eye it presented the appearance of what may be called a raining of fire, for I can compare it to nothing else."

People gaped at the extraordinary meteor showers, which could be seen all across the country, and wondered what they foretold. "Some in dreadful affright predicted the end of the world," reported the *Daily National Intelligencer,* based in Washington, DC. "Others of more stern souls were sure that it at least prognosticated some dreadful war."

At St. Inigoes, the fiery showers left a lasting imprint on the people who witnessed it. Frank Campbell, an enslaved man not yet in his twenties, would remember it decades later. Anny's son, Arnold Jr., was about three or four, and baby Louisa was about one when the heavens opened. But a newspaper advertisement published the following day made it clear that Anny and her husband had troubles more immediate than anything the heavens foretold.

A terrible fate had befallen Arnold's brother Moses. His wife had been sold and his entire life turned upside down. Moses was a sailor, too, accustomed to the freedom of traveling the rivers. But he was powerless to save his bride. So he had requested and received permission to visit her in Baltimore. Like Arnold, he had long plied the waterways of the county and had always returned to his master.

This time, though, he didn't return home. An advertisement in the newspaper warned white readers across the state that a runaway from St. Mary's County was on the loose.

"After remaining some 4 or 5 days, he left Baltimore and I expected for home, but he has not been heard of since," wrote his enslaver, Thomas Smith, in the advertisement, offering a $100 reward to anyone who could secure Moses's capture. Smith, who lived near the St. Inigoes plantation, described Moses as a mulatto who "often smiles when spoken to, speaks softly and has a deceitful countenance." The runaway was "a first rate hand by water, knows the bay very well, and a good deal about the Potomac river," Smith said. Moses, who was about twenty-seven, was one of more than a dozen people enslaved by Smith in the early 1830s. As sailors, he and Arnold were Smith's most skilled laborers and his most valuable human possessions, each valued at $250. "I am induced to believe he has put for Philadelphia," Smith wrote. "Captains and owners of vessels will be particular not to employ the said boy. But should they meet with him to secure him in any jail so I can get him."

Philadelphia was a haven for free Blacks, an important stop on the Underground Railroad, and a welcoming sanctuary for a Black man on the run. Harry Mahoney's brother had moved there after he had purchased his freedom. But the notice in the newspaper meant that white men across Maryland would be hunting for Moses, who had last been seen wearing black pantaloons, coarse shoes, an old white hat, and "a very fine long overcoat such as all sailors use," the advertisement said. The notice warned that Moses would likely ditch those clothes, "except his big coat nearly new which I think he will not part with," in an effort to avoid detection.

Would he be captured? Would he be beaten or tortured? Would he ever see his wife and enslaved relatives again? Anny and her husband had little choice but to wonder and worry as they continued to work and care for their young children. By then, though, even the comparatively small degree of autonomy that the Mahoneys enjoyed at St. Inigoes seemed tenuous.

Earlier in the year, William McSherry, Thomas Mulledy's ally, had been selected as the new leader of the Maryland Jesuits, which had been elevated from a mission to a province within the Jesuits' international structure. Nearly two hundred years after first setting foot in Maryland, the Jesuits tended to a growing flock increasingly centered in the big cities of the Eastern Seaboard. New York counted 35,000 Catholics among its citizens; Philadelphia, 25,000; Baltimore, 19,000; and Boston, 11,000. And now, for the first time, the leadership was dominated by two American-born priests—Mulledy and McSherry—who were determined to sell off all of the enslaved people on the plantations.

McSherry was no intellectual. He had "modest intellectual gifts," one historian wrote. Even Kenney, who championed him, had described him only a few years earlier as "not endowed with that shrewdness and energy" required for a senior position at the college. Others had kinder views, describing him as "very amiable and kind" and as a priest with great potential. His connections with senior Jesuits, including Jan Roothaan and Kenney, cultivated during his time with Mulledy in Rome, would help smooth his path to power. In the early 1830s, McSherry had served for a time as the minister of the college, as the financial administrator of the Maryland mission, and as Kenney's assistant, and he had spent considerable time striding across the Jesuit estates and scrutinizing their often haphazard records.

A black-and-white portrait painted several years after he became the first provincial, the title given to the Jesuit leader in charge of the province, captured him staring into the distance, his hair swept back, his eyes fixed on something unseen, a striking man in a dark robe or jacket with a white collar. He was in his thirties—just thirty-three when he was appointed provincial, but lines had begun to creep across his forehead. No records have emerged to indicate what the enslaved people made of the priest with the deep-set eyes and narrow nose. But his promotion would have a profound impact on the Mahoneys and the other enslaved people on the Jesuit plantations.

McSherry had visited St. Inigoes and had walked the fields with

Kenney, who had described with delight the improvements under
Carbery. But McSherry shared none of Kenney's optimism. In a
series of reports about the plantations that he apparently penned
that year, McSherry mentioned none of Carbery's improvements.
He didn't discuss the unorthodox priest's energy and enthusiasm or
his decision to give enslaved people more power and incentive to
farm. He didn't mention that the plantation's debts had been wiped
out or that the plantation was finally becoming productive. Some
Jesuits would point to Carbery's experiment at St. Inigoes as a
model, as an example of how the plantations might become profitable farms. But McSherry emphasized that the estate was failing to
produce much income. Ninety enslaved people lived on the plantation, and only forty-three could work, he said. The rest were too
old or too young, "but all must be supported, clothed, there doctors fees paid (etc.)." He tallied up the rent collected from the white
tenant farmers, who turned over a third of their produce to Carbery. Then he turned to the lands cultivated by the enslaved workers, who produced tobacco, corn, and wheat. Altogether the farm
generated about $1,900 in annual income, he said. But the planta-
tion's expenses, which included the upkeep of the enslaved families,
repairs of the buildings and manor house, and agricultural equip-
ment, were "so large . . . that there are frequently not $600 clear
after the above expenses and the Procurator of the Province is frequently embarrassed for on account of the delay of the payment"
needed to cover the real estate taxes, he wrote.

His accounting of the state of the other plantations—Newtown
and St. Thomas Manor—was even more grim. Rome had declined
to approve a mass sale of slaves, but McSherry seemed undeterred.
Bit by bit, he was building his case. Mulledy was still pushing, too.
"We cannot have both flourishing colleges and flourishing missions," he wrote to Roothaan in that fall of 1833.

Meanwhile, Kenney was continuing to search for buyers, determined to sell people one by one, if necessary. He tried to sell enslaved people from St. Thomas Manor but was stymied by the priest

in charge, who dug in his heels. Undeterred, Kenney turned his attention to a woman who had earned his ire by flouting the mores of the Catholic Church. "Approved of selling Lucy, who is again pregnant of an illegitimate child," he wrote in his journal. An enslaved worker at Georgetown named Gabe was sold as well.

As one elderly man enslaved by the Jesuits learned, loyal service counted for little. His name was Thomas Brown, and he wrote to the Maryland Jesuits, pleading for help. A decade earlier, Brown, his wife, and two other enslaved couples had been forced to abandon their families to accompany a band of Maryland Jesuits heading to Missouri to establish a novitiate just north of a small school in St. Louis. They had trekked for eight hundred miles with the priests, lugging heavy supplies over land and on timber floats that bobbed precariously down a rushing river. In Missouri, the three couples were forced to live in a single cabin under dismal conditions. They endured whippings and worked from dawn to dusk. The settlement had prospered. The Jesuits had taken over the school, which would become Saint Louis University.

But in a letter sent to McSherry that fall, Brown said that he and his wife were suffering unbearable hardships under his Jesuit enslavers in St. Louis, despite decades of faithful service. "I have been a faithful servant in the Society going on 38 years; & my wife Molly has been born & raised in the Society," he said in the letter, which may have been written by someone else who transcribed his words. "Now we have not a place to lay our heads in our old age after all our Service. We live at present in rotten logg house so old & decayed that at every blast of wind we are afraid of our lives and such as it is it belongs to one of the neighbors." He said that other enslaved people had far better lodgings. But his enslaver, the Jesuit president of St. Louis University, "wants me and my wife to live in the loft of one of the outhouses where there is no fire place. Nor any way to warm us during the winter—and your Reverence Knows it is Cold enough here. I have not a doubt but cold will Kill both me and my wife here. To prevent the Evil, I am willing to Buy myself & wife free if you Accept of 100 dollars 50 dollars I can pay down in Cash, the rest as soon as I possibly can. Rev. Father, Consider this is as much as I can raise, & as much as our old Bones are worth; have pity on Us, let us go free for one hundred dollars or else we will Surely perish with the Cold. Oh!"

No records have emerged that suggest that Thomas Brown ever received any response or assistance from McSherry, who may have had little interest in the fate of individual slaves though he remained, as ever, set on finding a way to dispose of the enslaved people in his care in their entirety.

But Rome remained reluctant to move forward with a mass sale, perhaps, in part, because the average price of an enslaved person had fallen as the economy faltered. So in that fall of 1834, McSherry began considering a new option.

The state legislature had appropriated $200,000 to cover the cost of sending free and recently freed Black people to Africa with the assistance of the Maryland State Colonization Society. The plan had its roots in white anxieties inflamed by Nat Turner's Virginia rebellion, in which dozens of whites had been killed. Many free Blacks in Maryland viewed the plan with disdain and mounted protests against it. "The prejudices of the colored people in Baltimore and other large Towns, against African Colonization, are so strong that distributing literature among them would be to throw it away," a white supporter noted.

But McSherry smelled an opportunity. He wanted to keep his personal interest in colonization private, so he sent an emissary, Will Erkead, a Catholic layman with ties to the colonization society, to discuss the matter with the group's board. Erkead told the group that he represented "a large Catholic proprietor of slaves" who was interested in resettling enslaved people on the African continent. In October 1834, he reported back to McSherry, enthused about what he had learned. The society had purchased "twenty miles square" of land in what is now southern Liberia and created a new colony called Cape Palmas, he wrote in a letter to

McSherry. It was an extraordinary development: The state of Maryland, working with a private organization, had established a US territory overseas, a foreign policy move typically reserved for federal officials.

"The country is represented as fertile—and abounding in excellent water," he said, and was ideal for growing grains. The territory was free of the fevers and diseases that plagued other parts of the continent. Already, some sixty white settlers from Maryland had lived there for several months without falling ill. Recent reports indicated that everything was in place, and the colony was ready for new arrivals. "The government house & dwellings for the settlers had been set up, their land cleared, & the cassada crop planted, & the whole party had passed through their seasoning fever," he wrote. "The relations between the settlers & natives had continued thus far pacific." He told the colonization society's board that allowing his associate to move enslaved people to the colony might encourage other prominent Catholics to do the same, provided that the slaveholders could be assured that the Blacks would have the freedom to practice their faith. The response from the board was overwhelmingly enthusiastic.

In his report to McSherry, Erkead emphasized that he had "endeavored to confine (himself) to facts." But he acknowledged that he might be viewing the prospect of resettlement with rose-colored glasses, given his fervent support of colonization and his belief that "a vast deal of good will be accomplished by it, if it proves, as I think it will, the feasibility of the black man's emigration to the land of his fathers."

Erkead's rosy view would not be borne out by the reality on the ground. Life in Liberia, as the colony was called, turned out to be extraordinarily difficult. Nearly all of the settlers fell ill for several months. Many died. Those who survived struggled to make a living, planting subsistence crops in sandy soil because the area's most fertile lands were controlled by Africans, who viewed the new arrivals with hostility. From 1831 to 1851, only 1,025 emigrants were sent to Liberia, a fraction of the enslaved people who were freed during that period. (The number of recorded manumissions of enslaved people during that time frame was 5,571, and that was probably an undercount, since some slaveholders did not file in court.)

It turned out that the hundreds of people enslaved by the Jesuits would not be among the cohort. McSherry, who had commissioned Erkead to investigate the possibility, ended up reconsidering the idea of a mass resettlement. Father Stephen Dubuisson provided something of an explanation two years later when he described the views of some Jesuits who argued against resettlement, saying that "the colony of Liberia is far from offering the resources we hoped for." And some hoped that a mass sale would at least bring some cash into the Jesuits' coffers. So McSherry decided to bide his time, while Carbery prayed that he could protect his people.

THE WINTER OF 1835 was one of the harshest in memory. A January blizzard left Baltimore blanketed in twenty inches of snow, and the temperature plunged below zero. "We have had the longest and severest cold 'spell' that is recollected," one observer reported. At St. Inigoes, Father Fidelis de Grivel gave thanks for the brick manor house, "100 years old, but solid & tight," which protected its inhabitants from the chill and snow. But the people living in the slave quarters could not count on the manor's sturdy walls for protection from the harsh weather. One priest described them as living in "huts" that were "open to any wind."

But Anny and Arnold could still count their blessings. The Jesuits had recently sold "a negroe boy" at the Newtown plantation for $270. Under Carbery's watch, though, none of the St. Inigoes families had been sold.

Moses was gone, leaving a hole in their family that could never be filled. But the Mahoney family was still together. Arnold still had the freedom to sail the county's waterways on his own. Anny could marvel as she watched her children grow and spend time with Louisa, their parents, and their older siblings. The extended family would endure the cold and pray for spring, when the sun would once again warm the earth and their homes. For the time being, they were safe.

8

Saving Georgetown

THE EARLY SPRING OF 1835 BROUGHT LITTLE IN THE WAY OF relief from the frigid temperatures. At Georgetown, Mulledy huddled over his diary, describing yet another blast of arctic air that had left the Potomac "river closed up."

The following day found him in a gloomy mood. He was writing to Rome, recounting his struggles to get students to pay their fees, the illness afflicting the college's professor of moral theology ("he can hardly walk"), and his mounting frustrations with McSherry.

McSherry, the new provincial superior, had holed himself up at the plantation at St. Thomas Manor. "He hides himself quietly in a corner," Mulledy complained, describing McSherry's inclination to avoid the many problems facing the fledgling province. "The smallest difficulty seems to disturb the mind of our good Provincial Father—and sometimes he seems to be devoid of all energy."

It didn't take long for him to return to the subject of the enslaved people owned by the Jesuits, pointing to them once again as a source of the province's problems, reminding his superior of "what I have said about our plantations for several years."

"More and more, daily experience forces me to believe that these plantations will be a kind of curse for the society in this region," he wrote. "Blacks behave most wickedly in many plantations and priests themselves suffer ruin of both the soul and the body. For they are neither farmers nor priests nor religious, but some un- specified composite from all three." As a result, he said, many of the priests on the plantations "begin to drink *aqua vita*—many love that poison—they become drunks—and then many evils, along with many other types, follow."

The truth was that Mulledy himself often drank to excess, so much so that he was counseled on the problem by his superiors. The burdens of his job as rector of Georgetown seemed to weigh ever heavier on him, so much so that he pleaded to be reassigned, a request that Rome rejected. He was still struggling to find ways to cover the costs of the new building on campus that he had com- missioned and to get parents hit hard by the economic downturn to pay tuition. By summertime, though, the economy had begun to rebound, and the prices offered for enslaved people began to soar. The auction block had rarely seemed so enticing.

In early July, Mulledy and his allies finally had the opportunity to force a decision about the fate of the enslaved. The leadership of the newly established Maryland province was holding its first con- gregation, and Mulledy left little to chance. On July 2, he presided over a Mass in which he prayed for the "success of Congregation." No one who knew Mulledy had any doubt about what success meant to the leader of Georgetown College. If he had his way, the Mahoneys and all of the other enslaved families owned by the Jesu- its would be sold.

The meeting began on July 3, attended by some of the most prominent Catholic leaders in the country. The priests wrestled with a number of questions, ranging from the nuts and bolts to the profound. Should the novitiate be housed in Frederick? Should men who had abandoned Catholicism be excluded from the homes of the priests? Should the seminary in Washington be sold?

The most pressing question, whether to sell the plantations and the enslaved, left the men deeply divided. Around the country, in speeches and in newspapers, abolitionists were increasingly pressing their cause, and the debate had spilled over to Congress. William Lloyd Garrison's recently formed American Anti-slavery Society, the first to call for the immediate liberation of Black people, was growing, and Mulledy and his allies argued that the widening opposition to slavery in the country might lead the government to order the emancipation of Black people, resulting in a devastating financial loss for the Jesuits. He and his supporters also warned that the slaves might revolt.

Father James Ryder took another tack, arguing that slaveholding and the ministry were incompatible—not because of the immorality of slavery, but because life on the plantations exposed priests "to the dangers of solitude," giving them too much independence from their superiors. He also argued that the Jesuit plantation managers typically lacked the will to treat the enslaved with a forceful and stern hand, which was necessary for Blacks, who could well be considered "demons" because of their "immorality." "The negroes absorb half of the produce of the farms because the priests are too nice to them and do not make them work enough," he argued.

Most important, Mulledy and his supporters argued, the future of Catholicism lay in the cities, not in the countryside. A mass slave sale would enable the Jesuits to establish colleges in Philadelphia, Richmond, and beyond.

Father Fidèle de Grivel countered those arguments with arguments of his own, rooted in the time he had spent at St. Inigoes. He noted that Carbery and others dismissed the notion that the enslaved people owned by the Jesuits were lazy and immoral. "They say that our Negroes work as much as those of other farmers Catholics or Protestant and that their morals are less bad," he said, noting that they took Communion and confessed their sins.

He also pointed to Carbery's system of giving Black people control over land and their livelihoods, which had raised productivity at St. Inigoes. He urged the Jesuit leadership to adopt the strategy at all of the plantations, instead of moving to sell people. "The natural consequence of this operation," he pointed out, was that the enslaved had incentives to work harder "because [of] the profit being for them." "I visited these good people," he said, describing his time with the Mahoneys and the other enslaved people at the plantation, "and I argue that for clothing, beds, furniture, etc they are Lords in comparison to the negroes of White Marsh."

Grivel and his allies said that a mass sale would amount to nothing less than a betrayal of the Jesuit mission in the United States, which had been founded by priests "with the intention that we take care of souls in the country," he said. And though Mulledy and his supporters complained that the Black people on the plantations consumed too many of the province's scarce resources, Grivel noted that the Jesuits themselves squandered money.

The province and Georgetown College were deeply in debt. The problem was compounded by Mulledy's building campaign and wasteful spending. Georgetown owed $30,000 at 6 percent interest, Grivel pointed out. The "administration is poorly run," he wrote. "For example, at Georgetown College we spent in a year, it was 1833, 900 dollars on beer, 300 dollars on brandy or liquors, and 100 dollars on champagne."

The meeting lasted about six days, with the priests fiercely debating the issues on the table. In the end, Mulledy and McSherry emerged victorious. "The Provincial Congress decided that the project," the proposal to sell the plantations and the enslaved, "should be recommended," Grivel wrote in his report.

Father Aloysius Young complained that Mulledy had muscled the vote through, pressuring the province's financial administrator to vote in favor of the sale even though he personally opposed it. No matter. The proposal was sent to Rome along with a series of others for approval. But McSherry and Mulledy, buoyed by their success at the meeting, had no intention of waiting. Within days, McSherry had begun selling enslaved people. A notation describing the sales appeared on July 16, just eight days after the meeting's close, in a ledger that documented the province's income and expenditures.

"Received" of Father McSherry, the notation reads, from the "sales of 4 women of St. Thomas." The buyers paid McSherry $1,150.

The following month, Father Ryder traveled to Richmond, Virginia, to deliver a full-throated attack on the abolitionists who were challenging the slave system that the Jesuits had relied on for generations. The Jesuits had long viewed abolitionists with suspicion. In addition to threatening the priests' plantation system, many abolitionists were Protestants, and some—including prominent men such as Garrison and Elijah Lovejoy—sometimes attacked the Catholic Church in their writings and speeches. Speaking to a group of prominent Catholics, Ryder denounced the men and women calling for emancipation as fanatics and "misguided abettors of disorder" and said that he welcomed the opportunity to assure "my fellow citizens of the South that the Catholic body, both clergy and laity, North of the Potomac, will go heart and hand . . . in resistance to the unholy efforts of incendiary fanatics."

He described slaveholders as noble protectors of the enslaved, who could take comfort in the "kindness of his compassionate" enslavers. "He is clothed, maintained, and protected by his master, who looks upon him as a portion of his family," Ryder insisted. In his remarks, however, he made no mention of the families that the Jesuits planned to tear apart.

GRIVEL WOULD SAY later that it had all happened without warning.

July melted into August as the Mahoneys and other enslaved families on St. Inigoes labored in the wheat and tobacco fields, fished in the river's rushing waters, and tended their vegetable gardens. Leonard Cutchmore was about thirty-seven years old that summer. He was married to Maria, and they had had five children, ranging in age from two to eight years old. Bazil Hall, who was nearly six feet tall at twenty-three, had come to the plantation as a child. He was the father of a baby boy. By September, the two men would be bound together by a shared tragedy when eleven people, including their family members, would be sold.

Slave sales broke apart Black communities all across the South, searing themselves into the memories of witnesses. Slave traders dragged people from the fields. Slaveholders burst into slave quarters and grabbed weeping men, women, and children from their homes.

"You could hear men and women screaming to the top of their voices as either ma, pa, sister or brother was taken without any warning," remembered Susan Hamlin, an enslaved woman who had witnessed agonizing separations in South Carolina.

Clayborn Gantling, who had been enslaved in Florida, described "slaves sold in droves like cows" and the anguish of the people left behind to mourn those who had been lost. "I have heard slaves morning and night pray for deliverance," he recalled. "Some of 'em would stand up in de fields or bend over cotton and corn and pray out loud for God to help 'em."

The Cutchmores were kin to the Mahoneys, their family lines entwined. But the Mahoneys and the other enslaved people at St. Inigoes were powerless to prevent the two families from being taken. Even Father Carbery could do nothing. Rome had yet to respond to the province's proposal, but McSherry made it clear that he was just getting started. Outraged, Grivel wrote to Rome and described his concerns about the sales, including the earlier sales at St. Thomas Manor. The four women at St. Thomas Manor, he said, had been sold to slaveholders who planned to ship them to Georgia, "a region which all the slaves vehemently despise (especially the Catholic ones, because priests are lacking there) due to the climate, because of the heat and the unhealthy climate." He said that one enslaved girl had even been traded for a horse. "That was a grave offense to Catholics," he wrote, "for they were saying, 'Look at that! Even priests engage in the business of human flesh!' After a month the horse died! And the Catholics rejoiced, mocking the seller."

The Cutchmores and Halls were shipped to Louisiana, a state favored by the Jesuits who supported a mass sale in part because the state had a high concentration of Catholics. There, the priests hoped, the slaves might end up with someone who would allow them to practice their faith. The plantations there were also vast, which meant that a potential buyer might be willing to purchase multiple slaves, maybe scores of them, from the Jesuits.

Grivel worried about whether priests should be in the business of selling human beings at all, even as he seemed to move closer to accepting Mulledy and McSherry's idea that the province might be better off without them. "The most perplexing inquiry is whether it is suitable to sell our slaves!" he wrote. "For I admit that it is per-mitted, and that it is expedient in this region for the good of our society's plantations in their present state. But nevertheless, I have never heard that the society did this in Mexico, Peru, Tucumam [Argentina], or in the islands in the Gulf or Mexico."

He warned that McSherry had made it no "secret that he would proceed to sell the other slaves at his own pace." Buoyed by the resurgent economy and the expanding cotton and sugar planta-tions, the prices charged for human beings continued to rise. The Cutchmores and Halls were among the approximately 150,000 people shipped to the Southwest in just the six years from 1831 through 1836.

But even as he worried about whether it was suitable to sell people, Grivel took pains to emphasize that the enslaved people sold from St. Inigoes, unlike the women from St. Thomas, had at least been sold to two reputable men in Louisiana, one of whom was Catholic. The families had been sold together, he said. None had been split up. "The wife was not separated from the husband, nor the children separated from the parents," he wrote, adding that they had been sent "to the county Opelusas, into a place which they say is only miles from a most flourishing convent des Dames de Sacre Coeur . . . so the slaves would lack neither a church nor a priest." It is hard to imagine that such talk offered much comfort to

the Cutchmores or the Halls or to the Mahoneys and other enslaved families who had lived alongside them at St. Inigoes.

The enslaved people McSherry sold from St. Inigoes ended up
on the plantation of Henry Johnson. Johnson had a foot in two
worlds: the elite Catholic circles in the Chesapeake and the wealthy
planter community in Louisiana. He had won a seat in the US
House of Representatives and had served in the US Senate and as
governor of his home state. He owned dozens of slaves and regularly mingled with powerful lawmakers, government officials, and
merchants. And his marriage connected him with a prominent
Maryland family with deep roots in St. Mary's County and close
ties to the Jesuits.

His wife, Elizabeth Rousby Key, was related, through her mother,
to Father Charles Sewell, a prominent Jesuit who had served on
Georgetown College's first board of directors. Her cousin Francis
Scott Key had penned the poem that would provide the lyrics of
"The Star-Spangled Banner." Her father, Philip Barton Key, Sr., a
prominent lawyer, had represented Father John Ashton in the lawsuit filed by the Mahoneys back in the 1790s and had battled Louisa's and Anna's relatives in the Maryland courts.

Johnson had been trying to find his way back into public life ever
since he had left the governor's office. He was elected to Congress
as a Whig, and by December 1834 he began commuting between
the nation's capital and Louisiana. About four months before he
purchased the Cutchmore and Hall families, Johnson sold his plantation in LaFourche and purchased a new estate in St. James parish
on the right bank of the Mississippi River, just sixty miles from
New Orleans. It was a sugar plantation purchased at a public auction with a dwelling house, a sugar house, slave quarters, stables,
barns, and a blacksmith's shop.

That was where the Cutchmores and Halls would end up, along
with several other enslaved people who had traveled south from
Alexandria on the brig *Tribune*. The Jesuits at St. Inigoes felt some
relief that they had ended up in Johnson's hands, even as they raised

concerns about the sale itself. Though Johnson was an Episcopalian, he had a partner in the sale whose surname was Jamesson, a man described by Father Grivel as "a good Catholic." And he mentioned approvingly that "Johnson & Jamesson are prepared also to buy others to send there."

But not long after he wrote that, Grivel discovered that Johnson was a man with no qualms about revisiting a business deal. The Louisiana congressman wrote back to Father Carbery, complaining that one of his newly purchased human assets had been mislabeled, as it were. Grivel was outraged. "Father Carberry [*sic*] received letters from that <u>fine, very honest</u> Johnson in which it was asked whether there was an error from Father McSherry in the ages assigned to the slaves he bought," he wrote. "There was no error. Do not marvel, Father, if you hear that he has sold to others for a higher price the slaves which he bought from us for a lower price."

But Johnson was clearly undeterred by any feelings of pique on the part of the Jesuits. He negotiated a discount, which the Jesuits paid, noting in a ledger that $400 had been deducted from the original price paid for the enslaved people sold from St. Inigoes because of "physical defects."

The loss of the Cutchmores and Halls must have reverberated through the estate as the enslaved people at St. Inigoes struggled to get through the frigid early months of 1836. When spring came and the peach and cherry trees burst into bloom, Father Carbery cobbled together a description of the people who had been sold nearly seven months before. The Maryland province's financial ledgers simply described the number of people shipped away and the money received for them. But Father Carbery had lived alongside them and knew them by name. Some were children, as young as two years old. And the enslaved men, women, and children at St. Inigoes had been forced to adapt to life in Maryland without them, all the while wondering and worrying who might be sold next.

. . .

THE JESUITS CONTINUED to debate the right course forward as they waited for approval from Rome for a mass slave sale. The matter became more pressing when two planters put an offer on the table. "Two rich and distinguished individuals have expressed interest in buying our slaves," a priest wrote sometime in 1836. "One of them is Catholic, the other Protestant, but both would transport these Negros to Catholic establishments in Louisiana, where, we have all assurance, they would enjoy the free exercise of their religion."

The priest did not identify the two men, but he described one as "Catholic and the son of one of the governors," strongly suggesting that that prospective buyer was John Lee, a son of Maryland's former governor Thomas Sim Lee, who had converted to Catholicism. Both men, the priest wrote, "wish to purchase the slaves and they are offering very high prices. The opportunity is thus very favorable and a better opportunity might never present itself."

The prospect of such a lucrative endeavor cheered Mulledy, McSherry, and their allies, who once again tried to rationalize their plan to ship enslaved families off to the harsh plantations of the Deep South. "The slaves would be most able to enjoy a happy tranquility and the succors of religion by being together on a good plantation in Louisiana," one priest wrote, recounting their sentiments. To those priests, the suffering of Black people counted for nothing, so long as they had their faith.

But critics of the sales continued to raise doubts. What kind of impact would such a mass sale have on the enslaved? On the men, women, and children who had spent most of their lives on the plantations and feared the rigors of slavery in the Deep South? "There is, in general, a great repugnance among the blacks of Maryland towards being sold and transported to the South," the priest continued, this time summing up the arguments of those opposed to the sale. "Without doubt, our best slaves, those who have religious sentiments (and indeed there are some!), would be in despair to see themselves ripped away from their former manors, from their old churches. . . . Is it not cruel, this idea to force them to depart with new masters?"

That summer, Anny's husband, Arnold Jones, decided to follow his brother Moses's example and risk escape. He was in his midthirties by then and still plying the waterways in and around Maryland for white men. Who would be next? His wife? His children? He decided not to wait to find out.

We do not know whether he and Anny discussed his plan in whispers while their young children slept. We do not know whether he promised to find a way to bring the whole family to freedom, once he had established himself up north. But one day that summer, Arnold left the plantations of St. Mary's County, set out for Washington, DC, and never came back.

The news of his flight appeared in the *American and Commercial Daily Advertiser* that August under the headline "$600 Reward." "Arnold, who calls himself Arnold Jones, he ran away in Washington City, D.C., 26 July, 1836," the notice said. The advertisement described his height (five feet, eight inches), his color (light skinned, mixed race) and his "round face and flat nose."

The white men hunting for Arnold suspected that he might be with his brother. "Arnold and Moses are brothers and a great likeness, and no doubt they will meet somewhere to the north as they have been going by water together about 12 years," read the advertisement, which offered a cash reward to anyone who could capture the two men. Slave catchers would receive $600 if they caught the two men outside Maryland and $300 if they snared them within the state.

The wanted ad was republished in Philadelphia, New York, and Boston but to no avail. For the Jesuit priests, who recorded his absence, it was a financial loss. It certainly meant more to Father Carbery, who was close to the Mahoneys and empathized with the enslaved on the plantation, but he still had to make sure that the estate's papers remained in order. So he requested and received a reduction in his taxes from the county for "Arnold (salor)," human property he no longer owned. And later, as the priests put together a list of the people they owned in preparation for a possible sale, they would note that Arnold "ran away." But for the Mahoneys, his disappearance was much more profound, creating a gaping hole in the family he left behind at St. Inigoes plantation.

Anny, who was about twenty-five that summer, was left without a husband. Her young children, Arnold Jr., who was about seven, and Louisa, who was about four, were left without a father. Whether Anny wept in the dilapidated slave quarters or secretly celebrated her husband's daring escape as she continued to labor for the Jesuits and tried to comfort her children that summer is unknown. But if she clung to the hope that Arnold would return to carry her and their children to a life of liberty in the North, she would be deeply disappointed.

Several weeks after Arnold's escape, Father McSherry wrote a much delayed update to his superiors in Rome. Word had trickled back to Rome about the families who had been sold the previous year, news passed on by McSherry's fellow priests who had been outraged by the sale. Now Jan Roothaan, the leader of the Jesuits worldwide, was raising uncomfortable questions for McSherry.

McSherry picked up his pen in late August in his own defense. He argued that his critics had falsely suggested that he had separated husbands and wives in the sales that had included the Cutchmores and the Halls. ("One woman out of these slaves had a big family, but never had a husband," he wrote.) And he insisted that he had had no choice but to ship the enslaved people to plantations in the Deep South. "It was not possible for the slaves to be sold into the neighboring regions," he said, arguing that it had been "necessary to find some master in Louisiana where the opportunity for religion would not be lacking for them where also they would be able to be together."

As for his decision to push for the mass sale of all of the Jesuit slaves, he rejected the notion that he should have consulted with men such as Father Carbery who worked on the plantations and knew the enslaved men and women personally before pressing for Rome's approval. He dismissed the Jesuit plantation managers as "overseers" who "can make trouble." And he grumbled that it was a scandal that a man such as Carbery, who was viewed by some Jesuits as unsophisticated and unlettered, "should have been ordained" at all. "I know well enough how they feel," he wrote of Carbery and the other managers. "I know the sort of value to give to their sentiments. . . . Fathers who are simultaneously missionaries and overseers are not able to be called truly missionaries, or truly overseers."

McSherry urged Roothaan to approve the mass sale, despite the concerns laid out by its critics. Pressing the case he had been making for years, he insisted that the very survival of the college and seminary depended on it, writing, "If the blacks are kept, so much of what is profited from the farms is required for their sustenance, and the novitiate and the scholastics cannot exist." He sent the letter off to Rome and waited for a reply.

Classes resumed at Georgetown in September, and the following month Mulledy made plans to visit St. Inigoes. An unexpected blizzard swept through much of the Northeast that October—"a great snow storm," Mulledy wrote—that left sections of the country buried in snow. He headed out to the plantation two days after the storm. By then, as he passed time with Father Carbery and walked the beautiful estate still coated in abundant white drifts of untrodden snow, word had come back from Rome. Roothaan had finally come to a decision. Mulledy, McSherry, and their allies had won the day. All of the Jesuits' slaves were to be sold.

Mulledy returned to Georgetown only to find that McSherry had fallen ill. He prayed for his recovery. The young provincial superior rallied, perhaps buoyed by the news, and then the two men awaited the details from Rome so that they could set their long-awaited plan into motion. Roothaan had decided that the mass sale could take place only if a series of conditions—twenty in all—were met. Father Francis Vespre, who would serve as the province's treasurer, shared them with the Jesuit leadership.

Roothaan's rules were intended to safeguard both the spiritual lives of the people who were to be sold and the money earned from the transaction. The enslaved people, Vespre advised, "should be transported to a place where they can practice their religion and receive spiritual aids, as would be the case in the state of Louisiana, which is considered most Catholic." Families should be kept together. "Not only must married couples who are both owned by us not be separated from one another, but also, as far as it is possible, for no parents to be separated from children, especially if the parents are already elderly or the children still young," he continued. In instances where enslaved people had spouses owned by neighboring planters, the Jesuits would need to purchase those spouses so that the couples could be sold together as part of the mass sale or sell the Jesuit slave to the neighboring planter so that the couple could remain together in Maryland.

Vespre made it clear, though, that Roothaan believed that such humanitarian concerns should go only so far. Some Jesuits had argued that elderly people should be spared from the mass sale. But in the conditions set by Roothaan, Rome made it clear that the old people should be sold, too, as long as "they do not have an infirmity that can impede their transport." Vespre, in recounting Roothaan's conditions, tried to put the best light on what many Jesuits would view as an outrageous decision, suggesting that the elderly would be pleased to be torn from their homes and shipped to Louisiana, where "they shall find a very beautiful climate where Maryland's ice and snow (so feared by blacks) are unknown."

As for the buyers, Vespre said, they need not restrict the sale to Catholic planters, but emphasized that any buyer would have to commit to providing the enslaved people with "every convenience for practicing" their faith, "especially on festival days, and in the event of illness, to provide the slaves with the assistance of the nearest Catholic priest." He singled out Henry Johnson, who had purchased the Cutchmores and Halls, for praise in that regard. Johnson was a Protestant but had "accurately carried out" his commitment to tend to the families' spiritual needs, he said.

Then Vespre got down to the profits from the sale. Payment should be made up front in cash, if possible, he said. If that was not possible, half should be paid up front with the remainder paid within three years. The proceeds should be carefully safeguarded, he said, ticking off a list of risky investment options to be avoided. In all of these issues, he said, McSherry should proceed with "the utmost caution possible with regards to a matter so delicate and of such importance for his Province."

Roothaan himself weighed in on the matter in December 1836, writing to McSherry to express his personal support for the sale— "We are persuaded that they can be sold and should be sold, whenever the opportunity should present itself"—and to reiterate and in some instances expand on the strict conditions that he had set for the sale. The enslaved families should be sold to wealthy planters to ensure that they would not be resold or separated. Elderly people who could not be sold "on account of burdensome age or incurable illnesses" should continue to be cared for on the plantations "in keeping with charity and justice."

He emphasized again the importance of keeping families together, particularly husbands and wives, who "in no way must be separated." But he offered McSherry a little wiggle room when it came to the sale of children, saying that they should remain with their parents "as much as is possible." As for the proceeds from the sale, he made the restrictions clear. The money "ought to be invested so that it may grow," he wrote. And, perhaps aware of the concerns about reckless spending and mismanagement, he emphasized that the cash "absolutely must not be spent on making expenditures, nor in paying off debts." As he ticked off the list of conditions, the moral implications of the decision he had made to permit the sale of nearly three hundred human beings seem to have weighed on him. He said he was reviewing the conditions explicitly and carefully with McSherry to "satisfy my own conscience."

But he expressed no hesitancy or ambivalence about the step he had chosen to take. He knew that the stakes were high. The continued existence of the American province depended on the sale. "The survival of this Province depends to a large degree on this being done well, clearly for the benefit of the Novitiate and the school," he wrote. "Consider therefore what is to be done, and deliberate, and pray, so that it may turn out for the good of the Province and the glory of God."

On the plantation at St. Inigoes, Father Carbery watched the unfolding plans with alarm. He had been working with the Mahoneys and the other enslaved families on the estate for nearly two decades. He believed that he had proven that the Jesuit plantations could be profitable and disproven the notion that Black people were lazy and immoral. So as the Jesuit leadership discussed the plans for the sale, he traveled to Georgetown to voice his opposition. He pleaded with the senior Jesuits, begging them to change course. He told his entire parish that he was praying and urged parishioners to pray with him, asking the Lord to allow the Black families on the plantation to remain in their homes.

After the meeting, the priest returned home to St. Inigoes. He seemed quiet and downcast as he sat down at the dinner table. Harry Mahoney, the patriarch of the Mahoney family, who had saved the estate's young women and valuables during the War of 1812, was serving his meal. But Carbery couldn't eat. Harry Mahoney knew it then. "We're sold!" he cried.

The Sale

ON MONDAY, JANUARY 9, 1837, JOHN QUINCY ADAMS TOOK to the floor of the Capitol to decry the evils of slavery before his fellow members of the House of Representatives. The southerners in the room tried to shout him down as the former president, now nearly seventy years old, presented a petition signed by 228 women in Massachusetts. Ignoring the outcry, he pressed on reading from the document, which assailed "the sinfulness of slavery" and urged Congress "immediately to abolish slavery in the District of Columbia and to declare every human being free who sets foot upon its soil."

Former Louisiana governor Henry Johnson listened as Adams spoke and then as his fellow lawmakers argued over whether the petition should be considered. A vote was called. One by one, the powerful men called out their ayes and nays, and when the votes were finally tallied, Adams, a fierce opponent of slavery, and his allies had prevailed, ensuring that the lawmakers would cast another vote, this time on whether the petition should proceed to committee.

The procedural victory would give little comfort to the more than 2 million enslaved people across the country or the dozens of enslaved men and women that Johnson owned in Louisiana. Johnson and the other slaveholders in the House were determined to ensure that this petition—and any others that challenged the legitimacy of slavery—died in the halls of Congress without ever receiving a full hearing on their merits. After all, Johnson's wealth, his prestige, his social standing, his very identity as a planter and a man of consequence in Louisiana politics were rooted in the enslavement of Black people. So when the vote was called, he joined forces with like-minded compatriots in the House, including some lawmakers from the North. They emerged victorious. The petition from the women of Weymouth was tabled.

Johnson's stance would come as little surprise to those living on his home plantation in St. James parish. To the Cutchmores and the Halls, who now labored there along with dozens of other enslaved laborers, Johnson would always be the man who had torn them away from Maryland, shattering their families and their community. But to the Jesuit leadership, the haughty Louisiana lawmaker was no monster. He was the man who would help save their college and their mission.

The fierce debate over the petitions calling for an end to slavery would consume Congress for weeks. In early February, Johnson took to the floor himself, denouncing efforts that Adams had made to suggest the unthinkable: that enslaved people should be allowed to present petitions to Congress. Adams had argued that "the God of Nature" had bestowed that right on "every man when he created him; it is the right to implore favor, to seek for mercy!" And that right, he insisted, belonged "to every human creature . . . which cannot be denied to man in any condition."

His stance outraged Johnson and other southerners, who vehemently rejected the notion that God had given enslaved men and women the same rights as whites. Johnson warned the men assembled in the Capitol that if the House recognized the rights of the slaves to petition, "the Union was virtually dissolved; and when that day came, he should feel it his duty to leave that House and go home to his constituents."

For Johnson, the debate hit uncomfortably close to home. While the arguments over the rights of enslaved Black people raged in the nation's capital, he was making arrangements to use the human beings that he owned as collateral for a $30,000 loan. Just two days before he made his arguments before the House, his attorney had been in New Orleans, signing legal papers on his behalf. If Johnson failed to repay what he owed, the bank could seize both his plantation and his human property. The document listed the first names of the enslaved men and women he held captive, including Len and Maria Cutchmore and Bazil and Eliza Hall.

More than a year had passed since the two families had been shipped to Louisiana. The winter of 1837 found them living on Johnson's sugarcane plantation in St. James parish. The families woke up each morning in the slave quarters on a sprawling estate equipped with stables, barns, a blacksmith's shop, and a manor home for Johnson and his wife. The enslaved served the Johnsons and their guests and tended to the horses, mules, and cattle as well as the brutal business of raising and harvesting sugarcane. Even as they adjusted to their new lives the Cutchmores and Halls never forgot the people and the community they had left behind in Maryland. But there is no account of their grief and despair. Instead, they are accounted for on a list of Johnson's many possessions, livestock, carts, tools, and the plantation itself.

The Maryland Jesuits praised Johnson for ensuring that the enslaved men and women he purchased from them could continue practicing their Catholic faith. In fact, his plantation in St. James parish bordered property owned by the local Catholic Church, ensuring that a priest could easily minister to his laborers. But like most wealthy southerners at the time, Johnson, an Episcopalian, saw no conflict between his religious beliefs and slavery. For him, Black people were assets to be bought, sold, mortgaged, and used as collateral. Decades later, he would have a reputation as a kindly master, who cared for the people he owned. But in 1837, the year that he stood up in the Capitol, he ended up with thousands of dollars in his pocket from selling more than a dozen people he held in bondage.

The Jesuits were also counting on a windfall from slave sales, but in the spring of 1837, the country entered into the throes of a financial panic and a subsequent national depression. Once again the market value of enslaved people plunged, leaving McSherry despondent. The banks in New York, Philadelphia, Baltimore, and the nation's capital had stopped issuing credit and cash. The mass sale that he and Mulledy had so long sought was out of the question, at least for the time being.

The warmer weather brought terrible news for the Mahoney family as well. Anny's husband, Arnold, had been hunted down and captured. Everyone knew that runaways were often whipped— even maimed—and promptly sold. But Father Carbery stepped in, saving Anny's husband from being shipped down south. He purchased him for $250 and brought him to St. Inigoes, where he was reunited with his wife and children. The reunion, though, must have been bittersweet. Would the Jesuits resurrect their plans for a mass sale? They were all living on borrowed time.

By that summer, Henry Johnson was back on the Jesuits' radar. He had joined like-minded members of the House in their charge to defeat John Quincy Adams's bill and had returned home to his plantation in St. James parish. Congress would convene in September, and he would have to head to Washington sooner than he had planned. But he did not plan to travel alone. He hoped to use his wealth and connections to place his nephew in one of the best colleges in the nation's capital. "If you shall send your son Joseph here against the first next month, I will place him at George Town College, and attend to his education," Johnson wrote his brother on July 10, 1837. He had pressed his brother on the subject a year earlier, describing the Jesuit school as "an institution equal, perhaps, to any in the Union."

Across the country, economic hardships were mounting. Hundreds of banks collapsed. People lost jobs and went hungry. The planter class in Louisiana, where Johnson spent much of the summer, was far from immune. Wealthy planters had watched the price of cotton plunge from a high of 15.5 cents per pound in 1835 to 9 cents per pound. A New York correspondent described the hard times in New Orleans, reporting that "it can no longer be concealed that the commercial community at New Orleans is altogether in a complete state of bankruptcy or suspension." Johnson had described his own financial struggles a few years earlier in a letter to his brother, weighing whether to consider a run for Congress. He still relied on loans and mortgages to come up with needed cash. But although credit had completely dried up for many ordinary people, Johnson had powerful friends and acquaintances who were willing to loan him thousands of dollars. He had enough to help cover the cost of tuition and living expenses for his nephew at Georgetown. And he had a valuable asset—scores of enslaved men, women, and children—who could be sold or mortgaged along with his plantations.

About two weeks after he wrote to his brother, Johnson bought a new plantation in Ascension parish, paying $4,000 for a two-hundred-acre estate alongside the Mississippi River, about twelve miles from Donaldsonville. He raised part of the money by selling seven people—two men, two women, and three children aged eight, six, and two—for $3,525. He promised to pay the balance later. A day later, he sold much of the land on his home estate in St. James parish for $10,500, reserving for himself the sugar house, the brick kiln, the garden, and the crops in the fields. He would eventually move to Ascension, but at the end of July 1837, he owned land in at least three parishes.

By the time he returned to the Capitol in September for a special session called by President Martin Van Buren to try to tackle the nation's economic crisis, Johnson had bought one plantation and sold a portion of another. But he remained deeply in debt. The plantation in St. James parish was mortgaged to the hilt—to the tune of about $35,000—all owed to Citizens Bank of Louisiana. He had to find a way to pay off the mortgages in order to finalize the sale. Once again, he turned his attention to his human property.

Many wealthy planters and their wives prided themselves on caring for their enslaved laborers. And in October, the Johnsons reached out to the priest at St. Michael's Catholic Church. Even as he juggled the lofty affairs of the nation and his home state, Johnson arranged for the infants of six of his enslaved women to be baptized, tending to the souls of the children who would someday labor in his fields. The priest welcomed the three baby girls and three baby boys—all of them six months or younger—into the faith in a mass baptism on a single day. But the Catholic Church would not save its faithful from the fate they feared most.

Johnson had already begun to sell off some of his enslaved people. He started with Milly, who was fourteen. She garnered him a little more than $600. In September, he sold Peter, who was about twenty-two, for nearly double that sum. In November, six weeks after the mass baptism, Johnson sold five more people: Dafney, a twenty-two-year-old woman, her six-year-old daughter and two-year-old toddler, and two other girls, both under the age of thirteen. For Dafney, the sale must have felt particularly cruel. Records suggest that her three-month-old infant was among those admitted to the Catholic faith in the mass baptism that Johnson had arranged. But when Johnson sold Dafney, he sold her without her baby girl. The sale netted him $2,500.

By year's end, he had sold eighteen people and raised nearly $13,000. The sales destroyed families but not Johnson's reputation. In the books and articles that would describe him more than a century after his death, he would be called an aristocrat, a wily political tactician, an elder statesman. In Washington, the Jesuits at Georgetown who discussed business with him—his nephew's enrollment at the college and his purchase of the Cutchmore and Hall families from St. Inigoes—viewed him as eminently respectable. He was just the kind of man who they hoped might purchase all of their enslaved people, not just a dozen or so.

In December, as Johnson wrapped up his slave sales for the year, there was a changing of the guard among the Maryland Jesuits. For months, McSherry had been appealing to Rome to be relieved of his position as the first leader of the Maryland province. He had stomach cancer, and his health was deteriorating. So he relinquished his position as provincial superior, taking instead the role of Georgetown's president. Mulledy, who had reinvigorated the college but left it burdened with debt, stepped into McSherry's shoes, becoming the new leader of the province. Mulledy had, in the past, criticized McSherry, suggesting that he lacked backbone. But the criticism went both ways, particularly as McSherry began to look more closely at Georgetown's finances.

By January 1838, the extent of Mulledy's fiscal neglect became painfully clear. A month earlier, Mulledy had reported to Rome that the college's debts amounted to $25,000. But when McSherry dug into the books, he was stunned to discover that the debts were nearly twice that. As the new head of Georgetown, he was inheriting a debt of $47,654.54. He managed to bring that down to $23,857.36 with the help of a large donation and other funds. But even that debt left the Jesuits' leadership uncertain as to whether the college could survive.

McSherry and Mulledy had their differences, but they remained united on one critical point: They were convinced that the only way to save the college was to sell the people they had enslaved. Mulledy had been feeling unwell for months, missing Mass to tend to his health. But his new position as leader of the Maryland province seemed to give him newfound energy and momentum. He spent much of late February and early March 1838 traveling to the plantations, visiting Newtown, St. Inigoes, and St. Thomas Manor. By late April, he was gearing up for a large slave sale. It would have to be piecemeal, not the mass sale he had been dreaming of but at least a start.

Mulledy began that "disagreeable work," as a Jesuit described it more than half a century later, with a sale at the St. Thomas Manor plantation on March 4. The Jesuit accounting book recounts the event in spare terms, focusing on the resulting revenue: "From same [St. Thomas] for sale of Negro boy 450." Two months later, another opportunity presented itself when Henry Johnson stopped by Georgetown's campus. He arrived, not in his official capacity as a lawmaker, but to assess the progress of his nephew Joseph. "The professors at the Institution entertain a favorable opinion of him, and say that his talents are good, & that he improves well in his studies," he wrote to his brother afterward. "Indeed, I consider Joseph a very fine boy, and hope that your expectations with respect to him will be fully realized. Today being Sunday, he has visited me with several boys at the College, from Louisiana, and is now here. He has grown considerably and is in fine health & spirits."

Joseph's well-being and academic progress may have been foremost on Johnson's mind when he first sat down with the faculty at Georgetown that day. But it seems likely that they turned to business, and a few days later, he accepted Mulledy's invitation to St. Mary's County, Maryland. The priest had also invited a doctor, Jesse Batey, who had established himself as a planter in Louisiana, to join them. Batey, who happened to be in the nation's capital that month, owned a plantation in Terrebonne parish not far from Johnson's estate and was hoping to buy more labor. When the two men disembarked from the stagecoach that carried them south from the capital to the countryside of southern Maryland, they found Mulledy waiting to give them a tour of the plantations and the scores of people he'd put up for sale.

The Jesuits owned two plantations in St. Mary's County. The Newtown plantation extended for about 750 acres and produced wheat and other grains along with what the priests described as an inferior grade of tobacco. It was run by Father Peter Havermans, the Dutch priest who objected to the idea of selling off the roughly forty-five members of Newtown's enslaved community. He had pleaded with Fathers Mulledy and McSherry, telling them that he had the agricultural experience necessary to ensure that the plantation would be "better, productive," and more "suitable" than it had been in previous years.

Havermans's advocacy was accompanied by some of the racist views common to the Jesuits. He wrote that the enslaved people's resistance and refusal to abide by the priests' rules had, in part, led to the decision to sell. "God likely allowed for the punishment for the Black men themselves, for many of them were bad." Still, he vehemently opposed the sale and Mulledy's visit with Johnson and Batey would have been decidedly unwelcome.

The same was true at St. Inigoes, where Father Carbery had asked the faithful to pray for divine intervention to stop the sale. The arrival of the buyers from Louisiana would have sent waves of terror through the fields, the stables, and the manor house where the enslaved people worked. It had been nearly three years since the Cutchmores and Halls had been sold, and the memory of the sale was still fresh.

In preparation for a mass sale, the Jesuits had put together a census of their human property, plantation by plantation, carefully documenting the names and ages of their inhabitants, noting whether they were married to people on other plantations and whether they had special skills or infirmities. From that simple handwritten document, Johnson and Batey could perceive the complexity of the Black communities that had emerged over the generations on the Jesuit plantations.

The list of nearly three hundred enslaved people included a shoemaker, a blacksmith, and three carpenters. One elderly man was described as lame. A twelve-year-old boy was called "an Idiot." Nearly two dozen of the enslaved had wives or husbands who were owned by other slaveholders. At least five were married to free people of color. And despite the priests' multiple accounts of the kindly and paternalistic care they provided to the people they owned, at least a dozen enslaved people, including three women, had decided they could no longer abide life under Jesuit rule. In their notes describing those people, the priests wrote simply, "ran away." Among them was

Anny's husband, Arnold, who had escaped for a second time sometime between June 1837 and the spring of 1838. Perhaps after tasting freedom, he could no longer bear to be treated as property.

But Johnson and Batey wanted more than just a list. As one Jesuit put it decades later, the men from Louisiana needed "to take a look at our negroes." At St. Inigoes, they found more than eighty people, including the Mahoneys. There were toddlers and young mothers, young men in the prime of their lives, middle-aged couples, and elderly men and women approaching their sunset.

Harry Mahoney, the patriarch of the extended Mahoney clan, was described as the oldest enslaved person on the plantation. He might well have served the men if they stopped in the manor house to dine with Father Carbery before perusing the people on display in the fields. Would the Jesuits keep the pledge they had made to his family decades ago that his family would never be sold? His daughter Nelly seemed safe. She was working in Alexandria, Virginia, helping the Jesuit priest who was tending to the flock at St. Mary's Church. But what about his wife, Anna? What about his daughters Louisa and Anny and the rest of his children? One of his sons, Gabriel, a blacksmith, was married to a woman on another plantation. Would he be safe?

No records have emerged to describe the details of the visit that Johnson and Batey made to the plantations in St. Mary's County. But in cases like these, enslaved people were sometimes made to line up in the fields so that the potential buyers could assess the human wares firsthand. Did the young women look as though they would bear many children? Would the young men be strong enough to handle the backbreaking labor on a plantation in the Deep South? At slave auctions, white men often handled the people on display, running their hands over the bodies of young women while their fathers, brothers, and husbands watched helplessly. What is known about Batey and Johnson's visit is that the men returned to Washington afterward and haggled over the number and price of the people they might purchase.

Johnson went back to his work in the Capitol while Batey found lodgings at Brown's Indian Queen Hotel, a first-class establishment on the north side of Pennsylvania Avenue, midway between the White House and the Capitol, which boasted about its spacious dining room, "equal if not superior to any in the U.S."

Mulledy, meanwhile, had been on the road. At Newtown, where both the enslaved and the free were expected to attend Mass, Mulledy preached about the sinfulness of men, even good men, and about the power of God's grace to overcome that sinfulness. For a moment, as he stood before the parishioners, he seemed to consider his own soul and his own shortcomings. "This mixture of good & evil I find even in myself," he told the congregants. "I see what is good & right—but I always adhere to what is evil & wrong. I would wish to be good, but I am always bad. There are then within me two principles—two men who cannot live in peace," he continued. "What a monster then am I—what a chimera, what an abyss—what a capricious compound of discordant elements—that are ever engaged in an implacable & an unceasing war?"

But by the time he preached in Newport, Maryland, on May 30, he had put that talk aside. He focused instead on the triumph of the Catholic faith over its many detractors and enemies. The mass sale, and the constellation of Catholic colleges it would allow him to build and support, would be his legacy.

By mid-June, Mulledy was inching closer to finalizing the deal. He was so busy that he had to put off a trip to Frederick, Maryland, to visit a fellow priest. He apologized in a letter on June 12: "I am now so busily engaged in trading off our negroes, that I know not when I shall be in Frederick." He wrote that he had found it difficult "to dispose of our servants in a Catholic neighborhood" but had come across "a fine opportunity if we agree upon prices."

One of the buyers had started off with an offer of $800 for each of the young men and $650 for each of the young women, he explained, with lower prices for anyone over twenty-five or under eighteen. Mulledy countered that he wanted an average price for each person. The buyer came back with his next offer: $345 per person. Mulledy's response? No deal. "I told him that he must make his average come to $400 at least—before I would even deign to consider his proposition," he wrote. "Tell me what do you think of $400 round for young & old—leaving out all of 60 & above for separate agreement—& counting all under one year with the mother as one. Fr. McSherry thinks it a fair price—let me know what you think of it. I would be willing to take $450."

The decision weighed on him. On each of the next three days, he dedicated Masses to prayers for his own soul. But on Saturday evening, June 16, he took time away from self-reflection to hobnob with some of the most powerful men in the country at a meeting of the Columbian Horticultural Society, a group established to promote and improve gardening. The men gathered at the home of General Nathaniel Towson, the society's president, who served as paymaster general of the US Army, to sample some domestic wines produced in different parts of the country. Mulledy sipped his drink and enjoyed "the pleasures of social and scientific conversation" with the president of the United States, the Treasury, war, and navy secretaries, and several members of Congress.

Mulledy, who had worked long and hard to boost both George-town's profile and his own, must have been pleased at the invitation and at its coverage in the *Daily National Intelligencer* on Tuesday, June 19, 1838. That very same day, he would have more substantive news. After years of dreaming, months of planning, and weeks of intense negotiations, he was finally ready to put his vision into motion. The three men—Mulledy, Johnson, and Batey—had come to an agreement.

They met in Washington, to put the deal into writing: 272 men, women, and children—many of whom belonged to families that had been enslaved by the Jesuits for generations—were to be sold for the sum of $115,000, roughly $422 per person. The handwritten agreement, signed by all three men, ran to eight pages. There were the financial details, of course—a payment plan in installments with interest—and there was a delivery plan, which described when and how the enslaved people would be handed over. The men agreed that $25,000 would be paid on the delivery of the first group of fifty-one people, who were to be shipped to the port of Alexandria, Virginia, "as soon as practicable."

The rest of the people in the deal were to be delivered in the fall, between October 15 and November 15. Johnson and Batey would have ten years to pay the remaining $90,000 at an annual interest rate of 6 percent. The men promised to start paying the interest immediately and to pay off the balance in five annual installments of $18,000 each, beginning in 1843. They also promised to mortgage their lands and to use the land and the newly purchased people as collateral, to ensure that Mulledy could recoup his human property if they failed to make good on their payments.

But nearly half of the agreement was devoted to scores of names, those of nearly every enslaved person owned by the Jesuits: grandfathers such as Isaac, a sixty-five-year-old man enslaved on the White Marsh plantation, and his extended family; children such as Francis, an eight-year-old boy enslaved at St. Thomas Manor; mothers such as Susan, a twenty-year-old woman, and her seven-year-old daughter.

Mulledy, in his zeal to wrap up the deal, left out some important details. He failed to mention that several of the men listed in the agreement had run away and no longer lived on the plantations—a detail that Johnson and Batey would discover soon enough. The agreement also failed to note that a number of the enslaved on the list had spouses who were owned by other slaveholders and that Rome had ordered the Jesuits not to separate such couples. The document provided the first hint that Mulledy was prepared to do what many Jesuits viewed as unconscionable and immoral: to break up families, if necessary, to get the money he needed to save Georgetown and his dream of expansion.

Johnson and Batey did get some assurances written into the agreement to ensure that they would be protected if the enslaved people turned out to be sickly or older—and therefore less valuable—than Mulledy claimed. The priest promised to reduce the purchase price of the enslaved people purchased "for such difference in age, or for such defects as shall lessen their value" and to go to arbitration if the parties could not come to an agreement on a reasonable reduction in price. With that, the deal was done. The three men signed the document one after another—first Mulledy, then Batey, then Johnson—setting into motion the machinery of what would become one of the largest documented slave sales in the nation.

The people most deeply affected by the deal were miles away, laboring in the plantations in Maryland. The sale document included only their first names, but to one another, they were the Queens, the Goughs, the Hawkinses, the Campbells, the Butlers, the Browns, the Dorseys, and the Wests. And all of them had been sold, including, despite a decades-long pledge, the Mahoneys.

Within days of Mulledy, Batey, and Johnson signing the agreement, Horatio Trunnell, the man hired to handle the roundup, headed out to St. Inigoes. He and his men arrived without warning and swept through the plantation rounding up frantic families, about forty-one people in all. The youngest were toddlers. The oldest were two men, both aged about forty-five, both with wives and children. One of those men was Robert Mahoney, Harry Mahoney's oldest son. A similar roundup took place at the White Marsh plantation, where nearly a dozen people were forced to leave their homes and their extended families. Word spread from one estate to another, radiating through the enslaved communities and the small circle of clergy responsible for the plantations. "Without any notice or preparation the slaves were seized violently and by heathen hands," Father Thomas Lilly wrote, describing what had happened at St. Inigoes and White Marsh. "They were treated as animals in every respect."

The Jesuit financial ledgers recorded the dollars and cents, the $38.06 paid on June 25 for "Trunnel's [sic] bill for St. Inigoes negroes," the $85.00 paid the same day "for same negroes & Traveling expenses," and the money paid for transporting the enslaved people from White Marsh. Their destination was the port in Alexandria, where they would be imprisoned as they waited to board the *Uncas,* the ship that would carry them to Louisiana.

The *Uncas* had been built to order for Isaac Franklin and John Armfield, who had built the nation's largest slave-trading operation. The 155-ton, two-masted ship had transported the Cutchmores and Halls in 1835 and had been purchased a year later by William H. Williams, a slave trader based in Washington, DC. During the very week that Robert Mahoney, his family, and the others were imprisoned in the port city, Williams announced in the pages of the *Alexandria Gazette* that his ship would be sailing "FOR NEW ORLEANS." No record has survived of Robert's thoughts as he and the others descended into the hold of the ship. But on June 29, the newspaper carried the news of the ship's departure: "Sailed, June 28, Brig Uncas, Cross, New Orleans."

Mulledy was visiting St. Inigoes when the news of the *Uncas's* departure appeared in the newspaper. The following day, he dedicated his Mass to the "poor negroes," but his prayers did little to assuage the outrage of the priests who managed the Jesuit plantations. A few days later, Lilly wrote an urgent letter to Rome. "It is with the greatest pain of spirit that I take up the pen," he wrote before he described the sale. "Those men, I believe, had assured humane and Christian treatment, but I discovered their nature," he continued. "What distress! What a scandal not only for the Catholics, but also for the Protestants! Many of them detest this sale as much as possible. And it will dispense such a wound to this religion and to this order." Worse still, he wrote, was the news that it was only the beginning, that the "remaining entirety" of the enslaved population had also been sold. It was only a matter of time before the slave traders returned for the rest. Could Rome have "permitted and approved" such an inhumane plan? Could Jan Roothaan himself have given such a horrific sale his blessing?

Mulledy was well aware of the outrage bubbling up among his

fellow priests, particularly those stationed on the plantations. But he was determined not to let their protests stop him. Four days after Lilly wrote to Roothaan in Rome, he was back in Washington, signing another document confirming his sale of the first group of people. "The whole of the said slaves have been delivered and have been shipped to New Orleans, on board the Brig Uncas, for the said J. Batey [*sic*]," he said, "except the last five." He promised to round up the missing people and to deliver them to Batey in the fall. But the stress of what priests would later describe as the ugly business of selling human beings was clearly taking its toll. Mulledy felt so "fatigued" and "unwell," as he recorded in his journal, that on five occasions that summer he did not officiate at Mass.

Still he remained unbowed, and in August, he struck back against his critics. In a defiant letter to Roothaan, he addressed the mounting criticism of his leadership. He dismissed Lilly and the other priests criticizing him on the plantations, suggesting that their objections to the sale stemmed from their self-serving distress at losing their authority over scores of enslaved people. "In no way is this matter pleasing to them," he wrote on August 9, 1838, "because they will not be the great masters they were before, but I hope they will be better Jesuits." The lay Catholics who lived alongside the plantations supported his decision to sell off the enslaved people, he continued. "I am carrying out a good work, as they say," he wrote. "They also say that this should have been done 20 years ago." He described the sale and the money that would flow into the province. He mentioned Johnson but not Batey, perhaps hoping that Johnson's stature as a congressman might impress his boss and noted that McSherry had sold enslaved people to Johnson before. He emphasized that the enslaved people would continue to practice their faith in their new homes in Louisiana. "Entire families will stay together, just as among us," he wrote. "They have the ability to go to Catholic mass every Sunday and holiday."

But the resistance he was encountering from the priests on the plantations, he wrote, was forcing him to handle the nuts and bolts of the mammoth transaction almost entirely on his own. He described riding on horseback from one plantation to another, some-times in the searing heat, as well as his mounting levels of stress and strain. ("One time," he wrote, "the thermometer read 98 degrees Fahrenheit.") He kept the problems he had encountered to himself, offering up instead a prettier (and clearly inaccurate) portrait of a subservient people who had willingly submitted to their fate. "Thanks be to God," he told Roothaan, they all "departed peace-fully." "I hope that the remaining ones depart as peacefully," he added.

Mulledy knew he couldn't expect any help from the priest plan-tation managers even though they knew the neighboring commu-nities and farmers best. He spoke bitterly of what he described as the "cowardice" of men such as Carbery, Lilly, and Havermans who challenged him. But he planned to clip their wings. "The adminis-trator fathers will have no jurisdiction as to the plantation" once the mass sale was completed, he vowed. The "upright and honest" white tenant farmers he planned to hire to replace the enslaved la-borers would answer to one of their own, who would supervise the plantations and report directly to him. The priests would become nothing more than spiritual caretakers, responsible only for the souls of the faithful, not powerful administrators of the vast estates.

It was vintage Mulledy, defiant and impetuous, proud and self-important, a man determined to force his vision on the world around him. He presented himself as a lonely warrior for the Mary-land province and for the Jesuits, a fighter who was forging ahead in the battle despite defections from unfaithful allies. The prize—the Catholics in the northeastern cities who would soon flock to Jesuit colleges—was clearly in sight. "This place, very Reverend Father, is an enormous field for us, and now it approaches harvest," he wrote, asking for one or two priests from Rome who could serve as reinforcements, trusty lieutenants who would stand by his side. "It only lacks workmen." In the meantime, he planned to head once more to the estates on horseback, visiting them one by one, to make sure all was in order for the next shipments of people. "Tomorrow I will begin my circuit of the plantations, alone but not sorrowful—for God protects me, almost openly," he wrote.

But his fellow Jesuits refused to buckle. One day after Mulledy wrote his vigorous defense of the sale, Father Dubuisson, now the pastor at St. Mary's in Alexandria, warned Roothaan that it was attracting unfavorable attention in Catholic circles. "Father Mulledy has his share of worries; this business of selling our Negroes en masse is giving him even more!" he wrote on August 10, 1838. "Alas! I still tremble at what will be the outcome. I mentioned it to two of our fathers from the lower counties; their response was an outcry of sorrow. They told me that a gang of these unfortunates going through Washington, making their way to a ship that was tied up at Alexandria greatly excited emotions among our separated brethren," he continued. "Out of politeness no one here speaks about it, but one person did tell me, 'Oh, what a terrible affect [*sic*] this is going to have, if it becomes publicly known!'" He felt particularly worried about the reaction to the sale in Philadelphia. He had good relations there with members of the Quaker community, who abhorred slavery. "The sale there will bring on a storm," he wrote. "May God avert it!"

On the plantations that summer, the enslaved were uneasy, as unsettled as the weather in the Chesapeake, where the temperature soared to nearly 100 degrees in the villages that surrounded the Jesuit estates while floods ravaged a community in Virginia not far from Mulledy's hometown. At St. Inigoes, the cadence of country life continued to ebb and flow. The sun rose in the early-morning sky. Horses shuffled and snorted in their stables. Wailing babies found comfort in their mothers' arms. Elderly couples tended to their gardens. Sailors plied St. Mary's River, and fishermen availed themselves of its bounty. At the manor house on the plantation, the Mahoneys continued to tend to Father Carbery and the visiting priests. And then, after sunset, chatter, whispers, and murmurs once again filled the slave quarters as families settled into their cramped lodgings for the night. But the day-to-day routines that felt as familiar as the soil underfoot were pierced by the agony of loss.

Many of the dilapidated homes that had once sheltered families were empty. Familiar faces and voices no longer rang out. The two sisters Louisa and Anna awoke each morning to the unbearable realization that their big brother was gone. Robert had been there when they had taken their first steps, when they had started serving the priests in the manor house, when Anna had gotten married and had children, when Louisa had left girlhood behind and become a young woman. They knew his wife, Mary. They knew his children, and the familiar faces and voices of their cousins. Robert carried hints of the Mahoney family's history, a history of rebellion and resistance, in his name. He had been born during the heady decade after the Revolutionary War and the birth of the young American republic, when his kinfolk had taken to the courts to demand their liberty. He carried the name of his uncle, the carpenter who had managed to buy his own freedom. Perhaps his parents, Harry and Anna, had hoped that their firstborn son would someday taste freedom, too. Instead he would be forced to endure an even harsher servitude.

Jesuit administrators, meanwhile, made careful note of the money that poured into their accounts that summer, and where that money went. "July 6 Cash for Negroes," reads one line in one of the Jesuit cashbooks, describing the first payment of $23,214 from Johnson that came in from the slave sale. "8000 to Archbishop Of Balt. to extinguish debt," reads another, describing a payment made to the Bishop of Baltimore to settle an old claim.

The rest of the down payment—some $17,000—went to George-town. That hefty sum would help pay down the debts that Mulledy had incurred during his building campaign. And more money—much more—would be coming into the province over the next decade, Mulledy informed Rome, as Johnson and Batey made good on their payments to the Jesuits in annual installments. While money flowed into the Jesuit coffers, the priests and enslaved people on the plantations prayed and waited.

Only about thirty people remained in St. Inigoes's Black community. They had witnessed the end of the world as they knew it. But the trauma wasn't past. All of them—the young, the old, the married, the single, the strong, the feeble—had price tags on their heads. Who would be taken next?

ON A SWELTERING afternoon that September, the sky darkened as the moon obscured the sun and a sign appeared in the sky. Enslaved people looked up and saw a blazing red ring of light surrounding the moon like a shimmering halo. Some prayed that such heavenly spectacles meant that their liberation from endless enslavement was near. Others viewed solar eclipses as omens, signs of agony to come. At St. Inigoes, Louisa and Anny needed no celestial sign to know of the darkness that lay ahead.

The slave traders came to the Newtown plantation first, on a Saturday evening about a month after the eclipse. Mulledy turned up at the estate with Johnson and announced that he planned to round up the enslaved and load them on a ship the following day. Father Havermans protested, demanding to know if their plan complied with protocol. Mulledy backed down. But he vowed to send a law enforcement official to complete the job and ordered the enslaved families to prepare to leave.

The families washed their clothes and waited. One person took flight, hiding from the traders. The rest "handed themselves over to fate with heroic fortitude," Havermans wrote, and with what Havermans saw as "Christian resignation, relinquished themselves to God."

Two days later, the sheriff arrived, ready to load the people of the Newtown plantation onto a ship. Some people begged Havermans for rosaries and crosses before they were led away. One pregnant woman fell to her knees. "If ever there was some reason for despairing, do I now not have it?" she said. "I do not know on what day the child will come, whether on the road or at sea. What will happen to me? What did I do to deserve this?"

"Trust in God," Havermans told her.

The priest offered his blessings and watched helplessly as the men walked the plantation, choosing who would stay and who would go. Some enslaved people, mostly those with spouses on other plantations, were spared. The rest left the estate—and the world they knew—behind.

Witnessing the roundup at Newtown seemed to take a physical toll on Havermans; he was hit by waves of nausea and vomiting. He wrote to Rome on behalf of the enslaved, condemning the sale and marveling at the faith of the enslaved. "And with how much obedience they went to the boat," he reported. "Only one tried to run away. And the official was not compelled to bind him." Some of the enslaved "remain here so that either their wives or husbands might be bought, or there might be an arrangement concerning them by said Johnson," he continued. "I wish that he would not separate them from their partners and children. For this would . . . greatly hurt the faith."

Havermans had assailed the decision to move ahead with the mass sale just days earlier, calling it tragic and unacceptable. "For this is done by no one except by bad people (as merchants of blacks are), who crave nothing other than money, or by those who out of necessity, e.g., among otherwise blameless people, for repaying debts that must be resolved, are forced to it. Others, even Protestants, consider this forbidden." But he knew that his letters to Rome would not prevent what was coming next.

Back at Georgetown, Mulledy readied himself once again for the road. Roothaan had ordered him to keep families together and warned that missteps might provoke divine retribution: "It would be better to suffer financial disaster than suffer the loss of our souls with the sale of the slaves." Mulledy carried the weight of that warning with him as he prepared himself for the journey. But it would not deter him. On October 31, 1838, he picked up his diary. "Set out for St. Innigoes," he wrote.

Someone, somehow got word to Father Carbery. The slave traders were coming. He knew he could not mount a blockade to stop the roundup. But he decided he would do what he could to protect the people.

When Mulledy finally arrived at the plantation, he presided over a Mass for the faithful and prayed once again for his own soul. But the leader of the Maryland Jesuits had a mission to accomplish, and he did what he had come to do. Soon cries of terror and sorrow filled the air. Word spread through the dilapidated cabins where weary parents were sleeping with their children and through the fields where they were laboring.

But Carbery had taken matters into his own hands. In a flagrant act of defiance against his superior, he had sought out members of the Mahoney family. *Run!* he told them. *Run!*

Louisa ran with her mother. Anny gathered her children. Many of the Black people on the plantation hoped to flee, to fly from the approaching danger like the herons that circled and soared far beyond the Jesuit estate. But for most of the enslaved men and women, including Anny, the news came too late. She and her two young children, Arnold, who was about eight or nine, and Louisa, who was about six, were herded together with the rest of the enslaved people who would be loaded on the ship. Did she catch a glimpse of Louisa before Louisa ran? Did she try to run herself? Did she turn back to protect her children? Did she scream as she was taken?

Harry, now an old man and the patriarch of the family, was spared. But it was the bitterest of blessings. He had done all he could to keep his family safe. He had declined to resist as his ancestors and kinfolk had. He had worked faithfully for the Jesuits for decades, hidden the Church's wealth during the War of 1812, and secured a pledge that his family would never be sold. He had raised his children and watched his grandchildren grow, buoyed by that promise and the belief that they would all remain together. But now he was forced to endure the unbearable, the disintegration of his entire family. In June, his oldest son had been stolen from him. Now two of his daughters, Anny and Bibiana, and his grandchildren were being taken, torn from their homes and marched away from St. Inigoes, all of them victims of the mundane brutality of American slavery.

Mulledy, who orchestrated and oversaw the destruction of the families, witnessed it all. Then he clambered onto his horse and over the next two weeks continued his circuit of the plantations, heading to Newtown, St. Thomas Manor, and White Marsh. "I have been on horseback daily for the last twenty days with the exception of three days—All Saints & two Sundays," he wrote. "One day I rode 66 miles—God be praised I feel healthy & active."

Anny and her children and the dozens of other enslaved people were not so blessed. They marched. Their footprints in the soil have faded over the centuries, the precise path of their journey lost. But yellowing scraps of paper in the archives offer clues. Dr. James Roach, a medical doctor from a well-known family in the county, was paid to assist in the process. The enslaved families were herded aboard a seagoing craft, the *Stafford,* from which they caught their last glimpses of home before the boat carried them away from St. Mary's County.

Families were herded out of the other plantations as well. Father Grivel, who visited the slave quarters at White Marsh plantation in early November, found that Mulledy had already rented nearly the entire estate to white tenant farmers. Nearly all of the enslaved people were gone. Grivel expressed none of Havermans's or Lilly's outrage over the sale. He downplayed fears that the spiritual lives of the enslaved would be neglected by their new Protestant enslavers, as if that were all that mattered. He also expressed optimism that Johnson would tend to their religious needs in Louisiana. "Governor Johnson will have a Priest at his plantation every Sunday & H. Days," he wrote. "These last years, the priest had been there 35 times & he paid him $185 for his trouble. It's a fact."

And instead of describing the despair of the few enslaved people who remained on the estate, he described a joke that he had shared with an elderly Black man. He joked that the man's wife, who was heavyset, would need a wagon and five horses to carry her to Baltimore. "Old Isaac is quite cheerful," reported Grivel about the enslaved man, Isaac Hawkins, who had just lost nearly all of his children and grandchildren to the sale.

While Anny and her two children and the other enslaved men and women, imprisoned in a slave pen in the bustling port of Alexandria, waited for their departure to Louisiana, money poured into the Jesuits' accounts. On November 12, a day before their ship was set to sail, Johnson handed over an additional $2,000 in cash.

Franklin and Armfield, the slave traders who had shipped the Cutchmores and Halls, had largely retired from the business. But the jail they'd started still held scores of Black captives. An abolitionist who visited the jail in early 1838 saw "50 or 60 wretched prisoners" in what he described as "an immense slave factory." It was operated by George Kephart, who had assumed control of much of the trade, working out of the old Franklin and Armfield office. Kephart hired a bookkeeper and assistant named Robert Windsor, who had been in the business since at least the 1820s, when he had posted an advertisement in the *Alexandria Phenix Gazette* seeking "a few slaves."

Windsor, who also worked as a constable in Alexandria, had cut his teeth in the business working for Armfield, shipping enslaved people to New Orleans aboard the *Uncas* and the *Tribune,* and he ended up being the man who would handle the men, women, and children from the Jesuit estates.

Like Franklin and Armfield, the Kephart-Windsor team spun the same sugarcoated stories about slavery, telling the visitors who ventured within the walls of the compound on Duke Street "how kind they were to the prisoners" and "how mild southern slavery was." But Windsor knew the truth. He knew that the two-story building where the enslaved slept at night had "rings made of round iron, about three-fourths of an inch thick, fastened to the floor about as far apart as a man's length" and that people were generally kept chained there at night. He knew about the dungeon, the basement under the firm's offices, located directly below the parlor, which was equipped with "thumb-screws, and other instruments of coercion" designed to tame rebellious Black people. And he knew all too well the desperation and anguish of the enslaved people who were kept captive.

A year earlier, while he had been patrolling in the city, he had been called to the slave pen on Duke Street. Someone had heard children screaming. A young enslaved woman in her twenties, who had been granted the freedom to live with autonomy until she had recently been sold, had decided that she could not bear for her children to return to a life in slavery. She had already strangled her two youngest children in the pen and was attempting to murder her two older children, beating their faces and heads with bricks "by which they were horribly mangled." The killings and the trial that followed garnered headlines in local newspapers, briefly bringing the desperation of the enslaved families into the spotlight. Windsor testified before a judge, who ultimately found the woman not guilty by reason of insanity. But the slave trade continued unabated, and the pen on Duke Street continued to serve as a way station for the enslaved, including hundreds of frightened and bewildered mothers and children.

Given Windsor's ties to Kephart, it is likely that Anny and her young children, Arnold and Louisa, along with the scores of other people sold by the Jesuits, were among those confined within the tall white walls of the Duke Street slave pen. The jailers segregated the men and teenage boys from the women and younger children. But grief, fear, and a bitter sense of betrayal united them. In Alexandria, Anny encountered men, women, and children who like herself had spent their entire lives on Jesuit plantations, people from Newtown, White Marsh, and St. Thomas Manor, families that had spent generations serving the Jesuits. All of them had been owned by Catholic priests, religious men who often described themselves as kinder and more generous to the enslaved than ordinary slaveholders but nonetheless profited from their labor. But Anny and the others now knew firsthand that the hunger for profit had trumped the calls for compassion, even among the most powerful Jesuits in the country.

Sometime around November 13, Anny and her children woke to what for most people in Alexandria was an unremarkable morning. The pharmacist on King Street sold cough lozenges and Bermuda arrowroot. The bookseller hoped to draw customers interested in his latest offerings, schoolbooks and specialty items such as *History of the Horse* and *Religious Opinions of Washington*. And shoppers stopping by local stores and suppliers could find English walnuts and West Indian sugar, gunpowder and tea, curled hair and corn shuck mattresses, fancy cologne and Indian hair dye, all ready for purchase. White residents took pride in the town's paved roads and bustling commerce, the ordinary rhythms of day-to-day life. But nothing would be ordinary for Anny that day.

Windsor had rounded up the young mother and her children and the scores of other enslaved people for delivery to the wharf. Slave traders typically chained their human wares together for that last walk through Alexandria. Witnesses described Black men and boys lined up two by two, their wrists handcuffed together, a long chain running the length of the line. Women and girls followed, sometimes tied with rope. Some mothers carried babies in their arms. Others, like Anny, must have feared that they might never see their sons again.

Slave traders forced so many Black people to parade through the streets that some white people began to view the human chains as a nuisance. "Scarcely a week passes without some of these wretched creatures being driven through our streets," complained one white observer, who had grown weary of the ubiquitous slave coffles. "After having been confined, and sometimes manacled, in a loathsome prison, they are turned out in a public view, to take their departure for the South. The children, and some of the women, are generally crowded into a cart or wagon, while the others follow on foot, not infrequently handcuffed and chained together."

One Black witness, who recalled watching the horrific spectacle, said he had never forgotten the sight. Or the sounds. The people, he reported, had been "screaming and crying."

Jacob Stroyer, an enslaved man in South Carolina, remembered his own feelings of despair when his sisters were shipped to Louisiana. "Louisiana was considered by the slaves a place of slaughter, so those who were going there did not expect to see their friends again," he wrote.

The agony of the enslaved was seared into the bystanders' memory. "Imagine a mass of uneducated people shedding tears and yelling at the tops of their voices in anguish and grief," Stroyer wrote. "The colored people cried out with one voice as though the heavens and earth were coming together. We heard the weeping and wailing from the slaves, as far as human voice could be heard," he continued, "and from that time to the present I have neither seen nor heard from my two sisters."

But to Windsor, it was just another day at the office. His letters were matter-of-fact. The enslaved people were commodities, human property, faceless and often nameless. ("We have purchased upward of 30 Negroes suitable for shipping since Mr. Armfield left home, and we have a flattering prospect of purchasing more in the course of a few days," he wrote.)

When Anny and her children finally arrived at the wharf, they saw it: the *Katharine Jackson,* a 456-ton vessel with three masts and white billowing sails. Anny and her children and the other people sold by the Jesuits—some 130 in all—carried their clothing and bedding as they boarded. On November 13, the crew scrutinized each enslaved passenger and carefully noted his or her name, age, height, and color on a handwritten list that would be further scrutinized by customs inspectors. Among the desperate people marching onto the ship were children, teenagers, and elders in their sixties and seventies: mothers and fathers, grandmothers and grandfathers, babies and toddlers. The two oldest enslaved people to step onto the deck were seventy. The youngest, who was carried on board, was two months old.

For the crew and customs officials, it was all numbingly familiar: the crush of bodies, the wailing babies, the tear-streaked, terrified faces, the men, women, and children herded like cattle, listed by number. Anny, described as brown skinned and about five foot three, was no. 73. Her children, Arnold and Louisa, stood about four foot four and three foot eleven, respectively. They were listed on the shipping manifest as nos. 74 and 75. Anny's older sister Bibiana; Bibiana's husband, Nace; and their children boarded, too.

Anny stood amid the crowd of frantic people. What would the future hold for her and for her children? Could she and her sister Bibiana find a way to stay together in the new world on the other side of the water? Would she ever find her brother Robert? And what would become of Louisa, her parents, and the siblings she had left behind at St. Inigoes? Would she ever see them again?

Generations of Mahoneys had viewed Maryland as home, even as they resisted—through rebellion and lawsuits—and then endured enslavement, clinging to the promise that Harry Mahoney's loyal service had earned, the promise that his family would never be sold.

Now Anny stood on the deck of the slave ship *Katharine Jackson* taking her final glimpse of the Chesapeake region that had always been her home. Soon Alexandria's bustling wharf would fade from view until there was nothing on the horizon but sky and sea.

A Family Divided

THE RUSHING WATERS OF THE POTOMAC RIVER HAVE CAPtured the imaginations of the area's human inhabitants for thousands of years. Native Americans prized the abundant wildlife that swam in its waves and flocked to its banks. The early white settlers, including the first Jesuit priest to set foot in Maryland, extolled its bounty. George Washington, whose mansion in Mount Vernon offered stunning views of the Potomac, described it as "the nation's river" and "one of the finest Rivers in the world." Thomas Jefferson, who marveled at the sight of the river winding through the Blue Ridge Mountains, called it "one of the most stupendous scenes in nature."

The enslaved people at St. Inigoes knew the Potomac intimately. They fished and dug for oysters in St. Mary's River, which bathed the banks of the plantation and emptied into the Potomac. They knew the fish and wildlife that flourished in its waters and on its banks. They knew that the vital waterway carried vessels—filled with passengers, goods, and the wheat and tobacco they harvested— to places such as Alexandria, Washington, and Georgetown. But for Anny, who was imprisoned on board the *Katharine Jackson,* the twisting tributary must have seemed like a river of tears. It was the waterway that carried thousands of captive souls on the first leg of one of the largest forced migrations in the nation's history. Between 1800 and 1860, about a million enslaved people were forcibly relocated from the Upper South states, including Maryland and Virginia, whose soils had been depleted by generations of tobacco farming, to the states of the Deep South, such as Louisiana, Mississippi, and Alabama, whose booming cotton and sugarcane plantations had an insatiable hunger for labor.

This staggering figure is more than twice the number of people shipped to North America in the transatlantic slave trade and about twenty times the number of Native Americans driven from their homes along the Trail of Tears in the 1830s. At the height of the domestic trade, a young person born into slavery in the Upper South faced a one-in-three chance of being sold down south. In the United States during that time, someone was sold about every 3.5 minutes.

On plantations and farms in Maryland and Virginia, human beings had become one of the most lucrative commodities. And Virginia—with its bustling ports in Alexandria, Norfolk, and Richmond—had become one of the nation's primary departure points. Between 1810 and 1860, nearly 450,000 people were shipped south from that state alone. For many of them, that agonizing journey began on the river that carried Anny and her children from Alexandria into the unknown in November 1838.

The Potomac twists and turns as it runs past Prince William County, Virginia, and Charles County, Maryland, on its way to the Chesapeake Bay. If Anna was lucky enough to have been standing on the deck of the *Katharine Jackson,* she would have caught one last glimpse of home as the slave ship glided past St. Mary's County. Some slave ships made stops along the way, picking up additional cargo and enslaved passengers. Anny and her fellow prisoners may have prayed for such a miracle, for one last stop on familiar soil, for one last chance to escape. But the captain of the *Katharine Jackson* had one destination in mind: New Orleans. So he continued south without stopping, and before long, the ship was sailing through the Chesapeake and into the vast open waters of the Atlantic Ocean.

"I can see us now, riding on de water," recalled one enslaved woman, recalling the sea voyage she had taken when just a girl. "One morning, we come out lookin' an' see nothin', but sky an' water. Dey made us go by de sea because den we can't go back. God help us!"

The journey to New Orleans on board a slave ship, coursing around the Florida peninsula and streaming into the Gulf of Mexico, typically took about three weeks, depending on the weather. Some travelers might have savored the beauty of the sea, the flying fish, the endless sky. Solomon Northup, a free Black man who was kidnapped and enslaved just a few years after Anny and her family were sold, certainly remembered that the waters of the gulf seemed almost white. But for him and for thousands of other enslaved passengers, the extraordinary vistas were accompanied by hardship, brutality, and despair as they endured seemingly endless days in what amounted to floating prisons.

On the best of days, prisoners such as Anny and her children were able to walk on deck freely, without being handcuffed or chained, to stretch their legs and breathe the fresh air of the sea. But at night, Northup recalled, they had been forced below into the cramped, dank hold. The holds in the slave ships that Windsor used were specifically outfitted for human cargo. On the *Tribune,* for example, wooden platforms lined both sides of the hold. One was positioned a few inches above the floor, the other about halfway to the ceiling. They were, in effect, shelves for "human merchandise," hard wooden platforms where the enslaved passengers were forced to sleep at night. Slave traders often crammed as many people as possible into the ships. On the *Tribune,* a ship designed to hold 180 enslaved people, each captive was forced to squeeze into thirty-six cubic feet of space, roughly the size of a large desk. Northup and others described the interiors of the ships as nightmarish.

Sometimes fierce winds tossed the vessels between towering

waves. "The brig rolled and plunged until we feared she would go down," Northup recalled. "Some were sea-sick, others on their knees praying, while some were fast holding to each other, paralyzed with fear. The sea-sickness rendered the place of our confinement loathsome and disgusting. It would have been a happy thing for most of us—it would have saved the agony of many hundred lashes, and miserable deaths at last—had the compassionate sea snatched us that day from the clutches of remorseless men."

The sea did not swallow Northup, nor did it swallow Anny and the rest of the enslaved passengers on the *Katharine Jackson,* which continued its journey through the Gulf of Mexico. But even when the winds slackened, the heavens cleared, and the waters stilled, the suffering on the slave ships continued belowdecks. Smallpox sickened and killed one passenger aboard Northup's ship, and overcrowding and unsanitary living conditions rendered the weeks at sea unbearable. William Walker, an enslaved man who was forcibly relocated from Virginia to New Orleans only a few years after Anny and her family, never forgot the grim voyage on board the *Pelican,* a massive ship that held three times as many enslaved people as the *Tribune* did. In his memoir, he described retching passengers, fetid air, and unrelenting anguish. "It would be impossible for any man to draw the faintest idea of the horrible position in which we were placed while on the boat," he wrote. "Men, women and children were packed beneath the hatches like cattle. Think of six hundred human beings living six weeks in the hold of a vessel 180 feet long, 40 feet wide, and 10 feet high.

"There was no air to be had, for the only means of receiving air was by three small grated windows on either side of the boat, two feet long and eight inches wide," he continued, "and when sea sickness began among us it was surely one of the most horrible places ever visited by a human being." The stench from the ship, he said, seemed "poisonous to breathe."

Some people died on the journey. Walker reported that thirty-one perished on the *Pelican.* But the captain of the *Katharine Jackson* steered the slave ship into the mouth of the Mississippi River with all of his passengers alive. The river would carry Anny, her children, Arnold and Louisa, and Anny's sister Bibiana and her family north on the last hundred miles of their journey. By the time the ship pulled in to the clamorous wharf in New Orleans on December 6, 1838, it had spent more than twenty days at sea. A customs inspector stepped on board, and, taking the passenger list, he examined the captives on the ship one by one, making sure that the name and description of each person on board matched that of each individual who had been loaded on board in Virginia. After inspecting the human cargo, he scribbled his assessment on the bottom of the list: "Examined & found correct."

Bewildered and uncertain, Anny and her children, her sister Bibiana and Bibiana's family, and scores of other enslaved people stepped off the ship into the city that housed the largest slave market in America. It was the place where north and south, east and west intersected, where the Old World and the New World met and mixed. New Orleans, with its prime location on the Mississippi River, the gateway to the Gulf of Mexico and the Atlantic, had long been a nexus that linked the colonies in North America to the old cities of Europe. As the United States had expanded westward and white men hungry for hope and opportunity had migrated from the Chesapeake to Mississippi, Tennessee, Alabama, and Louisiana, New Orleans had boomed. From the Northeast arrived ships brimming with crates of textiles and guns, books and fine china, buttons and shoes to satisfy the hungers of the wealthy elite. From the Upper South arrived vessels crammed with captive families such as Anny's, Black people who would do the backbreaking labor to produce the precious commodities helping to fuel Louisiana's rapid expansion: cotton and sugar. By 1830, cotton exports from New Orleans accounted for more than half of the cotton shipped from the country. By 1834, New Orleans had surpassed New York City to become the nation's busiest port for foreign exports.

Above: Chesapeake Bay tobacco wharves, ca. 1750. Ann Joice, the matriarch of the Mahoney family, arrived in the Chesapeake sometime around 1676 as an indentured servant to Charles Calvert, Lord Baltimore, the proprietor of Maryland.
Collection of the Maryland State Archives

Above, right: Charles Calvert, 3rd Lord Baltimore.
John Closterman, Wikimedia Commons

Left: Rev. John Carroll, 1806. He was the nation's first Catholic bishop, its first archbishop, and the founder of Georgetown College.
Georgetown University Art Collection

Georgetown College in the District of Columbia, 1829.
Campus by W. Harrison after S. Pinistri, Booth Family Center for Special Collections, Lauinger Library, Georgetown University

UNITED STATES SLAVE TRADE.
1850.

Above: US slave trade, Washington, DC, 1830.
Library of Congress

Right: Rev. Thomas F. Mulledy, who served
as president of Georgetown College and leader
of the Maryland province. He helped to
orchestrate the mass slave sale of 1838.
Georgetown University Art Collection

Left: Rev. William McSherry, who
served as the first leader of the
Maryland province and as a president
of Georgetown. He worked with
Mulledy to organize the mass sale.
Georgetown University Art Collection

Above: Old St. Inigoes mansion, pre-1875. The Mahoney family was enslaved on the Jesuit plantation of St. Inigoes, and several family members served the priests in this mansion.

John Brosnan, S.J., Photographic Collection, Woodstock Theological College Archives, Georgetown University

Franklin and Armfield slave prison in Alexandria, Virginia, 1836. Scores of people enslaved and sold by the Jesuits were shipped from Alexandria to New Orleans, and some of the shipments were handled by slave traders and ship captains with ties to Franklin and Armfield, who ran the largest slave trading operation in the country. *Library of Congress*

Above: A document inside St. Ignatius Church in Port Tobacco, Maryland, lists the names of the enslaved people sold by the Jesuits in 1838 to help keep Georgetown University afloat.

Michael A. McCoy *for* The New York Times

Left: Rev. Thomas Lilly, one of the priests who criticized the Jesuits' 1838 mass slave sale.

Georgetown University Art Collection

Right: Painting of the *Katharine Jackson* in watercolor, 1844. The *Katharine Jackson* slave ship carried scores of the people sold by the Jesuits to Louisiana in 1838.

M. A. Thomas, Watercolor, 21.5 x 26.75 in. Collection of the Chesapeake Bay Maritime Museum, 2002.18.1. Collections.cbmm.org

Left: Gathering the Cane, Louisiana, 1853. Some enslaved members of the Mahoney family ended up on sugarcane plantations like this one in Louisiana.

Harper's New Monthly Magazine *(1853), vol. 9, p. 760. Copy in Special Collections Department, University of Virginia Library. Slavery Images: A Visual Record of the African Slave Trade and Slave Life in the Early African Diaspora, accessed December 1, 2021, http://slaveryimages .org/s/slaveryimages/item/1082*

Dr. John Dominique's Store near Chatham plantation in Ascension parish, Louisiana, 1857. Anna Mahoney Jones and her children were enslaved on Chatham plantation, which was adjacent to this store.

Marie Adrien Persac, courtesy of the Louisiana State Museum, Gift of Mr. Emile Dominique Jr., 1969.007

Below: Our Colored Troops at Work, Fort Macomb, Louisiana, 1863. Several of the men who were sold by the Jesuits joined the Union Army in Louisiana.

"Our Colored Troops at Work," Harper's Weekly (February 28, 1863), vol. 7, p. 133

Bob Mason and family, ca. 1900. Archivists believe that the elderly woman in this photograph is Louisa Mahoney Mason, mother of Bob Mason, who is standing behind her.

John Brosnan, S.J., Brosnan Photo Collection, Woodstock Theological Library, Georgetown University

Above: May procession, Black Catholic community in Woodstock, Maryland, 1927. Members of the Mahoney family migrated to Woodstock where they continued to work for the Jesuits, who had established a seminary there. They became members of the thriving Black Catholic community.

St. Peter Claver's Sunday School Diary: 1901–1906, I.P. 3.1, Woodstock Theological College Archives, box 38, folder 827, Georgetown University

Left: Sister Mary Theophane Bennett, great-granddaughter of Louisa Mahoney Mason. At least two women in the Mahoney family became nuns. They and other members of the family worked to make the Church more responsive to the needs of the Black community.

Oblate Sisters of Providence Archives, Baltimore, Maryland

Top: Georgetown University, 2016.
Annie Flanagan for The New York Times

Middle: Dr. John J. DeGioia, president of Georgetown, greets descendants in Maringouin, Louisiana.
Annie Flanagan for The New York Times

Bottom: Joseph M. Stewart, president of the Descendants Truth & Reconciliation Foundation. He was one of three descendant leaders who negotiated a historic agreement with the Jesuits. Jesuit leaders agreed to raise $100 million to atone for the Catholic order's participation in the American slave trade.
Saul Martinez for The New York Times

Rev. Timothy Kesicki, former president of the Jesuit Conference of Canada and the United States and chair of the trust created in partnership with Mr. Stewart and two other descendant leaders. He helped to broker the historic agreement between the Jesuits and the three descendant leaders.
Michael A. McCoy for The New York Times

Above: Melissa Kemp, direct descendant of Louisa Mahoney Mason.
Courtesy of Melissa Kemp

Left: Jeremy Alexander, direct descendant of Anna Mahoney Jones.
Georgetown University

Melissa Kemp and Jeremy Alexander discovered their ties to the 1838 slave sale, and to each other, in 2016.

Anny and her wide-eyed children would have seen it all as they stepped onto the dock: wharves teeming with sea captains, ship and dock workers, merchants and slave traders, all shouting and chattering in a half-dozen languages. She would have seen people of all shades, white, Black, and mixed race, jostling and hustling amid the thousands of flatboats anchored along the city's docks.

For the wealthy white elite, New Orleans was one of the finest cities in the nation. But for enslaved newcomers such as Anny, it was terrifying, the city known throughout the Upper South as the gateway to the country's harshest slave regimes. As she and the others were guided from the ship, she made her way through frenetic and cacophonous crowds after a lifetime of isolation among people she had known forever. Everywhere she turned, she saw a sea of unfamiliar faces, each one adding to the disorientation and despair that many enslaved people experienced.

"In all the crowd that thronged the wharf, there was no one who knew or cared for me. Not one," Northup wrote. "No familiar voice greeted my ears, nor was there a single face that I had ever seen. . . . My family, alas, should I ever see them more?" he continued. "There was a feeling of utter desolation in my heart, filling it with a despairing and regretful sense, that I had not gone down . . . to the bottom of the sea."

From the docks, Northup, like thousands of other Black captives, was marched to one of the many slave pens that drew traders and speculators from around the region. Enslaved people typically walked past gin houses and tenements to the stretch of jails only a few blocks away from New Orleans's historic cathedral, the heart of Catholicism in the city, where priests and nuns profited from the slave trade, just like their compatriots in Maryland. There they would encounter the open-air slave markets with scores of enslaved people in suits and calico dresses paraded before eager white buyers. Northup ended up in a slave pen run by Theophilus Freeman. Freeman had done business in the mid-1830s with Franklin and Armfield and with Windsor, the trader who had shipped Anny and her family to New Orleans. Northup recalled that the pen, like many of the others, was enclosed by wooden planks that often stood fifteen or twenty feet high. Inside, dozens of enslaved people were crammed together in yards that must have reeked of smoke, sweat, human waste, and the lye that was spread around to prevent infection. They were paraded like cattle either in showrooms or out on the street.

"He would make us hold up our heads, walk briskly back and forth while customers would feel of our hands and arms and bodies, turn us about, ask us what we could do, make us open our mouths and show our teeth, precisely as a jockey examines a horse which he is about to barter for or purchase," recalled Northup, describing how Freeman had presented his enslaved wares to his clients.

A New Orleans merchant company, Lambeth & Thompson, had agreed to take charge of Anny and the rest of the human cargo, who were destined for shipment to the plantations upriver owned by Henry Johnson and Jesse Batey. So after being held in New Orleans, Anny, her children, and the others boarded another vessel that carried them up the Mississippi River, the vast watery highway that traverses the state of Louisiana. The saga of the river journey taken by the Mahoney clan upriver was passed down from one generation to the next, tales of enslaved men, women, and babies forced onto flatboats that cruised along the river with alligators trailing in their wake.

The river carried them west and then north, snaking its way through the parishes of St. John the Baptist, St. James, and Ascension. As they traveled, they could see other flatboats as well as steamers crowding the waters and, on the shoreline, hints of what was to come. White travelers wrote about the plantations lining the riverbanks, the "groups of slave-dwellings, painted or unpainted, standing under the shade of sycamores, magnolias, live oakes [sic], or Pride-of-India trees. Many dusky gazing figures of men with the axe, and women with the pitcher." Enslaved men who worked on the steamboats recalled grimmer landscapes. One man described overseers shouting and threatening hundreds of enslaved workers. Another could not forget the sounds that emanated from the estates, the ringing of the "great bells" that signaled the start of the workday, and the "crack of the overseers whip."

Anny, her children, and the others finally stepped off the boat onto the banks of Iberville parish. There they had their first glimpses of their new world. It was a small, sleepy parish where white men planted both cotton and sugarcane, where Johnson and Batey had established estates nestled deep in the woods. As the enslaved people were taken from the river to their new homes, Anny was forced to confront yet another devastating blow: She would be torn from the only sibling she had left. The two sisters had traveled together on the slave ship from Alexandria to New Orleans. They would have prayed to stay together on what must have felt like the other side of the world. But Anny had been purchased by Johnson; her sister Bibiana by Batey.

Batey and some business partners had set their sights on land in the parish only four years earlier. Batey's portion had become a plantation called West Oak. In September 1838, just three months before Anna and the others arrived, Johnson, who was still living in St. James at the time, purchased some land from one of Batey's partners. Johnson's plantation would become known as Marengo. The two plantations, West Oak and Marengo, sat side by side. Anny would be close to her sister, at least for a time. There must have been some comfort in that, even as Anny struggled to make sense of her new reality, bewildering and alien.

She arrived at a plantation community in flux, one transitioning from cotton to sugarcane, the sweet commodity that would transform the collection of sleepy river estates into some of the most prosperous parishes in Louisiana. But Anny and her children quickly learned that cotton was still king on the estates that Johnson and Batey owned. Cotton was white gold, the nation's cash crop, and production had surged from 40 million pounds in 1800 to 322 million pounds in 1831, accounting for a majority of the value of the nation's exports. By 1835, cotton prices had surged to "fifteen year highs," fueling a furious demand for enslaved labor to clear land, sow, and harvest. Prices had plummeted during the Panic of 1837, but by 1838 they were on the rise, jumping from 9 cents a pound at the beginning of the year to almost 13 cents a pound as the year inched to a close, lifting the spirits of Iberville planters such as Johnson and Batey, who hoped to use their enslaved workers to cash in on the boom.

Cotton, the world's most valuable commodity, proved to be a boon to white plantation owners, northern merchants and factories, and the American economy as a whole. It fueled the Industrial Revolution at home and abroad. But producing such vast volumes of cotton required a completely new way of working; it required backbreaking labor and punishing work schedules that bore little resemblance to what enslaved people had endured in the Chesapeake. On Maryland plantations such as St. Inigoes, which produced wheat and tobacco, planters often allowed Black foremen such as Harry Mahoney to supervise small groups of laborers who tended to the crops. That did not mean that those enslaved people were not beaten or raped. Such brutal violations certainly took place. But it meant that they sometimes had some autonomy, dictating for themselves how they handled the work at hand. Old people and children might not have to work in the fields at all.

On cotton plantations, on the other hand, overseers carefully monitored Black people in the fields and required men, women, and older children alike to tend to the crop at a breakneck pace. To increase production, the men employed violence and savagery at levels typically unseen in the Upper South. "The conch shell blowed afore daylight and all hands better git out for roll call or Solomon bust the door down and git them out," recalled Mary Reynolds, who was enslaved on an estate on Louisiana's Black River, describing the overseer and the harsh labor regime he had imposed. "It was work hard, git beatins and half fed."

Anny and her family had heard the stories about the Deep South, but now she was about to experience it herself. She and her children were sent to the slave quarters on the Marengo plantation, uncertain and fearful of what was yet to come. What kind of master would dictate the order of their days? Would he be kindly, cruel, or indifferent? She would go to sleep that first night without knowing the answers to any of those questions. It would be months before she and the others laid eyes on their new enslaver.

Johnson, who had purchased the plantation in Iberville as an investment, was in Washington tending to the business of lawmaking in the Capitol when Anny and her family first set foot in Louisiana. He cast his vote for a new clerk of the House of Representatives on the day that customs inspectors in New Orleans inspected Anny and the other passengers on board the *Katharine Jackson*. Then, about a week after Anny stepped off the ship, he waded back into the turbulent debate over slavery once again.

The issue before Johnson and the other members of the House that time was yet another petition calling for an end to slavery in Washington, DC. The petitioners also wanted to bar the movement of enslaved people from one state to another. So Johnson joined with the majority of his fellow congressmen to assert "that all attempts on the part of Congress to abolish slavery in the District of Columbia or the Territories, or to prohibit the removal of slaves from State to State, or to discriminate between the institutions of one portion of the confederacy and another, with the views aforesaid, are in violation of the constitution."

With all the business at hand, it would be several months before he could visit his plantation, which sat alongside the waters of the Bayou Maringouin, but he was encouraged by the reports he heard, likely from his overseers and fellow planters in the community. "I have not yet visited my plantation on the Maringoin, where I placed a number of hands early in December last, but propose seeing them on my return home, or in the course of a few days afterwards," Johnson wrote to his brother in April 1839. "I am informed, however, that on that place, that I now have in cultivation more cotton, corn[,] pumpkin etc. than the hands there can save," he continued, writing from New Orleans. "All who have the place speak in high terms of it, and consider my prospects there very flattering."

Undoubtedly, Anny felt very differently. She woke every morning to the trilling of unfamiliar birds and the sounds, smells, and rhythms of an unfamiliar plantation. She bore the burden of struggling to explain the inexplicable to her children and to make sense of it herself. Why had they been sold? What had become of her mother? Her father? Her sister and brothers?

Anny left behind no letters or journals as some of her white contemporaries did. Her emotions can only be imagined, though they are the definition of unimaginable. Did she swallow her tears for the sake of her children? Did her body shake with sobs when she had a moment to herself? Or did she wail out loud in the black of the night? No one knows. What we do know is that she kept moving, kept surviving, even as she was haunted by all she had lost. Anny had named her daughter after her beloved sister Louisa, a name that evoked the joys of sisterhood and new motherhood. But now the name must have evoked a more complex mix of emotions, including heartbreak and unbearable longing. When Anny called out, "Louisa!" she knew that only her daughter would come running, not the sister she had left behind. Where was Louisa?

LOUISA AND HER mother were huddled in the woods, hiding from the slave traders who had taken Anny, Bibiana, and so many of their friends and relatives. For days, they had gone without food and slept beneath the trees, watching the sun rise and set, fearful that they were still being hunted.

When Mulledy and the slave traders swept through the Jesuit estates, the Jesuits paid local men to assist in the hunt. The faded receipts and records of those payments offer a glimpse of the enslaved people's last days in Maryland. The white man who handled the accounts at White Marsh received $15.50 to cover the cost of "supper . . . & breakfast" for "horses & servants." The local boat captain who ferried enslaved people aboard the *Stafford* seacraft and the local doctor who tended to them received a total of $57.50. Another captain received $75 for his troubles, sailing with thirty-two slaves to the port of Alexandria.

The Jesuits also rounded up stragglers, including Charles Queen. "Paid for taking Charles (srvt) sent to Alexandria 10.00," read one line in a Jesuit financial ledger. Charles ended up in the slave pen established by Franklin and Armfield and run by George Kephart. "Ten dollars for taking negro to Alexandria & depositing him in Kepharts Jail," read a receipt that documented the amount paid to transport him to the slave pen. Queen, who was brown skinned and stood five foot ten, was later forced on board the *Isaac Franklin,* which set sail from Alexandria and arrived in New Orleans sometime around December 22, 1838.

Louisa and her mother hoped to avoid such a fate. They must have considered running from Maryland. They had family living free in Philadelphia. Could they evade capture? Could they find their way? Finally, exhausted and famished, they emerged from the woods. Louisa and her mother had made up their minds. Louisa was about twenty-five, young enough and strong enough to make a run for it. But her mother was about sixty-three, one of the oldest people on the plantation. Her father was older still, about sixty-seven years old. What of him? What of her three brothers? Louisa would not leave them behind. So the two women crept back to St. Inigoes.

They found the once bustling slave quarters, always crowded and full of life, nearly empty. The people who had tended the fields, the mill, and the stable were gone. The blacksmith had vanished. The sounds of laughter, bickering, babies wailing, old women singing and calling to Jesus had been replaced by the lonely cries of migrating birds, the grunts of hogs and lowing cattle, the sounds of stomping horses, and the whistling wind that rippled through the trees and scattered the falling leaves. Nearly everyone in Louisa's community—two of her sisters, her oldest brother, her nieces and nephews, the elders and friends she had known since childhood—was gone. Sixty-nine enslaved Black people had lived on the plantation in 1838, tax records show. Only about a dozen remained. Among them were Harry, Louisa's father, and Gabe and young Harry, two of her brothers, who had wives on other plantations. Her older sister Nelly was safe, too, still keeping house for the Jesuit priest responsible for St. Mary's Church in Alexandria.

For a moment, at least, the joyous reunions must have swept away the overwhelming sense of fear and despair. The Mahoney family had been torn apart, and Louisa knew that she might never see her older sisters again. But on that day at St. Inigoes, she could sing hymns of gratitude and thanksgiving. She could embrace her father and two of her siblings. She could look into their eyes and savor the sounds of their voices. They were alive. They were together. But the jubilation would not last long.

By springtime, her brothers were gone. Gabriel Mahoney was sold to Joseph Harris, the longtime clerk of court in St. Mary's County. Young Harry Mahoney was sold to a local man named William Smith. (The fate of Daniel Mahoney, her youngest brother, remains unknown.) Louisa and her parents realized that even now they could not rest easy, despite their hopes. The roundup of the enslaved people who had not been shipped on the *Katharine Jackson* had begun.

Johnson managed to purchase the spouses of some of the enslaved people who had been left behind, clearing his way to claiming them as well. By springtime, he had prepared "a brig for carrying them & almost the rest at S. Inigoes W.M. & S. Thomas's servants" to Louisiana, wrote Father Grivel, using shorthand to describe the White Marsh and St. Thomas Manor plantations.

Despite some efforts to ensure that husbands and wives would be sold together, a grim reality was emerging. It was becoming clear that the Jesuit leadership had decided, in some instances, to defy Rome and God and prioritize profit over the promises the priests had made to their superiors. Some neighboring farmers were willing to buy the spouse of a Jesuit slave but unwilling to buy the couple's children. In such a situation, the conditions handed down from Rome, as well as the moral imperative, were clear: No sale should go forward. But Mulledy was determined to raise the money necessary to finance his expansionist vision, which mattered more to him than the sanctity of the Black families his order owned.

"Some children who could not be sold with their mothers, have been sent with the others to Louisiana," Father Grivel wrote without condemnation or judgment. Instead, he focused on the news that cast the Jesuits in a more positive light: the couples who were allowed to stay together and the elderly people, such as Harry and Anna Mahoney, who were allowed to remain on the Jesuit plantations in Maryland. "There remain in our farms only few old people, well provided for their life times," he wrote approvingly.

Positive reports also came in from Louisiana during that spring of 1839. Johnson, who was trying to get the son of a wealthy planter admitted to Georgetown, reached out on his behalf to McSherry and reported, as an aside, that Anny, her children, and the other enslaved people he had purchased were doing well. "The slaves I purchased from Mr. Mulledy, & transported to this state, are all healthy, and well pleased with their situation," he wrote.

In Rome, Jan Roothaan, the leader of the Jesuits worldwide, expressed satisfaction that most of the enslaved people had finally been sold, bringing to a close the Jesuits' long history as large slaveholders in the United States. Roothaan hoped that that would mark the beginning of a period of economic sufficiency for the Maryland province and an end to the chronic mismanagement that had contributed to its financial woes. "I rejoice that the matter of the negroes is concluded and the lands have been leased to good men," he wrote to Mulledy. "May they truly be good men, that is, upright men, the sort who make good their debt to justice at the proper times. And so at last this Province will be able to escape from its current hardships," he continued, "nor will it any more have need of charity."

But there was little celebration at St. Inigoes. Carbery spoke openly to the handful of remaining enslaved men and women at St. Inigoes of his disdain for Mulledy. He spoke so freely that word of his discontent traveled among his fellow Jesuits. It was Nelly, Louisa's older sister in Alexandria, who told Father Dubuisson about Carbery's response to the sale. Dubuisson responded disapprovingly. "The Superior of St. Inigoes would seem to have given in too much to his feelings," he wrote. "I have for a cook, in Alexandria, a black woman, full with religion and very intelligent, who was at the scene, and who heard the Father express himself, right at the table, about the Provincial in a very improper way."

But Carbery could not hide the outrage he felt, even as he followed Mulledy's orders and attended to the aftermath of the Jesuits' sale. In June, he reported to the county courthouse to give an accounting of the people who had been sold and to request a reduction in the taxes imposed on the St. Inigoes plantation. "I do hereby certify that all the negroes now assessed to me has [sic] been sold out of the state," he told the clerk. There were, he pointed out, a few notable exceptions, including Louisa's two brothers, who had been sold locally, and at least six enslaved men who were purchased by another local farmer.

Carbery sold off much of the livestock and leased out the bulk of the plantation to white tenant farmers. He would live on the remaining land with the enslaved people who remained, including Louisa, who did not even have the luxury of losing herself in her sorrow. She was still someone's property. Every morning, despite the loss of her sisters and brothers, nieces and nephews, aunts and uncles, she had no choice but to leave her shabby cabin and tend to the labor that, since her birth, had defined her value.

Exile

IT WAS THE DEAD OF SUMMER 1839 WHEN THOMAS MULLEDY boarded a ship in New York City. The *Commercial Advertiser* of New York took note and published a brief account, describing the prominent priest as one of several dignitaries setting out across the Atlantic on the packet ship *Iowa,* a "large vessel and a good sailer," to Le Havre, France.

What the newspaper's readers would not have known was that it was no grand European vacation for Mulledy. The priest, who had ascended to the highest clerical position in the Maryland province, was leaving the United States in disgrace.

It was a stunning turn of events. Only eight months earlier, Mulledy, exhausted after spending weeks on horseback, racing from plantation to plantation, had taken a moment to reflect. He had orchestrated the sale of scores of people, tearing families apart. He had witnessed their anguish and despair. But the leader of the Jesuits in Maryland expressed no misgiving, no regret. To his mind, he had accomplished something laudable. He'd ridded the province of what he had long lamented as the expensive burden of troublesome Black people and used the profits to help extinguish the debts he had incurred during his building campaign as president of Georgetown. In doing so, he had broken the rules laid out by his superiors in Rome. Some people might have worried about the consequences of such defiance. Mulledy was characteristically certain that his way was the right way.

But the steady stream of letters from horrified priests on the plantations had raised alarms in Rome. Archbishop Samuel Eccleston of Baltimore also wrote to Rome, expressing concern. And by the summer of 1839, condemnations of the sale were spreading even beyond the tight-knit Jesuit circles in Virginia and in Washington. The sheer size of the sale staggered and shocked people. "The effect of the size made us quite unfavorable, in Washington and in Alexandria!" Father Stephen Dubuisson, the pastor of St. Mary's, wrote to Jan Roothaan on June 21, 1839.

Louisa's older sister Nelly was Dubuisson's cook and housekeeper, so he had witnessed firsthand how the sale had impacted Black families. But he seemed more immediately concerned with the impact it would have on the Jesuits. "It is very much feared that the enemies of religion will take hold of this matter to use as a weapon against us," he wrote. He also suspected that Johnson and Batey would be unable to pay the rest of the money they had promised. If that were to come to pass, the Jesuits would have shattered families and damaged their reputations—for what? "To date, I do not know if anything has been published, but, I confess, I am not at all considering this thing finished," he warned.

That same month, William McSherry, now president of Georgetown, and Eccleston took stock of the decidedly unfavorable landscape. They considered the mounting opposition to Mulledy within the Jesuit order and the concerns about and criticism of the sale voiced by outsiders. Then they joined forces and told Mulledy that he could no longer lead the Maryland Jesuits. They wondered whether he might even be expelled from the order, and they urged him to go straight to Rome to plead his case before Roothaan in person.

On June 27, 1839, Eccleston wrote to Roothaan. He let the Jesuit leader know that Mulledy would be seeking an audience with him, and he asked him to show mercy and forbearance as he weighed Mulledy's fate. "My object in writing to you is to engage your paternal indulgence in behalf of Revd F. Mulledy," he wrote, expressing the hope that Roothaan would "receive him as a cherished although unfortunate son." He warned that banishing Mulledy from the Jesuit order would damage the order's reputation in the United States and hinder its mission. And he appealed to Roothaan's "paternal heart" in urging him to consider Mulledy's "spiritual interests & welfare." "If I may venture to speak of my own feelings," he continued, "you will, very Revd Father, spare me many a sorrowful moment by leaning to the side of clemency."

The news that he would be forced to abandon the most powerful post in the Maryland province and that he might be expelled from the Jesuit order altogether left Mulledy reeling. He had always been determined to steer Georgetown and the province in the direction of his own choosing, no matter what others, even his superiors, might think. And he had succeeded—excelled, even. He had accomplished what his early spiritual adviser, Father Kohlmann, had dreamed of but failed to do.

Some may have ridiculed Mulledy for his rough manners and rebuked him for his fiery temper. But his unbridled ambition had carried him from a rural hamlet in Virginia to Rome and to the leadership of the first Catholic college and of the first Jesuit province in the United States. Now, nearly twenty-five years after he had first set foot in the seminary, all of that was coming undone.

Mulledy was so shaken, so staggered by the devastating turn of events that he did not officiate at Mass on the day that Eccleston wrote to Roothaan. "No mass," he wrote in his journal, "unwell."

The disgraced priest booked his passage to Europe and packed his bags. He left Georgetown on Independence Day with $160 and stopped in Philadelphia on his way to the port of New York. He had no idea when, if ever, he might return.

After nearly three weeks at sea, he arrived in Paris on July 30 and officiated at Mass in Paris the following day. Anxious about his fate, uncertain as to the severity of the consequences he would pay for ignoring Rome's directives, he dedicated the church service that day to "myself."

The journey to Italy carried Mulledy across France with stops in Lyons, Avignon, Marseille, and Nice. By mid-September, he was in Rome and presented himself for an audience with his superior.

In the end, Roothaan decided not to expel Mulledy from the Jesuit order. But he also decided that the American priest could not return to the United States, given the scandal he had created with the slave sale. Roothaan assigned him to work with the English-speaking community in Nice, telling Mulledy that "all was now settled."

By the second week of October, Mulledy had arrived in southern France. During his first few days in Nice, he dedicated Masses to Roothaan, who had spared him from expulsion, and to himself, as he made peace with his fate and his new assignment so far from home. He had ascended to the pinnacle of power in the Jesuit order in the United States and had been toppled by his own pride and his disregard for his superiors. He had no idea when he might see his family, his beloved college, and his country again.

But Roothaan's disapproval of Mulledy's conduct—his separation of Black families and his use of the profits from the sale to pay off some of the debts he had incurred at Georgetown—did not mean that the Church was taking a stance against slavery itself. The decision not to formally censure Mulledy or to denounce the sale reflected the Church's long-standing acceptance of slavery, which had endured for centuries. The Catholic Church that Mulledy loved believed that Black people had eternal souls that should be nurtured. So they tended to the souls of the Black people on the plantations even as they bought and sold their bodies. The buying and selling of human beings was no sin in the eyes of the Church. American slavery, which had fueled the expansion of the Church in the United States, was simply not a priority in Rome.

The question of slave trading on an international level, however, reemerged as an issue in 1839, as Mulledy was settling into his new life in France. In December of that year, Pope Gregory XVI published an apostolic letter condemning the slave trade. He lamented the fact that Catholics, "blinded by the lust of sordid gain, in remote and distant lands, reduced to slavery, Indians, Negroes, or other miserable persons" and trafficked in human beings. He declared that such practices must end. "With apostolic authority," he wrote, "[we] do vehemently admonish and adjure in the Lord all believers in Christ, of whatsoever condition, that no one hereafter may dare unjustly to molest Indians, Negroes, or other men of this sort . . . or to reduce them to slavery; or to extend help or favor to others who perpetrate such things against them; or to exercise that inhuman trade by which Negroes, as if they were not men, but mere animals . . . are . . . bought, sold and doomed sometimes to the most severe and exhausting labors." The pope made it clear that he was speaking not only to Catholic lay members but also to priests and nuns, saying that "we, indeed, with apostolic authority . . . do strictly prohibit and interdict that any ecclesiastical or lay person shall presume to defend that very trade in Negroes as lawful under any pretext or studied excuse."

But the pope's letter came too late for Anna, her children, and the other families who had been sold by the Jesuits. That fall, Henry Johnson had continued transporting the enslaved people he had purchased as he wound down his time in Washington. On September 25, he visited Georgetown before heading home to Louisiana. He checked in on his nephew, who was still attending the college, and was pleased to find him "well & in fine spirits." "He has been prudent & economical," he wrote in a letter to his brother, William. "Indeed, he is in every respect a very promising youth, and will, no doubt, fulfil our expectations."

But for Johnson, the trip to Georgetown was more than just a chance to catch up with his nephew; it was also an opportunity to try to wrap up the messy business of the slave sale. Mulledy was gone, and a number of the enslaved people Johnson had purchased had yet to be delivered. It was frustrating for Johnson, who had moved to a new plantation in Louisiana's Ascension parish and needed to ensure that he had an adequate supply of enslaved laborers on his multiple estates.

He was trying to live up to the promise he had made to the Jesuits, that he would keep families together. But months after he had purchased more than eighty people from the priests, he still "could not succeed in obtaining many of them, in consequence of their wives & husbands belonging to persons in the neighbourhood, who would not sell," he lamented.

There were at least two Black people he had purchased from the Jesuits whom he could ship south immediately. Stephen, who was about forty-nine, and Sara, who was a year younger, had remained on the Newtown plantation. They may have prayed that they would be spared the fate of dozens of their friends and relatives who had already been shipped down south. But that was not to be. "The enclosed paper authorizes you or any person you may employ for the purpose to take possession of the two negroes," Johnson wrote to Robert Windsor, "and to ship them to N. Orleans."

He would continue his efforts to ship the remaining people to his Louisiana estates with the blessing of the Jesuits even after the pope's strongly worded language against slave sales. And there is no indication that the Jesuits viewed the pope's letter as a condemnation of their slaveholding. It came more than a year after the 1838 slave sale, and Catholic enslavers could easily view it as a ban on slave sales, not as a ban on slave ownership. Or they could ignore it altogether, which most did.

Bishop Benedict Fenwick of Boston suspected that the Maryland Jesuits had been warned in advance that the pope intended to condemn the slave trade. He thought that they had scrambled to sell off their enslaved people to ensure that the sale was complete before the pope released his letter. Whether that is true or not remains unknown. But the Catholic clergy in the United States remained mostly silent on the subject of the pope's letter until the following year.

The apostolic letter arrived as the Maryland Jesuits were marking the end of an era in the leadership of their province. Mulledy had been banished to France. And McSherry, his ally and the college president, was dying.

McSherry had been suffering from stomach cancer for five years. After Mulledy's departure, he was put in charge of the Maryland Jesuits once again. By then he was in constant pain. The priests consulted with six different doctors, hoping to save him. But by mid-December, the prognosis was grim. "They all agreed he may linger awhile," an observer reported, "however, there is no hope of recovery."

McSherry spent his last days almost completely bedridden, well aware that each day might be his last. Unable to eat solid foods, he still managed to eat chicken soup and joke with the priests who stood vigil. "You had appointed yr place in the grave yard," he told one of the brothers who tended to him. "I will take it." He asked his fellow Jesuits to pray for him and to forgive any "offenses he may have given or faults committed." But with the end looming, he concluded, "Nothing troubles my conscience."

On December 18, two weeks after the pope issued his apostolic letter condemning the slave trade, McSherry asked one of his attendants to help him roll over in bed. It was just past midnight, and the man tried to turn the ailing priest. In that moment, McSherry took his final breaths. He was only forty years old. "The fate is sealed," a Jesuit wrote, "our good Fr. McSherry died this morning ¼ past 12."

He was buried the next day, and word of his passing spread across the country. Over the next two months, newspapers in Washington, New York, Boston, and Newark, New Jersey, published notices about the death of Georgetown College's president. None of the notices mentioned his key role in organizing one of the largest slave sales of the time, one that had devastated hundreds of enslaved

families. But Mulledy knew, as did all of the senior Jesuits in Maryland and Washington.

The following year, Bishop John England of Charleston issued a
ringing defense of the Catholic Church's position on slavery in the
United States. He was responding to Secretary of State John For-
syth, who was using Pope Gregory XVI's denunciation of slave
trafficking to attack the Church, accusing the nation's priests of
siding with abolitionists. In a series of public letters, Bishop England argued that nothing could be further from the truth. "Slavery," he wrote, "is regarded by the church . . . when the dominion
of the slave is justly acquired by the master, to be lawful, not only
in the sight of the human tribunal, but also in the eye of Heaven."

Meanwhile, at St. Inigoes plantation, far from the public eye,
Father Carbery was using his limited power and resources to try to
undo Mulledy and McSherry's legacy. In particular, he and other
priests quietly sheltered the remaining members of the Mahoney
family, working to ensure that they would never be handed over to
Johnson.

Nelly, Louisa's older sister, continued to serve the Jesuit parish in
Alexandria, where the priest would buy her clothing, hire servants
to tend to her when she fell ill, and allow her time off and spending
money to cover the cost of trips to visit her family back home at St.
Inigoes.

Harry Mahoney, the elderly patriarch of the family, remained
safely on the Jesuit estate. He had been listed on the sale document,
but given his age, Johnson had probably felt little urgency in re-
couping him. The same held true for Anna, Harry's wife, who was
in her sixties. But Louisa was still vulnerable.

She was strong and healthy and only about twenty-five. (The
province's financial officer, who kept abreast of the attributes of
the Jesuits' human property, praised her "robust constitution.") She
could serve as a housemaid or a field worker. And she would likely
give birth to many children, who would expand her new master's
workforce. She would be very attractive to Johnson, who was still

trying to round up the enslaved people he had purchased, and both Carbery and Louisa knew it.

She may once again have considered running north to join her uncle and cousins in Philadelphia. But such a journey would have been especially perilous for a young woman. Slave catchers and traders and even Jesuits patrolled the thickets and winding roads. So Carbery came up with another strategy, one he thought might satisfy Johnson and keep Louisa out of harm's way: He decided to buy her back.

The priest knew he would have to persuade the Jesuits leadership to forgo the money they had received for Louisa at a time when cash wasn't easy to come by. And he didn't have the money himself. How he convinced his superiors and how they persuaded Henry Johnson remains unknown. But in March 1840, the transaction was formally recorded both in the county's tax books and in the Jesuits' ledgers. Carbery had handed Johnson a promissory note, pledging to pay $648 for Louisa, to ensure that she would remain safely in Maryland.

Louisa would be spared the fate of so many of her siblings. She would stay at her home at St. Inigoes and care for her elderly parents. Father Carbery had done what he could. He had tried to make good on the Jesuits' broken promise to Harry, ensuring that at least some of the Mahoneys would remain in place, their families intact.

But the truth was that he could do only so much. The Jesuit institution, which had expanded and profited from slavery, was not about to give up one of its prime assets. Freedom, which Louisa and her ancestors had so desperately longed for, still seemed out of reach. Carbery had saved Louisa from being sold, but he could not save her from slavery.

New Roots

OVER TIME, A STORY WOULD SPREAD ABOUT THE 1838 SALE: The people sold by the Jesuits had succumbed to either malaria or overwork in Louisiana, that faraway land where the enslaved toiled under the burning sun until they broke.

That story wasn't true. The broken branches of the tree that had flourished in Maryland had taken root in Louisiana, a state so unlike the world the displaced had known that it seemed to them like a different country. But no one knew whether the new roots would wither or grow. Certainly the fear of being sold again, of being separated from their children, haunted the newcomers, including Anna who shed her childhood nickname as she and the others struggled to find their footing on a new plantation.

Henry Johnson had promised the Jesuits that he would keep the families together. His prominence, his wealth, and perhaps the Jesuits' own wishful thinking had convinced them it would be true. Visitors to Chatham, his 1,100-acre estate in Ascension parish, certainly marveled at the "splendid plantation." And it was there that he attempted to further his political career, entertaining financiers and politicians such as Henry Clay, the US senator and former secretary of state, at elegant gatherings where "champagne flowed deep enough to float a man of war."

But the people sold by the Jesuits experienced another reality. The priests had reassured themselves that the enslaved people would be treated well, not subjected to the violence they had heard about in places such as Georgia and Louisiana. Johnson was viewed by his white contemporaries as a benevolent enslaver, a man who prided himself on the paternalistic care that he provided to the people he enslaved. He was, according to one account of his career, "always solicitous of the welfare of the slaves." But he, like many other wealthy slave owners, left the day-to-day operations of his estates mainly to overseers, who often used violence to ensure the productivity of the enslaved workforce. They flogged Black people who worked too slowly, questioned authority, or tried to lighten the load for children and the ailing.

In the mid–nineteenth century, white women in Johnson's genteel circles were viewed as precious flowers, to be protected from any indignity. But on the plantations, Black women such as Anna could count on no mercy. Mary Reynolds, the enslaved woman who had worked on the Black River estate in Louisiana, never forgot the overseer who had whipped her and the other Black people on the plantation. "I got the scars on my old body to show to this day," she said. ". . . I seed worse than what happened to me. I seed them put the men and women in the stock with they hands screwed down through holes in the board and they feet's tied together and they naked behinds to the world. Solomon the overseer beat them with a big whip and massa look on. The niggers better not stop in the fields when they hear them yellin'. They cut the flesh most to the bones and some . . . they never got up again."

The rest of the enslaved, who witnessed those horrors, had to continue working the cotton, a punishing crop that Anna and the other Jesuit slaves had never planted. She and her children knew the corn and wheat crops that filled the fields in the Chesapeake. But on Johnson's estate alongside the Bayou Maringouin, she and the others would learn cotton's relentless rhythms and feel how the bolls pricked their hands, leaving them cracked and bleeding. The Loui-

siana politician, the Jesuits would later say, had given his cruel overseer control of "all our people from W. Marsh & St. Inigoes."

Anna, who was about twenty-eight in 1839, was a stranger in
that new land, heartbroken and grieving. On top of that, she now
lived in a region where any misstep might lead to the lash and
where even her young children, Arnold and Louisa, might be vulnerable to an overseer's violence. But as she labored and tried to
protect her children, she also knew that accommodation was not
the only strategy that Black people used to survive. Her ancestors
had rebelled against slavery, using all the tools at their disposal: lawsuits, rebellion, and the fine art of diplomacy. At St. Inigoes, the
Black people in the county, including some free men who had
worked on the plantation with her parents, had risen up, starting an
insurrection, when Anna was just a girl. That rebellion had failed.
But on the plantation, the enslaved people she knew had still managed to oust the harsh religious brother who had managed the farm
before Father Carbery had taken charge of the estate's operations.

It remains unclear whether Johnson's hired man terrorized the
estate in Iberville parish, where Anna was enslaved, or whether he
worked on the estate in St. James parish, where Johnson had placed
the Cutchmore and Hall families he had purchased from the Jesuits.
But Anna wasn't the only one who had seen effective resistance at
St. Inigoes. And before long, some of the enslaved decided that
they would not suffer in silence. Word spread about the brutal
white overseer and somehow the news got to Johnson in his fine
manor home in Ascension parish.

The enslaved men and women may have enlisted a visiting priest
to intercede on their behalf. Father John Boullier, who was stationed about twelve miles away in the town of Donaldsonville in
Ascension parish, tried to visit the neighboring plantations weekly
or at least every other week to "give religious instruction to the
Negro slaves." He ventured to the corner of Iberville parish only
about once a month, but that might have been enough.

For some white planters, there was no shame in employing an

overseer who was handy with a bullwhip. But that was not the kind of reputation that Johnson cultivated. The Louisiana politician didn't go so far as to fire the cruel overseer, but he did move some people, including the Cutchmores and Halls, to another plantation. The enslaved men and women from the mid-Atlantic estates had found a way to ensure that their voices and concerns were heard. By the spring of 1840, word of that trickled back to the Jesuits in Washington.

"The last year they were unhappy, on account of a cruel overseer, but now they are pleased in their new place," Father Grivel wrote to a fellow Jesuit on May 30, 1840. "He praises them much," he said, describing Boullier's comments about the former Jesuit slaves. "He married 2 couples on Easter Sunday." The communication with Boullier left Grivel feeling upbeat about the future for the men, women, and children the Jesuits had once owned. Johnson, he emphasized in the letter, would make good on all of his commitments. "Govr. Johnson did not & will not sell any," he continued, referring to Anna and the others, "but this summer will build a chapel for them, & even pay a Priest, if he can get one."

Those promises reassured Grivel and may have eased the fears of other priests who had criticized the sale. Three of the people Johnson owned were baptized in Ascension parish that year, and six more would be baptized the following year. Their bodies and souls were in good hands, the priests hoped.

That was certainly the image that Johnson portrayed to Father Boullier and the others in his social circle. But even as Grivel was cheerfully reporting that Johnson had promised to build a chapel for the enslaved, Johnson was struggling to meet his financial obligations and was falling behind on his payments for Anna, her children, and the other people he had purchased from the Jesuits in 1838.

Johnson hoped that he could plant his way out of his financial troubles, relying on his enslaved laborers to produce a bumper crop of cotton. As he recovered from a bout of "chills and fevers," he wrote his brother in November 1840 to assure him that he was "now nearly restored" and expected "to plant from two to three hundred acres of cotton on Maringouin next year."

Despite his hopes, cotton prices continued to slide, and in March 1841, he was forced to take out another loan, this one for $6,000 from the Bank of Louisiana. He put up an estate he owned in La-Fourche parish—including the enslaved workers on it—along with another tract of land in Assumption parish as collateral.

It wasn't enough. Once again, he missed the deadline for the interest payment on the loan he had taken out to cover his purchase of Anna and the other Jesuit slaves. He paid what he could and implored the Jesuits once again to give him more time, suggesting that he would pay on a visit in May—news that was received with considerable frustration at Georgetown. "Although, as I must Sincerely tell you, that delay puts me to no small inconvenience, I shall however willingly bear with it to Show my desire of obliging you," the Jesuit financial administrator wrote from his office at the college. "But I earnestly request, that in case your intended visit should not take place, or be delayed, the remittance of said balance should be exactly made."

Johnson managed to make the payments by May, but the years of 1841 and 1842 would still be marked by financial struggle and personal and professional heartbreak. His only child, a daughter, had died in 1839 before reaching her second birthday, and the unbearable loss still weighed on his wife, Elizabeth. "What I suffered in the death of this child, it would be impossible for me to say," she wrote in 1841. "Alas how fleeting, and transitory, is every thing here, and upon how slender a thread, is our happiness suspended."

Meanwhile, Johnson's effort to return to political life, with a campaign for the governor's office, had ended in failure. The political defeat left him stunned and demoralized. "To have been thus defeated, whilst calculating with confidence upon success, is truly mortifying," he wrote his brother in July 1842. But he was determined to make the best of it, noting that he was "considerably enfeebled by age and other causes" and that the governor's salary had been reduced, which made the job considerably less appealing, given his chronic shortfalls of cash. "I never before found it as difficult to obtain money," he confided. "I have been, and still am pressed for small sums, to meet pressing engagements. I have recently visited the city several times in order to collect some money, but returned without a dollar even to pay my passage on board the Boat. It is believed that nearly the whole of the business men in the city will soon stop payment." Once again he pinned his hopes on the cotton crop on his plantation in Maringouin. "Although I am somewhat embarrassed, a change for the better, it is to be hoped, will take place, as the present crops are prepared for market," he concluded.

But his troubles continued unabated. In September, a violent storm swept through the estate near Bayou Maringouin, dashing the prospects for a bumper harvest. His chronic financial difficulties had already taken a toll. The deadline for his annual payment for the Jesuit slaves had come and gone. This time, he wasn't late; he just didn't pay at all.

In July 1843, Johnson wrote to his brother that he had decided to shift course from cotton to sugarcane and focus his efforts on Chatham, his home plantation in Ascension parish. "And it is probable, that I may next year withdraw all my hands from my cotton plantation on Maringouin," he wrote. "I now regret that I ever established that place."

No one knows exactly when or how Anna, Arnold, and Louisa learned that they would have to leave Maringouin for the Chatham plantation. But the news must have come as a blow, as the Maringouin plantation sat alongside Jesse Batey's plantation, where her older sister Bibiana worked.

The sisters did not work side by side or cook or sleep in the same slave quarters. But they lived close enough to see each other from time to time. They would have been able to share their memories, their anguish, and their strategies for survival. They could have marveled at how their children were growing, adjusting, adapting.

They had already lost so much, and now they would lose each

other. When Johnson moved Anna and her children to Chatham, his 1,100-acre estate in Ascension parish, the sisters would be forty miles apart, a world away from each other. And through their grief, Anna and her children would once again have to adjust to life on a new plantation.

By January 1844, Johnson had found his way back into national politics. His colleagues in the Whig Party selected him that month to fill a recently vacated seat in the US Senate. But he still needed to get his personal finances in order. So he decided to go back to the negotiating table with the Jesuits. In February of that year, he stood in a notary's office in New Orleans alongside the banker Edmund John Forstall, who was representing the Jesuits.

The Jesuits agreed to give Johnson a five-year extension to pay the balance he owed—$56,220 in total—for the enslaved people he had purchased. He would have to pay annual interest on the capital and make five annual payments of $11,244, starting in 1850. Three of Johnson's estates would serve as collateral—Chatham, the plantation in Maringouin, and another property in Pointe Coupee parish— as would the enslaved men, women, and children he had purchased from the Jesuits and some others.

That same month, he sold half of the Chatham plantation—and half of his interest in some of the enslaved people living there—to his brother-in-law, Philip Barton Key II. He did hold on to Anna and her daughter, but included among the dozens of people to be owned in partnership with Key was Anna's son, Arnold, who was only fifteen years old. Just six years after being sold by the Jesuits, Arnold had yet another enslaver who could determine his fate.

The arrangement raised the possibility of new perils for Anna and her family. Key owned property in LaFourche parish, some fifty miles away. Would he ship Arnold there? Would Anna be able to stay near her children? Or would she lose her son just as she had lost her parents and her baby sister?

Johnson's decision to shift from cotton to sugarcane would bring more hardship. Sugarcane made many planters wealthy, but their profits came at a terrible human cost. In Ascension parish, Anna's family was now subjected to the harshest, most punishing labor regime imaginable. Sugarcane is a delicate crop, and the acres of tall, green, swaying cane have to be harvested before the winter frost arrives and destroys it. In an effort to collect all the cane in time, planters and their foremen drove enslaved people in a race against the seasonal clock.

"Everybody worked, young, an ole', if yo' could carry two or three sugar cane yo' worked," recalled Ceceil George, describing her childhood in the cane fields of Louisiana. "Sunday, Monday, it all de same."

Men, women, and children were expected to work with military-style precision during harvesttime. White visitors marveled at what some described as the armies of Black workers slashing their way through the fields of cane stalks, which typically stood six to nine feet tall.

"And now may be seen the field hands, armed with huge cane knives, entering the harvest field," recounted Thomas Bangs Thorpe, a writer for *Harper's Magazine,* describing Louisiana's sugar plantations. "The cane is in the perfection of its beauty, and snaps and rattles its wiry-textured leaves, as if they were ribbons, and towers over the overseer as he rides between the rows on his good sized horse. Suddenly, you perceive an unusual motion among the foliage— a cracking noise, a blow—and the long rows of growing vegetation are broken, and every moment it disappears under the operation of the knife. The cane is stripped by the negroes of its leaves, decapitated of its unripe joints, and cut off from the root with a rapidity of execution that is almost marvelous. The stalks lie scattered along on the ground, soon to be gathered up and placed in the cane-wagons, which with their four gigantic mule-teams, have just come rattling on to the scene of action with a noise and manner that would do honor to a park of flying artillery."

Workers transported the freshly harvested cane to the sugarhouse and then, as Solomon Northrup described it, placed the stalks onto a mechanized conveyer. The conveyor took the cane high above the workers' heads toward rollers that crushed the cane and squeezed fresh cane juice into vats. The vats sent the sweet boiling liquid into kettles, and the kettles poured it into coolers.

It would not have been Anna's first glimpse of a sugar plantation. Cane fields filled the estates near the Maringouin plantation in Iberville parish. But everyone knew that tending cotton was far less dangerous than working cane. Peril lurked in every part of the process. For the enslaved, sugarcane harvesting meant hunger, disease, malnutrition, and workloads so arduous that some died in the fields and some died of heatstroke in the searing hot sugarhouses where granulated sugar was transformed into vats of boiling molasses. An enslaved woman at one of Jesse Batey's plantations perished in a horrific incident when she was ground to pieces in a sugar mill. On some sugar plantations, more than 55 percent of children died during their early years. Whereas the enslaved population grew rapidly in other parts of the South, Louisiana's high mortality rates resulted in a decline, despite the importation of thousands of human beings each year.

"The grueling rigors of the sugar industry placed an unfathomable strain on the human body," explained Richard Follett, a historian who studied the sugarcane fields in Louisiana. "Even if the planters replaced their dead with likely men and young, fertile women, they could not stem their dwindling slave populations."

If the threat of being killed or maimed was not enough, the threat of sale remained ever present. In June 1845, Johnson's brother-in-law, Philip Key, sold his interest in Chatham—and in the enslaved men and women on it—to yet another of Johnson's relatives, a man by the name of John Ryers Thompson, who owned an adjoining property. Anna's son, Arnold, and the others whom Key had co-owned with Johnson for sixteen months now had to contend with a new enslaver. Under the terms of the new partnership agreement, Johnson and Thompson would be "joint and equal owners" of Chatham, but Johnson would have nothing to do with its day-to-day operations. Thompson would have "the management and complete control of the estate."

Within the span of eighteen months, Anna and her family had been uprooted and separated from loved ones in Maringouin and forcibly relocated to a sugar plantation, where her son found himself controlled by two new slaveholders. The passing seasons—and the vicissitudes of one man's finances—had brought one heartbreak after another.

BUFFETED BY THE whims of their enslavers and powerless to hold their families together, many enslaved people turned to God, relying on their faith to sustain them and ease their troubles. It was the same God worshipped by those who had sanctioned, supported, and actively dealt in their enslavement for centuries. But enslaved believers saw God as distinct and apart from the men and women who bought and sold people in his name.

"No, sir, nothing could stop us from praying to Gawd," recalled Elizabeth Ross Hite of her days enslaved on a Louisiana plantation. "We didn't use light. We prayed in de dark, children an all."

Even though Anna and her children had been betrayed by the Jesuit leaders who owned them, there are signs that they held on to their Catholic faith nonetheless.

Father James Van de Velde, the priest in charge of the Jesuits' Missouri mission, visited Chatham in February 1848. Born in the Austrian Netherlands (now Belgium), Van de Velde had studied at Georgetown and worked as a professor and librarian at the college before climbing the ranks within the Jesuit order and the Catholic Church.

Van de Velde knew John Thompson, who had attended St. Louis University, the Jesuit college in Missouri, and during his visit to Chatham, he discovered, to his surprise, that Thompson had purchased many of the people who had been moved south in the mass sale and asked to meet with them. "Mr Thompson had the kind-

ness to assemble them & to allow me to inquire into their circumstances &c.," he recalled. But those conversations left him deeply
troubled. "They are all very good people, industrious, faithful,
moral, &c.," he wrote of the enslaved people that he met. "But they
have scarcely any chance to attend to their religious duties, & the
children, several of them not yet baptized, grew up without any
religious instruction whatever." Johnson, he reported, had "been
very unfortunate in business, & though he might be willing, is unable to build a church for those who live on his & on Mr Thompson's plantation."

The local priests were too busy with their white congregants to
attend to the Black people at Chatham on Sundays. And during the
week, the enslaved explained to the Jesuit priest, they "would have
to work, & many would not be permitted to attend," even if a priest
stopped by the plantation to offer Mass.

That meant that Anna and her children could attend Mass only
at the church in the town of Donaldsonville, which was ten miles
away. The Mass was offered only in French, a language that the
enslaved did not understand. And anyone embarking on that arduous journey would have to find a way to cross one of the many
bayous that traversed the region. "Some of the stoutest can walk it,
& do sometimes,—but very seldom,—as the distance is so great, &
their services are generally wanted at home," Van de Velde wrote.
"Some of the women told me weeping that they had not been to
Church for more than a year, & these women appeared strong &
healthy, but they have either to attend to their children, or to
household works, & cannot absent themselves so long," he continued. "Hence you may judge how it fares with the aged, infirm, the
children, &c."

Worse still, he reported, was the plight of the enslaved people
who had been purchased by Jesse Batey and lived on his estates in
Iberville and Terrebonne parishes, where they "never see a Catholic priest." He knew that the 1838 sale had been made under certain
conditions, and as he spoke to the weeping women, he could clearly

see that at least one of those conditions had been violated. "It seems that one of the conditions of the contract . . . made with Mr Johnson was that they should have a chapel & that they should be permitted to attend to their religious duties," he wrote in a letter sent to the new leader of Georgetown College. "The above account must convince yr Revce that this condition is not complied with."

But for the enslaved people on the Chatham plantation, at least, there was a solution. Van de Velde said that several planters in the community were willing to contribute funds toward the construction of a church that could be used by all of the enslaved people on the local estates, provided that the Maryland Jesuits would support their efforts.

Ironically, he addressed his plea for support to none other than Thomas Mulledy, the architect of the slave sales, who had returned to the United States after his banishment in Europe. There is no evidence that he received a response. So he appealed directly to the leader of the Maryland Jesuits, Father Ignatius Brocard. "I take the liberty of writing a word to you again in order to plead the cause of the poor negroes, who previously belonged to your Province, and who are now found destitute of nearly all religious succor in Louisiana," he wrote in November 1848 in a letter that suggested that it was not the first time he had contacted Brocard about the matter. "I may be mistaken, but it appears to me that the Province of Maryland is obligated by conscience to procure them succor and to make some sacrifices in this matter," he continued, describing "these poor people, particularly the children, who, bit by bit, lose religion." The priest pointed out that the Jesuits had benefited considerably from the sale of the people who now suffered in Louisiana and warned that spiritual harm might come to the Jesuits themselves for turning their backs on the enslaved. "All that is asked is that the Province of Maryland contribute $1,000, the neighbors will contribute the rest; and what is a mere $1,000 for the province that has the income from so many farms, and which has already received so large a sum for these poor exiles?"

A month later, he was appointed bishop of Chicago, but the chapel near Chatham plantation was never built.

Despite all of that, many of the enslaved people on the estate—including Anna, Louisa, and Arnold—appear to have held on to their faith. In 1848, the year that Van de Velde was imploring the Jesuits to send money for a chapel, eight people were baptized on the plantation. One of them appears to have been sponsored by Arnold. Two years would pass before a visiting priest would visit Johnson's portion of Chatham again for a baptism. So the enslaved had to make do, praying in the quiet of their cabins, calling to the heavens as they walked to the cane fields, singing their hallelujahs as they returned home, famished and weary, at nightfall. Johnson arranged for an overseer to perform marriages, and the faithful had no choice but to accept the arrangement, hoping that God would bless their unions without the presence of a priest.

"Sometime de slaves would hav marriages lak de people do today wid all de same trimmings," remembered Ms. Hite, who recalled from her time in captivity the veil, the gown, and the festivities in the slave quarters. "Den sometime dey would go to de master to git his permission an blessings an he would say, 'C'mon darky jump over dis brum an call yo'self man an wife,'" she said. "Shucks, some of dem darkies didn't care er bout master, preacher or nobody dey just went an got married, married demselves."

Amid the ever-present hardships, Anna and her children still found solace and support in the enslaved community around them. Sometime around 1849, a year after Arnold helped welcome a new member into the Catholic Church, he married Christina West, who had undergone many of the same trials he had. As a girl, Christina had been enslaved on the Jesuits' White Marsh plantation. Sometime before the 1838 sale, her mother had decided to escape. She had run away from the estate, making the agonizing decision to leave her four young children behind. She may have hoped to return for them, but she had never gotten the chance.

The Jesuits had sold her children, including Christina, who was only about seven years old, and shipped them to Louisiana on their own. There, their family was splintered further. Christina and her younger sister, Harriet Anne, ended up at Ascension. Her older siblings ended up on the plantation near the Bayou Maringouin.

Like Arnold, she found herself under the control of one enslaver after another, first Henry Johnson, then his brother-in-law, Philip Key, and then John R. Thompson. At Chatham, Arnold and Christina discovered the striking parallels in their lives. Both had parents who had escaped from slavery and knew the pain of growing up without them. Both had been enslaved by Catholic priests, shipped to Louisiana as children—torn from their extended families and communities in Maryland—and forced to make their way in an entirely new world.

Arnold was about twenty years old and Christina was about eighteen when they formed a bond that would last for decades. No record has survived to suggest that they solemnized their vows before a priest. Perhaps an overseer or a preacher on the plantation married them. But sometime around 1849, the couple was blessed with a child, a baby boy. They named him Henry.

Henry made Anna, who was about thirty-eight by then, a grandmother. She had lost her parents and her siblings, including her beloved sister Louisa. But she had survived. Her children had survived. And her growing family was now increasingly rooted in Louisiana soil. As baby Henry cooed and babbled and took his first steps, Anna could take pride in his father's steady progress.

Arnold was not relegated to the cane fields. At some point, he became a cooper—a barrel maker—and a carpenter, a member of the small, elite group of enslaved tradesmen who were essential to the operations of any sugar plantation.

Sugar planters relied on skilled Black workers—masons, blacksmiths, mechanics, and others—to keep their estates running. Coopers, in particular, served as vital linchpins in the production process because they crafted the wooden barrels that would carry a plantation's finished product—sugar or molasses—to market. A planter who developed a reputation for shipping out leaky barrels would find few repeat customers.

Skilled young men such as Arnold sat atop the hierarchy of the enslaved labor force and often received payments as incentives or rewards for their work, money that might allow them to help their relatives. Arnold may have displayed an early interest in carpentry as a teenager, attaching himself to one of the older men on the plantation, watching and learning as the craftsman hammered and shaped the cypress or hickory into casks. His mother may have encouraged him to learn a skill. The Mahoney men in Maryland, after all, had not done much in the way of field work. They had mostly worked for the priests, driving the clergy and tending the horses and stables. However he learned his trade, Arnold's role as a craftsman at Chatham made him more valuable to the white men who enslaved him.

Even so, Arnold knew that despite everything, despite his hard work, despite his skill, despite his faith, uncontrollable forces still dictated the lives of enslaved people. That became painfully clear once again in 1851, after Jesse Batey died. All the enslaved men and women that Batey had purchased were put up for sale, including Anna's brother Robert, who had labored on Batey's estate in Terrebonne parish. On the list of Batey's human property Robert is described as "a Negro man aged of sixty five years." That he belonged to a vibrant enslaved community and was the patriarch of a sprawling family meant little to the white man assigned to assess Robert's worth after Batey's death. Next to his perfunctory description of Robert, the appraiser reported that the older man was "of no value."

The death of a slave master often brought peril, not deliverance, to enslaved families, who could end up being sold at auction. But in Robert's case, an unlikely benefactor emerged to spare him that fate. Henry Johnson, who had imperiled Anna's family by selling Arnold, swooped in unexpectedly and purchased Robert, paying $5 for the older man and moving him and several others he had purchased—including Charles, Robert's son—to the Maringouin estate. Johnson's decision to save the older man from being handed over to a stranger would certainly have brought joy to the divided Mahoney clan. The move brought several members of the Mahoney family together again for the first time in more than a decade and allowed the older man to be close to his sister Bibiana, who still lived on the adjoining plantation.

Family members separated by slave sales knew that the chances of reunion were agonizingly slim. To be living near each other once again was nothing short of a miracle. Anna's siblings Bibiana and Robert had been lost to each other, but they would now spend the last years of their lives in close proximity, able to marvel at how the passage of time had transformed them, reminisce about the old days in Maryland, and compare notes about their new masters and overseers in Louisiana.

Solomon Northup described the moment when he was finally reunited with his family. "They embraced me, and with tears flowing down their cheeks, hung upon my neck," he recalled. "When the violence of our emotions had subsided to a sacred joy—when the household gathered round the fire, that sent out its warm and crackling comfort through the room, we conversed of the thousand events that had occurred—the hopes and fears, the joys and sorrows, the trials and troubles we had each experienced during the long separation."

Solomon had his liberty, of course, while Bibiana and Robert remained subject to the whims of their enslavers, just as Anna and her family did on Chatham plantation.

Twelve years had passed since Henry Johnson had purchased Anna and her family and scores of other men, women, and children from Maryland, and he was still burdened by debt. He had suffered one political defeat after another. He had lost his bid to hold on to his seat in the US Senate and in 1850 had waged an unsuccessful campaign for a seat in the House of Representatives, which one historian described as a "humiliating loss." With his political career behind him and nearing the age of seventy, he decided it was time to downsize.

In 1851, the year he reunited members of the Mahoney family in

Maringouin, Johnson sold nearly all of his remaining portion of Chatham, along with some of the enslaved people he owned, including Anna's daughter, Louisa, who was about nineteen years old. "She fell to his relatives who were Thompsons," recalled Henrietta Cutchmore, describing what had become of her cousin after the sale of the Chatham plantation.

It was no surprise that Johnson turned to Thompson. Thompson already managed the Chatham plantation and the nearly two hundred people who were enslaved there, and he was clearly wealthy enough to buy Johnson out. Thompson also agreed to take on a significant portion of Johnson's debts, notably "the payment of the sum of thirty seven Thousand six hundred & seventy four Dollars and thirty seven Cents ($37.474-37¢.) due by the Seller to Thomas F. Mulledy of Georgetown."

Johnson had shattered the families of scores of Jesuit slaves when he had purchased them in 1838. Now he was free of his debt to the Jesuits and wiping his slate clean. He was able to keep a portion of the land as well as some of the slaves; among them, it seems, was Anna.

She was about forty years old when Johnson finally sold her youngest child. She might have taken some comfort from knowing that Thompson owned an adjoining plantation and might keep the enslaved workforce at Chatham intact. She could only pray that her children, her daughter-in-law, and her baby grandchild would stay together and that Johnson would hold on to his sliver of Chatham so that she would always be close by.

BY THE TIME Anna's children were sold, newcomers had begun pouring into US cities. They came by the thousands, then by the tens of thousands. Between 1840 and 1850, about 500,000 Irish Catholic immigrants arrived in the United States, hungry for priests, churches, and schools. The religious center had shifted, and the future that Mulledy had envisioned, of Catholicism firmly rooted in its cities, was now a reality.

Catholicism, once a minority faith whose adherents had suffered persecution, had become the largest single denomination in the United States with a flock of 1.6 million followers. The Jesuits began funneling money, faculty, and supplies to create and support new schools, transforming themselves from an order known as one of the largest slaveholders in Maryland to one that would become synonymous with Catholic education. As Mulledy had hoped, the mass sale of 1838 would prove to be a critical turning point. The year would be known, one historian wrote more than a century later, as the year when Jesuit "slaveholding in Maryland had come to an end."

But in fact, the mass sale—and the waves of Irish migration that followed—did not bring an end to the Jesuits' involvement in America's system of forced bondage. The Maryland Jesuits continued to enslave Black people on several of the plantations that had sustained the Catholic Church in its infancy. And as slavery moved west with the expanding nation, the Jesuits followed, relying on slave labor in Missouri, Kentucky, Louisiana, Alabama, Illinois, and Kansas to help build churches and sustain the livelihoods of the clergy. In the Maryland province, the priests continued to curtail the lives of dozens of Black people in bondage, hunting down runaways, hiring enslaved laborers, and profiting from their labor.

The members of the Mahoney family who remained in Maryland would always be grateful to have escaped the slave ships, to have been allowed to remain in Maryland on the land that had been home to their families for generations. But they had been forced to witness the sale and then to endure the agonizing absence of so many of their kinsmen. Of the scores of enslaved people who had once lived on the plantation, only about eight remained. Harry Mahoney, the family patriarch, who had hoped that his loyal service would protect his family, was one of them. By then, he was an old man buffeted by a staggering loss. In June 1840, Father Carbery allowed him to visit his daughter Nelly, who was still serving the priests at St. Mary's Church in Alexandria. Nelly would return the favor in September of that year, traveling to St. Inigoes to spend time with what remained of her family. After that, Harry vanished from the Jesuit records. No records have emerged to describe his wife's death, his final days, or his own passing. What is known is that he never tasted freedom in his lifetime.

Louisa would not grieve on her own. She found companionship in the company of a suitor. He stood about five foot nine and had light skin and a mole below his left ear. His name was Alexander Mason, and he was born free.

Members of the Mason family had been living as free people of color in St. Mary's County for nearly two generations. They were mixed race, often described in county records as having "yellow" or "copper" complexions. The Mahoneys knew the Masons. Over the years, several members of the Mason clan had earned a living working off and on at St. Inigoes.

Freedom was still tenuous for people of color in Maryland. Their lives were hedged in by whites, who not only restricted their ability to work but required them to register with county officials and to carry certificates documenting their free status.

Father Joseph Zwinge, the Jesuit treasurer who decades later wrote about some of the Black people on the plantations, described those limitations: "The free negro could not travel without his papers of manumission sealed by the county court, and even then he had to have a responsible white man go security for him wherever he stayed, and failing in any of these, the negro was cast into jail, and after a certain time sold at auction to the highest bidder. At St. Inigo's we had such hangers-on," he continued, describing Alexander's relatives by name: "Robert, Joseph, Jesse and Gabe Mason, free negroes, and others."

But Alexander still experienced the kind of freedom that seemed glorious to many enslaved people: the freedom to come and go, to wake in the morning when he chose, to earn money from his labor. He was probably in his twenties when he started courting Louisa, who was several years older. No record of their wedding day, which likely took place in the early 1840s, has survived, but Zwinge noted it in his own writings: "Aunt Louisa, by and by, was married to a son of these Masons." Sometime around 1843, around the time she turned thirty, Louisa gave birth to a baby boy and named him John. Two years later, in September 1845, Alexander reported to the clerk in the county office for his freedom certificate. The county official took detailed notes about his physical appearance, describing his height, his light complexion, and the precise location of the moles and scars on his face and hands. A white man who lived in the community appeared on his behalf, testifying to the clerk that Alexander was, in fact, "born free & raised in St. Mary's County."

Now that he was a husband and father, Alexander's status as a free person was more important than ever. The wages he earned would help ensure that his wife and children had enough food to eat and clothing to wear if the Jesuits fell short.

Their family grew. Sometime around 1849, Louisa gave birth to a baby girl, Ann, who carried the same name as her beloved sister in Louisiana. Alexander's freedom papers allowed him to work as a laborer for white men in the community, while Louisa continued to serve Father Carbery in the manor house on the plantation.

By then, Carbery was in his seventies, having served at St. Inigoes for more than thirty years. He had survived a serious illness, which had prompted him to write his will, ensuring that the plantation and the enslaved people living on it would remain in Jesuit hands. He remained popular among his white congregants as well as among the Black people, who continued to describe him as a kindly and caring man.

Just a few weeks after his seventy-third birthday, he collapsed from a stroke as he walked in the garden at St. Inigoes. The doctor who tended to the men, women, and children on the plantation rushed to his side, but it was too late.

"I have this moment, received the sad intelligence of the sudden death of Rev. Fr. Carbery," wrote Father Robert Woodley to his Jesuit superior on May 25, 1849, promising "to bury him tomorrow afternoon, or forenoon."

Newspapers hailed Carbery as an amiable priest well known for his "Christian simplicity and benevolence" and "his unbounded hospitality and generous feeling."

For many in the St. Inigoes community, the passing of the priest left a hole that could not be easily filled. Louisa had known Carbery since she had been just three or four years old, and for her, he must have embodied many of the contradictions of Jesuit slaveholding. He was the white priest who owned her and her family, but he was also her champion and protector. He had given enslaved families unprecedented autonomy on the estate and had saved her and her parents from being sold and shipped down south. As she served him and the other priests in the plantation's manor house, he had watched her grow from childhood to womanhood, and she had watched him grow old.

In general, the death of an enslaver meant change, which was bound to create anxiety for the people he held captive. Carbery had done everything in his power to keep Louisa and her family from being sold, but there was no guarantee that her next master would do the same.

By September 1850, Father Thomas Lilly had taken charge of the plantation and the ten enslaved people who lived there. Lilly had been an outspoken opponent of the 1838 sale. But he was also known as a hard man, and under his rule, Louisa could no longer count on whatever privileged status the Mahoneys had enjoyed previously. Nor could any of those who still lived on the Jesuit plantations. Louisa's sister Nelly learned that the hard way.

That month, Father Woodley wrote to the Jesuit in charge of the Maryland province about his concerns about Nelly, who was still enslaved at the nearby Newtown plantation. Other priests had raised concerns, too. ("A colored woman has ruled and partly rules this house but she will not rule me," wrote one Jesuit stationed at Newtown in what seems to be a clear reference to Nelly.)

She had managed to withstand such criticism so far. But her sharp tongue and fierce sense of independence had finally put her into jeopardy. "I hope her conduct may be such, after the admonition I have given her, as to render it unnecessary to remove her," Woodley wrote on September 16, 1850.

Less than two weeks later, Woodley decided to send her away. Frantic, Nelly begged one of the other priests on the plantation to help her escape. When their efforts failed, she barricaded herself in his quarters. "She was harbored in his room, the door locked—and he wrote a pass or permit to run away—take the stage to—I don't know where," Woodley wrote on September 25, 1850. "I have cautioned the public against this unauthorized pass or permit." Woodley then shipped her to the home of a Catholic family "for an indefinite period," leaving it to the Jesuit leadership to decide whether to "ratify a sale, or dispose of her otherwise."

Louisa did what she could to ensure that she would not be sold or separated from her growing family. As her father had done before her, she embraced the role—outwardly, at least—of the diligent, faithful servant working to earn the trust of the priests who owned her and her children. She made sure that she would be viewed differently from her sister and from her ancestors, who had rebelled against their status as enslaved people.

But the heartbreak of her sister's plight was followed by a crisis that hit much closer to home. In May 1852, Louisa's son John fell ill. Father Lilly called in the medical doctor for the plantation, who tended to him. But the little boy's illness got worse, not better. By May 15, 1852, it was clear that the child could not be saved. "Our little black boy John, son of Elick Mason (free) and Louisa died to day about 11 A M," wrote Lilly in his diary, adding that "he was a good little boy & much regretted."

The entry in the priest's journal did not describe the boy's burial or Louisa's grief. By then she was nearly forty years old. She had at least two other children to care for, along with her work for the priests in the manor house. But she swallowed her pain somehow and kept on. Over the next few years, both she and Alexander worked for Lilly. Alexander worked off and on at the plantation's sawmill, at a rate of 50 cents a day, and did odd jobs on the estate, accepting payment in cash and in flour, tobacco, and an occasional shirt or pair of boots. He was one of a number of free men Father Lilly hired to supplement the labor of the enslaved people he owned.

Lilly felt responsible for the souls of the Black people on the plantation and in the community. He prayed with the sick and ailing and offered last rites to the dying. "Went to see a black man at Mrs. Ford's," he wrote in a typical journal entry, "very ill—assisted him for death."

And in the presidential election of 1852, he voted for General Winfield Scott, the losing candidate, who was widely viewed as opposed to the expansion of slavery. He condoned racial segregation, however, keeping congregants at the church at St. Inigoes separated, a common practice at the time and one that he had inherited. Black parishioners had long been relegated to the back of the church. Lilly expanded the available seating, overseeing the construction of new pews in side galleries for Black worshippers. But he did not challenge the notion that the church's best seating should be reserved for whites. And there is no evidence that slavery became more tolerable for those in bondage on St. Inigoes. In fact, about a month after Louisa's son died, one of the enslaved people on the plantation tried to escape but was caught. "My Black boy Bill absconded on Monday," Lilly wrote in his diary. The priest made sure that Bill understood that there was a price to pay for running away by having him imprisoned in a local jail for several days.

Louisa must have observed his contradictions as she worked for him, but Nelly's fate would have reminded her of the dangers of speaking too freely. She knew what happened to runaways. She knew that the Jesuits were willing to break their promises, to sell the people they owned, to tear families apart for profit. And she would never give anyone any reason to consider selling her.

As the years passed, Louisa burnished her reputation as an industrious and virtuous servant. She became a familiar figure in the plantation's church, and the priests who knew her praised her religious devotion. It is unclear whether she truly found comfort in the faith or whether she believed that a display of public devotion would keep her and her family safe. Maybe it was a bit of both. However she found it, she would need all the faith she could muster to endure what was yet to come.

ABRAHAM LINCOLN WON the presidency on November 6, 1860. White slaveholders were alarmed, sure that the new president and his Yankee allies intended to free their slaves, decimate their wealth, and destroy their society. In response, just one month after Lincoln's election, South Carolina seceded from the union. The state was followed by Mississippi a month later, in January 1861.

That same month, Church leaders in Rome put together a list of priorities for American bishops, calling on them to focus on the evangelization of Native Americans at their next plenary council. Tensions over the system of forced labor in the United States had reached a boiling point, yet neither the issue of American slavery nor the evangelization of Black people was on the Vatican's agenda.

By 1861, Louisa and Alexander had at least six children. They had been married for about twenty years and had settled into the familiar routines of family life on the plantation, even as the nation seemed poised for war. One day, Alexander headed off the plantation, leaving Louisa and the children behind. It was the last time they would see him alive. He was attacked as he traveled along the road between St. Nicholas Church and St. Mary's City. The assailant struck him with an ax and left him dead on the road.

"Alex Mason was an excellent man and without enemies, and was too poor to excite suspicion that he had money on his person," recalled a white man who served on the grand jury that tried and failed to identify either the murderer or the motive for the killing. "There was much excitement in the community on account of this tragedy, and very great sympathy for the excellent man who was murdered, and a very extensive amount of sympathetic feeling exhibited everywhere for his widow and children."

But sympathy could not change the harsh reality. A few months later, when the first shots of the Civil War were fired, Louisa was on her own.

Freedom

THE UNION NAVAL FLEET DARTED PAST THE CONFEDERATE forts just before dawn on April 24, 1862, and sailed up the Mississippi River. Before long, their prize was in sight: New Orleans, the jewel of the Confederacy. The Union ships charged through the rebels' chain and timber fortifications and surrounded the city.

"We landed on the levee in front of a howling mob, which thronged the river-front as far as the eye could reach," wrote Navy Captain Albert Kautz, who debarked New Orleans on April 26 with a letter for the mayor demanding its surrender. "I attempted to reason with the mob, but soon found this impossible," he recalled. "I then thought to clear the way by bringing the marines to an aim, but women and children were shoved to the front while the angry mob" raged behind them.

On April 29, Union soldiers lowered the Louisiana state flag atop City Hall. Thousands of people filled the streets outside the building, which was flanked by marines armed with heavy guns. "The vast crowd looked on in sullen silence as the flag came down," Kautz wrote.

Supporters of the Confederacy expressed their disdain for their occupiers, spitting on Union soldiers as they patrolled the streets.

(One woman even dumped the contents of her chamber pot on the head of a Union officer.)

But the enslaved people both in the city and in the rural parishes rejoiced. Hundreds abandoned the plantations and ran to Union camps, while others cheered the federal troops as they moved up-river, taking the city of Baton Rouge. "Thousands of negroes welcome us with various demonstrations of pleasure," wrote Rufus Kinsley, a corporal in the 8th Vermont Regiment. Another Union soldier described the jubilation of the Black people who watched the ships passing on the river. They "gathered to stare at us," he wrote, "and when there were no whites near, they gave enthusiastic evidence of good will, dancing at us, waving hats or branches and shouting welcome."

The naval fleet encountered no opposition when it cruised past the Chatham plantation in Ascension parish, where Anna and her children had lived for nearly two decades. But in August 1862, a Confederate sympathizer commandeered an old cannon hidden at the wharf in Donaldsonville, twelve miles south of Chatham, and fired on a passing Union steamer, killing the pilot. Union officers quickly made it clear that rebels and civilians alike would pay dearly for such deadly attacks. Days later, federal troops came ashore and torched the most prominent buildings in and around the town, leaving them ablaze.

The occupation by Union forces was radically transforming the world the slaveholders knew. In the parishes of St. Bernard and Plaquemines, planters were forced to agree to do the unthinkable: pay their enslaved workers for their labor. Under terms set by the Union leadership in Louisiana, the planters would pay $10 a month—with $3 of that sum allotted for clothing—and provide workers and their dependents with food, housing, and medical care. Any enslaved person who was whipped or physically abused would be freed.

Black people cheered the new rules requiring planters to provide some pay for their work. But they wanted freedom. Real freedom.

The freedom to move and live where they liked, the freedom to work for themselves, the freedom to decide when or how they would work. And they were determined to seize those freedoms.

"Revolt & Insurection among the negroes," one planter in Plaquemines wrote in the fall of 1862, describing the Black people on his estate who had refused to work in the cane fields and were demanding better rations, "flour biscuit beef etc," instead of "pork & cornbread." "They all went up to McManus's Plantation," he complained. "Returned with flags & drums shouting Abe Lincoln and Freedom."

Some of the enslaved dropped everything and followed the Union troops as they advanced through the countryside. "Found our negroes completely demoralized, some gone and more preparing to go," one white planter lamented. "I fear we shall lose them all." It was as if the entire world had turned "upside down," one enslaved man from Chatham would recall decades later.

But the Catholic Church was reluctant to embrace such transformative change. In Rome, many people clung to the belief that slavery could be reformed and that the Confederates were the ones to do it. "We are certain that [emancipation] will not come about from the benevolent initiative of the North," opined the editors of *L'Osservatore Romano,* a newspaper that often reflected the opinions of the Vatican leadership. Such reforms would come instead from the rebels, who had "always shown themselves to be . . . intelligent and chivalrous," the newspaper commented in the fall of 1862.

That Church leaders in Rome would favor the Confederacy would come as little surprise to Augustus Martin, the bishop of Natchitoches in northern Louisiana, who had delivered a full-throated defense of slavery just a year earlier. Most of the nation's Catholic leaders sympathized with the rebels and remained deeply suspicious of abolitionists, who sometimes espoused anti-Catholic views.

Martin described the enslavement of Africans as ordained by God and praised the institution of American bondage for bringing glory to people he viewed as savages and offering redemption to those who would otherwise be relegated to the "darkest intellectual night." Enslaved people received "not only the bread and clothes necessary to their material life," he proclaimed, "but also, and especially, their just share of truth and of the goods of grace" in exchange for their labor. He argued, in essence, that slavery was a gift, one that enabled Black people to shed "the curse of sin" for "the glorious hopes of an everlasting happiness."

But the ground was shifting, whether Martin and the Church's leaders in Rome liked it or not. In September 1862, Archbishop John Baptist Purcell of Cincinnati broke ranks and delivered a lecture in which he condemned "the sin of . . . holding millions of human beings in physical and spiritual bondage." He warned that the nation's contradictions were unsustainable, arguing that "a people could not long survive the fatal contrast between the Declaration of Independence and the Constitution of the United States, the one asserting that all men are born free, sovereign and independent, that the other millions may be slaves." He called for the emancipation of the enslaved, declaring that such a move would rapidly bring the war to an end. With that, he became known as the most prominent Catholic leader in the country to embrace abolition, a priest who used his diocesan newspaper, the *Catholic Telegraph,* to champion his cause. His was a lonely voice among Catholic leaders, and he soon found himself assailed by his fellow bishops and the Catholic press. But he would turn out to be far more prescient than his critics in the religious establishment.

On January 1, 1863, President Abraham Lincoln issued the Emancipation Proclamation, declaring "that all persons held as slaves" within the rebel states "are, and henceforward shall be free." The announcement unleashed waves of jubilation among Black people, free and enslaved, all across the country. But it also gave some hope to white planters in Louisiana. The proclamation exempted the sugar parishes in Louisiana, where Union troops remained in control and hoped to keep the vital industry running. In

Ascension parish, where Anna and her family had been enslaved, the community's prominent white men seized on that provision, hoping to salvage their livelihoods.

A week after the proclamation was issued, a group of white men met with General Nathaniel P. Banks, the new Union commander in the state, to explain "our necessities & what guarantees we wanted to enable us to undertake with safety to make a crop this year," reported William J. Minor, who owned an estate in Ascension parish. Banks found the men "full of theories, prejudices, opinions based on the old system" and told them to "look to the new state of things, to the future & not to the past."

But now that it was the occupier, the Union had an interest in maintaining the local economy, and that meant maintaining, in some form, the abundant cheap labor that slavery had provided. To accomplish that, Banks established new guidelines to govern the relationships between planters and the enslaved that pleased no one. Planters who wanted a return to the old ways were to pay wages to their enslaved workers, though less than they had been required to before. And Black people, who chafed at their bondage, were expected to display what one historian described as "faithful labor and perfect subordination."

But there was no turning back the clock. Many Black people simply refused to follow the guidelines. "Negroes doing next to nothing & I can't make them do any better by talking to them," one planter complained.

At Chatham plantation, a number of the Black men, including John Henry Brown and Thomas Hall, who had been sold by the Jesuits, abandoned the estate in the spring of 1863 and found their way to military camps, where they enlisted in the Union Army.

Union officials were deeply divided over the question of whether Black men should serve on the front lines. But all of that began to change after the battle at Port Hudson.

Port Hudson was a highly fortified rebel fort about twenty miles north of Baton Rouge. On May 27, 1863, segregated Black troops charged through a rain of enemy artillery and musket fire, crossing rough terrain, abatis, and a creek eight feet deep. Scores died as they "fought with the desperation of tigers," one white soldier recalled. "After firing one volley they did not deign to load again, but went in with bayonets."

Though it failed to capture the fort that day, the Union Army ultimately prevailed, and General Banks, who had doubted the capacity of the Black troops, marveled at their valor. He told Lincoln that "we could never have accomplished the conquest of Port Hudson *but for the presence* of the negro regiment." And he told his wife that the men had fought "splendidly." "Everyone is delighted that they did so well!" he wrote. "Their charges . . . exhibited the greatest bravery, and caused them to suffer great losses."

The troops' courage was hailed across the country, lauded by *The New York Times* and recognized even by some Confederates. The following year, urging the Confederate secretary of war to recruit Black troops, the governor of Louisiana wrote, "We have learned from dear-bought experience that negroes can be taught to fight."

Soon more men took flight from the Chatham plantation. At least six had been owned and sold by the Jesuits, and they made their way to military camps, where they volunteered to give their lives in the battle to overthrow slavery.

For many Black men, the fight provided a way, finally, to channel years of rage, heartbreak, and hardship. On the battlefield, there would be no kowtowing to any master, no swallowing the outrage burning inside.

When a white Union officer advised his Black troops to view the rebels with a forgiving spirit, one Black soldier responded sharply, reflecting the emotions of thousands of newly enlisted men. "Your back ain't cut up as mine is," the soldier replied, describing his scars from a white man's whip. "You ain't heard screamin' wimmin, and seen the blood run out at every lick, just 'cause a woman wouldn't leave her husband and sleep with the overseer. They never done you such things, but I could kill 'em easy."

The absence of the men from the Chatham estate left holes in the plantation's social fabric. Sons, brothers, husbands, cousins, all of them gone. And even in Union territory, the threat of violence lingered. People knew about the bombardment of Donaldsonville, about the Union soldiers who marched through the town, the rebels who fired on them, and the gunboats cruising along the Mississippi.

The bloody images of war were seared into the memories of the enslaved long after the battles ended and the sounds of war—the *pop-pop-pop-pop* of gunfire rang in their ears. "I seen some bad things," recalled Albert Patterson, who had been enslaved near Baton Rouge. "I seen de Rebel soldiers run, wid their leg most cut off to de knee, or de arm hangin', de blood pourin.'"

Robert St. Ann, who had been enslaved as a child in Plaquemines parish, remembered that the Confederate soldiers had "started throwing bullets like rain." "At night," he said, "it looked like hundreds o' fire crackers all lit up."

Those who remained on the plantations felt the shock waves of the conflict, enduring violence and hunger as battles raged and white planters struggled to keep their estates up and running. But hope and joy bloomed amid the hardship and uncertainty.

Some whispered it. Others shouted it, taunting their overseers and masters. And many prayed for it just as the wealthy white landowners who knew that emancipation would mean the loss of their most valuable assets prayed it would never happen. But the Black people on the plantations saw the Yankee soldiers—and the formerly enslaved men who fought along with them—and prayed that that victory was coming—and with it, liberation.

In January 1864, General Banks suspended the state's slavery laws and issued new rules that hinted at the future he and other Republicans envisioned for the state. Under the new regulations, Black people on the plantations could choose whom they would work for. Their children could go to schools financed by property taxes. Their wages were increased, and planters were required to provide them with garden plots.

But the regulations also addressed many of the concerns raised by

white planters, who complained that the emboldened Black workforce was undermining productivity. In response, Banks described
work as a "public duty" and idleness "a crime." He required laborers to sign work contracts that barred them from leaving the plantations, except under specific conditions. Black people who violated
the contracts would be required to work for the state without pay.

Banks's order also required half of workers' pay to be held until
the end of the planting season to ensure that necessary farm work
was completed. But if the goal was to tie Black people more closely
to the plantations, the effort failed. "They work less, have less respect, are less orderly than ever," one planter complained.

Newly empowered Black workers, determined to get their due,
filed complaints with Union Army officials. One planter described
a local provost marshal's office as "thronged with negroes claiming
their payment."

ANNA WAS IN her early fifties when war swept across the plantations. Her family appears only fleetingly in archival records in the
early 1860s, but records suggest that she remained enslaved by
Henry Johnson for the war's duration.

Johnson had retired from political life and, after selling his plantation in Ascension parish, had purchased a twelve-thousand-acre
sugarcane plantation in Pointe Coupee parish known as Woodley.
He had decided to spend his twilight years in the estate's elegant
Greek Revival mansion with white columns and ornate balconies.
He filled the grand home with paintings and books, including two
volumes on the presidential administrations of George Washington
and John Adams. Friends recalled that he spent much of his time
reading, particularly enjoying religious and historical texts, and kept
his mind active. With an eye to his legacy, he had pledged $40,000—
$1.5 million in today's dollars—to help establish Sewanee, the Uni-
versity of the South, an institution expressly designed to uphold
and protect the institution of slavery.

Dozens of enslaved people labored in his fields, and others tended to him in his home. Johnson continued to be viewed by his peers as a kindly master, the kind who required his overseers to consult with him before punishing any of the Black people on the plantation. (One imagines that the enslaved on the estate would have considered it kinder to bar whippings and other forms of punishment altogether.)

His wife provided some of the house servants with a rudimentary education and a grounding in the faith so that they might offer religious instruction to the others. John Battiste, who was born on the plantation during the Civil War, said that his mother had told him years later that she and the other enslaved people at Woodley had considered themselves "free Negroes" because of the relative freedom that they enjoyed. But that kind of "freedom," whether tangible to the people enslaved at Woodley or little more than the self-congratulatory views of a white man who liked to be seen as kind by his human possessions, would not have eased Anna's heartbreak. Woodley was about forty miles away from Chatham, the plantation now run by John R. Thompson, who still owned her children.

Johnson's wife traveled occasionally to Donaldsonville, the town closest to Chatham, to attend Mass at the Catholic Church there. If Anna worked as a house servant for the Johnsons, as she had done for the Jesuits, she may well have accompanied Mrs. Johnson on those trips and had the opportunity to visit her children. But those opportunities soon dwindled. The aging couple had done little in the way of socializing, and the death of Johnson's wife in 1860 left him with even fewer reasons to travel back to Ascension parish. He suffered from occasional bouts of illness, and as Union troops occupied large swaths of the state, including sections of Pointe Coupee parish, the retired politician began considering his own mortality. So on March 26, 1864, he sat down to write a will.

In the handwritten document, he parceled out his fortune—thousands of dollars in cash and real estate—to his friends, nieces and nephews, and other relatives. He gave away precious keepsakes and prized possessions, including a gold watch and his writing desk, his silver spoons and forks, his horses, and his wife's rosewood furniture.

Johnson funded his wife's favorite charities and causes, as she had requested before her death, including the missionary society of the Episcopal Church and the American Colonization Society, which was continuing to promote the removal of Black people from the United States. And he mentioned a lady's maid, whom he described as "an honest faithful servant, always obedient to her mistress in her lifetime."

The servant was a woman known as Louisey, who had a young daughter named Ann. This enslaved woman happened to have the same name as Anna's daughter, Louisa, who also happened to have a daughter named Ann. Had Anna Jones and her daughter been reunited at Woodley plantation?

Thompson occasionally moved his enslaved people from one estate to another, shipping a handful of people from Chatham to his son's estate in the 1850s, for instance. No records have emerged to suggest that he sold Louisa back to Johnson, but the two families were related and may have shared and exchanged servants as the Jesuits had done back in Maryland, without troubling themselves with formal bills of sale.

If the Louisey in the will was indeed Anna Jones's daughter, Louisa, the two women may have spent the tumultuous war years together, finding comfort in each other's company as Union troops marched through Pointe Coupee parish. At Woodley, Anna was still forced to live many miles away from her son, Arnold, who continued to labor on the Chatham plantation. But she had a granddaughter now, a child who carried her name and who may have even toddled through the big house where she worked.

In that summer of 1864, Johnson's close friends and relatives converged on the Woodley estate. The retired politician had fallen ill again, and this time, he told them, he did not believe he would recover. The sickness, he said, was "a messenger of death."

Soon word got out onto the plantation that Johnson, the former governor, congressman, and senator, was dead. The news appeared in newspapers across the country, in Washington, DC; Alexandria, Virginia; Springfield, Massachusetts; Houston, Texas; and beyond. The *Louisville Daily Democrat* hailed his "great legislative abilities." The *Times-Picayune* of New Orleans hailed his rise to power, his early days as a young lawyer, his participation in the state's constitutional convention, his years as governor, congressman, and senator. "For nearly thirty years he filled the highest offices in the State, and in every position," the reporter wrote, he "discharged his duty with an ability, integrity and disinterestedness which has few parallels." The newspaper also heralded Johnson's nurturing side, describing the time he had spent mentoring promising young people and helping them advance in their careers and praising him for "devoting himself to the welfare of his negroes."

What Anna and the other enslaved people he owned would have made of such a statement is unknown. Johnson had certainly purchased her elderly brother and placed him on a plantation where he would be close to his relatives, a decision that suggested he recognized and honored the importance of family ties among the enslaved. The newspaper made no mention, however, of his decisions to split up families for profit or to pay down his debts.

Anna was about fifty-three when Johnson died in his mansion on the Woodley estate. She had been in her twenties when he had purchased her, a single mother with two young children, already deeply rooted in her community. Johnson and his wife had controlled her life—deciding where she would live, what work she would do, and the fate of her children—for nearly three decades. Now he was gone. The burning question for many of the enslaved people on the plantation was: What will come next?

In his will, Johnson had bequeathed Louisey and her young daughter, Ann, to his niece, along with all the paintings and most of the furniture in the house. If Louisey was indeed Anna's daughter, she would yet again face the prospect of involuntary separation from her family. Only a decade earlier, Anna might have despaired.

But it was 1864. Union soldiers were camped all across the parish. Some Black people in Louisiana were already being paid for their labor. Some were fighting in the war. Enslaved people everywhere were talking about freedom. So as the community at Woodley wrestled with the complex mix of emotions—jubilation, fear, and uncertainty—that often swept a plantation after the death of its master, Anna could finally cling to something new: hope.

Change was coming, too, to the Catholic Church. That fall, the Vatican finally began to take a critical look at American slavery. It was a sharp change in approach.

Only a year earlier, Bishop Martin Spalding of Louisville had seemed to find a receptive audience in Rome to his complaints about Bishop Purcell and his allies, who were continuing to press for an end to slavery. In his twenty-three-page letter to Rome, Spalding acknowledged that slavery left a moral stain on the country. But he argued that those who pressed for abolition, as Purcell did, failed to consider the dangers that emancipation posed both to the economy and to Black people. He noted that some free Blacks in the North were struggling, and he accused northern abolitionists of hypocrisy, pointing out that several northern states had refused to allow free Black people to settle there. (Illinois, Indiana, Oregon, Iowa, and Indiana were among the states that passed laws barring Black migration. Northern proponents of such laws targeted free Blacks, arguing that they were necessary to prevent an influx of criminals and impoverished people.)

"Our philanthropists of the North," he wrote, "wish certainly to see the slaves freed, but they wish by no means to have them among themselves." He argued that the clergy should stand on the sidelines of the bloody conflict, which he described as Lincoln's "miserable war." The war, he wrote, "has now become a war of confiscation of property, of violent emancipation of the Negroes, of threatened and encouraged slave insurrection, of destruction and desolation of the vast and fair territory of the South, and finally of extermination of all the whites, and perhaps at the same time also of the Negroes themselves."

Spalding's missive was warmly received. In October 1863, *L'Osservatore Romano* serialized it. Then, in December of that year, Pope Pius IX outraged Union officials by addressing Jefferson Davis as "the illustrious and honorable" president of the Confederate States of America, which jubilant rebel leaders said amounted to formal recognition of their independence by the Holy See. When the Union officials protested, the pope backtracked and insisted privately that he did not support slavery. He did not make that position public.

But within the Holy See, dissent on the question of slavery was growing. In January 1864, the Vatican's consul in New York City urged the Church's leadership to take a stand. The consul, who had cheered Purcell's call for an end to slavery and questioned the Church's silence, said he could not understand those who opposed abolition. He described slavery as "the sole cause of our terrible civil war" and called on those in the Vatican to speak up. "The question of the future of slavery is the question of the day," he wrote.

His prodding seems to have had some impact. Rome finally addressed the question later that year, focusing on Bishop Martin's pastoral letter proclaiming that American slavery had God's divine imprimatur. Father Vincent M. Gatti, the Vatican official charged with examining Martin's letter, dissected the bishop's arguments one by one, issuing a report that amounted to Rome's most pointed and forceful critique of American slavery.

Gatti disputed Martin's contention that Black people were cursed by God, arguing that original sin, which was passed down the generations from Adam and Eve, affected all people, not just Black people. Gatti pointed out that Martin was suggesting that white people were "born with a certain kind of education or culture," which was clearly far from the truth, and that Black people were incapable of improving their circumstances through education, yet another falsehood, though one that was widely believed. "Experience shows that Negroes, placed among Catholics and educated like them, can become learned and virtuous people, fit for moral dignity and freedom," he observed. He dismissed the idea that enslavement could be justified if the enslaved received the gift of Christianity. There was, he wrote in his report, no "justification" for the gross injustice "which such traffic" entailed.

Gatti acknowledged that the Church had tolerated slavery in the past but said it could not condone a form of systemic bondage based solely on race. He concluded that Martin was contradicting Church teachings, which "condemned not only the enslavement of individuals, but the continued keeping of them as slaves." "We prohibit and strictly forbid any Ecclesiastic or lay person from presuming to defend as permissible this traffic in Blacks under no matter what pretext or excuse, or from publishing or teaching in any manner whatsoever, in public or privately," he wrote, quoting Pope Gregory XVI.

Gatti's conclusion, which would be supported by Pope Pius IX, marked a profound shift in the Church's position. He was explicitly criticizing slave ownership, in addition to the buying and selling of people. The condemnation of Father Martin's letter amounted to what one scholar has described as "a small revolution" in the Church's view of the institution of slavery in the United States. Vatican officials decided to order Bishop Martin to "correct the errors and inaccuracies" of his position and to warn him that "should there be undue delay, further and harsher measures be taken by the Holy See."

But it remains unclear whether the order was ever communicated to the bishop. And the new stance on slavery adopted by the Catholic leadership in Rome would not be publicly disseminated as Church doctrine for years. By then it would be far too late to influence American policy or to affect the lives of people who had been enslaved by Catholic priests and nuns with the full endorsement of the Catholic Church.

By November 1864, when Gatti released his report, Union officials in Louisiana had already approved a state constitution that formally abolished slavery. Since the Civil War was still raging, the new constitution affected only the parts of the southern states that were under Union control, the sugar regions, and the estates located along the Mississippi River.

In Maryland, where Louisa and her family were still enslaved, legislators took a similar step, rewriting the state constitution to ensure that slavery was ended once and for all. All across the state, planters and slaveholders struggled to make sense of the momentous change that was to come. At St. Inigoes, Father Basil Pacciarini wrote to the treasurer of the province, seeking guidance "about our darkies": "My plan would to be let them stay if they prefer with food, clothing and dwelling and $20 in wages but I will not come to any conclusion until I receive an answer."

But freedom was coming, whether the Jesuits were ready or not. On November 1, 1864, slavery was officially abolished in the state of Maryland. On that date, Louisa, her six children, and another enslaved man owned by the priests at St. Inigoes woke up and walked out of the slave quarters as free people for the first time. The Jesuits would later record their names, hopeful that they might be compensated by the state for the loss of their human property. They were not.

Louisa, born into an enslaved family that had dreamed of freedom for generations, was finally a free woman. She was about fifty-one years old, and she could finally live without the fear that she or her children, who ranged in age from about five to about fifteen, would ever be sold. She could leave the plantation, and the priests who had enslaved her, behind. She could establish herself in a new place, decide whom she would work for, and earn wages for her work. She could send her children to the new schools that would be established for freed people. The new world was rich with possibility.

But she was keenly aware that she was walking into this new world without many of the people who had supported her and loved her. Her parents were dead. Her husband, who had shown her what freedom could look like, was gone, too. She would be navigating on her own.

In Louisiana, Anna's family was finding its way as well. On February 20, 1865, on the Chatham plantation, John R. Thompson signed a contract promising to provide Anna's son, Arnold, and the other Black workers and their families with "good and sufficient quarters, a separate tenement for each family, fuel and medical attendance . . . [and] . . . a sufficient supply of wholesome food and proper clothing."

The contract also stipulated that Arnold and the other Black workers would work only ten hours a day, "except in cases of positive necessity," and in those instances they would receive additional pay. They would have Sunday and half of Saturday off each week and one holiday during the year, the Fourth of July.

Acknowledging the concerns of Black men and women determined to prepare their children for lives in a free society, Thompson also pledged "to co-operate in the establishment of any school for the education of the children of said Laborers." The workers committed to working under those terms at Chatham for another year, now as free people.

It was an exhilaratingly new framework. As a free man, Arnold had the right to wages and good living conditions. At least on paper, he had the right to leave, to abandon the contract, and his employer, if Thompson provided "bad or insufficient food, or insufficient or unhealthy quarters, or shall be guilty of cruelty."

Thompson had good reason to treat Arnold reasonably well. Not only did the authorities in the federally controlled sugar districts in Louisiana require it, but he was short on "first-class workers." Twenty-five men, thirteen women, and two boys lived on his plantation. Three of the men were sickly. One was lame. Even among the able-bodied men, Arnold stood out. He was a craftsman, a carpenter known for his skill, one of only two men classified as "first class." Most of the men earned $8 a month. Arnold earned $10.

On April 3, 1865, less than two months after Arnold and the other workers had struck the deal with Thompson, the Confederate capital of Richmond fell to federal forces. Six days later, General Robert E. Lee surrendered.

Jubilation swept the estates as the word spread. "Ev'rybody ran into de streets hollorin' we is free at last," recalled Elizabeth Ross Hite, who had been enslaved on Trinity plantation in Iberville parish, not far from Chatham. "De Yankees shook our hands, dere was singin, prayin an ev'rythin."

Harrison Camille remembered the celebrations that had taken place when the soldiers marched through the city "and all the beautiful ladies throw flowers to them from their balcony."

Shack Wilson never forgot the singing. "After freedom, Lor' how we did sing! We sang when we went to Church and when we were at work and all the time it seems like."

But those heady days would not last long. Anger simmered among the many white supporters of the defeated Confederacy whose lives had been upended by the war. Like Thompson, they now had to pay the Black men and women who had once been forced to work for nothing. They had to abide by rules that required minimum standards for housing, clothing, and feeding their workers. The new rules barred them from whipping or beating workers who decided to work elsewhere. Black people even spoke of educating themselves, and the federal government seemed ready to support schools for the millions of newly freed people. Outraged, some white men decided to do what they could to turn back the clock and ensure that Black people knew their place.

In October 1865, violence erupted in Ascension parish, where Arnold and his family were savoring their liberty. A Black man, Burtin Austin, was walking through a plantation that evening when the man who had enslaved him called out to him. Slavery was over, and it was a clear, beautiful night with the moon aglow above the cotton fields. So Austin ignored the calls of the white man and kept on toward his destination, the banks of the Mississippi River.

One of the last sounds he ever heard was the blast of gunfire. "I halted him three times and he never gave an answer," the white man later told the authorities. "So I shot him."

The white man, a well-known planter, described the cold-blooded killing matter-of-factly. He told the jury called to investigate the case that Austin had worked for him and that the Black man had died "on his belly."

In November 1865, the jury found that the planter, J. B. Marchand, had killed his Black worker but said that it "could not come to any final conclusion whether Mr. Marchand was or was not justified in shooting the said Austin or not." The jurors called on the authorities to investigate further. But Marchand was right to feel confident that he could tell the world he had shot a Black man in the back, even though he had posed no threat to him. The white planter was arrested, then released, and the authorities did nothing more.

"The Civil Authorities of the Parish (Ascension) have made a show of bringing murderers to justice after which they are permitted to go at large, and if need be to do the same act over again," wrote John H. Brough, a local Freedmen's Bureau official, who was assigned to Donaldsonville. "Shall these gross acts of murder be permitted to go unpunished? If so the people, especially the Freedmen, stand in dread."

In December, just a month after the authorities in Donaldsonville decided to turn a blind eye to the murder, the states ratified the Thirteenth Amendment, formally abolishing slavery. Slavery had ended, but it was increasingly clear that in small towns and rural communities across the South, white men could still kill or brutalize Black people without facing consequences.

Arnold had to take that into account as he pondered his future. That month, he lined up with dozens of other Black workers on the Chatham estate as Thompson, the man who had enslaved him, handed out the final payments for the year. "I have this day settled with all the Laborers in my employ," Thompson attested on New Year's Eve, "and paid them in accordance with existing Gen. Orders from Head Quarters."

Arnold walked away with $71.50 that day. He had earned $112.35 that year, more than anyone else on the plantation. Some of the Black workers had decided to move on, cutting their ties to the old plantation. Arnold, who had spent nearly two decades of his life on the estate, still deliberated. Should he commit to another year on the plantation? Or start a new life as a free man somewhere else?

All across Louisiana, formerly enslaved people took stock of the simmering tensions and eruptions of violence as they weighed their options. In the spring of 1866, a federal agent in nearby St. James parish raised concerns about "reports of cruelties practised on the freedmen by Employers and overseers." The wrongdoing included "not only those in which physical injury is inflicted," the Freedmen's Bureau agent there reported, but also instances "where improper and unjust restraints are imposed upon the liberty of the freedmen." "It is also reported that the overseers are in the habit of going armed to the field with the laborers," he continued, "and that they use their pistols and other weapons upon the slightest provocation and indeed without any provocation whatever."

By then Arnold had made his decision.

When his wife gave birth to a baby girl on April 15, 1866, they were miles away from Ascension parish. The couple had cut their ties to the Thompsons and had moved to New Orleans. Anna and her daughter, Arnold's sister Louisa, and several other people who had been owned by the Jesuits would also find their way to the bustling city. There the family would integrate themselves into the vibrant Black community.

Anna was a middle-aged woman by then. She had lived longer in Louisiana than she had in Maryland. But her newfound freedom could not erase the pain of the past. She had been torn from her family, her parents, her sister, and several of her brothers. She would never see them again.

Back at the St. Inigoes plantation, Louisa's struggle with the question of what to do next yielded a different answer. All around the country, Black people were moving, abandoning the plantations where they had been enslaved and the people who had enslaved them. Many, like Anna and her children, found their way to towns and cities where they would no longer have to work the land. They could transform themselves into urban workers there and put the plantation life far behind them. But Louisa was a widow, a single mother of six. And unlike her older sister, she still had young children, including two under the age of ten. She had to provide for them, feed them, and shelter them. Could she really build a new life in a new place?

For some Black people, staying on the plantations where they'd worked was hard to stomach. The joy of earning wages for the first time was simply not enough. The fields and the big houses where they had labored for years were filled with sorrow and harrowing memories. For some, it was simply unbearable.

For Louisa, St. Inigoes was both the place where she had been born and raised and the place where she had been enslaved for most of her life. It was the place where she had given birth to her children and the place where she had wept over the sale of her sister and so many other members of her family.

If she stayed, she would continue working for the Jesuits, the men who had owned her family for generations. Always she would be reminded of priests such as Joseph Carbery, who had given the Black men and women on the plantation unprecedented freedom and saved her from the sale, and Thomas Mulledy, who had sold her siblings, her cousins, and her friends. The priests who knew Louisa said she had never forgiven Mulledy for tearing her family apart.

But after the Civil War, she weighed her options and considered her place in the new world unfolding around her. She looked at the rolling fields of the estate where she had spent her entire life, at the faces of the priests who had enslaved her and the children who depended on her. She had no way of knowing how many years she had left on Earth or whether she would live to regret or to cherish her decision. But she made up her mind. She decided to stay.

The Profits

FOR DECADES, THE MONEY FROM THE 1838 SALE STREAMED into the Jesuits' accounts.

More than a century later, Georgetown's working group on slavery would say that it was unlikely that the Jesuits had ever received the full amount promised them for the Black people they sold. Henry Johnson had had such serious financial problems, the group reported, that the priests "appear to never have received the full $115,000."

The Jesuit financial ledgers from the period, worn and yellowing but still largely intact, tell a different story. The pages are filled with careful handwritten notations, the painstaking accounting of the cash that flowed into the priests' coffers long after the men, women, and children were sold. The records, discovered by Georgetown's archivists nearly two years after the working group offered its preliminary assessment, show that the buyers, who included local farmers, continued to send payments to the Jesuits in the 1840s, the 1850s, and even the 1860s. Those payments amounted to far more than the initial down payment of $25,000. By the time freedom finally came to the Mahoneys, the Jesuits had received more than $130,000 from the 1838 sale, about $4.5 million in today's dollars.

The money enabled Georgetown to survive and thrive and

helped stabilize the Maryland province's precarious finances. The priests invested in Treasury notes and bonds and garnered additional income from various sources: tuition at the newly resurgent Georgetown and the tenant farmers who had replaced the enslaved, among others. And the money helped the Maryland Jesuits to create and support new schools, bringing Mulledy's cherished dream to fruition.

Income from the Maryland province had already helped finance the school that would become St. Louis University in Missouri and established the Washington Seminary, which later became Gonzaga College High School, in the nation's capital. It also supported Georgetown Preparatory School, a private Catholic high school now located in North Bethesda, Maryland, which was once part of Georgetown College. But with cash flowing in from the 1838 sale, the Jesuits could finally turn their attention to the cities of the Northeast, where throngs of Irish immigrants looked to the Church for spiritual, economic, and educational opportunities.

Mulledy would not watch that happen from the sidelines. He had been brought home by Jesuit leaders, who needed capable men in the United States, and had shaken off the taint of the mass sale, in Jesuit circles at least. (The enslaved people would not forget his betrayal.) And he was determined to help drive the expansion himself.

In 1843, he was named president of Worcester College, which would later be renamed Holy Cross, the first Catholic college in New England. Over the next decade, the Maryland Jesuits funneled more than $30,000 to the college to cover construction costs, books, and travel expenses for faculty journeying to Boston from Washington, DC. In 1852, the Jesuits established Loyola College in Baltimore, now known as Loyola University Maryland, allocating more than $40,000 by 1860 to support its operations. In 1860, they expanded their reach in Massachusetts by opening a seminary, the Scholasticate, in Boston. Over the course of three years, they spent more than $27,000 there on books, wine, vestments, and a range of operational expenses before moving the institution to Woodstock, Maryland. All told, the Maryland Jesuits invested about $2.3 million in today's dollars in those institutions.

They also offered assistance to colleges that did not receive direct financial support from the province. They helped to supply Jesuits who assumed senior positions in emerging institutions, and trained priests and seminarians who served as teachers and leaders at newly established colleges, including Fordham in New York, St. Joseph's in Philadelphia, Boston College, and Santa Clara in Santa Clara, California. An influx of newly arrived priests, who arrived in the United States after escaping upheaval in Europe, buoyed the Maryland Jesuits' dreams. "Perhaps with their arrival," Ignatius Brocard, the Maryland provincial, wrote to Rome of the European priests, the Jesuits would be able to expand to "states where we have been unable to fulfil our hopes of having schools."

Meanwhile, Jesuits based west of the Mississippi River, who also relied on slave labor, ran colleges in Kentucky, Alabama, Louisiana, and Ohio. Some of them, including Xavier College in Cincinnati, survived the Civil War.

But the Jesuits were not the only ones determined to build institutions. Members of the Mahoney family, steeped in Catholicism, would step up and work to reshape the Church, to make it more responsive to and reflective of its Black flock. They did that even though, when freedom finally came, many of the leaders of the Catholic Church viewed the millions of newly emancipated people with skepticism, even disdain.

In October 1865, Father Spalding, now the archbishop of Baltimore, called for a discussion among Catholic leaders about "the future status of the negro." "Four million of these unfortunates are thrown on our Charity," he wrote in a letter to the archbishop of New York. "It is a golden opportunity for reaping a harvest of souls, which neglected may not return."

Spalding's call for the issue to be discussed at a national plenary council received support from officials in Rome, who proposed the creation of a position for a bishop or a national coordinator focused on Black Catholics. But at the meeting the following year, Spalding quickly learned that few of his fellow bishops shared his concerns. One by one, his counterparts dismissed the idea. The bishop of Richmond even asked whether Rome had given any consideration to the plight of white people in the United States: "Behold so strong was the desire for promoting the salvation of the blacks as if they alone were derelict and neglected."

The meeting closed without reaching a consensus. The idea of creating a national ministry dedicated to Black Catholics, one that would initiate a broad outreach to the community, was shelved. Instead, in a joint statement issued after the plenary council, the bishops exposed their racial biases, describing what they called the "peculiar dispositions and habits" of Black people and making it clear that the nation's Catholic leadership remained doubtful about the wisdom of the "sudden liberation of so large a multitude." "We could have wished," they wrote, "that . . . a more gradual system of emancipation could have been adopted, so that they might have been in some measure prepared to make a better use of their freedom, than they are likely to do now."

But in Louisiana and Maryland, the newly freed members of the Mahoney family and their children were not waiting for the bishops' approval. They had been betrayed by the Catholic Church, an institution that had profited from their enslavement, and betrayed by powerful priests who had sold them and ripped their family apart. But they did not abandon the Catholic faith that had sustained them during the darkest times. And when freedom came, Anna's family carried that faith with them as they established themselves in New Orleans, where they and other newly freed Black people would create a vibrant culture and brand-new institutions.

On June 13, 1870, Anna's daughter, Louisa, walked into St. Alphonsus Church in New Orleans' lower Garden District. She was a grown woman, about thirty-eight years old, and she had finally met the man with whom she would share the rest of her life. His name was John Johnson. He was a carpenter who had enlisted in the Union Army, and he had made his way to the city along with thousands of other newly freed people after the war. They had both grown up on plantations in Ascension parish, but he was Protestant and she was Catholic.

Louisa never forgot that Jesuit priests had sold her and her family. But her faith did not belong to those hard men. The prayers, the hymns, the rosary beads, the rituals of the faithful also belonged to her and to the throngs of Black Catholics who had settled in New Orleans. So Louisa took John Johnson to meet the priest. Father James Gleason married them that day in his own house—he refused to bless marriages between Protestants and Catholics at the altar—in front of witnesses who would remember the ceremony decades later.

Afterward, the newlyweds returned home to a tightly knit community that would support and sustain them. Louisa had been living with her mother, Anna, who was supporting herself as a washerwoman. An old friend, who had also been owned and sold by the Jesuits, lived next door. Her brother, Arnold, lived down the street with his wife and children.

By 1870, the Black population in New Orleans had doubled to 50,495, up from 24,074 a decade earlier. Amid the throngs of newcomers, many of the people who had been enslaved by the Jesuits stuck together. They lived in the same neighborhoods, they socialized with one another, and their children grew up together. They bought property. A number of the men from Maryland were skilled workers, working primarily as carpenters and barrel makers. And many of them, including Anna, Arnold, and Louisa, continued to find comfort in the Catholic Church. The newly freed Black people "cling to the faith in which they were raised with a tenacity that is wonderful," one Catholic reporter noted.

Outsiders praised the Catholic Church in New Orleans for its willingness to embrace its Black parishioners. "In her most aristocratic churches in this city, lips of every shade, by hundreds press with devout kisses the same crucifixes, and fingers of a great variety of color are dipped in the 'holy water,' to imprint the cross on as varied brows," a Methodist minister declared in 1874.

But Black Catholics in the city knew better. They knew, for instance, that Father Gleason, the Irish priest who had married Louisa and John, was widely regarded as racist. (Gleason was outraged when he discovered that another priest had displayed a picture of St. Patrick in a Black Catholic school, a move that Gleason described as an insult to Ireland and to St. Patrick.)

Catholic priests might invite the multicolored multitudes into their churches, but Black people knew exactly what they might encounter once they stepped inside. At St. Louis Cathedral, the soaring landmark in the heart of the city, a priest refused Communion to a Black soldier. In other parishes, Black and white children were often separated for catechism, First Communion, and Confirmation, as well as parish festivities. And as the years passed, the segregation of parishioners within interracial churches increasingly became the norm. Black parishioners at the cathedral, for instance, found themselves forced to sit on a bench called a "long board" that was placed along the rear and side walls. The Church would ultimately pay a steep price for its racism. Nearly twenty thousand African Americans left the church in the two decades after the Civil War. But Anna's family stayed, as did most Black Catholics, holding on to their religion despite the racism of the clergy and white parishioners as they built new lives as free people. Louisa and her new husband saved enough to purchase a plot of land and a house that would remain in the family for decades. She and her brother passed on their spiritual devotion to the next generation, who did more than simply absorb their faith; they harnessed it, becoming religious leaders who would strive to reshape the Church by building institutions that would be more reflective of and responsive to Black Catholics.

Anna would not live to see it. On January 30, 1874, John Henry Brown, a barrel maker sold by the Jesuits who had joined the Union

Army, walked into the office of the city's recorder of births, marriages, and deaths to report the news. Anna had suffered from chest pains at home a day earlier. She was about sixty-three years old, and she died as she had lived, nurtured by her family and a circle of longtime friends.

She was gone, but her faith burned inside her grandchildren. Louisa's son James Alphonse Johnson got involved in the movement to establish Black Catholic churches in New Orleans. He became a trustee of Holy Ghost Church in the Uptown neighborhood, one of the city's first Black parishes, and successfully petitioned the archdiocese to set aside the land where the church stands today.

Arnold's daughter Helene Jones joined one of the nation's first order of Black nuns, the Sisters of the Holy Family, where she adopted the name Mary and became known as Mary Austin Jones. By 1891, she had become the leader of the religious order, which ran schools and orphanages. Though she was only thirty years old, her fellow nuns described her as the "most capable" and "most successful" of the order's mother generals.

During her eighteen-year tenure, she drove the order's expansion. She raised enough money to purchase 123 acres of land that would be used for the sisters' headquarters and other facilities. She opened new schools and orphanages for Black children in New Orleans and established others in Texas and Arkansas. She also ran a mission school for Black children in Belize, which became the first overseas mission ever established by Black Catholics.

Bishop Salvatore Di Pietro, a Sicilian Jesuit responsible for the country, marveled at what she and her order of nuns had been able to accomplish. "Yesterday they opened the schools, both parochial and select ones," he wrote in 1898. "They had 177 [students] in the first and 7 in the second. Many more are expected." "It seems to me that the foundation of the Sisters of the Holy Family in Stann Creek will be a success," he continued, noting their work with adults as well as children. "I feel confident that in a short time we will see a remarkable change in the town."

. . .

LOUISA WAS STILL in Maryland, but after decades of heartbreaking separation, she had finally found a way to get news of her family in Louisiana—perhaps through letters passed through a network of priests. She was one of thousands of Black people who, after the war, searched for loved ones who had been sold, placing notices in newspapers and journeying for miles to search for lost relatives. Many searched in vain.

The lucky ones described joyous, tear-filled reunions. Frederick Douglass recalled his jubilation after receiving a letter from his brother, whom he had not seen in decades. He described their emotional meeting as "an event altogether too affecting for words to describe."

Louisa would never have that opportunity. She would never see her sister, her other siblings, or her nieces and nephews again. But she could find comfort in knowing that her people in Louisiana were doing just fine. "They were getting along pretty well," she told one Jesuit priest.

Her own sons and daughters were getting along pretty well, too. They educated their children and several bought plots of land. As in Louisiana, they and other Black worshippers continued to deal with segregation in the pews and racism on the part of the clergy and white parishioners. ("In the distribution of the Xmas presents care must be taken that no room be given for jealousy," wrote one priest, who worked in the Sunday school that some of Louisa's relatives attended. "The peculiar formation of a negro's character makes him a fit subject for this miserable vice.")

Despite those slights and humiliations, several members of Louisa's family continued to work for the Jesuits. And like her sister's family, they remained deeply involved in the Church, trying to shape it into an institution that would support Black families.

Louisa's daughter, Josephine, married into the Barnes family, whose ancestors had led the insurrection against whites back in 1817. Josephine's husband, Daniel O. Barnes, would run a parochial school for Black children and help establish the Knights of St. Jerome, a Catholic benevolent society that supported Black families in crisis.

Louisa's son Thomas and his wife, Ann, would teach catechism to Black children, passing on the Church's teachings to the next generation. Her son Robert continued to work for the priests at St. Inigoes, where the priests grumbled that he was far too independent minded for his own good.

And when the Jesuits established Woodstock College, a seminary near Baltimore, Louisa made sure that her grandson, Gabriel Bennett, went with them. He would serve as the head cook there for more than sixty years. His daughter, Mary, joined the Oblate Sisters of Providence, another early order of Black nuns, and ran Catholic academies for Black children in St. Louis and Wilson, North Carolina.

As for Louisa, she continued cooking and cleaning for the Jesuits until age and infirmity made it impossible, and then she lived with her daughter Josephine during the last years of her life. Her mind remained sharp well into her nineties, and she hobbled to Mass whenever she could, returning home with a small bottle filled with holy water. "On my last visit to her," one priest recalled, "she made me renew the promise every procurator had made her, namely, to pay for her burial."

Louisa was about ninety-six years old when she died in the summer of 1909. To reward her for a lifetime of service, the Jesuits honored her with a Mass in the church on the old plantation that July, which drew "a very large assemblage of all classes of residents," one observer recalled. One priest called it the largest funeral that St. Inigoes had ever seen.

The white people who knew Louisa praised her as a faithful Black woman who had known her place. The obituary in *St. Mary's Beacon* described her as "eminently honest, virtuous and obedient to her God, faithful to husband and children and all the duties of her station in life."

One priest recalled that she proudly referred to herself as a Jesuit slave as long as she lived, even after slavery ended. She never viewed herself as a free person, the priest said. "Aunt Louisa would never admit emancipation," he wrote.

Louisa had learned to tread carefully. Her family had been betrayed by the Jesuits, enslaved and sold to support their dreams of American expansion, but some of her kinfolk still relied on the priests for their livelihoods. So she told the white people what they wanted to hear.

But to her children and grandchildren, she told the truth.

Epilogue

ON THE FRIDAY AFTER THANKSGIVING IN 2016, JEREMY AL-
exander and Melissa Kemp got together in a shopping mall in Columbia, Maryland, about a two-hour drive from St. Mary's County,
where their ancestors had been enslaved by the Jesuits. The family
had been torn apart in 1838. Now, for the first time in more than a
century, the descendants of the two sisters, Louisa and Anna, were
reuniting.

Six months had passed since my first article about the 1838 slave
sale had appeared on the front page of *The New York Times,* and
Jeremy had watched the developments with astonishment.

The stories that I had written had generated a wave of coverage
by major newspapers, broadcasters, and other media outlets, focusing intense attention on Georgetown and its plans to reckon with
its past. Georgetown's president, John J. DeGioia, had reached out
directly to descendants, flying to Spokane, Washington; New Orleans; Baton Rouge, Louisiana; and the rural Louisiana community
of Maringouin with his chief of staff, Joseph Ferrara, to meet with
dozens of newly discovered descendants of the slaves who had been
sold.

"I think all of us need to get it right this time," Dr. DeGioia said
in July 2016, standing in a sugarcane field where the enslaved had
once labored.

Two months later, he announced that his university would award
preferential status in the admissions process to descendants of the
enslaved who had labored to benefit the college. That would be an
advantage akin to the legacy status offered to the children and

grandchildren of alumni. He also promised to offer a formal apology, create an institute for the study of slavery, and erect a public memorial to the slaves whose labor had benefited the institution, including those who had been sold in 1838 to help keep the university afloat. The two campus buildings that had carried Mulledy's and McSherry's names would be renamed—one for Isaac Hawkins, who had been enslaved by the Jesuits, the other for an African American educator who belonged to a Catholic religious order. Dr. DeGioia would also host a Mass of reconciliation in partnership with the Jesuit leadership in the United States and the Archdiocese of Washington.

"This community participated in the institution of slavery," said Dr. DeGioia, making his announcement at Georgetown's Gaston Hall before a crowd of hundreds of students, faculty members, and descendants, including Melissa and her mother. "This original evil that shaped the early years of the Republic was present here. We have been able to hide from this truth, bury this truth, ignore and deny this truth." But the time had come, he said, to recognize that truth and take action. "As a community and as individuals, we cannot do our best work if we refuse to take ownership of such a critical part of our history. We must acknowledge it."

By then, nearly six hundred descendants had been identified by the genealogists hired by Richard Cellini, the Georgetown alumnus who had founded the independent Georgetown Memory Project to determine what had happened to the people sold in 1838 and their progeny. The descendants praised the announcement, but they also said it did not go far enough. Some asked why scholarships weren't being offered to descendants. Others pointed out that the new admissions policy would benefit only people interested in and eligible for admission to Georgetown. They began pressing for a voice in the decision-making process about what should be done.

A week after Dr. DeGioia's announcement, a group of descendants called on the university and the Maryland Jesuits to create a $1 billion foundation to promote racial reconciliation and address the needs of the growing descendant community. "We appreciate the gestures of a proposed memorial to our enslaved ancestors on Georgetown's campus and President John DeGioia's visits with some descendants, but recommendations developed without the meaningful participation of descendants can only be seen as preliminary," said Sandra Green Thomas, the president of a new group, the GU272 Descendants Association, which she and others, including Melissa and Richard, had founded.

Jeremy had followed the developments from his office at Georgetown, watching Dr. DeGioia's announcement live on his computer and catching the news about the new group of descendants calling on Georgetown and the Jesuits to do more. Now he knew that this was his family, his story. His eyes filled with tears as he described the emotions that had swept over him. "I have a connection to all of this," he said.

But he still had more questions than answers. So he and Melissa sat down in the food court at the mall. Melissa had brought her mother, Zeita Kemp. Jeremy had brought his son, Jesse. Together, they started to unspool the separate threads of their shared story.

Jeremy was Anna's great-great-great-grandson. His father was descended from Anna's son, Arnold Jr., and carried Arnold's name. The generations had gone from Louisiana to Mississippi, where his father had been born, then up north to Chicago during the Great Migration. As the decades had passed, the story of the family's enslavement and sale had been lost. But his ancestors had passed on another inheritance from their time in bondage: their deeply held faith. Jeremy had attended a Catholic elementary school and a Catholic high school. He had gotten his graduate degree at DePaul University, which prides itself on being the largest Catholic university in the country.

Only about 4 percent of Catholic adults are Black, according to the Pew Research Center. But in Jeremy's home, Catholicism was deeply embedded in the fabric of family life, and he and his parents viewed several local priests as close advisers and friends. "Everybody was Catholic," Jeremy said of his family. "It was never a question of how we became Catholic."

He was no stranger, though, to racism within the Church. When he had decided as an adult to join the Knights of Columbus, a Catholic fraternal organization, his parents had described the group's history of racial exclusion. "They were very concerned," Jeremy recalled. "My dad was like 'I was never allowed to be a member, just being Black.' I was like 'Well, let me see how it goes.'"

Jeremy said he had been welcomed into the organization and had risen within its hierarchy, becoming a fourth-degree knight, the highest rank within the group. His personal experiences had persuaded him that the Catholic Church was willing and able to move beyond its past. But how far would it go? He had been deeply moved by Georgetown's decision to atone for its past and by the Jesuits' decision to apologize for enslaving his ancestors. But he was beginning to believe that it was not enough.

Melissa and her mother listened as they sat across the table from Jeremy in the shopping mall. Their family had lived in Maryland for generations, and they hadn't learned the details about their Louisiana connection until they had seen my story.

Melissa told Jeremy that there was a family story about her ancestors' ties to a place called Algiers. She had long assumed that that meant her ancestors had originated in the city of Algiers in Algeria in northern Africa. By the time she was in college, though, she had begun to suspect that the Algiers described by her forebears was actually in New Orleans. A relative had stumbled across a mention of a slave sale to Louisiana, too, but Melissa had never seen any evidence that it had actually happened. Now she understood that her forebears had probably been describing the Algiers neighborhood of New Orleans, the place where enslaved people—perhaps including Anna and her children—were often held captive before being shipped off to the plantations that lined the Mississippi River.

Discovering that Louisa's sisters and brothers had been sold and that her ancestors' labor and the profits from the sale of their bodies had fueled the growth of the early Catholic Church and George-town University was deeply unsettling. "It hurts knowing this history," she told me.

Unlike Jeremy, Melissa had known since she was a child that her ancestors had been enslaved by the Jesuits. Louisa had passed her story down to her children and grandchildren, among whom was Gabriel Bennett, Melissa's great-great-grand-uncle. Melissa was close to a great-aunt who had researched the family's history, so she knew about Ann Joice and Harry Mahoney and his valor during the War of 1812. She knew that Louisa had been saved by a Jesuit priest and that she had remained in Maryland. She had assumed that the entire family had remained in Maryland, enslaved by the very priests who had tended to their souls.

Her ancestral line embodied the contradictions of that painful experience. On his one hundredth birthday, the *Community Times,* a local newspaper, recorded Gabriel Bennett's thoughts on his family's time in bondage, describing what he must have learned from his grandmother Louisa, who had helped care for him after his parents had died. "Slavery was really something; some people suffered some awful lashes," he said. "It was a terrible period. There's just nothing like freedom."

It may be surprising that he and the rest of Louisa's descendants hadn't cut their ties to a church that had owned them and sold off their family members. But Melissa told Jeremy that her ancestors had maintained their connections to the Jesuits. Their shared faith and their need for steady work meant that their lives had remained interwoven with the priests' long after slavery had ended.

Gabriel and his younger brother, Daniel, had spent their adult lives working for the Jesuits in the seminary at Woodstock, Maryland, one of the biggest employers in the area. Though he'd hoped to work as a carpenter, Gabriel had been sent to the seminary's cramped kitchen as soon as he arrived. "Teach him all the tricks of the trade," he recalled the Jesuits telling the Frenchman in charge. "He's going to be the new cook."

Daniel's son, Marshall, had also worked for the Jesuits, tending the chickens in the coop at the seminary. Four of Marshall's children had worked there, too, while Gladys Kemp, Marshall's daughter and Melissa's grandmother, had served as the Jesuits' housekeeper and cook at the rectory at nearby St. Alphonsus Church. "Most all the Black people in the neighborhood" worked there, Gladys recalled of the seminary. "My sister worked over there when they started letting women over there to work; she worked in the infirmary over there," said Gladys, who remained a faithful Catholic just like her parents, grandparents, and great-grandparents. "My husband, he worked over at Woodstock College for a couple of years also."

Melissa was an altar server for years, assisting the priests during Sunday Mass. Many of the Jesuits she knew had advanced degrees and encouraged her academic studies. She would become the first in her family to attend college and the first to earn a PhD. "I've always been—I guess I would say—proud of the relationship my family had with the Jesuits," said Melissa, who would become a biology professor at the University of Texas at Austin. "So much of my worldview has been shaped by the Catholic Church, more so than probably a lot of average Catholics, just because it's not only my worldview but the worldview of my grandmother, my mother, and everyone before that," she said. "We've always been connected to this order, ever since we've been in this country, and it's kind of amazing to have that connection."

But the relationship was complicated and strained at times and always framed by what Melissa described as the long-standing "power differential" between her family and the priests. Some of the Jesuits became very close to the family. Melissa's grandmother described a beloved priest who had played baseball with her children, taken Black families in the community on weekend outings, and "did everything he could to make the Black people feel welcome in the church."

But Gladys also remembered other priests who had insisted that the church remain segregated, that Black families sit "in the last six or eight pews" in the back of the church. "They had May processions for Black kids; they had May processions for the white kids," she said. "They had holy names out there for the Black people; they had holy names for the white people."

When her father had died unexpectedly, she said, the priests had offered her mother nothing for his long years of service even though she was suddenly alone with little recourse. "When he died, they told my mom that after all the years he worked there, 'This is your last paycheck. Don't expect nothing from us,'" Gladys recalled. "I was really hurt."

Still, Gladys remained steadfast in her faith. She made a point of pushing back against the segregation she had grown up with, and she taught her children, whom she raised in the Church, to do the same. "When I had my kids, I marched them all the way up front," she explained, describing her refusal to sit in the last pews once she became an adult. "I said, 'I'm not having you all grow up thinking you have to sit in the back seat.'"

It was in 1963, around the same time that Gladys was pushing back against segregation, that the Jesuits in Maryland began to address their history. Using the proceeds from the sale of a portion of the White Marsh plantation, they established the Carroll Fund for needy Black students as a way to quietly offer what one Jesuit described as "private and unrecognized restitution." Over the years, the fund provided between $15 million and $25 million in scholarships to Black students at Jesuit schools, Jesuit officials said. But some of the money went to unrelated purposes—some was sent to students in India—and the Jesuits kept the fund's origins to themselves.

By the time Gladys finally retired in 2011, the Mahoney family had served the Jesuits for more than two centuries. Melissa, Jeremy, and the growing community of descendants were beginning to think about what their families had lost and about what was owed them. Melissa knew that the Jesuits had provided scholarships at

Jesuit colleges for Black students. Some of her relatives had been beneficiaries. But neither she nor Jeremy knew at the time about the Carroll Fund, which the Jesuits liquidated, disbursing all of its funds to Jesuit schools, shortly after my first story ran. Was the fund quickly disbursed to prevent families from trying to lay claim to it? The Jesuits deny that, saying it was an administrative decision tied to the pending merger of two of the order's provinces, but some descendants wondered. Though many of the stories being published focused on the university, a group of the descendants was increasingly focusing their attention on the Jesuits.

In April 2017, when Georgetown and the Jesuits formally apologized for their role in the American slave trade, Jeremy and Melissa were there, along with nearly a hundred descendants of the enslaved. Jeremy participated in the liturgy, carrying a flickering candle into the hall where the ceremony was held. "May our endeavors begin to restore the dignity of those from whom it was taken," he said as he stood before the crowd and read a passage from "Intercession for Hope." "May those who were counted as little be counted as much, and may their lives be an abiding testimony to these efforts."

And when the apology finally came, Jeremy felt deeply moved.

"Today the Society of Jesus, who helped to establish Georgetown University and whose leaders enslaved and mercilessly sold your ancestors, stands before you to say that we have greatly sinned," Father Timothy Kesicki, the then-president of the Jesuit Conference of Canada and the United States, said during the ceremony at Georgetown. "We pray with you today because we have greatly sinned and because we are profoundly sorry."

Afterward, Jeremy said, he sought Father Kesicki out and thanked him. "I never expected to hear a white person say they were sorry for enslaving my family," Jeremy said. "To hear Father Tim, to hear him go up and say, 'It was our fault, our fault, our most grievous fault,' and the way he did it through the prayer, the Act of Contrition, I felt it was truly sincere."

Still, Georgetown and the Jesuits, who were grappling with the emergence of a number of descendant groups, hadn't moved on the GU272 Descendant Association's idea to create a $1 billion foundation to address the needs of the growing community. So in May 2017, the leaders of the association decided to make its case to Rome. One month after the reconciliation ceremony at Georgetown, Joseph M. Stewart, a founding member of the association, and Cellini hammered out a letter to the leader of the Jesuit order worldwide, calling for formal negotiations.

"For eight months, we descendants of the GU272 enslaved people sold in 1838 have humbly, respectfully and repeatedly requested meaningful engagement from the Maryland Province, the Central & Southern Province, and Georgetown University," wrote Stewart, a retired corporate executive whose ancestors were sold in 1838. "We have literally been ignored." Stewart, who had served as senior vice president of corporate affairs for the Kellogg Company and chairman of the board of the Kellogg Foundation, urged Rome to intervene, arguing that the Church's values had been "gravely compromised" by the Jesuits' "willful destruction of the innocent and humble lives of our ancestors." "The effects of the impact of slavery on our ancestors continue to manifest themselves in the lives of descendants until this day," he wrote, "and will persist far into the future."

A month later, the Reverend Arturo Sosa, the superior general of the order, wrote back. In his letter, Father Sosa described Jesuit slaveholding as "a sin against God and a betrayal of the human dignity of your ancestors." "I have great concern for this tragic history and its continuing legacy two centuries later," he wrote.

Father Sosa called for a dialogue between Jesuits in the United States and descendants of the enslaved. The descendants would finally have a chance to sit across the table from the Jesuits and represent their ancestors as they helped to determine how the Catholic Church should make amends for enslaving their forebears and breaking their families apart.

In August of that year, Father Kesicki flew to Michigan to meet with Stewart and his wife, Clara. He blessed their home. Then the two men sat down for a conversation that would lay the groundwork for their negotiations. That fall, the first descendants admitted to Georgetown under the new legacy program—including two of Sandra's children—took their seats in the university's classrooms. University officials continued working with the Jesuits and working on their own plans, contending with a growing number of descendant groups with different goals and objectives. Meanwhile, members of the growing descendant community continued to organize and to connect.

In June 2018, Melissa and Jeremy flew to Louisiana to visit Iberville parish, where Anna and her siblings Bibiana and Robert had been enslaved for a time. They were joined by hundreds of descendants from across the country—including some with ancestral ties to the Mahoneys—in what most believed to be the largest family reunion since the 1838 sale.

Joyous and tearful, the descendants gathered at the North Iberville Community Center, where they embraced newfound relatives and shared memories and family lore. Jeremy and his son, along with Melissa and her husband, Jeremy Dorn, joined the families on a bus tour of Maringouin and Donaldsonville, where they saw Anna's name in the courthouse records describing Henry Johnson's plantation. Many attended a church service at Immaculate Heart of Mary Church, where some of the people sold by the Jesuits had once prayed. "It makes this whole history of slavery more real," Melissa said.

But even as the descendants celebrated their newfound family connections, they wanted to know when Georgetown and the Jesuits would offer more concrete reparations to a community that now numbered about six thousand people.

In April 2019, a group of Georgetown students, including some descendants of the 272, who had been pressing the administration to take action, voted for a resolution to impose student fees that would raise $400,000 a year for descendants. Six months later, the administration announced that it would raise that amount each year—without relying on student fees—to support community projects such as health clinics and schools that would benefit the descendants.

By that time, there was a growing wave of American institutions attempting to offer a measure of restitution for their involvement in slavery. More than a dozen universities were investigating their history, and two seminaries had recently announced plans to provide restitution. The Princeton Theological Seminary said that it would spend $27 million on scholarships and other initiatives to make amends; the Virginia Theological Seminary had pledged $1.7 million a month earlier. (In 2018, the Catholic sisters of the Society of the Sacred Heart, who had owned about 150 Black people, had created a reparations fund to finance scholarships for African Americans at their school in Grand Coteau, Louisiana.) Georgetown had been working with the Jesuits and descendants behind the scenes and was continuing those efforts to help the two sides come to an agreement. None of that was public, yet. But its own announcement was a milestone, marking the first time that a major American university had pledged to create a fund to atone for its role in the slave trade.

Craig Steven Wilder, a historian at MIT who has written extensively about universities and their ties to slavery, told me that "it's important because the conversation about institutional obligations to the descendants of the enslaved typically gets confined to a discussion of research and fact-finding." "It's the religious institutions that have started to lay out a path from there toward restorative justice," he added. "It's much harder for religious institutions to be silent on the moral implications of their own history."

Meanwhile, Jeremy, Melissa, and the other descendants were waiting to see how the Jesuits planned to respond to their call for action. After Rome called for dialogue, three descendant leaders, Stewart, Cheryllyn Branche, and Earl Williams, Sr., had taken the lead in the private negotiations with representatives from both the Jesuits and Georgetown. At last, in March 2021, they had an agreement.

The Jesuits said they would raise $100 million to benefit the descendants of the enslaved people it had once owned and to promote racial reconciliation initiatives across the United States. It was the largest effort by the Roman Catholic Church to make amends for the buying, selling, and enslavement of Black people in the United States. The money raised by the Jesuits would flow into a new foundation established in partnership with a group of descendants, Stewart and Kesicki announced. Roughly half of the foundation's annual budget would be distributed as grants to organizations engaging in racial reconciliation projects, they said. About a quarter of the budget would support educational opportunities for descendants in the form of scholarships and grants. A smaller portion would address the emergency needs of descendants who are old or infirm.

Father Kesicki said his order had already deposited $15 million into a trust established to support the foundation, whose governing board would include representatives from other institutions with roots in slavery. The Jesuits also hired a national fundraising firm with the goal of raising the rest within the next three to five years, he said. Georgetown, which currently holds a seat on the board of the foundation, had contributed $1 million to help get it off the ground.

The pledge fell far short of the $1 billion that descendant leaders had called for. But Kesicki and Stewart, the acting president of the newly created Descendants Truth & Reconciliation Foundation, said that the $1 billion figure would remain a long-term goal. "We now have a pathway forward that has not been traveled before," Stewart said.

Descendants greeted the plan with mixed emotions. Kevin Porter, an archivist, initially praised it as "an unprecedented step toward repairing the injustice of slavery." But he grew increasingly concerned about setting so much money aside for racial healing initiatives at the expense of other needs. "I wish there was more programming to benefit mental health, financial literacy and education, things that could empower African-Americans," he said.

Other descendants, including Melissa, Sandra, and Ronda Thompson, raised concerns that the deal had been negotiated in a series of private meetings without input from the wider descendant community and that Stewart and his partners had led the Jesuits to believe that they represented far more descendants than they actually did. (Stewart told me that a statement he had made in a signed agreement with the Jesuits, declaring that his group represented "a majority of descendants," reflected his hope that his organization would ultimately become a home for most descendants, not the group's actual membership.)

It is hard to know what will come of the two plans, the one announced by Georgetown and the other by the Jesuits, and what kind of impact they might have. Georgetown's plan to begin disbursing money was delayed, at least in part, by the COVID-19 pandemic that swept the nation in 2020. In the fall of 2022, Dr. DeGioia announced that the university planned to start distributing the annual grants for community projects intended to benefit the descendant community during the 2022–2023 academic year. Meanwhile, fundraising for the new foundation, which is expected to be up and running by 2026, had fallen far short of expectations by the summer of 2022, Father Kesicki told me.

"We still have to wait and see," Jeremy said of the initiatives.

But as he walks to work through Georgetown's leafy campus, Jeremy remains keenly aware of how much has changed. He feels the presence of his ancestors now, he said, and he feels confident that Louisa, Anna, and the others are guiding the descendants as they work to repair what was broken and reunite the families that the Jesuits tore apart. "It has been a spiritual journey," he said. "The ancestors want us back together."

Some descendants gather each week on Zoom. Others talk regularly by phone and share jokes on group chats. They share memories over meals at local restaurants and swap family stories and photographs across dining room tables. Jeremy and his wife, Leslie, and son, Jesse, attended Melissa's wedding, and he has grown close to some of his newfound cousins.

Some people ask Jeremy whether the revelations about Jesuit slaveholding have shaken his faith. He always shakes his head. If anything, it has deepened his connection. He knows now, and the nation knows, that his enslaved ancestors helped build the college where he works and the very foundations of the Catholic Church in America—his church. The people who labored there are no longer invisible, no longer forgotten. "We can call them by name," he said.

Acknowledgments

In January 2016, I received an email from a colleague at *The New York Times*. She told me that she had received a note from a corporate executive she knew, who happened to be an alumnus of Georgetown University. He was pitching a story about an 1838 slave sale that had benefited the college.

My colleague Louise Story was intrigued. She remembered that I had done archival research for my book *American Tapestry*, which had chronicled the lives of Michelle Obama's enslaved ancestors. So she forwarded the email to me to see if I thought it might lead to a story. I took one look at the email and I knew. My work on Michelle Obama's family had allowed me to explore how slavery had shaped American families. This story would allow me to take the next step, to explore how slavery had shaped American institutions. Weeks later, I was on a plane to Baton Rouge.

I will always be grateful to Louise for setting me on this path and to the many others who helped along the way.

My editors at *The New York Times,* Dean Baquet, Marc Lacey, and Michael Luo, gave me the space and encouragement to spend time digging into the nineteenth century. I want to thank Mike in particular, who didn't think I was crazy when I told him that exploring the connections between slavery and contemporary institutions could be an important line of coverage for the *Times.* Such reporting was quite rare back then, but he supported me and championed my work and I will always be grateful for that.

Flip Brophy, my agent, emailed me the day that my first story about the 1838 slave sale appeared in the *Times.* I will always be grateful for her support. Julie Grau acquired my book for Spiegel & Grau, and Hilary Redmon inherited it and brought me to Random House. Hilary is a wonderful editor, and I am grateful to her and her team for treating my manuscript with such care.

Richard J. Cellini is the corporate executive who contacted Louise. He was the one who asked: What happened to the people who were sold and their descendants? When no one could give him an answer, he built a nonprofit, the Georgetown Memory Project, to find out. None of this would have been possible without him and his team of amazing researchers, Judy Riffel and Malissa Ruffner. They got me started on the first story and have generously shared their ongoing research with me ever since. Judy also introduced me to Jari Honora, who helped me explore the lives of the Mahoney descendants in Louisiana in the early twentieth century.

Pamela Newkirk at New York University reached out to me just as I was getting started on this project and encouraged me to apply for a position on the faculty in the journalism department. I am so happy that she did. The department chairs—Perri Klass, Ted Conover, and Stephen Solomon—have championed me and my work. And the faculty, administrators, and staffers—too many to thank by name—have provided invaluable support and a welcoming and vibrant intellectual community. I feel blessed to work among such wonderful colleagues.

I completed this work over the course of seven years, and several organizations provided me with fellowships, grants, and other support that allowed me to focus on my research and writing. Darren Walker of the Ford Foundation was the first person to offer me a grant to support this project, telling me that I was writing a story that needed to be told. Arcelio Aponte at Rutgers University–Newark provided me with a quiet, comfortable office in the School of Public Administration. The Open Society Foundation selected me as one of the recipients of its inaugural Equality fellowship program, a program that pushed me to expand my vision of my work and myself. Many thanks to Alvin Starks, Andrew Maisel, and Shirley McAlpine and to the fellows in my cohort. NYU's Center for the Humanities, run by the amazing Ulrich Baer and Molly Rogers, gave me a respite from teaching, an amazing community of fellows, and invaluable feedback on my fledgling manuscript. The program also introduced me to Nicholas Boggs, a wonderful writer, thinker, and friend, who stuck with me long after the fellowship ended.

NYU's Office of Global Diversity, Inclusion and Strategic Innovation provided me with research grants and I will always be grateful to Lisa M. Coleman and Karen Jackson-Weaver for their support. The Sustainable Arts Foundation, which supports artists and writers with children, provided a grant that came just at the right time. The Biographers International Organization awarded me the inaugural Frances "Frank" Rollin research grant, and I would like to thank Eric K. Washington, who chaired that awards committee. Kai Bird and Thad Ziolkowski at the Leon Levy Center for Biography provided me with a yearlong fellowship, a wonderful community of fellows, and invaluable feedback as my manuscript was taking shape. They also connected me to Edward Charnley, a PhD student who provided much needed research assistance that year. MacDowell gave me a magical place to breathe, think, and write. It was at that writing retreat that my manuscript finally came together. And the National Endowment for the Humanities awarded me a Public Scholar grant, which helped me across the finish line.

Archival research is impossible without the assistance of expert archivists and librarians, and I remain indebted to the staff at a number of collections, including the Maryland State Archives, the National Archives, the Maryland Center for History and Culture, the Associated Archives of St. Mary's Seminary and University, the Oblate Sisters of Providence Archives, the Library of Virginia, the New York Historical Society, the Notarial Archives Research Center of Louisiana, the Archives of the Archdiocese of New Orleans, the Archives and Records Center of the Diocese of Baton Rouge, the Hill Memorial Library at Louisiana State University, the Cammie G. Henry Research Center at Northwestern State University, the courthouse archives in Ascension and St. James parishes in Louisiana, the Rubenstein Library at Duke University, the Mississippi Department of Archives & History, and the Irish Jesuit Archives in Dublin, to name a few. Edward O'Laughlin visited the Irish Jesuit Archives for me and pulled records that helped me illuminate the 1830s.

Mary Beth Corrigan and Lynn Conway at the Booth Family Center for Special Collections at Georgetown's Lauinger Library served as wonderful guides as I navigated the voluminous records of the Maryland Province Archives that document Jesuit slaveholding and other records related to the many priests tied to this history. Adam Rothman's digital archive—the Georgetown Slavery Archive—has been an invaluable resource for me and for many researchers. Adrian Vaagenes at the Woodstock Theological Library pointed me to records that offered insight into the Mahoney family in Maryland after the Civil War. Clifton Theriot at the Ellender Memorial Library at Nicholls State University shared documents that provided insights into Henry Johnson's life and slaveholdings before 1838. And Brett Landry at the Ascension parish courthouse helped me to find the records documenting Henry Johnson's business dealings and slave sales, and fielded phone calls from me after I got back home.

Tom Shroder read every word of my manuscript, and I am tremendously grateful for his time and feedback. Several historians also took the time to read and comment on my manuscript, or sections of it, and I benefited enormously from their expertise. Many thanks to Steven Hahn at New York University, Adam Rothman at Georgetown, Joshua D. Rothman at the University of Alabama, William G. Thomas, III, at the University of Nebraska, and James O'Toole at Boston College.

Special thanks to Molly Thacker, who spent five years with me, off and on, as a research assistant while she completed her doctorate in history at Georgetown. She pulled documents for me, did research, transcribed spidery nineteenth-century script, and read the entire manuscript from top to bottom. She is smart, dogged, and thoughtful, and her students are lucky to have her. Molly was one of several Georgetown students who aided with research, including Tom Foley, Cory Young, Emily Norweg, Tiana Mobley, and Greg Beaman, and I am grateful to them all. At NYU, Emilia Otte dug into Henry Johnson's congressional voting record, and Rebecca Blandon pored over slave narratives. I am grateful to them and to Lisa Rogers and Laura Lee Huttenbach, who also provided research assistance. Maya Shoukri went over every footnote and citation and I want to thank her for her time and attention to detail.

Many of the descendants of the people enslaved by the Jesuits shared their memories and family stories and the documents that they have collected over the years about their families, and I deeply appreciate their time and generosity. I want to offer special thanks to Maxine Crump, Patricia Bayonne Johnson, and Sandra Green Thomas, who were among the first descendants to share their stories with me, and to Melissa Kemp and Jeremy Alexander, the descendants of Louisa and Anna.

This is a book about family, and I could not have done this work, through the darkest days of the pandemic, without my own family. My husband, Henri Cauvin, and my boys, Gabriel and Julian, have been on this journey with me from the very beginning. None of this would be possible without them. I would not be who I am without the love and wisdom of my parents, Joseph and Lucille Swarns, and the companionship of my sisters, Christina and Jessica Swarns. Anne Cauvin, my mother-in-law, and J. L. Cauvin, my brother-in-law, helped us in so many ways, and I am particularly grateful for the time they spent with our younger son while I worked. Louis Cauvin, my father-in-law, and John McBrien, my uncle-in-law, passed away while I was working on this project. I will always be thankful for their love and support. I am also so very grateful for my friends. Evelyn Larrubia, Frenchie Robles, and

Marjorie Valbrun were here long before this book and will be there long after. Lynette Clemetson and Dana Canedy pushed me to take this project on and cheered me on and held me up. Yvonne Latty kept me going during the hardest of these tumultuous times and keeps me going still.

Ann Joice and Louisa Mahoney Mason were long gone when I started this project. They left behind no letters or journals to guide the people who followed them. But it was their determination to keep their legacy alive across the generations that made this book possible. It has been a privilege to tell their family's story.

Notes

Abbreviations

ABA   Archdiocese of Baltimore Archives, St. Mary's Seminary and University, Baltimore

ARSI   Archivum Romanum Societatis Iesu, Roman Jesuit Archives

BJA   British Jesuit Archives & Collections, London

GSA   The Georgetown Slavery Archive, http://slaveryarchive .georgetown.edu

GUL   Booth Family Center for Special Collections, Georgetown University Library, Washington, DC

IJA   Irish Jesuit Archives, Dublin, Ireland

MDAH   Mississippi Department of Archives and History, Jackson, MS

MPA   Maryland Province Archives of the Society of Jesus, Booth Family Center for Special Collections, Georgetown University Library, Washington, DC

MSA   Maryland State Archives, Annapolis, MD

NARA   National Archives and Records Administration, Washington, DC

Prologue

xiii *He was looking forward:* Interviews with Jeremy Alexander in person on July 10, 2017, and by phone on June 23, 2021, and May 19, 2022.

xiii *272 men, women, and children:* Rachel L. Swarns, "272 Slaves Were Sold to Save Georgetown. What Does It Owe Their Descendants?," *New York Times,* April 16, 2016, https://www.nytimes.com/2016/04/17 /us/georgetown-university-search-for-slave-descendants.html.

xiv *were probably his ancestors:* Telephone interviews with Melissa Kemp on September 3, 2016, May 17, 2017, and August 25, 2022.

xiv *Richard had become interested:* Multiple telephone interviews with Richard Cellini during the first four months of 2016, starting on January 7, 2016.

xiv *established a working group:* Swarns, "272 Slaves Were Sold to Save Georgetown."

xv *leaving no descendants:* Email from John Glavin, professor of English, Georgetown University, to Richard Cellini, November 16, 2015. Glavin said he had assigned students a research project a few years earlier to see if descendants could be found. "The best available evidence suggests that, used to the more temperate climate of Maryland, and the kind-ish oversight of the somewhat feckless Jesuits, almost all of them immediately succumbed to the hostile climate and the harsh labor conditions into which they were so suddenly and cruelly submitted." Glavin, who was listed among the working group members in November 2015, resigned from the group and was not mentioned in the group's final report. "Working Group Statement and Recommendations," Georgetown University, November 2015, https://president.georgetown.edu/update-on-slavery-memory-and-reconciliation-november-2015/#. "Report of the Working Group on Slavery, Memory and Reconciliation," Summer 2016, Georgetown University, https://georgetown.app.box.com/s/nz01tx4elaerg13akjwxuve3pv9sbo3a.

xv *University officials say:* Meghan Dubyak, Georgetown's associate vice president for strategic communications, interview with author, February 13, 2023.

xv *a short companion piece:* "Do You Think You Might Have a Connection to the 1838 Slave Sale That Kept Georgetown Afloat?," *New York Times,* April 16, 2016.

xv *Today, the Catholic Church:* U.S. Religion Census 2020, Association of Statisticians of American Religious Bodies, November 2022, https://www.usreligioncensus.org/node/1639; Center for Applied Research in the Apostolate, "Church Statistics, U.S. Data Over Time," 2022; David Masci and Gregory A. Smith, "Facts About U.S. Catholics," Pew Research Center, https://www.pewresearch.org/fact-tank/2018/10/10/7-facts-about-american-catholics/.

xvi *For more than a century:* The earliest known documentation of Jesuit slaveholding appears in 1717. The Jesuits continued to own and rent enslaved people until 1864. Deed of Gift between William Hunter and Thomas Jameson, Box 27, Folder 2, MPA. MSA, "Louise Mason and Her Children: The Last People Enslaved by the Maryland Jesuits," GSA, http://slaveryarchive.georgetown.edu/items/show/77. Robert Emmett Curran described how the plantations supported the Jesuits and their mission in *Shaping American Catholicism: Maryland and New York, 1805–1915* (Washington, DC: Catholic University of America Press, 2012), 32, and *The Bicentennial History of Georgetown University,* vol. 1: *From Academy to University, 1789–1889* (Washington, DC: Georgetown University Press, 1993), 112.

xvi *drive its expansion:* Sharon M. Leon, an associate professor of history and digital humanities at Michigan State University, who has studied the people enslaved by the Jesuits, estimates that the Jesuits enslaved about 1,150 people between 1715 and 1838.

xvi *the nation's first Catholic college:* Thomas Murphy, *Jesuit Slaveholding in Maryland, 1717–1838* (New York: Routledge, 2016), 37. Joseph Zwinge,

"The Jesuit Farms in Maryland, Facts and Anecdotes," *Woodstock Letters* 42, no. 1 (1913): 9. Working Group on Slavery, Memory, and Reconciliation, *Report of the Working Group on Slavery, Memory, and Reconciliation to the President of Georgetown University* (Washington, DC: Georgetown University, 2016), 12. In his PhD dissertation, Peter C. Finn described the critical role that the plantations played in providing the necessary financing for the establishment of the college, summarizing: "Without the financial aid of the Jesuit farms during those crucial early years of its history, Archbishop John Carroll's dream of establishing and maintaining a Catholic university in the new United States of America might never have been realized in his lifetime." "The Slaves of the Jesuits in Maryland," PhD dissertation, Georgetown University, 1974, 33.

xvi *the first archdiocese:* As early as 1794, the profits from the plantations were used to support John Carroll, the nation's first Catholic bishop. In February of that year, the Corporation of Roman Catholic Clergymen agreed to use the money raised from the estates to pay the bishop £210—roughly $32,488.52 in today's dollars—per year. Corporation of Roman Catholic Clergymen, minutes, Box 24, Folder 3, MPA. Conversion from pounds to dollars from Eric W. Nye, "Pounds Sterling to Dollars: Historical Conversion of Currency," University of Wyoming, https://www.uwyo.edu/numimage/currency.htm.

xvi *the first Catholic cathedral:* Thomas Hughes, *History of the Society of Jesus in North America, Colonial and Federal, 1605–1838,* vol. 1 (Cleveland: Burrows Brothers, 1908), 320–24.

xvi *establish two of the earliest Catholic monasteries:* Edward Devitt, "History of the Maryland–New York Province: St. Inigoes, St. Mary's County, Maryland, 1634–1915," *Woodstock Letters* 60, no. 3 (1931): 355; Susan Nalezyty, "The History of Enslaved People at Georgetown Visitation," *U.S. Catholic Historian* 37, no. 2 (2019): 23; Joseph G. Mannard, " 'We Are Determined to Be White Ladies': Race, Identity and the Maryland Tradition in Antebellum Visitation Convents," *Maryland Historical Magazine* 109, no. 2 (Summer 2014): 143.

xvi *The priests prayed for the salvation of the souls:* Deed of Gift from William Hunter to Thomas Jameson, January 30, 1717, Box 27, Folder 2, MPA.

xvi *The 1838 slave sale:* Adam Rothman, a historian at Georgetown and member of the university's working group that examined the 1838 sale and the history of Jesuit slaveholding, said, "The university itself owes its existence to this history." Swarns, "272 Slaves Were Sold to Save Georgetown."

xvi *helped stabilize the Jesuits:* Colleges that were built with financial support from the Maryland Jesuits include Holy Cross in Worcester, Massachusetts, and Loyola University Maryland in Baltimore: Annual Reports, Finances of the Province 1803–1893 [196B], MPA Additional

Materials, pre-1864, Box 3. The Maryland Jesuits expenditures on Holy Cross can be found on pages 31, 55, and 273; Loyola Maryland, 59, 60, 282, 286. A spokeswoman for Holy Cross said that accounting books in the college's archives describe student tuition and "other sources" as sources of revenue for this period. No explanation is provided for what the "other sources" were. Nicoleta Jordan, assistant director of media relations, Holy Cross, email message to author, January 27, 2023. The Maryland Jesuits also provided support to the school that would become known as St. Louis University in Missouri; the Washington Seminary, known today as Gonzaga College High School in Washington, DC, and Georgetown Preparatory School, a private Catholic high school in North Bethesda, Maryland.

Information on these institutions and their roots in slavery can be found here: St. Louis University in Missouri: "What We Have Learned: Missouri," Jesuit Conference of Canada and the United States, https://www.jesuits.org/our-work/shmr/what-we-have-learned/missouri/.

Gonzaga College High School: "Searching for Truth in the Garden: Gonzaga's History with Slavery," Gonzaga College High School, 2019, https://www.gonzaga.org/about/history/slavery-research-project.

Georgetown Preparatory School: "Endowment of Tears, Hope for Reconciliation: Georgetown Prep and Slavery," Georgetown Preparatory School, 2020, https://www.gprep.org/about/history.

The Maryland Jesuits also offered assistance to colleges that did not receive direct financial support from the province. They also helped to supply Jesuits who assumed senior positions in emerging institutions, and trained priests and seminarians who served as teachers and leaders at newly established colleges, including Fordham in New York, St. Joseph's in Philadelphia, Boston College, and Santa Clara in Santa Clara, California: Fordham: Ledger 1839–1864, 191A, 49–50, Box 1, Additional Materials, pre-1864, MPA.

St. Joseph's: The college's first presidents, Felix Barbelin, James A. Ward, and James Ryder. For information on Barbelin and Ryder: *Biographical Information about Maryland Province Members,* Lauinger Library, Georgetown University, 3, 5, https://library.georgetown.edu/sites/default/files/Biographical%20Information%20about%20Maryland%20Province%20Members%20and%20Other%20Jesuits.xlsx%20-%20Sheet1_0.pdf. For information on Ward, "James A. Ward, A Sketch," *Woodstock Letters* 25, no. 3 (October 1, 1896).

Boston College: Boston College's founder, Father John McElroy, both ministered to and educated Black people and was involved in their enslavement during his time at Georgetown and in Maryland. Father Robert Fulton, who was educated at Georgetown and taught there as well as at the Jesuit novitiate, became the college's first prefect of studies and its third president. Scholastics, or priests in formation, who were trained in Maryland, served as faculty in most of the new colleges, often moving from one to another, according to the needs of the time. One of the Maryland province's financial ledgers includes a list of the province's debts, including $22,000 owed to Boston College in 1869. The list offers no additional details. It remains unclear what the Maryland Jesuits had pledged to cover with that amount or whether Boston College ever received that money. Officials at Boston College say there is no evidence that the college received any financial support from the province. Maryland State Archives, "Runaway ad for Isaac, 1814," GSA, accessed February 15, 2023, http://slaveryarchive.georgetown.edu/items /show/51; Maryland Province Archives, "I overvalue her: Fr. McElroy disputes the price of slaves sold to Louisiana, February 18, 1840," GSA, accessed February 15, 2023, http://slaveryarchive.georgetown.edu/items /show/381; "Fulton, Father Robert, A Sketch," *Woodstock Letters* 25 (1896): 92–96; James M. O'Toole, *Ever to Excel: A History of Boston College* (Chestnut Hill, MA: Institute of Jesuit Sources, Boston College, 2021), 29–35, 46–47, 50; Curran, *The Bicentennial History of Georgetown,* Vol. 1, 130; List of Debts, December 31, 1869, Annual Reports, Finances of the Province 1803–1893 [196B], 357, Box 3, MPA; Jack Dunn, associate vice president, university spokesman for Boston College, interview with author, February 16, 2023; Seth Meehan, associate director of academic programs and special projects, Boston College Libraries, email message to author, February 16, 2023.

Santa Clara: Early presidents, Felix Cicaterri and Aloysious Masnata, *The University of Santa Clara: A History from the Founding of Santa Clara Mission in 1777 to the Beginning of the University in 1912* (Santa Clara, CA: University of Santa Clara, 1912) 23. More than a dozen priests and seminarians assigned to the California mission were trained by the Maryland Jesuits between 1854 and 1863. Some were already members of the faculty at Santa Clara; some would join the faculty after their training: Ledger 1839–1864, 191A, 111–114, 152–154, Box 1, Additional Materials, pre-1864, MPA. Jesuits based west of the Mississippi River, who also relied on slave labor, ran schools in Kentucky, Alabama, Louisiana, Illinois, Kansas, and Ohio, including Xavier College in Cincinnati, Ohio: "What We Have Learned: Missouri," Jesuit Conference of Canada and the United States, https://www.jesuits.org/our-work/shmr/what-we -have-learned/missouri/. Ohio was a free state so the Jesuits could not enslave people in Cincinnati. But a report published online by Xavier documents how the college's Jesuit administrators and faculty benefited financially from slaveholding: "Xavier's Historical Connections to Slavery," Xavier College, University Archives and Special Collections, https://libguides.xavier.edu/archives/historical-connections-slavery.

xvi *Their stories are rarely recounted:* As recently as 2020, the Catholic Conference of Bishops made no mention of slavery in its "History of the Catholic Church in the United States" page on its website, June 10, 2020, http://web.archive.org/web/20200610105839/http://www.usccb

.org:80/about/public-affairs/backgrounders/history-catholic-church
-united-states.cfm.

xvii *first arrived in Maryland:* Witnesses testified that Ann Joice arrived from
England with Charles Calvert, Lord Baltimore, who took up his posi-
tion as proprietor in 1676, in this court case: Charles Mahoney v. John
Ashton, Court of Appeals, Judgements. Description: A, June 1802,
No. 8, MdHR No. 683-2. S381-2, MSA. Ann Joice's arrival and en-
slavement are also described in the following texts: Eric Robert
Papenfuse, "From Recompense to Revolution: Mahoney v. Ashton
and the Transfiguration of Maryland Culture, 1791–1802," *Slavery &
Abolition* 15, no. 3 (December 1994): 38–62, https://doi.org/10.1080
/01440399408575138; William G. Thomas, *A Question of Freedom: The
Families Who Challenged Slavery from the Nation's Founding to the Civil
War* (New Haven, CT: Yale University Press, 2020).

xvii *Denied literacy:* "Legacy of Slavery in Maryland," Maryland State Archives, http://slavery.msa.maryland.gov/html/research/frequently-asked
-questions.html; Peter Kolchin, *American Slavery, 1619–1877,* 10th anni-
versary edition (New York: Hill and Wang, 2003), 128. The 1870 census described both Louisa and Anna as illiterate.

xvii *The elders passed their story:* Miriam Otterbein, "Born of Slave Parents,
100-Year-Old Woodstock Man Lauds Freedom," *Community Times,* August 10, 1972. Telephone interviews with Melissa Kemp, descendant of
Louisa Mahoney, September 3, 2016, May 17, 2017, and August 25,
2022.

Chapter 1: Arrivals

3 *The ship:* William McSherry, Andrew White, and N. C. Brooks, *A Relation of the Colony of the Lord Baron of Baltimore, in Maryland, near Virginia: A Narrative of the Voyage to Maryland* (Washington, DC: W. Q. Force,
1846).

3 *There were some 140 souls on board:* Raymond A. Schroth, *The American Jesuits: A History* (New York: New York University Press, 2007), 21.

3 *men and women, noblemen and indentured servants:* Robert Emmett
Curran, *Papist Devils: Catholics in British America, 1574–1783* (Washington, DC: Catholic University of America Press, 2014), 33.

3 *"I had scarcely ended":* McSherry et al., *A Relation of the Colony of the
Lord Baron of Baltimore,* 11.

3 *The Ark stopped at:* Curran, *Papist Devils: Catholics in British America,*
33.

4 *Disembarking, the voyagers found:* McSherry et al., *A Relation of the Colony of the Lord Baron of Baltimore,* 6–7.

4 *"We erected it":* Ibid., 19.

4 *They had been sent:* Curran, *Papist Devils,* 29.

4 *faced a raft of harsh restrictions:* Ibid., 4–9.

4 *impoverished white men:* Ibid., 40.

4 *Lord Baltimore would allocate:* Schroth, *The American Jesuits: A History*, 24.

4 *Father White brought somewhere:* Curran, *Papist Devils*, 33.

4 *"We had not come thither":* McSherry et al., *A Relation of the Colony of the Lord Baron of Baltimore*, 20.

4 *Four of the first fourteen priests . . . returned to England:* James J. Hennesey, *American Catholics: A History of the Roman Catholic Community in the United States* (Oxford, UK: Oxford University Press, 1983), 41.

5 *Among them was Ann Joice:* Charles Mahoney v. John Ashton, Court of Appeals, Judgements, Description: A, June 1802, no. 8. MdHR no. 683-2, S381-2, MSA. Witnesses testified that Ann Joice arrived from England with Charles Calvert, Lord Baltimore, who took up his position as proprietor in 1676.

5 *She was a teenager:* Testimony of Henry Davis, Charles Mahoney v. John Ashton, Court of Appeals, Judgements, Description: A, June 1802, no. 8, MdHR no. 683-2, S381-2, MSA.

5 *Charles had become:* Curran, *Papist Devils*, 116.

5 *Maryland had become:* Ira Berlin, *Many Thousands Gone: The First Two Centuries of Slavery in North America* (Cambridge, MA: Belknap Press, 2003), 29–33.

5 *less than 1 percent:* Demetri D. Debe and Russell R. Menard, "The Transition to African Slavery in Maryland: A Note on the Barbados Connection," *Slavery & Abolition* 32, no. 1 (March 2011): 131, https://doi.org/10.1080/0144039X.2011.538203.

5 *the charter generations:* Berlin, *Many Thousands Gone*, 29.

6 *George Alsop:* George Alsop and Newton Dennison Mereness, *A Character of the Province of Maryland* (Cleveland: Burrows Brothers, 1902), 52–61.

6 *"Mathias Sousa, a Molato":* David S. Bogen, "Mathias de Sousa: Maryland's First Colonist of African Descent," *Maryland Historical Magazine* 96, no. 1 (Spring 2001): 68.

6 *Living as a free man:* Ibid., 75–77, 80.

6 *In 1641, Massachusetts became:* "African American Trail Project," A Project of the Center for Race and Democracy at Tufts University, https://africanamericantrailproject.tufts.edu/17th-century-sites.

6 *Connecticut followed in 1650:* Peter Hinks, "Enslaved Africans in the Colony of Connecticut," Citizens ALL: African Americans in Connecticut 1700–1850, Gilder Lehrman Center for the Study of Slavery, Resistance, and Abolition, Yale University, https://glc.yale.edu/sites/default/files/files/mod_1_digging_deeper.pdf.

7 *By 1664, Maryland had:* Debe and Menard, "The Transition to African Slavery in Maryland," 135.

7 *some even took their employers:* Ross Kimmel, "Blacks Before the Law in Colonial Maryland," MA thesis, University of Maryland, 1974,

Maryland State Archives, https://msa.maryland.gov/msa/speccol /sc5300/sc5348/html/chap4.html.

7 *Charles Calvert lived:* Maryland State Archives, "Archives of Maryland (A Biographical Series): Charles Calvert, 3rd Lord Baltimore (1637–1714/15)," March 12, 2010, https://msa.maryland.gov/megafile /msa/speccol/sc3500/sc3520/000100/000193/html/calvert.html.

7 *Some of the old-timers said:* Testimony of Ann Cooke, Charles Mahoney v. John Ashton, Court of Appeals, Judgements, Description: A, June 1802, no. 8, MdHR no. 683-2, S381-2, MSA.

7 *others described her as "jet black":* Testimony of Henry Davis, Charles Mahoney v. John Ashton, Court of Appeals, Judgements, Description: A, June 1802, no. 8, MdHR no. 683-2, S381-2, MSA.

7 *"a pretty woman":* Testimony of Anne Hurdle, Charles Mahoney v. John Ashton, Court of Appeals, Judgements, Description: A, June 1802, no. 8, MdHR no. 683-2, S381-2, MSA.

7 *Ann told her children:* Testimony of Peter Harbard, grandson of Ann Joice, Charles Mahoney v. John Ashton, Court of Appeals, Judgements, Description: A, June 1802, no. 8, MdHR no. 683-2, S381-2, MSA.

7 *Calvert sailed home to England:* Julia King, Syklar A. Bauer, and Alex J. Flick, "The Politics of Landscape in Seventeenth-Century Maryland," *Maryland Historical Magazine* 3, no. 1 (Spring–Summer 2016): 18.

7 *Colonel Henry Darnall:* Garrett Power, "Calvert Versus Carroll: The Quit-Rent Controversy Between Maryland's Founding Families," Digital Commons, March 30, 2005, https://digitalcommons.law.umaryland .edu/fac_pubs/44.

7 *Baptism or conversion to Christianity:* Kimmel, "Blacks Before the Law in Colonial Maryland."

7 *viewed Black people's few remaining work contracts:* Darnall was sued by two Black people who accused him of disregarding their work contracts and forcing them into slavery. Kimmel, "Blacks Before the Law in Colonial Maryland."

8 *imported bricks from England:* Swepson Earle, *The Chesapeake Bay Country* (Baltimore, MD: Thomsen-Ellis, 1924), 210, https://catalog .hathitrust.org/Record/001268416.

8 *he relied on enslaved laborers:* Darrin Lythgoe, "Henry Darnall, 1645–1711," Early Colonial Settlers of Southern Maryland and Virginia's Northern Neck Counties, https://www.colonial-settlers-md-va .us/getperson.php?personID=I2149&tree=Tree1.

8 *Darnall had other plans:* Ann Joice was not the only one to accuse Darnall of violating the terms of her indenture. Darnall was also sued by two other Black people who accused him of disregarding their work contracts and forcing them into slavery. Kimmel, "Blacks Before the Law in Colonial Maryland."

8 *set them on fire:* Testimony of Peter Harbard, grandson of Ann Joice, Charles Mahoney v. John Ashton, Court of Appeals, Judgements, Description: A, June 1802, no. 8, MdHR no. 683-2, S381-2, MSA.

8 *He did not say:* Ibid.

9 *By the late seventeenth century:* Berlin, *Many Thousands Gone,* 109.

9 *"Slaves, be obedient":* "Ephesians, Chapter 6," United States Conference of Catholic Bishops, https://bible.usccb.org/bible/ephesians/6.

9 *Many Catholics saw these passages:* Thomas Murphy, *Jesuit Slaveholding in Maryland, 1717–1838* (New York: Routledge, 2016), 96–97.

9 *Other defenders of slavery:* John T. Noonan, "Development in Moral Doctrine," *Theological Studies* 54, no. 4 (December 1993): 665, https://doi.org/10.1177/004056399305400404.

9 *In 1435, Pope Eugene IV:* John Francis Maxwell, *Slavery and the Catholic Church: The History of Catholic Teaching Concerning the Moral Legitimacy of the Institution of Slavery* (London: Barry Rose, 1975), 51.

9 *"Some of these people":* Pope Eugene IV, "Sicut Dudum Against the Enslaving of Black Natives from the Canary Islands," 1435, Papal Encyclicals Online, https://www.papalencyclicals.net/eugene04/eugene04sicut.htm.

10 *In 1452, the pope explicitly gave:* "Pope Nicolas V and the Portuguese Slave Trade," Lowcountry Digital History Initiative, https://ldhi.library.cofc.edu/exhibits/show/african_laborers_for_a_new_emp/pope_nicolas_v_and_the_portugu.

10 *In 1493, just one year:* "The Doctrine of Discovery, 1493: A Spotlight on a Primary Source by Pope Alexander VI," The Gilder Lehrman Institute of American History, https://www.gilderlehrman.org/history-resources/spotlight-primary-source/doctrine-discovery-1493.

10 *Thousands of Native Americans died:* Ibram X. Kendi, *Stamped from the Beginning: The Definitive History of Racist Ideas in America* (New York: Bold Type Books, 2016), 26.

10 *Father Bartolomé de las Casas:* Ibid., 26–27; David Thomas Orique, O.P., *Bartolomé de Las Casas, OP: History, Philosophy, and Theology in the Age of European Expansion* (Leiden, Netherlands: Brill, 2018), 426.

10 *European powers used:* Kendi, *Stamped from the Beginning,* 26–27.

10 *In 1537, Pope Paul III condemned:* Pope Paul III, "Sublimus Deus: On the Enslavement and Evangelization of Indians," 1537, Papal Encyclicals Online, https://www.papalencyclicals.net/paul03/p3subli.htm.

11 *The "entire population":* Kendi, *Stamped from the Beginning,* 27.

11 *Las Casas would come to publicly regret:* Ibid.

11 *It would become:* John W. O'Malley, *The First Jesuits* (Cambridge, MA: Harvard University Press, 1995), 5–6, 15.

11 *Its members would also defend:* Adam Rothman, "The Jesuits and Slavery," *Journal of Jesuit Studies* 8, no. 1 (December 15, 2020): 4–6, https://doi.org/10.1163/22141332-0801P001. Rothman pointed out that Baltasar Barreira, the Jesuit who traveled to Africa and became a prominent defender of the enslavement of Africans during that period, argued that Africans themselves had participated in the slave trade. Barreira also argued that Portugal was justified in taking slaves as "compensation" for misdeeds committed by Africans. Rothman noted that the Jesuits had

enslaved more than twenty thousand people in the Americas, mostly in Brazil and Peru, by the mid-1700s.

11 *"It seems that nothing":* Quoted in P.E.H. Hair, "A Jesuit Document on African Enslavement," *Slavery & Abolition* 19, no. 3 (December 1998): 125, https://doi.org/10.1080/01440399808575258. Hair also noted that the Jesuits enslaved people in Angola, 110.

11 *Rome once again condemned:* Maxwell, *Slavery and the Catholic Church,* 72.

11 *Ann Joice spent five or six months:* Testimony of Peter Harbard, grandson of Ann Joice, Charles Mahoney v. John Ashton, Court of Appeals, Judgements, Description: A, June 1802, no. 8, MdHR no. 683-2, S381-2, MSA.

12 *she became a mother:* Testimony of Henry Davis, Charles Mahoney v. John Ashton, Court of Appeals, Judgements, Description: A, June 1802, no. 8, MdHR no. 683-2, S381-2, MSA.

12 *"an elderly mulatto woman":* Testimony of Ann Cooke, Charles Mahoney v. John Ashton, Court of Appeals, Judgements, Description: A, June 1802, no. 8, MdHR no. 683-2, S381-2, MSA.

12 *She decided to tell her descendants:* Testimony of Anne Hurdle and Henry Davis, Charles Mahoney v. John Ashton, Court of Appeals, Judgements, Description: A, June 1802, no. 8, MdHR no. 683-2, S381-2, MSA.

12 *She would share it:* Testimony of Peter Harbard, Charles Mahoney v. John Ashton, Court of Appeals, Judgements, Description: A, June 1802, no. 8, MdHR no. 683-2, S381-2, MSA.

Chapter 2: A Church's Captives

13 *By the early 1700s:* Allan Kulikoff, *Tobacco and Slaves: The Development of Southern Cultures in the Chesapeake, 1680–1800* (Chapel Hill: University of North Carolina Press, 1986), 40–41; Geoffrey V. Scammell, *The First Imperial Age* (New York: Routledge, 2003), 96.

13 *The handwritten deed:* Deed of Gift from William Hunter to Thomas Jameson, Box 27, Folder 2, MPA.

14 *including Quakers for a time:* Katharine Gerbner, "Slavery in the Quaker World," Friends Journal, September 1, 2019, https://www.friendsjournal.org/slavery-in-the-quaker-world/.

14 *Having removed the Calverts:* Robert Emmett Curran, *Papist Devils: Catholics in British America, 1574–1783* (Washington, DC: Catholic University of America Press, 2014), 135–36.

14 *"all Irish Papist Servants":* Thomas Murphy, *Jesuit Slaveholding in Maryland, 1717–1838* (New York: Routledge, 2016), 22.

14 *The servant tax touched off fears:* Ibid., 35.

14 *Within six years:* Ibid.

14 *Maryland's Protestant leaders barred:* Curran, *Papist Devils,* 155, 166.

14 *the colony's wealthiest men:* Ibid., 154.

14 *Ann Joice's children and grandchildren:* Eric Robert Papenfuse, "From Recompense to Revolution: Mahoney v. Ashton and the Transfiguration of Maryland Culture, 1791–1802," *Slavery & Abolition* 15, no. 3 (December 1994): 39, https://doi.org/10.1080/01440399408575138.

15 *Two of his nephews became:* Murphy, *Jesuit Slaveholding in Maryland, 1717–1838*, 39.

15 *the first Catholic bishop:* Herbert Brewer, "From Sierra Leone to Annapolis: The 1718 Journey of the *Margaret,* an Eighteenth Century Slave Ship," GSA, 2018, 9, http://slaveryarchive.georgetown.edu/files/show /336.

15 *The Jesuits also inherited:* Charles M. Flanagan, "The Sweets of Independence: A Reading of the 'James Carroll Day Book, 1714–1721,'" PhD dissertation, University of Maryland, 2005, 405, https://drum.lib .umd.edu/bitstream/handle/1903/2456/umi-umd-2323.pdf?sequence =1&isAllowed=y.

15 *He listed twenty-seven:* Murphy, *Jesuit Slaveholding in Maryland, 1717–1838*, 39.

15 *In 1756, the Jesuits purchased:* Maryland Province Archives, "The Jesuits of Bohemia Purchase Tom, April 1756," GSA, http://slaveryarchive .georgetown.edu/items/show/267.

15 *Five years later:* Ibid.

15 *By the mid-1700s:* Sharon M. Leon, "Jesuit Slaveholding," Jesuit Plantation Project, 2019, https://jesuitplantationproject.org/s/jpp/page/sj -slaveholding.

15 *In an accounting:* Murphy, *Jesuit Slaveholding in Maryland, 1717–1838*, 45.

16 *In 1749, Father George Hunter:* Ibid., 17.

16 *They often required them:* Robert Emmett Curran, *Shaping American Catholicism: Maryland and New York, 1805–1915* (Washington, DC: Catholic University of America Press, 2012), 37.

16 *For their part, enslaved men and women:* Laura E. Masur, "A Spiritual Inheritance: Black Catholics in Southern Maryland," *International Symposia on Jesuit Studies,* no. 2019, Symposium (March 2021): 2.

16 *In West African traditions:* Ibid., 3–6.

16 *Of the roughly twenty:* Ibid., 6–8.

16 *But they surely found:* Ibid., 7–8.

16 *When one priest discovered:* Ibid., 6–9.

17 *West owned several stores:* Edward C. Papenfuse et al., "A Biographical Dictionary of the Maryland Legislature, 1635–1789," vol. 426, 879, https://msa.maryland.gov/megafile/msa/speccol/sc2900/sc2908 /000001/000426/html/am426--879.html.

17 *he also manufactured cloth:* Ibid.

17 *including Tom Crane:* "Annapolis," *New York Journal,* July 12, 1770.

17 *"They thought themselves above":* Deposition of Peter Knight, Mahoney v. Ashton, Judgement Record, June 25, 1802, 7, Court of Appeals, S381-2, MSA.

17 *One man described the brothers as:* Deposition of Henry Davis, Ma-

honey v. Ashton, Judgement Record, June 25, 1802, 8–9, Court of Appeals, S381-2, MSA.

17 *Tom was so fair skinned:* Deposition of John Wheat, Mahoney v. Ashton, Judgement Record, June 25, 1802, 5–6, Court of Appeals, S381-2, MSA.

17 *a newspaper would later report: The Maryland Gazette,* June 28, 1770, https://www.newspapers.com/clip/18559313/pg-county-william-elson-murder-stephen.

18 *Jack was charged with killing:* Lord Proprietary v. Negroes Jack Wood, Davy & Jack Crane, Indictment for Murder, June Court 1770, Prince George's (Maryland) County Court, CM780-33: 1768–1770, Book AA1, 589–90, MSA.

18 *all three men initially declared:* A True Bill, Isaac Sansdale foreman, June Court 1770, Prince George's County Court, CM780-33: 1768–1770, Book AA1, 590, MSA.

19 *On July 2, 1770:* Ibid.

19 *Then they were hanged:* "Hanged, Slaves by Date, 1726–1775," 10, Maryland State Archives, https://msa.maryland.gov/megafile/msa/speccol/sc2900/sc2908/000001/000819/pdf/chart28.pdf.

19 *"in the most public places":* A True Bill, Isaac Sansdale foreman, June Court 1770, Prince George's (Maryland) County Court, CM780-33: 1768–1770 (Book AA1), 590, MSA.

19 *In 1773, Pope Clement XIV:* Curran, *Papist Devils,* 240.

19 *which by then was running:* John W. O'Malley, *The First Jesuits* (Cambridge, MA: Harvard University Press, 1995), 16.

19 *The move came in response:* John T. McGreevy, *Catholicism: A Global History from the French Revolution to Pope Francis* (New York: W. W. Norton, 2022), 10–11.

19 *The suppression order left:* Curran, *Papist Devils,* 240.

20 *Most Catholics supported the Revolutionary War:* Ibid., 243–44.

20 *Charles Carroll of Carrollton:* Ibid., 154.

20 *His cousin Father John Carroll:* Ibid., 248.

20 *"the fullest & largest":* Robert Emmett Curran, *The Bicentennial History of Georgetown University,* vol. 1: *From Academy to University, 1789–1889* (Washington, DC: Georgetown University Press, 1993), 8.

20 *"The object nearest my heart":* Ibid., 9.

20 *That same year, Carroll successfully pressed:* Ibid.

20 *The priests who gathered:* Ibid.

21 *Father Patrick Smyth:* Patrick Smyth, *The Present State of the Catholic Mission Conducted by the Ex-Jesuits in North America* (Dublin: P. Byrne, 1788), 17–18.

21 *"Are they obliged to live":* Ibid.

21 *"Besides the advantage":* John Carroll, *The John Carroll Papers,* vol. 1: *1755–1791,* ed. Thomas O'Brian Hanley (Notre Dame, IN: University of Notre Dame Press, 1976), 337–45.

21 *By the time Smyth published:* Murphy, *Jesuit Slaveholding in Maryland, 1717–1838,* 69.

22 *"I think I am rendering":* Curran, *The Bicentennial History of Georgetown University,* vol. 1, 15, 24.

22 *"Amongst other difficulties":* Carroll, *The John Carroll Papers,* vol. 1, 243.

22 *Carroll, who would become:* Curran, *The Bicentennial History of Georgetown University,* vol. 1, 15–16.

22 *At a meeting with Carroll:* Thomas Hughes, *History of the Society of Jesus in North America, Colonial and Federal, 1605–1838,* vol. 2 (New York: Longmans, Green, 1910), 695.

22 *"That there being great danger":* Maryland Province Archives, "Proceeding of the General Chapter Met at the White Marsh, May 1789," GSA, http://slaveryarchive.georgetown.edu/items/show/36.

23 *The clergy directed:* Ibid.

23 *the profits generated:* Curran, *The Bicentennial History of Georgetown University,* vol. 1, 19.

23 *Even the salary:* Ibid.

23 *Fourteen months after:* Maryland Province Archives, "The sale of Nell and Her Son Perry, July 1790," GSA, https://slaveryarchive.georgetown.edu/items/show/206; Maryland Province Archives, "A Payment for Esther, July 15, 1790," GSA, https://slaveryarchive.georgetown.edu/items/show/207; Maryland Province Archives, "The Sale of Sarah and Jerry from Bohemia, 1791," GSA, http://slaveryarchive.georgetown.edu/items/show/271; Maryland Province Archives, "The Sale of Kate, Jonathan, and Bob to John Carty, July 1791," GSA, http://slaveryarchive.georgetown.edu/items/show/199; Maryland Province Archives, "The Sale of William to Robert Milligan, Bohemia, March, 1792," GSA, http://slaveryarchive.georgetown.edu/items/show/250; Maryland Province Archives, "The Sale of Dina, Jacob, and Jemima for Tools and a Gray Mare, 1792," GSA, http://slaveryarchive.georgetown.edu/items/show/279.

23 *the priests, who had established a civil corporation:* In 1792, Maryland's General Assembly passed "An Act for securing certain estates and property for the support and uses of ministers of the Roman Catholic religion." The charter enabled the priests to establish the Corporation of Roman Catholic Clergymen. Curran, *Bicentennial,* 16.

23 *They had decided to allocate:* Hughes, *History of the Society of Jesus in North America, Colonial and Federal, 1605–1838,* vol. 2, 747.

23 *By 1793, the enslaved:* Craig Steven Wilder, "War and Priests: Catholic Colleges and Slavery in the Age of Revolution," in *Slavery's Capitalism: A New History of American Economic Development,* ed. Sven Beckert and Seth Rockman (Philadelphia: University of Pennsylvania Press, 2018), 237.

24 *two of his grandnephews:* Ibid., 229.

24 *Carroll, whose own annual pension:* In 1794, the Corporation of Roman Catholic Clergymen decided that the rents and profits from St. Inigoes and Cedar Point would cover the annual "pensions allotted to certain Clergymen," including the bishop and other priests. Corporation of Roman Catholic Clergymen, minutes, Box 24, Folder 3, 26, MPA.

24 *The Sulpicians were given control:* Bohemia, Box 42, Folder 9, MPA, https://repository.library.georgetown.edu/handle/10822/1065221.

24 *over the next four years sold:* Maryland Province Collection, "People Bought and Sold at Bohemia Plantation, 1794–1795," GSA, http://slaveryarchive.georgetown.edu/items/show/331.

24 *In one instance:* Ibid.

24 *The Church frowned on:* Murphy, *Jesuit Slaveholding in Maryland, 1717–1838,* 34, 39.

24 *But they weren't being reprimanded:* Maryland Province Collection, "Money Arriving from the Sale of Negroes," Proceedings of the Corporation of Roman Catholic Clergy, Aug. 25, 1795," GSA, http://slaveryarchive.georgetown.edu/items/show/169.

24 *At least one woman ran away:* Maryland Province Collection, "People Bought and Sold at Bohemia Plantation, 1794–1795."

24 *"lack of docility":* March 15, 1794, SMSU Faculty Meeting Minutes—Registre Du Resultat Des Assemblées Du Seminaire De Baltimore, 1791–1886, entries for 1793–1794, Archives of Mary's Seminary & University, Associated Archives at St. Mary's Seminary & University.

25 *"sound financial basis":* Ibid. Christopher J. Kauffman wrote that by mid-1799 the Sulpician priests had spent more on the plantation than they had recouped. He said the seminary "had yet to receive any income from the estate" though "the investment promised to yield profits in time." But the former Jesuits reclaimed the property and the seminary's "income from the manor, which was estimated to have been almost 900 pounds in 1799, was cut off." Christopher J. Kauffman, *Tradition and Transformation in Catholic Culture: The Priests of Saint Sulpice in the United States from 1791 to the Present,* (New York: MacMillan Publishing, 1988), 45–47. The Sulpicians continued to rely on enslaved laborers in Maryland through at least 1840: Thomas R. Ulshafer, "Slavery and the Early Sulpician Community in Maryland,'" *U.S. Catholic Historian* 37, no. 2 (Spring 2019): 1–21.

Chapter 3: Freedom Fever

26 *For generations, the priests spoke:* Joseph Zwinge, "The Jesuit Farms in Maryland, Facts and Anecdotes," *Woodstock Letters* 39, no. 3 (1910): 380.

26 *Larks and robins filled the mornings:* Joseph Mobberly, diary, Memoranda (1 of 5), 25–26, 1823, Box 1, Folder 1. Joseph P. Mobberly, SJ Papers, Georgetown University Manuscripts, GUL.

26 *Visiting Jesuits stopped to marvel:* Zwinge, "The Jesuit Farms in Maryland," 380.

26 *Some of the priests who knew him:* St. Inigoes Day Book, Rents Principally, 1816–1832, 53, 57, MPA.

26 *Another priest described him:* Maryland State Archives, "St. Inigoes Tax
Assessment, 1804," GSA, https://slaveryarchive.georgetown.edu/items
/show/344.

26 *a man with a sweet tooth:* St. Inigoes Day Book, Rents Principally,
1816–1832, 57, MPA.

26 *a leader among the enslaved:* Francis Michael Walsh, S.J., "Resurrection:
The Story of the St. Inigoes Mission, 1634–1994," Unpublished manu-
script, 2016, 91; Edwin Warfield Beitzell, *The Jesuit Missions of St. Mary's
County, Maryland,* 2nd ed. (self-published, 1976), 205.

27 *he and many of the other:* Records suggest that the Mahoney family's
time at St. Inigoes dates back to at least 1791. Baptism records indicate
that Harry Mahoney's daughter Bibiana was baptized in St. Mary's
County, where St. Inigoes plantation is located, in 1791. Judy Riffel,
"Bibiana Mahoney Report," Working Paper, January 27, 2019, Georgetown Memory Project, https://www.georgetownmemoryproject.org/.

27 *And they swayed some white judges:* Ira Berlin, *Slaves Without Masters:
The Free Negro in the Antebellum South* (New York: New Press, 2007),
30–35.

27 *On the White Marsh plantation:* Harry Mahoney was enslaved at White
Marsh, along with his kinsmen, before the Jesuits moved him to St. Inigoes. Walsh, "Resurrection," 82.

27 *But the Queen family still triumphed:* William G. Thomas, *A Question of
Freedom: The Families Who Challenged Slavery from the Nation's Founding
to the Civil War* (New Haven, CT: Yale University Press, 2020), 77–80.

27 *They petitioned for their freedom:* Mahoney v. Ashton, Judgement Record, June 25, 1802, Court of Appeals, S381-2, MSA; Thomas, *A Question of Freedom,* 86.

27 *Harry knew the story:* Eric Robert Papenfuse, "From Recompense to
Revolution: Mahoney v. Ashton and the Transfiguration of Maryland
Culture, 1791–1802," *Slavery & Abolition* 15, no. 3 (December 1994): 46,
https://doi.org/10.1080/01440399408575138.

27 *light skin was often accompanied:* Ann Joice's descendants were described
as mulatto in depositions filed in the lawsuit that Charles and Patrick
Mahoney filed against John Ashton. See the deposition of John Wheat,
Mahoney v. Ashton, Judgement Record, June 25, 1802, Court of Appeals, S381-2, MSA.

28 *Harry felt sorry for her:* John LaFarge, *The Manner Is Ordinary* (New
York: Harcourt, 1954), 163–64.

28 *The manor house:* Joseph P. Mobberly, S.J., Papers, "Map of St. Inigoes,
The Mobberly Diaries, Part I, ca. June 1, 1820," GSA, http://slavery
archive.georgetown.edu/items/show/149.

28 *Harry and his wife had:* Harry and Anna Mahoney's first child, Bibiana, was born around 1791. Judy Riffel, "The Mahoney Family," GU272 Memory Project, American Ancestors, https://gu272.americanancestors .org/family/mahoney.

28 *The jurors declared:* William G. Thomas, "Charles Mahoney v. John Ashton, Special Verdict from October 1797 Trial," O Say Can You See: Early Washington, DC, Law & Family, https://earlywashingtondc.org /doc/oscys.mdcase.0008.048.

29 *"They pretend that they":* "Sixteen Dollars Reward," *Maryland Gazette,* January 8, 1798, Maryland State Archives, https://msa.maryland.gov /megafile/msa/speccol/sc5400/sc5496/041700/041715/images /19780108mdg1.pdf.

29 *At the time, the Maryland Abolition Society:* Berlin, *Slaves Without Masters,* 28.

29 *In the decade between 1790 and 1800:* Ibid., 46.

29 *Ashton, perhaps mindful:* "Sixteen Dollars Reward."

29 *an enslaved carpenter:* LaFarge, *The Manner Is Ordinary,* 164.

29 *hunting for Black people:* Ibid.

30 *In 1799, a second jury:* Mahoney v. Ashton, Judgement Record, June 25, 1802, Court of Appeals, S381-2, 30–31, MSA.

30 *"had obtained such proof":* Charles Carroll of Carrollton to Robert Goodloe Harper, July 11, 1802, Charles Carroll of Carrollton Papers, Maryland Center for History and Culture.

30 *"The rats got at it":* Papenfuse, "From Redcompense to Revolution," 54.

30 *It was a remarkable turn of events:* William G. Thomas III, email to author, May 23, 2022.

30 *freeing Patrick Mahoney in December 1803:* Charles County Court (Land Records) Liber IB 6, 117–18, MSA.

30 *Charles, who had been living:* Ibid.

30 *Daniel the following year:* "Rev. John Ashton," Archives of Maryland, Biographical Series, Maryland State Archives, MSA SC 5496-041715, https://msa.maryland.gov/megafile/msa/speccol/sc5400/sc5496 /041700/041715/html/041715bio.html.

31 *As the flurry of manumissions:* Berlin, *Slaves Without Masters,* 102.

31 *In describing slaves sales:* Robert Emmett Curran, *The Bicentennial History of Georgetown University,* vol. 1: *From Academy to University, 1789–1889* (Washington, DC: Georgetown University Press, 1993), 119.

31 *Enrollment at Georgetown College had plummeted:* Ibid., 54–56, 397.

31 *Economic woes in the capital:* Ibid., 56.

31 *"The College," the trustees wrote:* Ibid., 55.

31 *To compensate:* Corporation of Roman Catholic Clergymen, minutes, May 5, 1801, Box 24, Folder 3, MPA.

32 *"dispose of unruly slaves":* "'The Power of Managers to Dispose Un-

ruly Slaves,' May 24, 1803," Proceedings of the Corporation of Roman Catholic Clergymen, May 24, 1803, Box 24, Folder 1, MPA.

32 *"Sale of Nigroe Frank from St. Inigoes":* Unprocessed materials, January 1804, Agent Accounts, 3L, Box 2, MPA. GSA has it this way: "Agent's Cashbook Kept by Francis Neale, Box 69, Addenda to the Maryland Province, Provincial Procurator Series, Maryland Province Archives, Booth Family Center for Special Collections, Georgetown University."

32 *But he was captured:* "By cash paid for Runaway, Matt $3.77," February 15, 1804, Agent's Cash Book, 1802–1820, Box 69, Unprocessed Materials, pre-1864, MPA.

32 *That spring, fear descended:* Maryland State Archives, "St. Inigoes Tax Assessment, 1804," GSA, https://slaveryarchive.georgetown.edu/items /show/344.

32 *In 1805, the Jesuit order:* Raymond A. Schroth, *The American Jesuits: A History* (New York: New York University Press, 2007), 52, https:// ebookcentral.proquest.com/lib/nyulibrary-ebooks/detail.action?docID =865343.

32 *"The sale of a few unnecessary negroes":* Thomas Murphy, *Jesuit Slave-holding in Maryland, 1717–1838* (New York: Routledge, 2016), 76.

33 *In 1806, St. Inigoes began:* Corporation of Roman Catholic Clergy-men, minutes, November 3, 1807, Box 24, Folder 3, 60, MPA.

33 *"Disagreeable as this truth is":* Curran, *The Bicentennial History of Georgetown University,* vol. 1, 60.

33 *the average price of a slave:* Edward E. Baptist, *The Half Has Never Been Told: Slavery and the Making of American Capitalism* (New York: Basic Books, 2016), 174.

33 *"This man came up to me":* Charles Ball, *Slavery in the United States: A Narrative of the Life and Adventures of Charles Ball, a Black Man, Who Lived Forty Years in Maryland, South Carolina and Georgia, as a Slave Under Various Masters, and Was One Year in the Navy with Commodore Barney, During the Late War* (New York: John S. Taylor, Brick Church Chapel, 1837), 36, https://docsouth.unc.edu/neh/ballslavery/ball.html.

34 *"I asked if I could":* Ibid., 36.

34 *In the first decade of the 1800s:* Baptist, *The Half Has Never Been Told,* xxv, 3.

34 *Anna was pregnant with her sixth:* The Jesuits recorded the ages of the Mahoney family members and the other enslaved people at St. Inigoes in 1813. Maryland State Archives, "St. Inigoes Tax Assessment, 1813," GSA, http://slaveryarchive.georgetown.edu/items/show/346.

35 *At St. Inigoes:* "Sales—Negro Watt at St. Inigoes Apr, Negro Pete & family St. Inigoes May," Annual Reports of Finances of the Province, Box 3, page 47, Additional Materials, pre-1864, MPA; Maryland Prov-ince Archives, "The Sale of George and Two Families, June 1809," GSA, http://slaveryarchive.georgetown.edu/items/show/193.

35 *The Jesuits at St. Inigoes:* Ibid.

35 . *William Green, a Maryland man:* William Green, *Narrative of Events in the Life of William Green, (Formerly a Slave.) Written by Himself* (Springfield, IL: L. M. Guernsey, 1853), 6, https://docsouth.unc.edu/neh /greenw/greenw.html.

36 *He became the plantation foreman:* Walsh, "Resurrection," 91.

Chapter 4: A New Generation

37 *By the time he took his seat:* John Gilmary Shea, *Memorial of the First Century of Georgetown College, D.C.* (Washington, DC: P. F. Collier, 1891), 34.

37 *black, curly hair:* Shea, *Memorial of the First Century of Georgetown College, D.C.,* 93.

37 *hazel gray eyes:* His eye color and height are described at "U.S. Passport Applications, 1795–1925 for Thomas F. Mulledy," Ancestry, https:// www.ancestry.com/interactive/1174/USM1371_2-0177?pid=1160906.

37 *would not hesitate to use his fists:* Anecdote of Thos. Mulledy, Box 1, Folder 10, Mulledy Papers, MPA.

37 *They had helped establish:* Edward Devitt, "History of the Maryland– New York Province: St. Inigoes, St. Mary's County, Maryland, 1634–1915," *Woodstock Letters* 40, no. 2 (1931): 355; Susan Nalezyty, "The History of Enslaved People at Georgetown Visitation," *U.S. Catholic Historian* 37, no. 2 (2019): 23.

37 *The nuns would enslave:* Rachel L. Swarns, "The Nuns Who Bought and Sold Human Beings," *New York Times,* August 2, 2019. Mannard, "'We Are Determined to Be White Ladies': Race, Identity and the Maryland Tradition in Antebellum Visitation Convents," *Maryland Historical Magazine* 109, no. 2 (Summer 2014): 133–157; Nalezyty, "The History of Enslaved People at Georgetown Visitation," *U.S. Catholic Historian* 37, no. 2 (2019): 23–48.

38 *The priests had opened:* Robert Emmett Curran, *The Bicentennial History of Georgetown University,* vol. 1: *From Academy to University, 1789–1889* (Washington, DC: Georgetown University Press, 1993), 64–66.

38 *By 1813, the mission's leaders:* Peter C. Finn, "The Slaves of the Jesuits in Maryland," PhD dissertation, Georgetown University, 1974, 33–34.

38 *It was clear:* Curran, *The Bicentennial History of Georgetown University,* vol. 1, 64–66.

38 *Father Giovanni Grassi:* Ibid., 64.

38 *War had broken out:* "The War of 1812," Smithsonian National Museum of American History, https://amhistory.si.edu/starspangledbanner/the -capital-captured.aspx.

38 *Within a year, students would see:* Ibid.

38 *He had grown up:* Shea, *Memorial of the First Century of Georgetown College, D.C.,* 162.

38 *His father, an Irish immigrant:* "Hampshire County, Virginia (now West

Virginia): Volume I—Minute Book Abstracts, 1788–1802," Ancestry, 7, 83, 96, 98, 99, https://www.ancestry.com/interactive/49178/FLHG _HampshireCntyVAVol1-0098, https://www.ancestry.com/interactive /49178/FLHG_HampshireCntyVAVol1-0099.

38 *By 1810, three years before:* "1810 United States Federal Census," Ancestry, 2010.

39 *"raising cattle and making a fortune":* Quoted in Curran, *The Bicentennial History of Georgetown University,* vol. 1, 359.

39 *Mulledy taught school:* "History of Hampshire County, West Virginia: From Its Earliest Settlement to the Present," Ancestry, 2005, https:// www.ancestry.com/interactive/28838/dvm_LocHist012674-00151-0.

39 *Mulledy appears to have paid:* Curran, *The Bicentennial History of Georgetown University,* vol. 1, 107.

39 *One year, Samuel gave the college:* Ibid.

39 *Grassi, who had become:* Ibid., 65.

39 *"The people are mobilized for war":* Ibid., 73.

39 *One of the British soldiers:* Anecdote of Thomas Mulledy, Box 1, Folder 10, Mulledy Papers, MPA.

40 *classes started on time:* Curran, *The Bicentennial History of Georgetown University,* vol. 1, 71–73.

40 *Grassi had reduced:* Ibid., 66, 71.

40 *the highest number ever enrolled:* Ibid., 397.

40 *Grassi boosted the profile:* Ibid., 69–70, 75.

41 *Grassi, who was a mathematician:* Ibid., 70, 83.

41 *Grassi enhanced the college's facilities:* Ibid., 67.

41 *In 1815, he decided:* Shea, *Memorial of the First Century of Georgetown College, D.C.,* 162.

41 *Mulledy left Georgetown:* Ibid., 162.

41 *The young men studied:* J. Wilfrid Parsons, "Rev. Anthony Kohlmann, S.J. (1771–1824)," *Catholic Historical Review* 4, no. 1 (April 1918): 38–51.

41 *only the second in the United States:* Ibid., 44–48; Joyce Mendelsohn and James E. Garrity, "History," Basilica of St. Patrick's Old Cathedral, 2015, https://oldcathedral.org/history.

41 *had drawn faculty and financial resources:* Curran, *The Bicentennial History of Georgetown University,* vol. 1, 60–62.

41 *taking charge of the seminary in 1815:* Parsons, "Rev. Anthony Kohlmann, S.J. (1771–1824)," 49.

42 *Kohlmann believed that the Church's future:* Curran, *The Bicentennial History of Georgetown University,* vol. 1, 88.

42 *He wanted the Jesuits:* Ibid., 60.

42 *To accomplish that:* Ibid., 88.

42 *Under the plan:* Maryland Province Archives, "The Maryland Jesuits Discuss and Resolve to Sell the Majority of Their Enslaved Community, 1813–1814," GSA, http://slaveryarchive.georgetown.edu/items /show/410.

42 *The priests may have been weary:* William G. Thomas, *A Question of Freedom: The Families Who Challenged Slavery from the Nation's Founding to the Civil War* (New Haven, CT: Yale University Press, 2020), 186.

42 *the need to come up with cash:* Thomas Murphy, *Jesuit Slaveholding in Maryland, 1717–1838* (New York: Routledge, 2016), 78.

42 *Archbishop Carroll also happened:* Robert Emmett Curran, *Shaping American Catholicism: Maryland and New York, 1805–1915* (Washington, DC: Catholic University of America Press, 2012), 96–99.

42 *After all, the plan:* Thomas, *A Question of Freedom,* 187.

43 *Under his direction:* Cornelius M. Buckley, *Stephen Larigaudelle Dubuisson, S.J. (1786–1864) and the Reform of the American Jesuits* (Lanham, MD: University Press of America, 2013), 68.

43 *They prayed together:* Shea, *Memorial of the First Century of Georgetown College, D.C.,* 46.

43 *They even traveled:* Ibid., 46.

43 *"good and sufficient clothing":* Buckley, *Stephen Larigaudelle Dubuisson, S.J.,* 71.

43 *at least one seminarian noted:* Ibid., 72.

43 *William McSherry:* History of the McSherry Family, Box 5, Folder 23, Carbery Family Collection, GUL.

43 *owned a large estate:* Ibid.; Curran, *The Bicentennial History of Georgetown University,* vol. 1, 108.

43 *McSherry stood over six feet tall:* Ibid., 109.

43 *Mulledy was about five foot eight:* His eye color and height are described at "U.S. Passport Applications, 1795–1925, for Thomas F. Mulledy," Ancestry, 2007, https://www.ancestry.com/interactive/1174/USM1371_2 -0177?pid=1160906.

43 *was better known:* Curran, *The Bicentennial History of Georgetown University,* vol. 1, 109; Thomas J. Morrissey, *As One Sent: Peter Kenney SJ, 1779–1841: His Mission in Ireland and North America* (Blackrock, Co. Dublin: Four Courts Press, 1996), 244.

43 *many older priests:* Murphy, *Jesuit Slaveholding in Maryland, 1717–1838,* 135.

43 *who by early 1817:* Hughes, 320–24.

44 *By the summer of 1817:* Buckley, *Stephen Larigaudelle Dubuisson, S.J.,* 84–85.

44 *Mulledy, who had entered:* Shea, *Memorial of the First Century of Georgetown College, D.C.,* 54.

44 *After supper one evening:* Buckley, *Stephen Larigaudelle Dubuisson, S.J.,* 89.

44 *"fearless action and skill contributed":* Ibid., 89–90.

44 *Kohlmann promoted Mulledy:* Ibid.

44 *In 1819, Mulledy's name:* Peter Kenney, "Statement for the Consultors of the Mission on Its Actual State and All Its Concerns," April 1820, Box 126, Folder 7, MPA.

45 *In a letter written just two months:* Ibid.

45 *what one historian described as:* Robert Emmett Curran, email to author, August 15, 2019.

45 *Even Kohlmann, who had groomed:* Anthony Kohlmann to Giovanni Grassi, June 2, 1820, ARSI, MD, 2.VII.5.

45 *"a final experiment to save him":* Peter Kenney, "Statement for the Consultors of the Mission on Its Actual State and All Its Concerns."

45 *On the morning of June 6, 1820:* Curran, *The Bicentennial History of Georgetown University,* vol. 1, 89–90.

46 *"At present":* Anthony Kohlmann to Giovanni Grassi, June 2, 1820, Maryland, 2.VII.5, ARSI.

46 *he was being celebrated:* Ibid.

46 *"A fair breeze":* Charles Constantine Pise, journal, June 6, 1820–September 3, 1820, Box 1, Folder 5, Charles Constantine Pise Papers, GUL.

46 *By September, Mulledy:* Curran, *The Bicentennial History of Georgetown University,* vol. 1, 90.

46 *"They are all well":* Giovanni Grassi to John McElroy, August 27, 1820, Box 3, Folder 7, MPA.

46 *"First Fruits of the American Mission":* Anthony Kohlmann to Giovanni Grassi, June 2, 1820, MD, 2.VII.5, ARSI.

46 *"Oh! am I thus":* Thomas Mulledy, poem, Box 1, Folder 11, Mulledy Papers, MPA.

47 *property values plunged:* S. Mintz and S. McNeil, "The Growth of Political Factionalism and Sectionalism, Panic of 1819," Digital History, https://www.digitalhistory.uh.edu/disp_textbook.cfm?smtID=2&psid=3531.

47 *James Neil, a Jesuit scholastic:* Curran, *The Bicentennial History of Georgetown University,* vol. 1, 79.

47 *"in the greatest misery":* Ibid.

47 *"Our affairs wear":* Adam Marshall to Enoch Fenwick, August 14, 1820, Box 59, Folder 6, MPA.

47 *Grassi himself was accused:* Marshall to Aloysius Fortis, February 6, 1821, Maryland 2 II 5, ARSI.

47 *Enrollment plunged from 108:* Curran, *The Bicentennial History of Georgetown University,* vol. 1, 397.

47 *"one foot in the grave":* Ibid., 92.

47 *Father Peter Kenney, sent:* Peter Kenney, "Report on the State of the Mission of the Society of Jesus Made into the United States of America to the General Congregation Congregated in the House of Professors in Rome," 1820, Peter Kenney, S.J., Papers, XT3, XK, MPA.

47 *The priests seemed:* Curran, *The Bicentennial History of Georgetown University,* vol. 1, 86.

48 *And still they argued:* Ibid.

48 *very heart of their mission:* Ibid., 88.

48 *In Rome, Kenney delivered:* Peter Kenney, (XK) "Relatio de statu mis-

sionis in America [XT3]," October 1820, Peter Kenney, S.J., papers, MPA.

48 *"There is not any where":* Peter Kenney, "Statement for the Consultors of the Mission on Its Actual State and All Its Concerns," April 1820, Box 126, Folder 7, MPA.

48 *Between 1820 and 1824:* Adam Marshall, "Full Report of Adam Marshall on Financial Condition of Province, 1820–1824," Box 60, Folder 7, MPA.

48 *The Jesuits even mortgaged:* Mortgage of White Marsh, Prince George's County Land Record, October 16, 1822, Liber AB3, 235–39, MSA.

48 *"common embezzler":* Thomas Hughes, "History of the Society of Jesus in North America, Colonial & Federal Text, Volume 3, from 1773 till 1822," MPA, 778–79.

49 *"Instead of a Constellation":* Curran, *The Bicentennial History of Georgetown University,* vol. 1, 96.

49 *But in Rome, too:* Ibid.

49 *His defenders described him:* Buckley, *Stephen Larigaudelle Dubuisson, S.J.,* 150.

49 *The Maryland Jesuits were so strapped:* Curran, *The Bicentennial History of Georgetown University,* vol. 1, 101.

49 *The voyage took 171 days:* Shea, *Memorial of the First Century of Georgetown College, D.C.,* 77.

49 *It was not until December:* The ship arrived in Philadelphia on December 31, 1828. *Pennsylvania,* U.S., Arriving Passenger and Crew Lists, 1798–1962, Ancestry.com, https://www.ancestry.com/discoveryui -content/view/10453392:8769?tid=&pid=&queryId=4cd56e74b623ae 649f85a219fddc3308&_phsrc=LRP22&_phstart=successSource.

49 *By January, those promising:* Shea, *Memorial of the First Century of Georgetown College, D.C.,* 77.

49 *In the fall of 1829:* *United States' Telegraph,* September 22, 1829.

50 *"The College is situated":* Ibid.

50 *he wrote a letter:* Thomas Mulledy to Jan Roothaan, January 7, 1830, Maryland 3 IV 20, ARSI.

Chapter 5: The Promise

51 *Louisa was only a year or two younger:* Anna "Anny" Mahoney was born sometime around 1811. The 1821 tax record for St. Inigoes plantation describes her as ten years old that year, which would put her year of birth in 1811.

51 *some eight children in all:* Judy Riffel, "The Mahoney Family," GU272 Memory Project, American Ancestors, https://gu272.americanancestors .org/family/mahoney.

51 *born into slavery around 1813:* Louisa Mahoney's precise year of birth remains unknown. An 1821 tax record for St. Inigoes plantation de-

scribes her as eight years old that year, which would put her year of birth in 1813. Her 1909 obituary said she was born in 1812. Maryland State Archives, "St. Inigoes Tax Assessment, 1821," GSA, http://slaveryarchive.georgetown.edu/items/show/79; GSA, "Louisa Mason Obituary, 1909," GSA, http://slaveryarchive.georgetown.edu/items/show/91.

51 *Louisa and Anny would learn:* Louisa Mahoney shared her family story, some of which was recorded by Jesuit priests. The family story was passed down to her children and grandchildren. Joseph Zwinge, "The Jesuit Farms in Maryland, Facts and Anecdotes," *Woodstock Letters* 41, no. 2 (1912): 195; John LaFarge, *The Manner Is Ordinary* (New York: Harcourt, 1954), 163–64; Miriam Otterbein, "Born of Slave Parents, 100-Year-Old Woodstock Man Lauds Freedom," *Community Times,* August 10, 1972.

52 *their warships streamed into:* Joseph Zwinge, "The Jesuit Farms in Maryland, Facts and Anecdotes: The War of 1812," *Woodstock Letters* 42, no. 3 (1913): 336–34.

52 *Panicked, the clergy:* Edwin Warfield Beitzell, *The Jesuit Missions of St. Mary's County, Maryland* (self-published, 1976), 158–59.

52 *Joseph Mobberly, the religious brother:* Ibid.

52 *"They have burnt every house":* Ibid., 160–61.

52 *The soldiers had also:* Zwinge, "The Jesuit Farms in Maryland, Facts and Anecdotes: The War of 1812," 337.

52 *which numbered about forty people in all:* Maryland State Archives, "St. Inigoes Tax Assessment, 1813," GSA, http://slaveryarchive.georgetown.edu/items/show/346.

53 *"In twelve hours":* Zwinge, "The Jesuit Farms in Maryland, Facts and Anecdotes: The War of 1812," 337.

53 *"robbing even the women and children":* William Matthew Marine and Louis Henry Dielman, *The British Invasion of Maryland, 1812–1815* (Baltimore: Genealogical Publishing Company, 2009), 53.

53 *Many enslaved men and women ran:* Beitzell, *The Jesuit Missions of St. Mary's County, Maryland,* 159.

53 *On April 2, 1814:* "African Americans and the War of 1812," MSA, https://msa.maryland.gov/msa/mdstatehouse/war1812/html/afam_war.html.

53 *"This is therefore":* "Annapolis & the War of 1812: 'The Enemy Nearly All 'Round Us,'" MSA, https://msa.maryland.gov/msa/mdstatehouse/war1812/html/afam_war.html.

53 *Hundreds ran:* Ibid.

54 *the Jesuits sold yet another:* Maryland Province Archives, "The Maryland Jesuits Decide to Sell Jem and His Family to Pay a Debt to Rev. Pasquet, 1814," GSA, http://slaveryarchive.georgetown.edu/items/show/412.

54 *word came:* Francis Neale to Giovanni Grassi, July 4, 1814, Box 58, Folder 11, MPA.

54 *"It was on the duty":* Ibid.

55 *Decades later, Louisa would tell:* Francis Michael Walsh, S.J., "Resurrection: The Story of the St. Inigoes Mission, 1634–1994," 2016, 91, footnote.

55 *the soldiers disembarking:* Joseph Mobberly to Giovanni Grassi, November 1–5, 1814, Box 58, Folder 8, MPA.

55 *leading them into the relative safety:* Beitzell, *The Jesuit Missions of St. Mary's County, Maryland,* 133.

55 *"Great God":* Joseph Mobberly to Giovanni Grassi, November 1, 1814, Box 58, Folder 8, MPA.

55 *"I took two wagon loads":* Joseph P. Mobberly, S.J., Papers, vol. 1, 98, Box 1, Folder 1, GUL.

56 *Harry and a team:* Joseph P. Mobberly to Giovanni Grassi, November 5, 1814, Box 58, Folder 8, MPA.

56 *"We must then purchase":* Ibid.

56 *"We can scarcely sleep":* Ibid.

57 *Father Rantzau reported a loss of his own:* Ibid.

57 *"I led them two miles":* Ibid.

57 *They promised that he would never be sold:* Walsh, "Resurrection," 91, footnote.

58 *"It appears that they":* Zwinge, "The Jesuit Farms in Maryland, Facts and Anecdotes: The War of 1812," 350.

58 *The enslaved families they knew:* Joseph P. Mobberly, diary, "State of the farm when I left it," 1820, 128–38, Box 1, Folder 1, Joseph P. Mobberly, S.J., Papers, GUL.

58 *Black worshippers relished:* Laura E. Masur, "A Spiritual Inheritance: Black Catholics in Southern Maryland," *International Symposia on Jesuit Studies,* no. 2019, Symposium (March 2021): 14–16.

58 *"hived":* Zwinge, "The Jesuit Farms in Maryland, Facts and Anecdotes, The Negro Slaves," *Woodstock Letters* 41, no. 2 (1912), 197.

58 *Enslaved children on plantations:* David K. Wiggins, "The Play of Slave Children in the Plantation Communities of the Old South, 1820–1860," *Journal of Sport History* 7, no. 2 (Summer 1980): 21–39, https://www.jstor.org/stable/43610352; Clint Smith, *How the Word Is Passed: A Reckoning with the History of Slavery Across America* (New York: Little, Brown, 2021).

59 *They could explore woods:* Joseph P. Mobberly, diary, 1820, 23–30, Box 1, Folder 1, Joseph P. Mobberly, S.J., Papers, GUL.

59 *As they grew older:* John LaFarge, *The Manner Is Ordinary* (New York: Harcourt, 1954), 164.

59 *he and his wife had:* Judy Riffel, "Bibiana Mahoney Report," Georgetown Memory Project, January 27, 2019, in author's possession.

59 *at least two of their daughters:* Maryland Province Archives, "Belonging to Us": Fr. Dzierozynski Recommends Nelly as Housekeeper for Fr. Lancaster, January 1843," GSA, http://slaveryarchive.georgetown

.edu/items/show/139; GSA, "Louisa Mason Obituary, 1909," GSA, http://slaveryarchive.georgetown.edu/items/show/91.

59 *their childhoods were marked:* Zwinge, "The Jesuit Farms in Maryland, Facts and Anecdotes," 212–13.

59 *"[We] were surprised":* Maryland Province Archives, " 'Sales of Negroes for Life': Archbp. Carroll Expresses His Surprise That Slaves Were Sold Against the Corporation's Orders, Oct 1815," GSA, accessed August 3, 2019, http://slaveryarchive.georgetown.edu/items/show/111.

60 *"This is not allowed":* Robert Emmett Curran, *Shaping American Catholicism: Maryland and New York, 1805–1915* (Washington, DC: Catholic University of America Press, 2012), 102–03.

60 *The Catholic Church continued:* Ibid., 102, 110.

60 *In the same letter:* Maryland Province Archives, " 'Sales of Negroes for Life.' "

60 *But now he was gone:* Edward Devitt, "History of the Maryland–New York Province: St. Inigoes, St. Mary's County, Maryland, 1634–1915," *Woodstock Letters* 40, no. 2 (1931): 226.

61 *"We are in the dark":* Joseph P. Mobberly to Giovanni Grassi, February 5, 1815, Box 58, Folder 6, MPA.

61 *Earnings from the sale:* Ellen Marks Bayly, "Economics and Society in a Staple Plantation System: St. Marys County, Maryland, 1790–1840," PhD dissertation, University of Maryland, 1979, 66.

61 *"apprehensions of the gloomiest kind":* Ibid., 69.

61 *But in 1816:* Walsh, "Resurrection," 94.

62 *In a strikingly frank letter:* Robert Fenwick to Giovanni Grassi, September 22, 1816, Maryl.-1001-VII_0328-_030, ARSI.

62 *"been accustomed":* Joseph P. Mobberly, SJ Papers, " 'Cham's Descendants': The Mobberly Diaries, Part II, August 1823," GSA, http://slaveryarchive.georgetown.edu/items/show/154.

62 *"Vices the most notorious":* Peter C. Finn, "The Slaves of the Jesuits in Maryland," PhD dissertation, Georgetown University, 1974, 43.

63 *"Where slavery exists":* Joseph P. Mobberly, SJ Papers, "Slavery Is Good, Is Necessary: The Mobberly Diaries, Part II, August 1823," GSA, accessed June 17, 2022, http://slaveryarchive.georgetown.edu/items /show/157.

63 *Carbery had attended Georgetown:* Robert Emmett Curran, *The Bicentennial History of Georgetown University*, vol. 1: *From Academy to University, 1789–1889* (Washington, DC: Georgetown University Press, 1993), 119.

63 *painting and plastering:* Joseph Carbery's History of St. Inigoes, 1844, Box 8, Folder 5, MPA.

63 *Carbery would become known:* LaFarge, *The Manner Is Ordinary*, 166.

63 *In his diary, he suggested:* Joseph P. Mobberly, SJ Papers, " 'Masters Must Answer,' The Mobberly Diaries, Part I, 1820," GSA, http://slaveryarchive .georgetown.edu/items/show/152.

63 *Father Ashton, who had been sued:* Maryland State Archives, "Rev. John Ashton, Slave Owner, Prince George's Maryland," Archives of Maryland, Biographical Series, http://msa.maryland.gov/megafile/msa/speccol/sc5400/sc5496/041700/041715/html/041715bio.html.

63 *Father Grassi decided:* Catholic Historical Manuscripts Collection, "'I Send You the List of the Negroes': Fr. Grassi Arranges the Transport of 11 Enslaved People to St. Inigoes, February 6, 1817," GSA, http://slaveryarchive.georgetown.edu/items/show/355.

63 *valued at $3,675:* Maryland Province Archives, "'Valuation of Rev. Ashton's Negroes,' November 11, 1816," GSA, http://slaveryarchive.georgetown.edu/items/show/146.

64 *At St. Inigoes, enslaved families:* Finn, "The Slaves of the Jesuits in Maryland," 77.

64 *Mobberly went through five overseers:* Craig Steven Wilder, "War and Priests: Catholic Colleges and Slavery in the Age of Revolution," in *Slavery's Capitalism: A New History of American Economic Development,* ed. Sven Beckert and Seth Rothman (Philadelphia: University of Pennsylvania Press, 2018), 239.

64 *"Some years ago":* Joseph P. Mobberly, SJ Papers, "'Masters Must Answer.'"

64 *Dick and Gabe worked:* Entries 14 and 19, St. Inigoes blacksmith accounts for 1810, 170-E, Box 43, Folder 3, MPA.

64 *"Free Charles & Stephen":* Entries 37 and 53, St. Inigoes mostly blacksmith shop acc'ts 1811–1814, 170-F, Box 43, Folder 3, MPA.

65 *In Maryland, free Blacks routinely:* Berlin, *Slaves Without Masters,* 93–97; Zwinge, "The Jesuit Farms in Maryland, Facts and Anecdotes," 215.

65 *"Suddenly":* "Riot Among the Negroes in St. Mary's," *New York Evening Post,* April 21, 1817.

65 *When a constable tried:* Criminal Court St Mary's 1-57- 9-88 Maryland Special Court 1817 (Riot) Criminal Papers C 1573 1817-1851, May 1817 Special Court, Folder 19836-3, MSA.

66 *By 1810, they accounted:* Nancy Radcliffe, "St. Mary's County Slave Revolt of 1817: Possible Religious Connections," Unpublished ms, St. Mary's College, St. Mary's City, Md., November 13, 1996, 5.

66 *more than a dozen were apprehended:* "Riot Among the Negroes in St. Mary's."

66 *Some were whipped:* Ibid.

66 *including three members:* Criminal Court St Mary's 1-57- 9-88 Maryland Special Court 1817 (Riot), Criminal Papers C 1573 1817-1851 May 1817 Special Court, Folder 19, 836-1, May 1817, Criminal 1817 MSA.

66 *"a free negro":* Charles Barnes, True Bill, Riot, May 1817, Verdicts, Folder 19836-3, Special Court, St. Mary's County, MSA.

66 *On May 12, 1817:* MSA S1107 Governor and Council Pardon Records 2/26/5/26 1817, S1107, MSA.

67 *"I do hereby order":* Governor and Council Pardon Records, February 26–May 26, 1817, S1107, MSA.

67 *Southern enslavers had developed:* Edward E. Baptist, *The Half Has Never Been Told: Slavery and the Making of American Capitalism* (New York: Basic Books, 2016), 111–22.

67 *"The sugar and cotton plantations":* Ibid., 105.

67 *"Many [of the accused] were flogged":* "Riot Among the Negroes in St. Mary's," *Daily National Intelligencer,* April 18, 1817.

67 *But Stephen Barnes:* Rick Boyd, "Those Enslaved in Southern Maryland Resisted," *Southern Maryland News,* September 30, 2016.

67 *In November, the estate shipped:* "St. Inigoes Day Book, 1804, Rents principally, 1816, Rents & Blacksmith, 1818–1832," Box 44, Folder 1, 50, MPA.

68 *The archbishop, who spent:* Beitzell, *The Jesuit Missions of St. Mary's County, Maryland,* 169.

68 *The following year:* Thomas J. Morrissey, *As One Sent: Peter Kenney SJ, 1779–1841: His Mission in Ireland and North America* (Blackrock, Co. Dublin: Four Courts Press, 1996), 148.

68 *In February 1820:* Ibid., 161.

69 *"presented a nice appearance to the eye":* Zwinge, "The Jesuit Farms in Maryland, Facts and Anecdotes," 196.

69 *"very bad":* Adam Marshall to Aloysius Fortis, March 5, 1821, Maryland 2 II 5, ARSI.

69 *"They are furious":* Peter Kenney, "Statement for the Consultors of the Mission on its Actual State and All Its Concerns," April 1820, Box 126, Folder 7, MPA.

69 *"should not be inflicted":* Ibid.

69 *He told the Jesuit leaders:* Ibid.

69 *"to promote morality":* Ibid.

70 *"in the very threshold":* Ibid.

70 *Finding a way to replace:* Ibid.

70 *But the American Jesuits:* Maryland Province Archives, "The Maryland Jesuits Repeal the Decision to Sell Their Enslaved Community, 1820," GSA, http://slaveryarchive.georgetown.edu/items/show/411.

70 *Back in Rome later that year:* Peter Kenney, "Report on the State of the Mission of the Society of Jesus, October 1820, Box 126, Folder 8, MPA.

71 *"in a very wretched condition":* Adam Marshall to Aloysius Fortis, February 6, 1821, Maryland 2 II 5, ARSI.

71 *Mobberly was ousted from the estate:* Morrissey, *As One Sent,* 169.

71 *Father Carbery, the priest:* Edward Devitt, "Biographies of Notable Jesuits," October 1866, Box 7, Folder 6, MPA.

71 *The priest, who came:* "Biographical Notes About Members of the Carbery Family," Box 1, Folder 12, Carbery Family Collection, GUL.

Chapter 6: A College on the Rise

72 *the number of boarding students:* Robert Emmett Curran, *The Bicentennial History of Georgetown University,* vol. 1: *From Academy to University, 1789–1889* (Washington, DC: Georgetown University Press, 1993), 109.

72 *"The College increases":* Thomas Mulledy to Jan Roothaan, January 7, 1830, Maryland 3 IV 20, Maryl.-1003-IV_0343–45, ARSI. Archivum Romanum Societatis Iesu, "Questions Regarding Slavery: Rev. Thomas Mulledy, SJ to the Jesuit Superior General, January 7, 1830," GSA, accessed January 24, 2023, http://slaveryarchive.georgetown.edu/items/show/408.

72 *The new students included:* Curran, *The Bicentennial History of Georgetown University,* vol. 1, 110.

72 *"I write to you":* Ibid.

73 *All three were first- or second-generation:* Ibid., 112.

73 *Between 1830 and 1835:* Joshua D. Rothman, *The Ledger and the Chain: How Domestic Slave Traders Shaped America* (New York: Basic Books, 2021), 157.

73 *The number of enslaved:* Edward E. Baptist, *The Half Has Never Been Told: Slavery and the Making of American Capitalism* (New York: Basic Books, 2016), 3.

74 *"and use the revenue":* Curran, *The Bicentennial History of Georgetown University,* vol. 1, 113.

74 *"He tells me":* Peter Kenney to John McElroy, November 23, 1830, Box 62, Folder 15, MPA.

74 *Mulledy, who was beginning:* "Georgetown College," *United States' Telegraph,* September 11, 1830.

75 *"By the grace of God":* Thomas J. Morrissey, *As One Sent: Peter Kenney SJ, 1779–1841: His Mission in Ireland and North America* (Blackrock, Co. Dublin: Four Courts Press, 1996), 244.

75 *He was also impressed:* Curran, *The Bicentennial History of Georgetown University,* vol. 1, 171.

75 *debts had been markedly reduced:* Morrissey, *As One Sent,* 244.

75 *"Nothing escapes his hands":* Curran, *The Bicentennial History of Georgetown University,* vol. 1, 110.

75 *Mulledy wanted:* Ibid., 111.

75 *Mulledy used the change:* Ibid., 114.

75 *"The greatest threat":* Archivum Romanum Societatis Iesu, "Slavery at St. Thomas Manor: Fr. Grivel to Fr. Roothaan, 1831," GSA, http://slaveryarchive.georgetown.edu/items/show/292.

76 *He said that the priests:* Ibid.

76 *Kenney visited the Bohemia plantation:* Notes compiled by Peter Kenney during his visitation to the Maryland and Missouri Missions, November 29, 1831, IE J474, 16, IJA.

76 *One man had married:* Maryland Province Archives, "Peter Kenney, SJ's Observations on Slave Families at Bohemia, 1831," GSA, http://slavery archive.georgetown.edu/items/show/65.

76 *"Not one has been":* Ibid.

77 *Roothaan had decided against:* Curran, *The Bicentennial History of Georgetown University,* vol. 1, 115.

77 *He was soon talking openly:* Peter Kenney to Thomas Mulledy, December 11, 1831, Mulledy Papers, Box 1, Folder 4, GUL.

77 *"Sale of boy Jery & little Mary":* Copy of note dated December 16, 1832, included in Peter Kenney's journal during his visitation to the Maryland and Missouri Missions, 506/17, 24, IJA.

77 *"Sould the little Boy Jery":* Joseph Zwinge, "The Jesuit Farms in Maryland, Facts and Anecdotes: The Negro Slaves," *Woodstock Letters* 41, no. 3 (1912): 277.

78 *"a boy" named Bill:* Ibid.

78 *That summer, Kenney celebrated:* Morrissey, *As One Sent,* 277.

78 *Mulledy had embarked on:* Curran, *The Bicentennial History of Georgetown University,* vol. 1, 115–16.

78 *Grivel heard about it:* Fidèle de Grivel to Nicholas Sewall, May 30, 1832, Letters from Maryland and America, 1772–1835, MSB.38, Folio 147–148, BJA.

78 *President Andrew Jackson:* Curran, *The Bicentennial History of Georgetown University,* vol. 1, 111.

78 *One senior Jesuit:* Ibid., 115.

79 *"I need not say":* Peter Kenney to Thomas Mulledy, February 29, 1832, Box 1, Folder 4, Mulledy Papers, GUL.

79 *offered a $12,000 loan:* Curran, *The Bicentennial History of Georgetown University,* vol. 1, 116.

79 *"Began foundation":* Thomas Mulledy, journal entry, July 9, 1832, Mulledy Papers, GUL.

79 *Several days after:* Peter Kenney, journal entry, July 18, 1832, J/474/17/4, IE, IJA.

79 *the "flourishing" college:* Morrissey, *As One Sent,* 316.

79 *He reported to Mulledy:* Peter Kenney to Thomas Mulledy, July 16, 1832, Box 1, Folder 4, Mulledy Papers, GUL.

79 *Father Peter Havermans:* Peter Havermans to George Fenwick, July 17, 1832, Box 63, Folder 18, MPA.

Chapter 7: Love and Peril

80 *Arnold Jones worked:* In 1831, Arnold Jones is listed as a thirty-year-old sailor on a list of people enslaved by Thomas Jones, who lived on nearby St. Inigoes plantation. He and his brother, Moses, were valued at $250 each, more than any of the others on the list. "A List of Slaves the Property of Thos. Smith," Assessment Record/Slaves, 1831, St. Mary's

County Levy Court, Book Name: S, Districts 1-5, Legacy accession No. C1545, MSA: CE453-16.

80 *Arnold was nearly thirty:* In 1836, Arnold Jones is described as a thirty-five-year-old sailor who had traveled to Washington, DC, and other places up north for more than a decade. His brother, Moses, is described as someone who had sought his freedom. "$600 Reward," *American and Commercial Daily Advertiser,* August 5, 1836.

80 *one day, he caught:* A marriage record for Arnold Jones and Anna Mahoney has yet to be found. Their first known child, Arnold Jones, Jr., was born sometime around 1830, according to Arnold Jones, Jr., death certificate, Orleans Parish Deaths, vol. 96, p. 356, Louisiana State Archives.

80 *Some Jesuit priests tried:* Maryland Province Archives, "Fr. Francis Neale Describes Difficulties Arranging Slave Marriages and British Pillaging During the War of 1812," GSA, http://slaveryarchive.georgetown .edu/items/show/368.

81 *he had decided:* Fidèle de Grivel, "Memoire Sur la Congregation Prov. du Maryland Commences le 3 Mai le 8 Juillet 1835," 1835, MD 5-I-21, ARSI.

81 *He divided the plantation:* Ibid.

82 *"I am much delighted":* Peter Kenney, journal entry, July 18, 1832, IE IJA/J/474/17/4, Irish Jesuit Archives, Dublin, Ireland.

82 *"I had no objections":* Joseph Carbery to George Fenwick, January 19, 1831, Box 64, Folder 3, MPA.

82 *He expressed admiration:* St. Inigoes ledger, 1804–1832, Box 44, File 1, MPA.

82 *And he praised Black Catholics:* Joseph Carbery to Stephen Dubuisson, April 27, 1838, Box 66, Folder 5, MPA.

82 *William Gaston:* Information about William Gaston, his enslaved young man, his views on slavery, and his decision to entrust Carbery with his slave come from J. Fairfax M'Laughlin, "William Gaston: The First Student of Georgetown College," *Records of the American Catholic Historical Society of Philadelphia* 6, no. 3 (September 1895): 225–51, https:// www.jstor.org/stable/44208793. While he affirmed that free Blacks could be citizens, Gaston also ruled that free Blacks could be treated unequally on the basis of their race. He ruled that an enslaved person's use of self defense was almost always unlawful. And by the time of his death, he held at least 163 Black people captive. John Mikhail, Adam Rothman, "Slaveholding and Judicial Opinions of William Gaston (2022)," GSA, accessed March 1, 2023, https://slaveryarchive .georgetown.edu/items/show/537.

83 *"I place my boy Augustus":* Georgetown University Library, "William Gaston Entrusts Augustus to Joseph Carberry, S.J., 1824," GSA, http:// slaveryarchive.georgetown.edu/items/show/33.

83 *Carbery kept his word:* The manumission record provides more details

about the enslaved young man, Augustus, including his age in 1824. He was not a "boy." Legacy of Slavery in Maryland, http://bit.ly /2FGdrPa.

83 *his brother served:* "Biographical Notes about Members of the Carbery Family," Box 1, Folder 12, Carbery Family Collection, GUL.

83 *and counted slaveholders among his kinsmen:* Will of John Baptist Carberry [paternal grandfather of Joseph Carbery], July 15, 1777, JJ1, f47 [the patriarch], proven 17 February 1778; Will of Peter Carberry [another son of John Baptist Carberry, uncle of Joseph], December 6, 1810, JJ3, f272.

83 *"an ignoramus":* Robert Emmett Curran, *Shaping American Catholicism: Maryland and New York, 1805–1915* (Washington, DC: Catholic University of America Press, 2012), 62.

83 *a skilled farmer:* Ibid.

83 *"Many speak in favor":* Peter Kenney, "Statement for the Consulters of the Mission on Its Actual State and all its Concerns," April 1820, Box 126, Folder 7, MPA.

83 *Carbery was elected:* Francis Michael Walsh, S.J., "Resurrection: The Story of the St. Inigoes Mission, 1634–1994," 2016, 99.

84 *He collected jokes:* Joseph Carbery, diary, Box 15, Folder 4, MPA.

84 *"Take of Wallnut tree bark":* Joseph Zwinge, "The Jesuit Farms in Maryland, Facts and Anecdotes," *Woodstock Letters* 41, no. 1 (1912): 63.

84 *Black people described Carbery:* John LaFarge, *The Manner Is Ordinary* (New York: Harcourt, 1954), 166.

84 *The Mahoney women cooked:* Joseph Agonito, "St. Inigoes Manor: A Nineteenth Century Jesuit Plantation," *Maryland Historical Magazine* 72, no. 1 (Spring 1977): 85.

84 *were blessed with two children:* Arnold Jones, Jr., was born sometime around 1830, according to his death certificate. Orleans Parish Deaths, vol. 96, p. 356, Louisiana State Archives.

84 *She named her baby girl:* Louisa Jones was six years old in 1838, thus born sometime in 1832, according to the passenger manifest of the *Katharine Jackson*. National Archives, Fort Worth, TX, "Manifest of the *Katharine* Jackson, 1838," GSA, http://slaveryarchive.georgetown.edu /items/show/2.

84 *Carbery's handwritten list:* Maryland State Archives, "St. Inigoes Tax Assessment, 1831," GSA, http://slaveryarchive.georgetown.edu/items /show/78.

85 *On November 13: Daily National Intelligencer,* November 15, 1833, 3, https://www.genealogybank.com/nbshare/AC01161217022016103941579195819.

85 *Thousands of fiery meteors:* "Shower of Fire," *Torch Light,* November 21, 1833, https://www.genealogybank.com/nbshare/AC01161217022016103941658226489.

85 *"the most grand and alarming spectacle":* "Singular Phenomenon," *Easton*

Star, November 19, 1833, https://www.genealogybank.com/nbshare/AC01161217022016103941658226590.

85 *Frank Campbell, an enslaved man:* Rachel L. Swarns, "A Glimpse into the Life of a Slave Sold to Save Georgetown," *New York Times,* March 12, 2017, https://www.nytimes.com/2017/03/12/us/georgetown-university-slaves-life-campbell.html.

85 *Anny's son, Arnold Jr.:* Louisa, the daughter of Anna Mahoney Jones, may have been born in 1832 or 1833. The Jesuit census of 1838 lists her as five years old that year. The passenger manifest of the *Katharine Jackson* lists her as six. Arnold, Jr., Anna Mahoney Jones's son, appears to have been between the ages of two and four. The census of 1838 lists him as seven that year. The manifest of the *Katharine Jackson* lists him as ... Jesuit Plantation Project, "List of Slaves Sold by Thomas Mulledy in 1838," GSA, https://slaveryarchive.georgetown.edu/items/show/9; National Archives, Washington, DC, Manifest of the *Katharine Jackson,* 1838.

85 *But a newspaper advertisement:* "$100 Dollars Reward," *American and Commercial Daily Advertiser,* November 13, 1833.

86 *Moses, who was about twenty-seven:* "A List of Slaves the Property of Thos. Smith," Assessment Record/Slaves 1831, St. Mary's County Levy Court, Book Name, E, Districts 1–5, Legacy accession no. C1545, MSA CE453-16.

87 *the Jesuits wanted:* Thomas J. Morrissey, *As One Sent: Peter Kenney SJ, 1779–1841: His Mission in Ireland and North America* (Blackrock, Co. Dublin: Four Courts Press, 1996), 228.

87 *"modest intellectual gifts":* Robert Emmett Curran, *The Bicentennial History of Georgetown University,* vol. 1: *From Academy to University, 1789–1889* (Washington, DC: Georgetown University Press, 1993), 109.

87 *Even Kenney, who championed him:* Morrissey, *As One Sent,* 244.

87 *Others had kinder plans:* Robert K. Judge, "First Years of the Maryland Province," *Woodstock Letters* 88, no. 4 (November 1959): 379.

87 *In the early 1830s:* Ibid.

87 *A black-and-white portrait:* GUL, http://repository.library.georgetown.edu/bitstream/handle/10822/551143/gu_archives_presidents_0012.jpg?sequence=1&isAllowed=y

88 *Some Jesuits would point:* "Memoire sur la Congregation Prov. du Maryland commence ... Mai ... 8 Juillet 1835" [1835], MD, 1-21, AD.

88 *But McSherry emphasized:* Maryland Province Archives, "Report ... Indigos 1833–7 by McSherry," GSA, https://slaveryarchive.georgetown.edu/items/show/20.

88 *Newtown:* Maryland Province Archives, "Report of Newtown 1833–7 by McSherry," GSA, http://slaveryarchive.georgetown.edu/items/show/19.

88 *St. Thomas Manor:* Maryland Province Archives, "Report ... of St. Thomas Manor, 1833, by McSherry," slaveryarchive.georgetown.edu/items/show/18.

88 *"We cannot have":* Curran, *Shaping American Catholicism: Maryland and New York, 1805–1915,* 112.

88 *He tried to sell:* Morrissey, *As One Sent,* 320–21.

89 *"Approved of selling Lucy":* Undated entry in Peter Kenney's journal; appears to have taken place in November 1832. Journals written by Fr. Peter Kenney during his visitation to the Maryland and Missouri Missions, 506/17, IJA.

89 *An enslaved worker at Georgetown:* Georgetown University Archive, "Georgetown College Sells Gabe, March 20, 1833," GSA, https://slaveryarchive.georgetown.edu/items/show/223.

89 *A decade earlier:* "Beyond the 272 Sold in 1838, Plotting the National Diaspora of Jesuit-Owned Slaves," *Hoya,* April 29, 2016. https://web.archive.org/web/20190202234049/https://features.thehoya.com/beyond-the-272-sold-in-1838-plotting-the-national-diaspora-of-jesuit-owned-slaves.

89 *But in a letter:* The letter from Thomas Brown is dated October 21, 1833. Maryland Province Archive, "Thomas Brown Letter, 1833," GSA, http://slaveryarchive.georgetown.edu/items/show/39.

90 *the average price of an enslaved person:* Edward E. Baptist, *The Half Has Never Been Told: Slavery and the Making of American Capitalism* (New York: Basic Books, 2016), 174.

90 *The state legislature had appropriated $200,000:* Ira Berlin, *Slaves Without Masters: The Free Negro in the Antebellum South* (New York: New Press, 2007), 202–03.

90 *"The prejudices of the colored people":* Ibid., 205.

90 *He wanted to keep:* Maryland Province Archives, "The Liberia Option," GSA, http://slaveryarchive.georgetown.edu/items/show/41.

91 *It was an extraordinary development:* "Maryland State Colonization Society Case Studies," Legacy of Slavery in Maryland, http://slavery.msa.maryland.gov/html/casestudies/mscscountycs.html.

91 *"The country is represented":* Maryland Province Archives, "The Liberia Option," GSA, http://slaveryarchive.georgetown.edu/items/show/41.

91 *Life in Liberia:* "Maryland State Colonization Society Case Studies."

92 *Father Stephen Dubuisson:* Archivum Romanum Societatis Iesu, " 'Is It Expedient to Sell These 300 Slaves?': The Dubuisson Memorandum, 1836," GSA, http://slaveryarchive.georgetown.edu/items/show/95.

92 *The winter of 1835:* The American Almanac and Repository of Useful Knowledge (Boston: Gray and Bowen, 1836), 178–81.

92 *Father Fidelis de Grivel gave thanks:* Fidelis de Grivel to Joseph Tristram, March 10, 1835, BJA.

92 *But the people living in the slave quarters:* Maryland 5 II 1 (Maryl.-1005-II_0149–52), ARSI.

92 *recently sold "a negroe boy":* November 24, 1834, Procurator Letter Books, 1831–1836, 1839–1843, MPA.

Chapter 8: Saving Georgetown

94 *"river closed up":* Thomas Mulledy, diary, March 7, 1835, GUL.

94 *He was writing to Rome:* Thomas Mulledy to Jan Roothaan, March 8, 1835, ARSI.

95 *The truth was:* Robert Emmett Curran, "'Wave Her Colors Ever!': Writing Georgetown's History," *U.S. Catholic Historian* 28, no. 3 (2010): 71.

95 *so much so:* Robert Emmett Curran, *The Bicentennial History of Georgetown University,* vol. 1, *From Academy to University, 1789–1889* (Washington, DC: Georgetown University Press, 1993), 116.

95 *the prices offered for enslaved people:* Edward E. Baptist, *The Half Has Never Been Told: Slavery and the Making of American Capitalism* (New York: Basic Books, 2016), 174.

95 *On July 2, he presided:* Thomas Mulledy, diary, July 2, 1835, MPA.

95 *The most pressing question:* Archivum Romanum Societatis Iesu, "Report on the Maryland Provincial Congregation, 1835," GSA, http:// slaveryarchive.georgetown.edu/items/show/273.

96 *the debate had spilled over:* Kate Masur, *Until Justice Be Done: America's First Civil Rights Movement, from the Revolution to Reconstruction* (New York: W. W. Norton, 2021), 86.

97 *Father Aloysius Young complained:* Robert Emmet Curran, "'Splendid Poverty': Jesuit Slaveholding in Maryland, 1805–1838," in *Shaping American Catholicism: Maryland and New York, 1805–1915* (Washington, DC: Catholic University of America Press, 2012), 43–44.

98 *"Received" of Father McSherry:* Entry, July 16, 1835, Cash Book 1835–1839, Box 1, p. 8, Additional Materials, pre-1864, 190D, MPA.

98 *sometimes attacked the Catholic Church:* John T. McGreevy, *Catholicism and American Freedom: A History* (New York: W. W. Norton, 2004), 57–62.

98 *Ryder denounced:* "Meeting of the Roman Catholic Congregation of the City of Richmond and County of Henrico," *Richmond Examiner;* GSA, "Proslavery Oration by Rev. James Ryder, SJ, August 30, 1835," GSA, http://slaveryarchive.georgetown.edu/items/show/88.

98 *Grivel would say later:* Fidèle de Grivel to Aloysius Landes, October 24, 1835, Maryland 5 II 1 (Maryl.-1005-II_0149–52), ARSI.

98 *Leonard Cutchmore was about:* The names, ages, and heights of the Cutchmores and Halls appear on the October 17, 1835, passenger manifest of the *Tribune* slave ship, which carried enslaved people from Alexandria, Virginia, to New Orleans. The surname of the Cutchmore family appears variously in records for the family. In this manifest, they appear as Cuckumber.

98 *He was the father:* Bazil Hall was the father of Thomas Hall, who is listed on the manifest of the brig *Tribune* along with Thomas's mother, Eliza. Judy Riffel, a genealogist at the Georgetown Memory Project, said that baptismal records in Ascension parish, Louisiana, document

the father/son relationship between Bazil and Thomas Hall. Email from Judy Riffel, May 23, 2018.

99 *eleven people, including:* Ledger entry, September 21, 1835, Cash Book 1834-1839, 190D, Additional Materials, Pre-1864, MPA. Also, Joseph Zwinge, "The Jesuit Farms in Maryland, Facts and Anecdotes: The Negro Slaves," *Woodstock Letters* 41, no. 3 (1912): 280–81.

99 *Slave sales broke apart:* Spencer Crew, Lonnie Bunch, and Clement Price, eds., *Slave Culture: A Documentary Collection of the Slave Narrative from the Federal Writers' Project* (Santa Barbara, CA: Greenwood/ABC-CLIO, 2014), 410–46.

99 *The Cutchmores were kin:* Henrietta Cutchmore, widow of Robert Brown, Certificate No. 627,817, Case Files of Approved Pension Applications of Veterans Who Served in the Army and Navy Mainly in the Civil War and the War with Spain, Civil War and Later Survivors' Certificates, 1861–1934; Civil War and Later Pension Files; Records of the Department of Veterans Affairs, Record Group 15; National Archives, Washington, DC.

100 *"The most perplexing inquiry":* Fidèle de Grivel to Aloysius Landes, October 24, 1835, Maryland 5 II 1 (Maryl.-1005-II_0149–52), ARSI.

100 *The Cutchmores and Halls were among:* Baptist, *The Half Has Never Been Told,* 256.

100 *"The wife was not separated":* Fidèle de Grivel to Aloysius Landes.

101 *Johnson had a foot:* Joseph G. Dawson III, ed., *The Louisiana Governors: From Iberville to Edwards* (Baton Rouge: Louisiana State University Press, 1990), 99–102.

101 *He owned dozens of slaves:* Mortgage records from 1835 indicate that Henry Johnson enslaved ninety-two people in LaFourche parish before he relocated to St. James parish, where the Cutchmores and the Halls ended up. Mortgage by Henry Johnson and wife, Elizabeth Key, to the Bank of Louisiana, April 17, 1835, accession record 001-009-007, La-Fourche Parish Courthouse Records, Ellender Memorial Library, Nicholls State University, Thibodaux, LA.

101 *His wife, Elizabeth Rousby Key:* Sewell and Elizabeth Key had common ancestors. Nicholas Sewell, who emigrated from England, was the father of Henry and Elizabeth Sewell. Henry was Charles's grandfather. Elizabeth Sewell was Elizabeth Key's great-great-grandmother. "Early Colonial Settlers of Southern Maryland and Virginia's Northern Neck Counties," https://www.colonial-settlers-md-va.us/familychart.php ?personID=I15294&tree=Tree1.

101 *a prominent Jesuit:* Curran, *The Bicentennial History of Georgetown University,* vol. 1: *From Academy to University, 1789–1889,* 402.

101 *had battled Louisa's and Anna's relatives:* William G. Thomas, *A Question of Freedom: The Families Who Challenged Slavery from the Nation's Founding to the Civil War* (New Haven, CT: Yale University Press, 2020), 89.

101 *Johnson had been trying:* Dawson, *The Louisiana Governors,* 100–01.
101 *About four months:* Johnson sold his plantation in Lafouche parish in
       1835: Henry Johnson to Henry Bibb, May 16, 1835, accession record
       001-009-011, Box 26, Folder 2, LaFourche Parish Courthouse Records,
       Ellender Memorial Library, Nicholls State University, Thibodaux, LA.
       Johnson purchased a plantation in St. James parish at around the same
       time and relocated there that year. The purchase is described in this
       mortgage record: Mortgage by Henry Johnson to Citizens Bank, Feb-
       ruary 9, 1837, Mortgage Book C, 300–05, St. James parish, LA.
101 *The Jesuits at St. Inigoes:* Fidèle Grivel to Aloysius Landes, October 24,
       1835, Maryland 5 II 1 (Maryl.-1005-II_0149–52), ARSI.
102 *He negotiated a discount:* Entry, September 7, 1836, Cash Book,
       1834–1839, Box 1, 49, 190D, Additional Materials, Pre-1864, MPA.
102 *When spring came: The American Almanac and Repository of Useful Knowl-
       edge for the Year 1837* (Boston: Charles Bowen, 1837), 188.
102 *Father Carbery cobbled together:* Maryland State Archives, "Fr. Carbery
       Requests a Tax Deduction for the Value of Seventeen Slaves Sold by
       the Maryland Jesuits, 1836," GSA, http://slaveryarchive.georgetown.edu
       /items/show/311.
103 *"The slaves would be most able to enjoy":* Dubuisson, Archivum Roma-
       num Societatis Iesu, " 'Is It Expedient to Sell These 300 Slaves?': The
       Dubuisson Memorandum, 1836," GSA, http://slaveryarchive.georgetown
       .edu/items/show/95.
103 *"There is, in general, a great repugnance":* Ibid.
104 *The news of his flight:* "$600 Reward," *American and Commercial Daily
       Advertiser,* August 5, 1836.
104 *So he requested and received:* Maryland State Archives, "St. Mary's
       County Deducts Two Slaves from St. Inigoes' Tax Burden, 1837," GSA,
       http://slaveryarchive.georgetown.edu/items/show/307.
105 *McSherry picked up his pen:* William McSherry to Jan Roothaan, Au-
       gust 30, 1836, Maryl.-1005-II_0156-0158, ARSI.
106 *An unexpected blizzard*: Bowen, *The American Almanac and Repository of
       Useful Knowledge for the Year 1837,* 323. The storm took place on Octo-
       ber 5, 1836.
106 *"a great snow storm":* Thomas Mulledy, diary, October 5, 1836, Box 8,
       Folder 4, Mulledy Papers, GUL.
106 *He headed out:* Thomas Mulledy, diary, October 7, 1836, Mulledy Pa-
       pers, GUL.
106 *word had come back from Rome:* Thomas Murphy, *Jesuit Slaveholding in
       Maryland, 1717–1838* (New York: Routledge, 2016), 199. Murphy said
       that Roothaan made the decision in October. Roothaan wrote to
       McSherry in December, discussing the decision, but indicated that
       Father Vespre had already informed McSherry.
106 *He prayed for his recovery:* Thomas Mulledy, diary, October 14, 1836,
       Mulledy Papers, GUL.

106 *Father Francis Vespre:* Undated note from Reverend Francis Vespre describing Roothaan's conditions for the sale, Maryl.-1005-II_0171-0175, ARSI.

108 *Roothaan himself weighed in:* Maryland Province Archives, "Fr. Roothaan, S.J. Lays Out the Conditions for the Sale of Slaves, 27 December 1836," GSA, http://slaveryarchive.georgetown.edu/items/show/94.

109 *he traveled to Georgetown:* Francis Michael Walsh, S.J., "Resurrection: The Story of the St. Inigoes Mission, 1634–1994," 2016, 121.

109 *He pleaded with the senior Jesuits:* John LaFarge, *The Manner Is Ordinary* (New York: Image Books, 1957), 166–67.

109 *After the meeting:* Walsh, "Resurrection," 121.

Chapter 9: The Sale

110 *On Monday, January 9:* David C. Frederick, "John Quincy Adams, Slavery, and the Disappearance of the Right of Petition," *Law and History Review* 9, no. 1 (1991): 152, https://doi.org/10.2307/743661.

110 *"the sinfulness of slavery":* William Henry Seward, *Life and Public Services of John Quincy Adams: Sixth President of the United States* (Auburn: Miller, Orton & Mulligan, 1856), 284.

110 *"immediately to abolish":* "John Quincy Adams: Gag Rule Controversy, Question of Non-Reception, House of Representatives, Monday, January 9, 1837," Wake Forest University, https://users.wfu.edu/zulick/340/gagrule1.html.

110 *A vote was called:* "A Century of Lawmaking for a New Nation: U.S. Congressional Documents and Debates, 1774–1875," Register of Debates, House of Representatives, 24th Congress, 2nd Session, Monday, January 9, 1837, Library of Congress, https://memory.loc.gov/cgi-bin/ampage?collId=llrd&fileName=026/llrd026.db&recNum=660.

111 *Adams had argued:* David C. Frederick, "John Quincy Adams, Slavery, and the Disappearance of the Right of Petition," *Law and History Review* 9, no. 1 (Spring 1991): 137.

111 *Johnson warned the men:* "A Century of Lawmaking for a New Nation: U.S. Congressional Documents and Debates, 1774–1875."

112 *he was making arrangements:* Mortgage Book C, February 9, 1837, 300–05, St. James parish, LA.

112 *a sprawling estate equipped:* Ibid. The mortgage describes the plantation in detail.

112 *the Cutchmores and Halls never forgot:* The Cutchmores' daughter Henrietta would describe the family's origins in Maryland in a filing for a Civil War pension. Henrietta Cutchmore, widow of Robert Brown, Certificate No. 627,817, Case Files of Approved Pension Applications of Veterans Who Served in the Army and Navy Mainly in the Civil War and the War with Spain, Civil War and Later Survivors' Certificates, 1861–1934; Civil War and Later Pension Files; Records of the Depart-

ment of Veterans Affairs, Record Group 15; National Archives, Washington, DC.

112 *St. James parish bordered property:* Mortgage Book C, February 9, 1837, 300–05.

113 *in the spring of 1837:* Robert Emmet Curran, *The Bicentennial History of Georgetown University,* vol. 1: *From Academy to University, 1789–1889* (Washington, DC: Georgetown University Press, 1993), 120.

113 *Once again the market value:* William McSherry to Jan Roothaan, May 13, 1837, Maryl.-1005-I_0122, ARSI.

113 *Anny's husband, Arnold:* Alienations and Transfers, St. Mary's County, Levy Court, 1832–1838, 277, C1511-1, MSA.

113 *"If you shall send":* Henry Johnson to William Johnson, July 10, 1837, Z0058, William Johnson Papers, MDAH.

113 *"an institution equal":* Henry Johnson to William Johnson, September 25, 1836, William Johnson Papers, MDAH.

114 *the price of cotton:* John M. Sacher, *A Perfect War of Politics: Parties, Politicians, and Democracy in Louisiana, 1824–1861* (Baton Rouge: Louisiana State University Press, 2003), 86.

114 *"it can no longer be":* Ibid.

114 *Johnson had described:* Henry Johnson to William Johnson, April 7, 1834, Z0058, William Johnson Papers, MDAH.

114 *Johnson bought a new plantation:* Henry Johnson, land purchase in Ascension parish, July 25, 1837, Notarial Acts, vol. 14, 167–68, Ascension Parish Courthouse, Donaldsonville, LA.

114 *he sold much of the land:* Henry Johnson, land sale, July 26, 1837, CB 16, 359–63, St. James Parish Clerk of Court, Convent, LA.

114 *he owned land:* In addition to the land that Henry Johnson owned in St. James and Ascension parishes, he also still owned land in LaFourche parish. Johnson land purchase, A. G. Gilbert to H. Johnson, recorded July 25, 1837, 025-005-022, LaFourche Parish Courthouse Records, Ellender Memorial Library, Nicholls State University, Thibodaux, LA.

114 *The plantation in St. James parish:* Henry Johnson, mortgage to Citizens Bank, July 25, 1837, CB 16, 359–63, St. James Parish Clerk of Court.

115 *Johnson arranged:* Baptisms in Convent, St. James parish, 1837–1840, email from Ann Boltin, Archivist/Records Manager, Diocese of Baton Rouge, Louisiana, July 10, 2020.

115 *He started with Milly:* Slave sale, July 31, 1837, CB 21, 291, St. James Parish Clerk of Court.

115 *In September, he sold Peter:* Notarial Acts, September 21, 1837, vol. 14, 215–16, Parish of Ascension, LA.

115 *In November, six weeks:* Notarial Acts, November 25, 1837, vol. 15, 182–83, Parish of Ascension, LA.

115 *In the books and articles:* Joseph G. Dawson III, ed., *The Louisiana Governors: From Iberville to Edwards* (Baton Rouge: Louisiana State University Press, 1990), 101–03; Sacher, *A Perfect War of Politics,* 103.

116 *He had stomach cancer:* Curran, *The Bicentennial History of Georgetown University,* vol. 1, 121.

116 *taking instead the role:* Ibid.

116 *By January 1838:* Ibid., 118–19.

116 *missing Mass:* Thomas Mulledy, diary, September 12, October 4–6, 16, and December 23, 1837, Mulledy Papers, GUL.

116 *He spent much:* Ibid. Mulledy visited the plantations between February 12 and March 3, 1838.

116 *"disagreeable work":* Joseph Zwinge, "The Jesuit Farms in Maryland, Facts and Anecdotes: The Negro Slaves," *Woodstock Letters* 41, no. 3 (1912): 282.

117 *"From same [St. Thomas]":* Ledger entry, May 4, 1838, Cash Book 1834–1839, 18L, Additional Materials, Box 1, 190D, Additional Materials, Pre-1864, MPA.

117 *"The professors at the Institution":* Henry Johnson to William Johnson, May 6, 1838, William Johnson Papers, MDAH.

117 *he accepted Mulledy's invitation:* Zwinge, "The Jesuit Farms in Maryland, Facts and Anecdotes: The Negro Slaves," 282.

117 *produced wheat and other grains:* Maryland Province Archives, "Report of Income &c Newtown 1833+7 by McSherry," GSA, http:// slaveryarchive.georgetown.edu/items/show/19.

117 *He had pleaded:* Peter Havermans to Jan Roothaan, February 14, 1840, Maryl.-1007-VI_0361cENGLISH, ARSI.

118 *In preparation for a mass sale:* Maryland Province Archives, "Census of people to be sold in 1838," GSA, accessed January 28, 2023, http:// slaveryarchive.georgetown.edu/items/show/71.

118 *carefully documenting:* Jesuit Plantation Project, "List of People Sold by Fr. Thomas Mulledy in 1838," GSA, http://slaveryarchive.georgetown .edu/items/show/9.

118 *Among them was Anny's husband:* A notation after Arnold Jones's name indicates that he "ran away." Ibid.

119 *"to take a look at our negroes":* Zwinge, "The Jesuit Farms in Maryland, Facts and Anecdotes: The Negro Slaves," 282.

119 *At St. Inigoes, they found:* Jesuit Plantation Project, "List of People Sold by Fr. Thomas Mulledy in 1838."

119 *Nelly seemed safe:* The priest purchased shoes for Nelly on May 19, 1838. Account Book, St. Mary's Church, 1831–1856, Box 79, MPA.

119 *One of his sons, Gabriel:* Ibid.

119 *At slave auctions, white men:* Walter Johnson, *Soul by Soul: Life Inside the Antebellum Slave Market* (Cambridge, MA: Harvard University Press, 1999), 149–52.

120 *Batey found lodgings:* "Jesse Batey Advertisement, Washington Globe, May 29, 1838," GSA, http://slaveryarchive.georgetown.edu/items/show /224.

120 *Brown's Indian Queen Hotel:* A lithograph of the hotel, with a caption

describing it, can be found on the Library of Congress website, https://www.loc.gov/pictures/item/93506552/.

120 *"This mixture of good & evil":* Thomas Mulledy, sermon at Newtown, May 20, 1838, Box 5, Folder 1, Mulledy Papers, GUL.

120 *He focused instead:* Thomas Mulledy, sermon at Newport, Maryland, May 30, 1838, Box 5, Folder 1, Mulledy Papers, GUL.

120 *He was so busy:* Maryland Province Archives, " 'I Would Be Willing to Take $450': Fr. Mulledy to Fr. McElroy on Pricing People, June 12, 1838," GSA, http://slaveryarchive.georgetown.edu/items/show/100.

121 *he dedicated Masses:* Thomas Mulledy, diary, June 13, 14, and 15, 1838, Mulledy Papers, GUL.

121 *But on Saturday evening: Daily Intelligencer,* June 19, 1838, 3, Genealogy Bank, https://bit.ly/2xsHZoa.

121 *served as paymaster general:* Francis B. Heitman, *Historical Register and Dictionary of the United States Army, 1789–1903,* vol. 1 (Washington, DC: Government Printing Office, 1903), 968.

121 *had come to an agreement:* Maryland Province Archives, "Articles of Agreement Between Thomas F. Mulledy, of Georgetown, District of Columbia, of One Part, and Jesse Beatty and Henry Johnson, of the State of Louisiana, of the Other Part. 19th June 1838," GSA, http://slaveryarchive.georgetown.edu/items/show/1.

121 *272 men, women, and children:* The 1838 agreement described the sale of 272 people, but the Georgetown Memory Project has found that as many as 314 people would ultimately be sold. "The Lost Jesuit Slaves of Maryland: Searching for the people left behind in 1838, Update," Georgetown Memory Project, June 19, 2019, https://www.georgetownmemoryproject.org/wp-content/uploads/Research-Memo-2019-Update.pdf.

123 *one of the largest documented slave sales:* The sale of 429 people in Georgia in 1859 has been described by historians as the nation's largest recorded slave sale. Michael E, Ruane, "It was the nation's largest auction of enslaved people. Now, a search for descendants of the 'weeping time,'" *Washington Post,* October 12, 2019.

123 *Horatio Trunnell, the man hired:* Reports of Committees, 16th Congress, 1st Session–49th Congress, 1st Session, vol. 2, United States Congress, House, January 1834, 313–14, 799–800.

123 *"Without any notice":* Thomas Lilly to Jan Roothaan, July 2, 1838, Maryl.-1007-II_0191cENGLISH, ARSI.

123 *The Jesuit financial ledgers:* Ledger entries, June 25, 1838, Cash Book, 1834–1839, Box 1, 18R, Additional Materials, MPA.

124 *purchased a year later by:* Jeff Forret, *Williams' Gang: A Notorious Slave Trader and His Cargo of Black Convicts* (New York: Cambridge University Press, 2020), 74.

124 *Williams announced:* "For New Orleans," *Alexandria Gazette,* June 21, 1838, 4, https://www.genealogybank.com/nbshare/AC0116121702201610394160016212I.

124 *But on June 29:* "Ship News," *Alexandria Gazette,* June 29, 1838, 3, https://www.genealogybank.com/nbshare/AC01161217022016 103941600163055.

124 *"poor negroes":* Thomas Mulledy, diary, June 29 and June 30, 1838, Mulledy Papers, GUL.

124 *"It is with the greatest pain":* Thomas Lilly to Jan Roothaan, July 2, 1838, Maryl.-1007-II_0191c, ARSI.

125 *"The whole of the said":* Agreement between Thomas Mulledy and Jesse Batey, July 6, 1838, H/293, Washington, DC.

125 *on five occasions that summer:* Thomas Mulledy, diary, July 5, July 25, 27, and 28 and August 9, 1838, Mulledy Papers, GUL.

125 *In a defiant letter:* Thomas Mulledy to Jan Roothaan, August 9, 1838, Maryl.-1007-I_0014c, ARSI.

127 *"Father Mulledy has his share":* Quoted in Cornelius Michael Buckley, *Stephen Larigaudelle Dubuisson, S.J. (1786–1864) and the Reform of the American Jesuits* (Lanham, MD: University Press of America, 2013), 236–37.

127 *where the temperature soared:* Thomas Mulledy to Jan Roothaan, August 9, 1838, Maryl.-1007-I_0014c, ARSI.

127 *while floods ravaged:* Charles Bowen, *The American Almanac and Repository of Useful Knowledge for the Year 1840* (Boston: Gray and Bowen, 1839), 312.

128 *$23,214 from Johnson:* Cash Book 1834–1839, Box 1, 190D, Additional Materials, pre-1864, MPA.

128 *The rest of the down payment:* Thomas Mulledy to Jan Roothaan, August 9, 1838, Maryl.-1007-I_0014c, ARSI.

129 *On a sweltering afternoon:* "The Eclipse," *American and Commercial Daily Advertiser,* September 21, 1838, 2, https://www.genealogybank.com /nbshare/AC01161217022016103941601561913.

129 *Some prayed:* Peter Wheeler, an enslaved man, described an eclipse as a sign to run for freedom: Peter Wheeler and Charles Lester Edwards, *Chains and Freedom: Or, The Life and Adventures of Peter Wheeler, a Colored Man Yet Living. A Slave in Chains, a Sailor on the Deep, and a Sinner at the Cross* (New York: E.S. Arnold & Co, 1839), 11. Nancy Whallen, an enslaved woman in Kentucky, described witnessing a solar eclipse and the reaction among the enslaved. Many feared the world was coming to an end: Works Progress Administration, *Slave Narratives: A Folk History of Slavery in the United States From Interviews with Former Slaves: Indiana Narratives,* Project Gutenberg EBook, 2004: https://www .gutenberg.org/files/13579/13579-8.txt.

129 *Father Havermans protested:* Peter Havermans to Jan Roothaan, October 20, 1838, Maryl.-1007-I_0032c.pdf, ARSI.

129 *"handed themselves over to fate":* Ibid.

130 *He wrote to Rome:* Ibid.

130 *"Set out for St. Innigoes":* Thomas Mulledy, diary, October 31, 1838, Mulledy Papers, GUL.

131 *prayed once again for:* Ibid, November 1, 1838.

131 **Run!** *he told them.* **Run!**: John LaFarge, *The Manner Is Ordinary* (New York: Harcourt, 1954), 166.

131 *Louisa ran with her mother:* Francis Michael Walsh, S.J., "Resurrection: The Story of the St. Inigoes Mission, 1634–1994," 2016, 124.

132 *"I have been":* Thomas Mulledy to John McElroy, November 11, 1838, Box 66, Folder 3, MPA.

132 *The enslaved families were herded:* Receipt for payment to Dr. James Roach and Captain John Gibson, November 12, 1838, Agent Accounts, Bills Kept for History, Box 1, Additional Materials, pre-1864, MPA.

132 *"Governor Johnson will have":* Fidelis Grivel to John Lancaster, November 6, 1838, Box 66, Folder 3, MPA.

133 *On November 12:* Ledger entry, November 12, 1838, Cash Book 1834–1839, Box 1, 20L, 190D, Additional Materials, pre-1864, MPA.

133 *"an immense slave factory":* Joshua D. Rothman, *The Ledger and the Chain: How Domestic Slave Traders Shaped America* (New York: Basic Books, 2021), 273.

133 *"a few slaves":* Ibid., 86.

133 *Windsor, who also worked:* Alison T. Mann, "Slavery Exacts an Impossible Price: John Quincy Adams and the Dorcas Allen Case, Washington, DC," PhD dissertation, University of New Hampshire, 2010, 38.

133 *"how kind they were to the prisoners":* Rothman, *The Ledger and the Chain,* 273.

133 *"rings made of round iron":* Ibid., 100.

133 *He knew about the dungeon:* Ibid.

134 *Someone had heard children screaming:* Mann, "Slavery Exacts an Impossible Price," x.

134 *"by which they were horribly mangled":* Ibid., 21.

134 *found the woman not guilty:* Ibid., 2, 83.

135 *Sometime around November 13: Alexandria Gazette,* November 14, 1838, 1, https://bit.ly/315vN92.

135 *White residents took pride:* "Discovering the Decades: The 1830s," City of Alexandria, VA, https://www.alexandriava.gov/historic/info/default .aspx?id=28398.

135 *Witnesses described Black men:* Edward Ball, "Retracing Slavery's Trail of Tears," *Smithsonian Magazine,* November 2015, https://www .smithsonianmag.com/history/slavery-trail-of-tears-180956968/.

135 *"Scarcely a week passes":* Quoted in Jeff Forret, *Williams' Gang: A Notorious Slave Trader and His Cargo of Black Convicts* (Cambridge, UK: Cambridge University Press, 2020), ProQuest Ebook Central, http:// ebookcentral.proquest.com/lib/nyulibrary-ebooks/detail.action?docID =6028977.

136 *One Black witness:* Rothman, *The Ledger and the Chain,* 202.

136 *Jacob Stroyer:* Jacob Stroyer, *My Life in the South* (Salem, NC: Salem Observer Book and Job Print, 1885), 42–44.

136 *"We have purchased":* Robert Windsor to Rice C. Ballard, Septem-

ber 24, 1834, Folder 15, Rice C. Ballard Papers, Collection 04850, Southern Historical Collection, Louis Round Wilson Special Collections, University of North Carolina, Chapel Hill.

136 **the Katharine Jackson:** Jenifer Dolde, "Fleshing Out a Disconcerting History: The Hidden Years of the Ship *Katherine Jackson,*" *Sea History* 165 (Winter 2018–19): 22–23, https://seahistory.org/wp-content /uploads/CBMM-Katherine-Jackson-SH-165.pdf.

136 *Anny and her children:* National Archives, Fort Worth, TX, "Manifest of the Katharine Jackson, 1838," GSA, http://slaveryarchive.georgetown .edu/items/show/2.

137 *Anny, described:* Ibid.

Chapter 10: A Family Divided

138 *George Washington:* Joel Achenbach, *The Grand Idea: George Washington's Potomac and the Race to the West* (New York: Simon & Schuster, 2005), 5.

138 *Thomas Jefferson:* Ibid., 43.

138 *They fished and dug:* Mobberly, diary, 1820, Box 1, Folder 1, 128–38, Joseph P. Mobberly, S.J., Papers, GUL.

139 *Between 1800 and 1860:* Joshua D. Rothman, *The Ledger and the Chain: How Domestic Slave Traders Shaped America* (New York: Basic Books, 2021), 3.

139 *more than twice the number:* Ibid.

139 *Trail of Tears:* Edward Ball, "Retracing Slavery's Trail of Tears," *Smithsonian Magazine*, November 2015.

139 *someone was sold about every 3.5 minutes:* Rothman, *The Ledger and the Chain,* 7.

139 *The Potomac twists and turns:* Norfolk and Washington Steamboat Company, "Route Map of the Norfolk & Washington Steamboat Company: Showing the Potomac River, Chesapeake Bay, and Adjacent Territory in Maryland and Virginia," Library of Congress, https://www .loc.gov/item/89694335/.

139 *Some slave ships made stops:* Calvin Schermerhorn, "The Maritime United States Slave Trade, 1807–1850," *Journal of Social History* 47, no. 4 (Summer 2014): 897–921.

140 *"I can see us now":* DaNean Olene Pound, "Slave to the Ex-Slave Narratives," master's thesis, Northwestern State University of Louisiana, 2005, 17.

140 *Solomon Northup:* Solomon Northup, *Twelve Years a Slave* (New York: 37 Ink, 2013), 46.

140 *But at night, Northup recalled:* Ibid., 45.

140 *wooden platforms lined:* Calvin Schermerhorn, *The Business of Slavery and the Rise of American Capitalism, 1815–1860* (New Haven, CT: Yale University Press, 2015), 147.

140 *a ship designed to hold:* Schermerhorn, Ibid., 139.

141 *"The brig rolled and plunged":* Northup, *Twelve Years a Slave,* 45.

141 *Smallpox sickened and killed:* Ibid., 49.

141 *In his memoir, he described:* Jeff Forret, *Williams' Gang: A Notorious Slave Trader and His Cargo of Black Convicts* (New York: Cambridge University Press, 2020), 80–81.

142 *The river would carry:* Rothman, *The Ledger and the Chain,* xx.

142 *By the time the ship:* National Archives, Fort Worth, TX, "Manifest of the Katharine Jackson, 1838," GSA, http://slaveryarchive.georgetown.edu/items/show/2.

142 *the city that housed the largest slave market:* Walter Johnson, *Soul by Soul: Life Inside the Antebellum Slave Market* (Cambridge, MA: Harvard University Press, 1999), 2.

142 *By 1830, cotton:* Rothman, *The Ledger and the Chain,* xx.

142 *By 1834, New Orleans:* Forret, *Williams' Gang: A Notorious Slave Trader and His Cargo of Black Convicts,* 91.

143 *thousands of flatboats:* Johnson, *Soul by Soul: Life Inside the Antebellum Slave Market,* 1.

143 *For the wealthy white elite:* Rothman, *The Ledger and the Chain,* 116.

143 *"In all the crowd":* Northup, *Twelve Years a Slave,* 52.

143 *Enslaved people:* Johnson, *Soul by Soul,* 2.

143 *Northup ended up:* Northup, *Twelve Years a Slave,* 53–56.

144 *A New Orleans merchant company:* National Archives, Fort Worth, TX, "Manifest of the Katharine Jackson, 1838."

144 *The saga of the river journey:* Sharon Litwin, "Helping Hand: At 83, She's Still Dishing Out Love and Care," *Times Picayune* (New Orleans), August 11, 1980. This is an interview with Geneva Taylor Smith, a descendant of Robert Mahoney, the older brother of Anna and Louisa, who ended up on Batey's plantation in Terrebonne parish.

144 *White travelers wrote about:* Thomas C. Buchanan, *Black Life on the Mississippi: Slaves, Free Blacks, and the Western Steamboat World* (Chapel Hill: University of North Carolina Press, 2004), 31–33.

145 *had established estates:* Judy Riffel, "History of Marengo Plantation," Report, Georgetown Memory Project, June 17, 2022, 2, in author's possession.

145 *Anny had been purchased:* Judy Riffel, "Bibiana Mahoney," Report, Georgetown Memory Project, January 27, 2019, 1, in author's possession.

145 *only four years earlier:* Ibid., 1–2.

145 *Cotton was white gold:* Edward E. Baptist, *The Half Has Never Been Told: Slavery and the Making of American Capitalism* (New York: Basic Books, 2016), 112–19.

146 *Prices had plummeted:* Ibid.

146 *It fueled the Industrial Revolution:* Ibid., 113.

146 *Old people and children:* Ibid., 116.

146 *unseen in the Upper South:* Ibid., 116–17.

147 *Anny and her family had heard:* Stephen Dubuisson, memorandum, 1836, Maryl.-1005-II_0159-0167, ARSI.

147 *"that all attempts":* Journal of the House of Representatives of the United States, 1836–1837, Tuesday, December 11, 1838, A Century of Lawmaking for a New Nation: U.S. Congressional Documents and Debates, 1774–1875, Library of Congress, https://memory.loc.gov/cgi-bin /query/D?hlaw:28:./temp/~ammem_y2Kl::.

147 *"I have not yet visited":* Henry Johnson to William Johnson, April 24, 1839, William Johnson Papers, 1811–1859, MDAH.

148 *Louisa and her mother:* Joseph Zwinge, "The Jesuit Farms in Maryland, Facts and Anecdotes The Negro Slaves," *Woodstock Letters* 41, no. 2 (1912): 195.

148 *For days, they had gone:* John LaFarge, *The Manner Is Ordinary* (New York: Harcourt, 1954), 166.

149 *received $15.50:* Receipt, November 10, 1838, Agent Accounts, Bills Kept for History, Box 2, Additional Materials, pre-1864, MPA.

149 *a total of $57.50:* Receipt for payment to Dr. James Roach and Captain John Gibson, November 12, 1838, Agent Accounts, Bills Kept for History, Box 2, Additional Materials, pre-1864, MPA.

149 *received $75:* Receipt, November 23, 1838, Agent Accounts, Bills Kept for History, Box 2.

149 *"Paid for taking Charles":* Entry, November 29, 1838, Cash Book, 1834–1839, 20R, 190D, Additional Materials, pre-1864, MPA.

149 *"Ten dollars for taking negro":* Receipt, December 8, 1838, Agent Accounts, Bills Kept for History, Box 2, Additional Materials, pre-1864, MPA.

149 *sometime around December 22, 1838:* Charles Queen appears on the passenger manifest of the *Isaac Franklin,* which departed Alexandria on December 1, 1838, and arrived in New Orleans around December 22, 1838. Information provided by Judy Riffel on February 9, 2016.

149 *Finally, exhausted and famished:* LaFarge, *The Manner Is Ordinary,* 166.

150 *Among them were Harry:* The Jesuits' census of 1838 describes Harry and Gabriel Mahoney as married to women on other plantations. Jesuit Plantation Project, "List of People Sold by Fr. Thomas Mulledy in 1838," GSA, http://slaveryarchive.georgetown.edu/items/show/9.

150 *Her older sister Nelly:* Nelly visited her father, Harry, at St. Inigoes in June 1840, and her sister visited her the following year. Box 79, Account Book, St. Mary's Church, 1831–1856, Maryland/Virginia Chapter, MPA.

150 *Young Harry Mahoney was sold:* Maryland State Archives, "Fr. Carbery Identifies Ten St. Inigoes Slaves Who Were Not Sold to Louisiana in 1838," http://slaveryarchive.georgetown.edu/items/show/312.

150 *"a brig for carrying them":* Fidèle de Grivel to Charles Lancaster, February 8, 1839, Box 66, Folder 2, MPA.

151 *"Some children":* Maryland Province Archives, "Old Isaac Remained:

Fr. Grivel to Fr. Lancaster, May 4, 1839," GSA, http://slaveryarchive
.georgetown.edu/items/show/156.

151 *"The slaves I purchased":* Maryland Province Archive, "'Healthy and
Well Pleased': Henry Johnson to Fr. McSherry, April 27, 1839," GSA,
http://slaveryarchive.georgetown.edu/items/show/155.

151 *In Rome, Jan Roothaan:* Maryland Province Archives, Society of Jesus,
"'I Rejoice That the Matter of the Negroes Is Concluded': Fr. Roothaan to Fr. Mulledy, March 4, 1839," GSA, http://slaveryarchive
.georgetown.edu/items/show/383.

151 *"I rejoice":* Ibid.

152 *"The Superior of St. Inogies":* Stephen Dubuisson to Jan Roothaan,
June 21, 1839, Maryl.-1007-I_0047-0049, ARSI.

152 *"I do hereby certify":* Maryland State Archives, "Fr. Carbery Identifies
Ten St. Inigoes Slaves Who Were Not Sold to Louisiana in 1838."

152 *Carbery sold off:* Ibid.

Chapter 11: Exile

153 *It was the dead of summer:* Commercial Advertiser, July 9, 1839.

153 *"large vessel and a good sailer":* "The Journey to Found Notre Dame,"
Notre Dame Trail, August 13–26, 2017, University of Notre Dame,
https://trail.nd.edu/story/father-sorins-journey/.

154 *also wrote to Rome:* Robert Emmett Curran, *The Bicentennial History of
Georgetown University,* vol. 1: *From Academy to University, 1789–1889*
(Washington, DC: Georgetown University Press, 1993), 120–21.

154 *"The effect of the size":* Stephen Dubuisson to Jan Roothaan, June 21,
1839, Maryl.-1007-I_0047-0049, ARSI.

154 *Then they joined forces:* Curran, *The Bicentennial History of Georgetown
University,* vol. 1, 120–21.

154 *On June 27, 1839:* Samuel Eccleston to Jan Roothaan, June 27, 1839,
Maryland 7 I, ARSI.

155 *left Mulledy reeling:* Curran, *The Bicentennial History of Georgetown University,* vol. 1, 120–21.

155 *"No mass":* Thomas Mulledy, diary, June 27, 1839, Mulledy Papers,
GUL.

155 *He left Georgetown on Independence Day:* Thomas Mulledy, diary,
July 4–8, 1839, Mulledy Papers, GUL; "Paid to R. F. Thos F. Mulledy
Provl for his journey to Europe $160," July 3, 1839, Cash Book 1834-
1839 (190D), Additional Materials, pre-1864, MPA.

156 *he dedicated the church service:* Thomas Mulledy, diary, July 31, 1839,
Mulledy Papers, GUL.

156 *In the end:* Curran, *The Bicentennial History of Georgetown University,*
vol. 1, 120–21.

156 *By the second week of October:* Thomas Mulledy, diary, October 11,
1839, Mulledy Papers, GUL.

157 *In December of that year:* The letter was published on December 3, 1839. Kenneth J. Zanca, *American Catholics and Slavery, 1789–1866: An Anthology of Primary Documents* (Lanham, MS: University Press of America, 1994), 27–29.

157 *"well & in fine spirits":* Henry Johnson to William Johnson, September 25, 1839, MDAH.

158 *"could not succeed":* Ibid.

158 *had remained on the Newtown plantation:* Henry Johnson to Robert Windsor, Sept. 24, 1839, Papers of Robert N. Windsor, 1839–1845, Accession no. 2867, University of Virginia Library, Charlottesville, Virginia.

158 *"The enclosed paper":* Henry Johnson to Robert Windsor, Sept. 25, 1839, Papers of Robert N. Windsor, 1839–1845, University of Virginia Library, Charlottesville, Virginia.

158 *Bishop Benedict Fenwick:* Curran, *Shaping American Catholicism,* 101.

159 *McSherry had been suffering:* Ibid., 121.

159 *The priests consulted:* Joseph Zwinge to William McSherry, June 1, 1913, Box 5, Folder 21, Carbery Family Papers, GUL. The letter from Zwinge includes an excerpt of a letter that describes McSherry's last days. The extract is dated December 14, 1839, with postscripts dated December 18 and 20, 1839.

159 *"You had appointed":* Ibid.

159 *"The fate is sealed":* Ibid.

159 *Over the next two months:* Notices appeared in the *Daily National Intelligencer,* the *New-York Weekly Whig,* the *Boston Courier,* the *Newark Daily Advertiser,* and other newspapers.

160 *"is regarded by the church":* Curran, *Shaping American Catholicism,* 93–94.

160 *the priest would buy her clothing:* Multiple ledger entries, including on August 10, November 21, and December 6, 1839; September 4, 1840; and January 29, 1841, Account Book, St. Mary's Church, 1831–1856, Box 79, MPA.

160 *Harry Mahoney:* Ledger entry, June 27, 1840, and handwritten note dated sometime in 1841 mention Nelly's father, Harry Mahoney, Account Book, St. Mary's Church, 1831–1856, Box 79, MPA.

160 *"robust constitution":* John McElroy to Jesse Batey, February 18, 1840, Box 3, 147–48, 194–1, Additional Materials, pre-1864, MPA.

161 *Carbery had handed Johnson:* Ledger entry, September 29, 1839, Day and Cash Book, 1839-1860 (190E), Box 1, Additional Materials, pre-1864, MPA.

Chapter 12: New Roots

162 *Over time, a story:* Lee Hawkins and Douglas Belkin, "For George-town, Jesuits and Slavery Descendants, Bid for Racial Healing Sours over Reparations," *Wall Street Journal*, March 25, 2022.

162 *who shed her childhood nickname:* Anna Mahoney Jones was described as "Young Anny" in the 1831 St. Inigoes tax assessment and as "Anny" in the 1838 Jesuit slave census. She appears without the nickname soon after leaving Maryland. Whether she chose to be known as Anna or Anne, or whether the white men who imprisoned and enslaved her simply described her that way, perhaps unaware of her nickname, re-mains unknown. She appears as Anna Jones on the passenger manifest for the *Katharine Jackson* in 1838 and as Anne in Henry Johnson's records in 1844. In the 1870 Census and on her death certificate, she appears as Ann Jones and Anna Jones, respectively. Maryland State Archives, "St. Inigoes Tax Assessment, 1831," GSA, accessed March 9, 2018, http://slaveryarchive.georgetown.edu/items/show/78. Jesuit Planta-tion Project, "List of people sold by Fr. Thomas Mulledy in 1838," GSA, accessed February 13, 2023, http://slaveryarchive.georgetown .edu/items/show/9. Maryland Province Archives, "Henry Johnson re-negotiates the terms of sale, February 17, 1844," GSA, accessed June 1, 2021, http://slaveryarchive.georgetown.edu/items/show/63. Orleans Deaths, 1874, vol. 60, Louisiana State Archives 3851 Essen Lane Baton Rouge, LA 70809, 298.

162 *"1,100-acre estate":* Henry Johnson's plantation in Ascension parish is described as 1,380 arpents or about 1,100 acres. "Henry Johnson's sales of enslaved persons, 1844–1851," GSA, accessed February 11, 2023, http://slaveryarchive.georgetown.edu/items/show/73.

162 *"splendid plantation":* "The Old Generation of Ascension," *Donaldson-ville Chief,* August 19, 1882.

162 *Henry Clay:* "Biographies of the Secretaries of State: Henry Clay (1777–1852)," Office of the Historian, https://history.state.gov /departmenthistory/people/clay-henry.

163 *He was, according:* Anna Marie Schmidt, "The Political Career of Henry Johnson," MA dissertation, Louisiana State University, 1935.

163 *They flogged Black people:* Edward E. Baptist, *The Half Has Never Been Told: Slavery and the Making of American Capitalism* (New York: Basic Books, 2016), 135.

163 *Mary Reynolds:* "Narrative of Mary Reynolds," National Humanities Center Resource Toolbox, *The Making of African American Identity,* vol. 1, *1500–1865,* http://nationalhumanitiescenter.org/pds/maai /enslavement/text1/maryreynolds.pdf.

163 *The Louisiana politician:* Fidelis de Grivel to John Lancaster, May 30, 1840, Box 67, Folder 10, MPA.

164 *Father John Boullier:* Roger Baudier, *The Catholic Church in Louisiana* (New Orleans: A. W. Hyatt, 1939), 352.

165 *"The last year"*: Fidelis de Grivel to John Lancaster, May 30, 1840, Box 67, Folder 10, MPA.

165 *were baptized:* Baptisms of Henry Johnson's enslaved people in Ascension parish, 1840–1850. Email from Ann Boltin, archivist, Diocese of Baton Rouge, August 14, 2020.

165 *"Johnson was struggling"*: Unsigned letter to Henry Johnson, March 29, 1840, June 1, 1840, Box, 163, 186, Letter Book of Financial Transactions of Md-NY Province 1833–1843, Additional Materials, pre-1864, MPA.

165 *As he recovered:* Henry Johnson to William Johnson, November 3, 1840, William Johnson Papers, MDAH.

166 *in March 1841:* Mortgage by Henry Johnson to the Bank of Louisiana, March 12, 1842, CB 17, 7, Clerk of Court, Ascension parish, Donaldsonville, LA.

166 *"I must Sincerely tell you"*: Unsigned letter to Henry Johnson, March 29, 1840, Box 3, 163, Letter Book of Financial Transactions of Md-NY Province 1833–1843, Additional Materials, pre-1864, MPA.

166 *"that delay puts me"*: Unsigned letter to Henry Johnson, April 8, 1841, Box 3, 249, Letter Book of Financial Transactions of Md-NY Province 1833–1843, Additional Materials, pre-1864, MPA.

166 *"What I suffered"*: Elizabeth Johnson to William Johnson, February 25, 1841, William Johnson Papers, MDAH.

166 *had ended in failure:* John M. Sacher, *A Perfect War of Politics: Parties, Politicians, and Democracy in Louisiana, 1824–1861* (Baton Rouge: Louisiana State University Press, 2003), 103–04.

166 *"To have been thus defeated"*: Henry Johnson to William Johnson, July 18, 1842, William Johnson Papers, MDAH.

167 *In July 1843, Johnson wrote:* Henry Johnson to William Johnson, July 26, 1843, William Johnson Papers, MDAH.

168 *By January 1844:* Sacher, *A Perfect War of Politics,* 108.

168 *The Jesuits agreed to give:* Maryland Province Archives, "Henry Johnson Renegotiates the Terms of Sale, February 17, 1844," GSA, http://slaveryarchive.georgetown.edu/items/show/63.

168 *That same month:* "Henry Johnson's Sales of Enslaved Persons, 1844–1851," GSA, http://slaveryarchive.georgetown.edu/items/show/73.

169 *"Everybody worked"*: DaNene Olean Pound, "Slave to the Ex-Slave Narratives," MA dissertation, Northwestern State University, 2005, 167.

169 *"And now may be seen"*: Richard Follett, *The Sugar Masters: Planters and Slaves in Louisiana's Cane World, 1820–1860* (Baton Rouge: Louisiana State University Press, 2005), 101–02.

170 *"perished in a horrific incident"*: Untitled, *Picayune,* December 13, 1850.

170 *"more than 55 percent"*: Follett, 78.

170 *"Louisiana's high mortality rates"*: Ibid., 77–79.

170 *"The grueling rigors"*: Ibid., 79.

170 *had to contend with:* "Henry Johnson's Sales of Enslaved Persons, 1844–1851."

170 *Under the terms:* Notarial Acts, June 4, 1845, Book 19, 327–28, Ascension parish, LA.

171 *"No, sir, nothing":* Pound, "Slave to the Ex-Slave Narratives," 186.

171 *Father James Van de Velde:* Maryland Province Archives, "Letter from James Van de Velde, S.J. to Thomas Mulledy, S.J., March 28, 1848," GSA, http://slaveryarchive.georgetown.edu/items/show/3.

171 *had studied at Georgetown:* "Biographical Note," James O. Van de Velde Papers, 1819–1855, Jesuit Archives & Research Center, http://jesuit archives.org/wp-content/uploads/2018/08/MIS-5-003-Van_de_Velde -Finding_Aid.pdf.

171 *asked to meet with them:* James Van de Velde to Thomas Mulledy, March 28, 1848, GSA.

173 *"I take the liberty":* Maryland Province Archives, "Letter from James Van de Velde, S.J. to Ignatius Brocard, S.J., November 27, 1848," GSA, http://slaveryarchive.georgetown.edu/items/show/90.

174 *One of them appears:* Judy Riffel, email to author, November 2020.

174 *Johnson arranged:* William Ware, pension application no. 411,488, 1861–1934, Civil War and Later Pension Files, Department of Veterans Affairs, Record Group 15; National Archives, Washington, DC.

174 *"Sometime de slaves":* Pound, "Slave to the Ex-Slave Narratives," 194.

174 *Sometime around 1849:* Henry Jones, the son of Arnold Jones and Christina West, was born sometime around 1849. "The Jones Family," GU272 Memory Project, New England Historic Genealogical Society, https://gu272.americanancestors.org/family/jones.

174 *her mother had decided to escape:* Christina's mother, Betsy West, is described as a runaway in the census of enslaved people compiled by the Jesuits in preparation for the 1838 sale. Maryland Province Archives, "Census of People to Be Sold in 1838," GSA, http://slaveryarchive .georgetown.edu/items/show/71.

175 *Her older siblings ended up:* Email from Judy Riffel, September 18, 2017.

175 *then John R. Thompson:* "Henry Johnson's Sales of Enslaved Persons, 1844–1851."

175 *They named him Henry:* Judy Riffel, "Descendants of Jones, Arnold," GU272 Memory Project, New England Historic Genealogical Society, https://gu272.americanancestors.org/family/jones.

175 *essential to the operations:* Arnold Jones is described as a cooper in the 1875 New Orleans City Directory and the 1880 census. In 1865, after Emancipation, he was one of the highest-paid workers on J. R. Thompson's plantation. Payroll of laborers employed on Chatham plantation, records of the field offices for the State of Louisiana, Bureau of Refugees, Freedmen, and Abandoned Lands, 1863–1874, National Archives microfilm publication M1905, Reel 30. He is described as a carpenter in the 1870 Census.

175 *Coopers, in particular:* Follett, 124–25, 139.

176 *the appraiser reported:* Email from Judy Riffel, June 28, 2020. Sale of Jesse Batey's Bayou Terrebonne plantation, Civil & Probate vol. 23, probate no. 240, Terrebonne parish, LA.

177 *The move brought:* Email from Judy Riffel, September 18, 2017. Iberville Parish Clerk of Court, Conveyance Book 3, Part 2, #291, 21 January 1854.

177 *"They embraced me":* Solomon Northup, *Twelve Years a Slave. Narrative of Solomon Northup, a Citizen of New-York, Kidnapped in Washington City in 1841, and Rescued in 1853,* Electronic Edition (Chapel Hill: University of North Carolina at Chapel Hill, n.d.), 320.

177 *He had suffered:* Joseph G. Dawson III, ed., *The Louisiana Governors: From Iberville to Edwards* (Baton Rouge: Louisiana State University Press, 1990), 101–02.

178 *"She fell to his relatives":* Henrietta Cutchmore, widow of Robert Brown, Certificate No. 627,817, Case Files of Approved Pension Applications of Veterans Who Served in the Army and Navy Mainly in the Civil War and the War with Spain, Civil War and Later Survivors' Certificates, 1861–1934; Civil War and Later Pension Files; Records of the Department of Veterans Affairs, Record Group 15; National Archives, Washington, DC.

178 *the nearly 200 people:* 1850 census, Iberville, Louisiana, Roll 231, 331b, Ancestry.com, https://www.ancestry.com/discoveryui-content/view/2725334:8054?tid=&pid=&queryId=d5629293e465ade5921a7dc9ae7a145d&_phsrc=LRP23&_phstart=successSource.

178 *"the payment of the sum":* "Henry Johnson's Sales of Enslaved Persons, 1844–1851."

178 *hungry for priests, churches, and schools:* Thomas Murphy, *Jesuit Slaveholding in Maryland, 1717–1838* (New York: Routledge, 2016), 166.

179 *a flock of 1.6 million followers:* Ibid.

179 *"slaveholding in Maryland":* Ibid., 209.

179 *The Maryland Jesuits continued:* Malissa Ruffner, Georgetown Memory Project, "St. Mary's County Plantation Census Analysis," Baltimore, MD, August 24, 2016; Malissa Ruffner, "Identification of St. Thomas Manor Priests as Slaveholders: 1830 Through 1860 Censuses," Baltimore, MD, 2016; Malissa Ruffner, "Whitemarsh Plantation Census Analysis," Baltimore, MD, September 5, 2016 in author's possession. In 1840, there were seventeen enslaved people at St. Thomas Manor, eight at St. Inigoes, four at White Marsh, and four at Newtown. In 1850, there were two enslaved people at St. Thomas Manor, ten at St. Inigoes, four at White Marsh, and six at Newtown. In 1860, there were two enslaved people at St. Thomas Manor, four at White Marsh, eight at St. Inigoes, and one at Newtown.

179 *relying on slave labor:* "About Us," Jesuits Slavery, History, Memory, and Reconciliation Project, https://www.jesuits.org/our-work/shmr/about/.

179 *In June 1840:* Unsigned notation, 1841, and ledger entry, September 4, 1840, Account Book, St. Mary's Church, 1831–1856, Box 79, MPA.

180 *he was born free:* Jerry M. Hynson, *Free African-Americans of Maryland, 1832* (Westminster, MD: Heritage Books, 2007), 137; Certificate of Freedom for Thomas Alex Mason, September 15, 1845, Certificates of Freedom, 1806–1853, C1540df, St. Mary's County Court, MSA, http://guide.msa.maryland.gov/pages/item.aspx?ID=C1540-1.

180 *Members of the Mason family:* Benjamin Mason was described as a "free Nigoroe" who owed 4 shillings to the St. Mary's County estate of Richard Forris in about 1760. Paul Heinegg, *Free African Americans of Virginia, North Carolina, South Carolina, Maryland and Delaware Free African Americans of Virginia, North Carolina, South Carolina, Maryland and Delaware* (Baltimore: Genealogical Publishing Company, 2005) https://www.freeafricanamericans.com/Kelly-Owens.htm.

180 *"yellow" or "copper" complexions:* Certificates of Freedom, 1806–1852, St. Mary's County, Maryland, C1541-1, MSA, http://guide.msa.maryland.gov/pages/series.aspx?id=C1541.

180 *several members of the Mason clan:* Zwinge specifically mentions the Masons in his writings about St. Inigoes. A Joseph Mason "free" is mentioned in St. Inigoes Day Book, 1804, Rents principally, 1816, Rents & Blacksmith, 1818–1832," Box 44, Folder 1, MPA.

180 *"The free negro":* Joseph Zwinge, "The Jesuit Farms in Maryland, Facts and Anecdotes, The Negro Slaves," *Woodstock Letters* 41, no. 2 (1912): 215.

181 *"Aunt Louisa, by and by":* Zwinge, Ibid.

181 *Louisa gave birth to a baby boy:* The available records do not provide a precise date of birth for Louisa's son John. Tax records for the plantation indicate that there were no children on the estate in 1842. The 1850 census indicates that an enslaved seven-year-old boy is living on the plantation, which would mean that the child was born around 1843. Father Lilly described the death of Louisa and Alex's little boy John without describing his age in his diary in 1852. St. Inigoes Assessment, 1842–1843, 13, Board of County Commissioners, St. Mary's County, C1528-2, HR 17139, MSA; Ruffner, Georgetown Memory Project, St. Mary's County Plantation Census Analysis, 2016, in author's possession; Thomas Lilly, diary, May 15, 1852, Diary of Father Thomas Lilly, Box 8, Folder 3, MPA.

181 *"born free & raised":* Certificate of Freedom for Thomas Alex Mason, September 15, 1845, Certificates of Freedom, 1806–1853, C1540df, St. Mary's County Court, MSA, http://guide.msa.maryland.gov/pages/item.aspx?ID=C1540-1.

181 *who carried the same name:* One source of estimates of the years of birth for Louisa's and Alex's children comes from Maryland State Archives, "Louise Mason and Her Children: The Last People Enslaved by the Maryland Jesuits," GSA, http://slaveryarchive.georgetown.edu/items

/show/77. Also, Judy Riffel, "The Louisa Mahoney Family," GU272 Memory Project, American Ancestors, https://gu272.americanancestors .org/family/mahoney48.

181 *He had survived:* January 12, 1840, Procurator Letter Books, 1831–1836, 1839–1843, MPA.

181 *Just a few weeks: Sun* (Baltimore), May 31, 1849.

181 *"I have this moment":* Robert Woodley to Ignatius Brocard, May 25, 1849, Box 70, Folder 18, MPA.

182 *Newspapers hailed Carbery: Daily National Intelligencer,* May 30, 1849; *Sun* (Baltimore), May 31, 1849.

182 *By September 1850:* 1850 census.

182 *But he was also known:* John LaFarge, *The Manner Is Ordinary* (New York: Harcourt, 1954), 166.

182 *"A colored woman has ruled":* Maryland Province Archives, " 'She Will Not Rule Me': Fr. Steinbacher Airs His Grievances Against the Female Slaves of Newtown, April 1848," GSA, http://slaveryarchive.georgetown .edu/items/show/144.

183 *"I hope her conduct":* Robert Woodley to Ignatius Brocard, September 16, 1850, Box 71, Folder 10, MPA.

183 *"She was harbored":* Maryland Province Archives, " 'I Have Parted from Nelly': Fr. Woodley to Fr. Brocard, September 25, 1850," GSA, http://slaveryarchive.georgetown.edu/items/show/165.

183 *In May 1852:* Thomas Lilly, diary entries describing John Mason's illness and death, May 9–15, 1852, Diary of Father Thomas Lilly, Box 8, Folder 3, MPA.

184 *50 cents a day:* St. Inigoes ledger, Box 44, Folder 1, MPA.

184 *offered last rites to the dying:* Thomas Lilly, diary, April 28 and November 29, 1852; February 1, March 6, March 13, and April 3, 1853, Diary of Father Thomas Lilly, 1852–1854, MPA Box 8, Folder 3, MPA.

184 *he voted for General Winfield Scott:* Thomas Lilly, diary, November 2, 1852, Diary of Father Thomas Lilly, 1852–1854, MPA.

184 *He condoned racial segregation:* Thomas Lilly, diary, October 31, 1852, Diary of Father Thomas Lilly, 1852–1854, MPA.

184 *Lilly expanded:* Francis Michael Walsh, "The Story of St. Inigoes Mission: 1634–1994," unpublished manuscript, 2016, 131.

184 *"My Black boy Bill":* Thomas Lilly, diary, June 30, 1852, Diary of Father Thomas Lilly, 1852–1854, MPA.

184 *an industrious and virtuous servant:* "Almost a Centenarian," *St. Mary's Beacon,* July 22, 1909.

185 *The state was followed:* James M. McPherson, *Battle Cry of Freedom: The Civil War Era* (Oxford, UK: Oxford University Press, 2003), 234–35.

185 *Church leaders in Rome:* Curran, *Shaping American Catholicism,* 103.

185 *left him dead on the road:* GSA, "Louisa Mason Obituary, 1909," GSA, http://slaveryarchive.georgetown.edu/items/show/91.

185 *"Alex Mason was":* Ibid.

Chapter 13: Freedom

187 *"We landed on the levee"*: Quoted in Albert Kautz, "Incidents of the Occupation of New Orleans," in *Battles and Leaders of the Civil War: Being for the Most Part Contributions by Union and Confederate Officers,* ed. Robert Underwood Johnson and Clarence Clough Buel, vol. 2 (New York: Thomas Yoseloff, 1956), 91, https://ehistory.osu.edu/books/battles.

188 *One woman even dumped:* Michael E. Ruane, "New Orleans Seethed Under Union Occupation," *Washington Post,* May 19, 2017.

188 *But the enslaved people:* Adam Rothman, "'Nothing to Stay Here For': How Enslaved People Helped to Put Slavery to Death in New Orleans," *Slate,* September 22, 2015, https://slate.com/human-interest /2015/09/the-end-of-slavery-in-new-orleans.html.

188 *Days later, federal troops:* Sidney A. Marchand, *The Story of Ascension Parish, Louisiana* (Donaldsonville, La.: J. E. Ortlieb, 1931), 63–64.

188 *Any enslaved person:* John C. Rodrigue, *Reconstruction in the Cane Fields: From Slavery to Free Labor in Louisiana's Sugar Parishes, 1862–1880* (Baton Rouge: Louisiana State University Press, 2001), 35.

189 *"Revolt & Insurection":* Ibid., 36.

189 *It was as if:* Deposition of Thomas Hall, Henrietta Brown pension file.

189 *"We are certain":* Robert Emmett Curran, *Shaping American Catholicism: Maryland and New York, 1805–1915* (Washington, DC: Catholic University of America Press, 2012), 104.

189 *Martin described the enslavement:* Maria Genoino Caravaglios, "A Roman Critique of the Pro-slavery Views of Bishop Martin of Natchitoches, Louisiana," *Records of the American Catholic Historical Society of Philadelphia* 83, no. 2 (1972): 71–72.

190 *Archbishop John Baptist Purcell:* "A Closer Look: The Purcell Brothers, Abolition, and the Catholic Telegraph," *Catholic Telegraph,* November 12, 2020, https://www.thecatholictelegraph.com/purcell-brothers -abolition-and-the-catholic-telegraph/70302.

190 *He warned that the nation's:* David J. Endres, "Rectifying the Fatal Contrast: Archbishop John Purcell and the Slavery Controversy Among Catholics in Civil War Cincinnati," *Ohio Valley History* 2, no. 2 (March 2002): 29–30.

190 *"that all persons held as slaves":* "The Emancipation Proclamation," National Archives, https://www.archives.gov/exhibits/featured -documents/emancipation-proclamation.

191 *a group of white men met:* Rodrigue, *Reconstruction in the Cane Fields,* 39.

191 *"full of theories":* Ibid.

191 *"faithful labor":* Ibid., 40.

191 *"Negroes doing":* Ibid., 41.

191 *they enlisted in the Union Army:* Josephine Brown, widow of John Henry Brown, certificate no. 613,714/614,466, Case Files of Approved Pension Applications of Veterans Who Served in the Army and Navy

Mainly in the Civil War and the War with Spain, Civil War and Later Survivors' Certificates, 1861–1934; Civil War and Later Pension Files; Records of the Department of Veterans Affairs, Record Group 15; National Archives, Washington, DC. Thomas Hall, certificate no. 796,970, Case Files of Approved Pension Applications of Veterans Who Served in the Army and Navy in the Civil War and the War with Spain. At least eight men sold by the Jesuits and enslaved at Chatham plantation in Louisiana joined the Union Army: Judy Riffel, "Union Soldiers among the GMP Ancestor and Descendants Database," Report, October 9, 2022, Georgetown Memory Project, in possession of author; Riffel, email to author, March 1, 2023.

191 *But all of that began to change:* John W. Blassingame, *Black New Orleans, 1860–1880* (Chicago: University of Chicago Press, 2008), 41–42.

192 *"we could never have accomplished":* Ibid., 42.

192 *When a white Union officer:* Ibid., 41.

192 *"Your back ain't cut up":* Ibid.

193 *"I seen some bad things":* Lynette Ater Tanner, ed., *Chained to the Land: Voices from Cotton & Cane Plantations: From Interviews of Former Slaves* (Winston-Salem, NC: John F. Blair, 2014), 112.

193 *"started throwing bullets":* Ibid., 116.

193 *In January 1864:* Eric Foner, *Reconstruction: America's Unfinished Revolution, 1863–1877,* New American Nation Series (New York: Perennial Classics, 2002), 55. Rodrigue, *Reconstruction in the Cane Fields,* 44–45.

194 *"They work less":* Foner, *Reconstruction,* 55.

194 *Newly empowered Black workers:* Rodrigue, *Reconstruction in the Cane Fields,* 46.

194 *Greek Revival mansion:* Henry Johnson purchased the Woodley plantation in Pointe Coupee parish, now known as the Valverda plantation, in 1855. "National Register of Historic Places Nomination: Valverda Plantation House, Pointe Coupee, LA," National Park Service, https://npgallery.nps.gov/GetAsset/fa74e7e6-82b1-4c0e-9f45-af471345e5c7.

194 *He filled the grand home:* Last will and testament of Henry Johnson, March 1864, "Louisiana Governors," http://www.la-cemeteries.com/Governors/Johnson,%20Henry/Will/Johnson,HenryWill.shtml.

194 *an institution expressly designed:* Woody Register and Benjamin King, "A Research Summary on Slavery and Race at the University of the South and in the Community of Sewanee," Sewanee, the University of the South, https://new.sewanee.edu/roberson-project/learn-more/research-summary/.

195 *Johnson continued to be viewed:* Anna Schmidt, "The Political Career of Henry Johnson," MA thesis, Louisiana State University, 1935, 74–77.

195 *His wife provided:* Ibid., Appendix, 16.

195 *his mother had told him years later:* Ibid., Appendix, 17.

195 *He suffered from occasional bouts:* *Times-Picayune* (New Orleans), October 30, 1864.

195 *So on March 26:* Last will and testament of Henry Johnson, March 1864.

195 *In the handwritten document:* Ibid.

196 *Thompson occasionally moved:* Pension file of Eliza Green, widow of Miles Green, certificate no. 468,798, Case Files of Approved Pension Applications of Veterans Who Served in the Union Army and Navy Mainly in the Civil War and the War with Spain, National Archives, Washington, D.C.

196 *In that summer:* Schmidt, "The Political Career of Henry Johnson," 76–77.

196 *The retired politician:* Ibid.

197 *The news appeared:* Daily National Republican, September 15, 1864; Springfield Daily Republican, September 23, 1864; Houston Telegraph, October 26, 1864.

197 *"great legislative abilities":* Louisville Daily Democrat, September 15, 1864, 1.

197 *"For nearly thirty years":* Times-Picayune (New Orleans), October 30, 1864.

198 *In his twenty-three page letter:* Curran, Shaping American Catholicism, 104–05.

199 *Spalding's missive:* Ibid, 104–105.

199 *He did not make that position public:* Richmond Times Dispatch, January 23, 1864, 6.

199 *urged the Church's leadership:* Curran, Shaping American Catholicism, 106.

199 *Rome finally addressed:* Ibid., 107–08; Caravaglios, "A Roman Critique of the Pro-Slavery Views of Bishop Martin of Natchitoches, Louisiana," 69.

199 *one that was widely believed:* Ibid., 79.

200 *"a small revolution":* Ibid., 70.

200 *By November 1864:* Rodrigue, Reconstruction in the Cane Fields, 50. The new constitution was approved in September 1864.

201 *Father Basil Pacciarini wrote:* The date on this letter is extremely difficult to read. Letters from Basil Pacciarini to C. C. Lancaster, 1864–1865, Box 15, Folder 3, MPA.

201 *On November 1, 1864:* "Chronology of Emancipation During the Civil War," Freedmen and Southern Society Project, University of Maryland, http://www.freedmen.umd.edu/chronol.htm.

201 *The Jesuits recorded their names:* Maryland State Archives, "Louise Mason and Her Children: The Last People Enslaved by the Maryland Jesuits," GSA, http://slaveryarchive.georgetown.edu/items/show/77.

201 *her children, who ranged:* Judy Riffel, "The Louisa Mahoney Family," GU272 Memory Project, American Ancestors, https://gu272 .americanancestors.org/family/mahoney48.

202 *"good and sufficient quarters":* National Archives, Washington, DC,

"Agreement with Freedmen of Chatham Plantation in Ascension Parish, La., February 2, 1865," GSA, http://slaveryarchive.georgetown.edu /items/show/81.

203 *"Ev'rybody ran":* Tanner, *Chained to the Land,* 197.

203 *"After freedom":* Ibid., 121.

203 *In October 1865:* "Copy of Findings of Jury of Inquest in the case of Burtin Austin Killed by J. B. Marchand," November 1, 1865, RG105, M1905, Roll 71, 293, Records of the Field Offices for the State of Louisiana, Bureau of Refugees, Freedmen, and Abandoned Lands, 1863–1872, National Archives, Washington, DC.

204 *"on his belly":* "Copy of Findings of Jury of Inquest in the case of Burtin Austin Killed by J. B. Marchand."

204 *"The Civil Authorities":* John H. Brough to S. O. Parker, 8 July 1867, Letters Sent, RG105, M1905, Roll 71, 293, Records of the Field Offices for the State of Louisiana, Bureau of Refugees, Freedmen, and Abandoned Lands, 1863–1872, National Archives, Washington, DC.

204 *That month, he lined up:* National Archives, Washington, DC, "Final Pay Roll, Chatham Plantation, Ascension Parish, La., December 31, 1865," GSA, http://slaveryarchive.georgetown.edu/items/show/82.

204 *He had earned $112.35:* Ibid.

205 *In the spring of 1866:* Circular from John Irwin Gregg, New Orleans, April 9, 1866, Records of the Field Offices for the State of Louisiana, Bureau of Refugees, Freedmen, and Abandoned Lands, 1863–1872, RG105, M1905, Roll 71, 878–9, National Archives, Washington, DC.

205 *When his wife gave birth:* Martha Jones was born on April 15, 1866, in New Orleans. "The Jones Family," GU 272 Memory Project, New England Historic Genealogy Society, https://gu272.americanancestors.org /family/jones.

206 *she had never forgiven:* John LaFarge, *The Manner Is Ordinary* (New York: Harcourt, 1954), 166.

Chapter 14: The Profits

207 *For decades, the money:* Day and Cash Book, 1839–1860, Box 68, Additional Materials, pre-1864, MPA.

207 *Georgetown's working group on slavery:* Georgetown University Working Group on Slavery, Memory, and Reconciliation, "What We Know Booklet," GSA, http://slaveryarchive.georgetown.edu/items/show/4.

207 *The Jesuit financial ledgers:* Day and Cash Book, 1839–1860, Box 68, Additional Materials, pre-1864, MPA.

207 *the Jesuits had received:* Ibid.

208 *St. Louis University in Missouri:* "What We Have Learned: Missouri," Jesuit Conference of Canada and the United States, https://www.jesuits .org/our-work/shmr/what-we-have-learned/missouri/.

208 *Gonzaga College High School:* "Searching for Truth in the Garden:

Gonzaga's History with Slavery," Gonzaga College High School, 2019, https://www.gonzaga.org/about/history/slavery-research-project.

208 *Georgetown Preparatory School:* "Endowment of Tears, Hope for Reconciliation: Georgetown Prep and Slavery," Georgetown Preparatory School, 2020, https://www.gprep.org/about/history.

208 *in Jesuit circles at least:* The Mulledy/Healy Legacy Committee, "What We Know: Report to the President of the College of the Holy Cross," College of the Holy Cross, March 18, 2016, 6, https://www.holycross .edu/sites/default/files/files/mulledy-healy/mulledycommittee reportfinal.pdf.

208 *The enslaved people would not forget:* LaFarge, *The Manner Is Ordinary,* 166.

208 *Worcester College:* The Mulledy/Healy Legacy Committee, "What We Know," 6–7.

208 *Loyola College:* "History and Traditions," Loyola University Maryland, https://www.loyola.edu/about/history-traditions.

209 *All told, the Maryland Jesuits invested:* Annual Reports, Finances of the Province 1803–1893 [196B], MPA Additional Materials, pre-1864. Box 3. The Maryland Jesuits expenditures on Holy Cross can be found on pages 31, 55, and 273; Loyola Maryland, 59, 60, 282, 286; the Scholasticate in Massachusetts, 138, 139, and 371. A spokeswoman for Holy Cross said that accounting books in the college's archives describe student tuition and "other sources" as sources of revenue for this period. No explanation is provided for what the "other sources" were. Nicoleta Jordan, assistant director of media relations, Holy Cross, email message to author, January 27, 2023.

209 *They helped to supply Jesuits:* See notes on pages 240 and 241 for information about Fordham, St. Joseph's College, Boston College, and Santa Clara.

209 *Xavier College:* Kelly L. Schmidt, " 'Without Slaves and Without Assassins': Antebellum Cincinnati, Transnational Jesuits, and the Challenges of Race and Slavery," *U.S. Catholic Historian* 39, no. 2 (2021): 1–26, https://doi.org/10.1353/cht.2021.0010. "Xavier College's Historical Ties to Slavery," Xavier College, University Archives and Special Collections, https://libguides.xavier.edu/archives/historical-connections -slavery.

209 *"Four million of these":* Cyprian Davis, *The History of Black Catholics in the United States* (New York: Crossroad, 2021), 118.

210 *"Behold so strong":* Ibid., 118–19.

210 *"sudden liberation":* Ibid., 120–21.

210 *"We could have wished":* Ibid.

210 *would create a vibrant culture:* John W. Blassingame, *Black New Orleans, 1860–1880* (Chicago: University of Chicago Press, 2008), Appendix, Table 1.

210 *June 13, 1870:* Marriage record, Louisa Jones and John Johnson,

St. Alphonsus Marriages, Vol. 1, Jan. 2, 1866, to Nov. 29, 1877, 270, #22, Office of Archives and Records, Archdiocese of New Orleans.

211 *He was a carpenter:* The pension file of John Johnson and Louisa Jones Johnson includes depositions and other records that describe their marriage, Louisa's father and her first child, the plantation where he was enslaved, and the home she lived in after his death in addition to his military record. John Johnson and Louisa Jones Johnson, certificate nos. 973,852/550,560, Case Files of Approved Pension Applications of Veterans Who Served in the Army and Navy Mainly in the Civil War and the War with Spain, (Civil War and Later Survivors' Certificates), 1861–1934, Civil War and Later Widows Certificates.

211 *many of the people:* Anna Jones, 1870 Census, Ancestry.com, https://www.ancestry.com/discoveryui-content/view/32778881:7163?tid=&pid=&queryId=45bcc41386bc7eb69f0a7ec43549052f&_phsrc=LRP26&_phstart=successSource; Anna Jones, Orleans Deaths, 1874, vol. 60, Louisiana State Archives 3851 Essen Lane Baton Rouge, LA 70809, 298.

211 *"In her most aristocratic":* Ibid., 200.

212 *They knew, for instance:* Michael Doorley, "Irish Catholics and French Creoles: Ethnic Struggles Within the Catholic Church in New Orleans, 1835–1920," *Catholic Historical Review* 87, no. 1 (2001): 47.

212 *a priest refused Communion:* James B. Bennett, *Religion and the Rise of Jim Crow in New Orleans* (Princeton, NJ: Princeton University Press, 2005), 153, http://ebookcentral.proquest.com/lib/nyulibrary-ebooks/detail.action?docID=4562468.

212 *Black parishioners at the cathedral:* Ibid., 153–69.

212 *Nearly twenty thousand:* Ibid., 168.

212 *as did most Black Catholics:* Ibid.

212 *a house that would remain:* John Johnson purchased land on September 25, 1882. John Bendernagel, notary, vol. 11, act 205 01, Notarial Archives, New Orleans.

213 *successfully petitioned the archdiocese:* Holy Ghost parish file, Central Files (Prior to 1935), Archdiocese of New Orleans Office of Archives & Records, New Orleans, LA.

213 *her fellow nuns described her:* Edward T. Brett, *The New Orleans Sisters of the Holy Family: African American Missionaries to the Garifuna of Belize* (Notre Dame, IN: University of Notre Dame Press, 2012), 26.

213 *She raised enough money:* "Brief History of the Sisters of the Holy Family," Sisters of the Holy Family, https://www.sistersoftheholyfamily.com/history.

213 *the first overseas mission:* Brett, *The New Orleans Sisters of the Holy Family,* 27.

213 *"Yesterday they opened":* Ibid., 31–32.

214 *Many searched in vain:* "About the Project," The Last Seen Project, https://informationwanted.org/about-the-project.

214 *"an event altogether too affecting":* "Frederick Douglass Reunites with

His Brother Perry After 40 Years Separation," *Loyal Georgian,* July 28, 1867, https://informationwanted.org/items/show/3671.

214 *"They were getting along":* Joseph Zwinge, "The Jesuit Farms in Maryland, Facts and Anecdotes: The Negro Slaves," *Woodstock Letters* 41, no. 3 (1912): 285.

214 *continued to deal with segregation:* Laura E. Masur, "A Spiritual Inheritance: Black Catholics in Southern Maryland," *International Symposia on Jesuit Studies,* no. 2019, Symposium (March 2021): 14–15.

214 *"In the distribution":* Diary, 1886–1887, St. Peter Claver's Sunday School General Hints &c, Saint Peter Claver's Sunday School: General Notes, Box 38, Folder 827, Woodstock College Archives, MPA.

214 *Josephine's husband:* Walsh, "Resurrection: The Story of the St. Inigoes Mission, 1634–1994," 145–46.

215 *would teach catechism:* Undated entry, General Notes Diary 1886–1887, Saint Peter Claver's Sunday School, Box 38, Folder 827, Woodstock College Archives.

215 *the priests grumbled:* Zwinge, "The Jesuit Farms in Maryland, Facts and Anecdotes: The Negro Slaves," 290–91.

215 *He would serve:* Miriam Otterbein, "Born of Slave Parents, 100-Year-Old Woodstock Man Lauds Freedom," *Community Times,* August 10, 1972.

215 *His daughter, Mary:* Assignments, Sr. M. Theophane/Mary Cecilia Bennett, SS-220-60-8304, Archives, Oblate Sisters of Providence, Baltimore, MD.

215 *As for Louisa:* Zwinge, "The Jesuit Farms in Maryland, Facts and Anecdotes: The Negro Slaves," 291.

215 *small bottle filled with holy water:* Walsh, "Resurrection," 165.

215 *"On my last visit to her":* Zwinge, "The Jesuit Farms in Maryland, Facts and Anecdotes: The Negro Slaves," 291.

215 *"a very large assemblage":* St. Mary's Beacon, July 22, 1909.

215 *one observer recalled:* Ibid.

215 *One priest called it:* Zwinge, "The Jesuit Farms in Maryland, Facts and Anecdotes: The Negro Slaves," 291.

216 *"Aunt Louisa would never admit":* John LaFarge, *The Manner Is Ordinary* (New York: Harcourt, 1954), 163.

216 *But to her children and grandchildren:* Otterbein, "Born of Slave Parents, 100-Year-Old Woodstock Man Lauds Freedom."

Epilogue

217 *On the Friday after Thanksgiving:* Interviews with Jeremy Alexander in person on July 10, 2017, and by phone on June 23, 2021, and May 19, 2022.

217 *my first article:* Rachel L. Swarns, "272 Slaves Were Sold to Save Georgetown. What Does It Owe Their Descendants?," *New York Times,*

April 16, 2016, https://www.nytimes.com/2016/04/17/us/georgetown
-university-search-for-slave-descendants.html.

217 *John J. DeGioia had reached out:* Rachel L. Swarns, "Intent on a Reckoning with Georgetown's Slavery-Stained Past," *New York Times,*
July 11, 2016, https://www.nytimes.com/2016/07/11/us/intent-on-a
-reckoning-with-georgetowns-slavery-stained-past.html.

217 *"I think all of us need":* Ibid.

217 *he announced that his university:* "Next Steps on Slavery, Memory, and
Reconciliation at Georgetown," September 1, 2016, https://president
.georgetown.edu/slavery-memory-reconciliation-september-2016/#.

218 *"This community participated":* Rachel L. Swarns, "Georgetown University Plans Steps to Atone for Slave Past," *New York Times,* September 1, 2016, https://www.nytimes.com/2016/09/02/us/slaves
-georgetown-university.html.

219 *GU272 Descendants Association:* Susan Svrluga, "Descendants of Slaves
Sold to Benefit Georgetown Call for a $1 Billion Foundation for Reconciliation," *Washington Post,* September 9, 2016, https://www
.washingtonpost.com/news/grade-point/wp/2016/09/08/descendants
-of-slaves-sold-by-georgetown-call-for-a-1-billion-foundation-for
-reconciliation/.

219 *the largest Catholic university:* "About DePaul University," DePaul University, https://www.depaul.edu/about/Pages/default.aspx.

219 *Only about 4 percent:* Jeff Diamant, Besheer Mohamed, and Joshua Alvarado, "Black Catholics in America," Pew Research Center, March 15,
2022, https://www.pewresearch.org/religion/2022/03/15/black
-catholics-in-america/?utm_source=Pew+Research+Center&utm
_campaign=ccdc8bf704-R%26E_2022_03_18&utm_medium=email&
utm_term=0_3e953b9b70-ccdc8bf704-399366889.

220 *his parents had described:* Cyprian Davis, *The History of Black Catholics in
the United States* (New York: Crossroad, 2021), 219, 234.

220 *Melissa and her mother:* Melissa Kemp shared her family story in telephone interviews on September 3, 2016, May 17, 2017, and August 25,
2022.

221 *"Slavery was really something":* Miriam Otterbein, "Born of Slave Parents, 100-Year-Old Woodstock Man Lauds Freedom," *Community
Times,* August 10, 1972.

221 *"Teach him all the tricks":* Tom Morton, "Looking Back: Woodstock
Resident to Mark 100th Year," *Baltimore Sun,* August 4, 1972.

221 *"My sister worked":* Gladys Kemp, interview by Linda Mann, April 17,
2017, in Granite, MD, Georgetown Memory Project, transcript in author's possession. The quotations and recollections from Mrs. Kemp in
this chapter come from this oral history.

223 *"private and unrecognized restitution":* Sean Toole, "Institutional Peculiarity: Jesuit Slave Trading in Maryland," MA thesis, Santa Clara University, Santa Clara, CA, 2015, 77.

223 *Over the years, the fund provided:* Mike Gabriele, director of communications, USA East Province, Society of Jesus, emails to author, March 9, 2021.

223 *the Jesuits kept the fund's origins to themselves:* Toole, "Institutional Peculiarity: Jesuit Slave Trading in Maryland," 77–78.

223 *the Mahoney family had served:* Eighteenth century documentation of the Jesuits' enslavement of the Mahoneys can be found in the lawsuit filed by Charles and Patrick Mahoney in the 1790s. Charles Mahoney v. John Ashton, Court of Appeals, Judgements. Description: A, June 1802, No. 8, MdHR No. 683-2. S381-2, MSA.

224 *But neither she nor Jeremy knew:* Was the fund quickly disbursed to prevent descendants from trying to lay claim to any of it? The Jesuits emphatically deny that, saying that the money was disbursed in June and July of 2016 as the order was preparing for the unification of the Maryland and USA Northeast Provinces, which took place in July of 2020. Mike Gabriele, a spokesman for the USA East Province, said that the disbursement ensured that the funds would "remain and grow for those schools" in the Maryland province. "The schools must continue to report to the province how the funds are spent—that they continue to support minority scholarships," he said. Gabriele, emails to author, February 22, 2023.

224 *In April 2017:* "Georgetown Apologizes for 1838 Sale of More than 270 Enslaved, Dedicates Buildings," Georgetown University, April 18, 2017, https://www.georgetown.edu/news/georgetown-apologizes-for-1838 -sale-of-272-slaves-dedicates-buildings/.

224 *"Today the Society of Jesus":* Ibid.

225 *"For eight months":* Joseph M. Stewart to Arturo Sosa, May 5, 2017. Letter provided by Mr. Stewart.

225 *"a sin against God":* Arturo Sosa to Joseph M. Stewart, June 20, 2017. Letter provided by Mr. Stewart.

226 *Then the two men sat down:* Interviews with Timothy P. Kesicki and Joseph M. Stewart, February 22, 2021, and March 1, 2021.

226 *the largest family reunion:* Olivia McClure, "About 500 Descendants of Slaves Sold by Jesuit Priests Gather for Unique Reunion in Iberville Parish," *Advocate,* June 9, 2018.

226 *"It makes this whole history":* Ibid.

227 *there was a growing wave:* Rachel L. Swarns, "Is Georgetown's $400,000-a-Year Plan to Aid Slave Descendants Enough?," *New York Times,* October 30, 2019.

227 *scholarships for African Americans:* Rachel L. Swarns, "The Seminary Flourished on Slave Labor. Now It's Planning to Pay Reparations," *New York Times,* September 12, 2019, https://www.nytimes.com/2019/09/12 /us/virginia-seminary-reparations.html.

227 *"it's important because":* Interview with Craig Steven Wilder, September 9, 2019.

228 *The Jesuits said they would raise:* Rachel L. Swarns, "Catholic Order Pledges $100 Million to Atone for Slave Labor," *New York Times,* March 15, 2021, https://www.nytimes.com/2021/03/15/us/jesuits -georgetown-reparations-slavery.html.

228 *the goal of raising the rest:* Ibid.

228 *"We now have":* Ibid.

228 *"an unprecedented step":* Rachel L. Swarns, "A Catholic Order Pledged $100 Million to Atone for Taking Part in the Slave Trade. Some Descendants Want a New Deal," *New York Times,* April 17, 2021, https:// www.nytimes.com/2021/04/17/us/catholic-church-jesuits-reparations .html.

229 *raised concerns that the deal:* Stewart and his descendant partners said that their organization, the GU 272 Descendants Association, represented "a majority" of descendants in a memorandum of understanding that they and the Jesuits signed in 2019. At the time, about 490 people had signed the group's declaration, but fewer than 50 had become members, according to Karran Royal, the association's former executive director and a founder of the group. About five thousand living descendants of the people sold by the Jesuits in 1838 to keep Georgetown University afloat have been identified by genealogists at the Georgetown Memory Project, the independent nonprofit group. The group estimates that about ten thousand descendants of the other people enslaved by the Jesuits are alive today. Ibid.

229 *Stewart told:* Ibid.

229 *In the fall of 2022:* "Georgetown Launches $400,000 Annual Fund to Support Descendants of the Enslaved," October 26, 2022, https://www .georgetown.edu/news/georgetown-launches-400000-annual-fund-to -support-descendants-of-the-enslaved/.

229 *had fallen far short:* Rachel Swarns, "Catholic Order Struggles to Raise $100 Million to Atone for Slave Labor," *New York Times,* August 16, 2022.

Bibliography

"About DePaul University." DePaul University. https://www.depaul.edu /about/Pages/default.aspx.

"About the Project." Last Seen: Finding Family After Slavery. https:// informationwanted.org/about-the-project.

"About Us: Slavery, History, Memory and Reconciliation Project." Jesuit Conference of Canada and the U.S. https://www.jesuits.org/our-work /shmr/about/.

Achenbach, Joel. *The Grand Idea: George Washington's Potomac and the Race to the West*. New York: Simon & Schuster Paperbacks, 2005.

"African Americans and the War of 1812." Maryland State Archives. https:// msa.maryland.gov/msa/mdstatehouse/war1812/html/afam_war.html.

Agonito, Joseph. "St. Inigoes Manor: A Nineteenth Century Jesuit Plantation." *Maryland Historical Magazine* 72, no. 1 (Spring 1977): 83–98.

Alsop, George. *A Character of the Province of Maryland*, Image No. 57. https:// msa.maryland.gov/megafile/msa/library/014300/014309/html/alsop-0057 .html.

———. *A Character of the Province of Maryland*. Cleveland: Burrows Brothers Company, 1902.

"The American Mission: Maryland Jesuits from Andrew White to John Carroll." Booth Family Center for Special Collections, Georgetown University Library. https://library.georgetown.edu/exhibition/american-mission -maryland-jesuits-andrew-white-john-carroll.

"Annapolis." *New York Journal*, July 12, 1770.

Ball, Charles. *Slavery in the United States: A Narrative of the Life and Adventures of Charles Ball, a Black Man, Who Lived Forty Years in Maryland, South Carolina and Georgia, as a Slave Under Various Masters, and Was One Year in the Navy with Commodore Barney, During the Late War*. New York: John S. Taylor, Brick Church Chapel, 1837. https://docsouth.unc.edu/neh/ballslavery /ball.html.

Ball, Edward. "Retracing Slavery's Trail of Tears." *Smithsonian Magazine*, November 2015.

Baptist, Edward E. *The Half Has Never Been Told: Slavery and the Making of American Capitalism*. New York: Basic Books, 2016.

Baudier, Roger. *The Catholic Church in Louisiana*. New Orleans: A. W. Hyatt, 1939.

Beckert, Sven, and Seth Rockman, eds. *Slavery's Capitalism: A New History of American Economic Development.* Philadelphia: University of Pennsylvania Press, 2016.

Beckett, Edward F. "Selling the Slaves." *Studies in the Spirituality of Jesuits* 28, no. 5 (November 1996): 35–39.

Beitzell, Edwin Warfield. *The Jesuit Missions of St. Mary's County, Maryland.* 2nd ed. Self-published, 1976.

Bennett, James B. *Religion and the Rise of Jim Crow in New Orleans.* Princeton, NJ: Princeton University Press, 2005.

Berlin, Ira. *Many Thousands Gone: The First Two Centuries of Slavery in North America.* Cambridge, MA: Belknap Press, 2003.

———. *Slaves Without Masters: The Free Negro in the Antebellum South.* New York: New Press, 2007.

"Biographies of the Secretaries of State: Henry Clay (1777–1852)," Office of the Historian. https://history.state.gov/departmenthistory/people/clay-henry.

Blassingame, John W. *Black New Orleans, 1860–1880.* Chicago: University of Chicago Press, 2008. http://www.SLQ.eblib.com.au/patron/FullRecord.aspx?p=408193.

Bogen, David S. "Mathias de Sousa: Maryland's First Colonist of African Descent." *Maryland Historical Magazine* 96, no. 1 (Spring 2001): 68–85.

Bowen, Charles. *The American Almanac and Repository of Useful Knowledge for the Year . . .* Boston: Gray and Bowen, 1839.

———. *The American Almanac and Repository of Useful Knowledge for the Year 1837 . . .* Nabu Press, 2012.

Brett, Edward T. *The New Orleans Sisters of the Holy Family: African American Missionaries to the Garifuna of Belize.* Notre Dame, IN: University of Notre Dame Press, 2012.

Brewer, Herbert. "From Sierra Leone to Annapolis: The 1718 Journey of the *Margaret,* an Eighteenth Century Slave Ship." GSA, 2018. http://slaveryarchive.georgetown.edu/files/show/336.

"Brief History of the Sisters of the Holy Family." Sisters of the Holy Family. https://www.sistersoftheholyfamily.com/history.

Buckley, Cornelius M. *Stephen Larigaudelle Dubuisson, S.J. (1786–1864) and the Reform of the American Jesuits.* Lanham, MD: University Press of America, 2013.

Caravaglios, Maria Genoino. "A Roman Critique of the Pro-Slavery Views of Bishop Martin of Natchitoches, Louisiana." *Records of the American Catholic Historical Society of Philadelphia* 83, no. 2 (1972): 67–81.

Carroll, John. *The John Carroll Papers.* Vol. 1: *1755–1791.* Edited by Thomas O'Brian Hanley. Notre Dame, IN: University of Notre Dame Press, 1976.

———. *The John Carroll Papers.* Vol. 2: *1792–1806.* Edited by Thomas O'Brian Hanley. Notre Dame: University of Notre Dame Press, 1976.

———. "The Present State of the Catholic Missions Conducted by the Ex-Jesuits in North America: Unpublished Reply by Rev. John Carroll, 1788."

American Catholic Historical Researches, New Series, 1, no. 3 (July 1905): 193–206. https://www.jstor.org/stable/44374531?seq=1#metadata_info _tab_contents.

"Charles Calvert, 3rd Lord Baltimore (1637–1714/15)." Maryland State Archives, March 12, 2010. https://msa.maryland.gov/megafile/msa/speccol /sc3500/sc3520/000100/000193/html/calvert.html.

Condon, Sean. "The Significance of Group Manumissions in Post-revolutionary Rural Maryland." *Slavery & Abolition* 32, no. 1 (March 2011): 75–89. https://doi.org/10.1080/0144039X.2011.538199.

"Correspondence Between His Excellency, President Davis, and His Holiness Pope Pius IX," *Richmond Times Dispatch.* January 23, 1864.

Craycraft, Kenneth. "A Closer Look: The Purcell Brothers, Abolition and the Catholic Telegraph." *Catholic Telegraph,* November 12, 2020. https://www .thecatholictelegraph.com/purcell-brothers-abolition-and-the-catholic -telegraph/70302.

Curran, Robert Emmett. *The Bicentennial History of Georgetown University.* Vol. 1: *From Academy to University, 1789–1889.* Washington, DC: Georgetown University Press, 1993.

———. *Shaping American Catholicism: Maryland and New York, 1805–1915.* Washington, DC: Catholic University of America Press, 2012.

———. " 'Wave Her Colors Ever!': Writing Georgetown's History." *U.S. Catholic Historian* 28, no. 3 (2010): 65–78.

Davis, Cyprian. *The History of Black Catholics in the United States.* Illustrated edition. New York: Crossroad, 2021.

Dawson, Joseph D., III., ed. *The Louisiana Governors: From Iberville to Edwards.* Baton Rouge: Louisiana State University Press, 1990.

Debe, Demetri D., and Russell R. Menard. "The Transition to African Slavery in Maryland: A Note on the Barbados Connection." *Slavery & Abolition* 32, no. 1 (March 2011): 129–41. https://doi.org/10.1080/0144039X .2011.538203.

DeGioia, John J. "Next Steps on Slavery, Memory, and Reconciliation at Georgetown." Georgetown University, September 1, 2016. https:// president.georgetown.edu/slavery-memory-reconciliation-september -2016/#.

Depuydt, Peter. "The Mortgaging of Souls: Sugar, Slaves, and Speculation." *Louisiana History: The Journal of the Louisiana Historical Association* 54, no. 4 (Fall 2013): 448–64.

Devitt, Edward. "History of the Maryland–New York Province: St. Inigoes, St. Mary's County, Maryland, 1634–1915." *Woodstock Letters* 40, no. 2 (1931): 199–376.

Diamant, Jeff, Besheer Mohamed, and Joshua Alvarado. "Black Catholics in America." Pew Research Center, March 15, 2022. https://pewrsr.ch /3wpoiYj.

"The Doctrine of Discovery, 1493: A Spotlight on a Primary Source by Pope Alexander VI." The Gilder Lehrman Institute of American History, https://www.gilderlehrman.org/history-resources/spotlight-primary -source/doctrine-discovery-1493.

Doorley, Michael. "Irish Catholics and French Creoles: Ethnic Struggles Within the Catholic Church in New Orleans, 1835–1920." *Catholic Historical Review* 87, no. 1 (2001): 34–54.

"Do You Think You Might Have a Connection to the 1838 Slave Sale That Kept Georgetown Afloat?," *New York Times,* April 16, 2016. https://www .nytimes.com/interactive/2016/04/16/us/georgetown-university -descendants-of-slaves.html.

Duhamel, Elizabeth. "Col. Darnall and His Family." *Records of the Columbia Historical Society* 26 (1924): 123–45.

Earle, Swepson. *The Chesapeake Bay Country.* Baltimore, MD: Thomsen-Ellis, 1924.

"Endowment of Tears, Hope for Reconciliation: Georgetown Prep and Slavery." Georgetown Preparatory School, 2020. https://www.gprep.org/about /history/gu272.

Endres, David J. "Rectifying the Fatal Contrast: Archbishop John Purcell and the Slavery Controversy Among Catholics in Civil War Cincinnati." *Ohio Valley History* 2, no. 2 (March 2002): 23–33.

"Ephesians, Chapter 6." United States Conference of Catholic Bishops. https://bible.usccb.org/bible/ephesians/6.

Pope Eugene IV. "Sicut Dudum Against the Enslaving of Black Natives from the Canary Islands." 1435. Papal Encyclicals Online. https://www .papalencyclicals.net/eugene04/eugene04sicut.htm.

Farrelly, Maura Jane. "American Slavery, American Freedom, American Catholicism." *Early American Studies* 10, no. 1 (2012): 69–100.

Fede, Andrew T. "Not the Most Insignificant Justice: Reconsidering Justice Gabriel Duvall's Slavery Law Opinions Favoring Liberty." *Journal of Supreme Court History* 42, no. 1 (January 2017): 7–27. https://doi.org/10.1111/jsch .12132.

Finn, Peter C. "The Slaves of the Jesuits in Maryland." PhD dissertation, Georgetown University, 1974.

Flanagan, Charles M. "The Sweets of Independence: A Reading of the 'James Carroll Day Book, 1714–1721.' " PhD dissertation, University of Maryland, 2005, https://drum.lib.umd.edu/bitstream/handle/1903/2456/umi -umd-2323.pdf?sequence=1&isAllowed=y.

Foner, Eric. *Reconstruction: America's Unfinished Revolution, 1863–1877.* New American Nation Series. New York: Perennial Classics, 2002.

Forret, Jeff. *Williams' Gang: A Notorious Slave Trader and His Cargo of Black Convicts.* Cambridge, UK: Cambridge University Press, 2019.

Frederick, David C. "John Quincy Adams, Slavery, and the Disappearance of the Right of Petition." *Law and History Review* 9, no. 1 (1991): 113–55. https://doi.org/10.2307/743661.

"Frederick Douglass Reunites with His Brother Perry After 40 Years Separation." *Loyal Georgian,* July 28, 1867. Last Seen: Finding Family After Slavery. https://informationwanted.org/items/show/3671.

"Frequently Requested Church Statistics: U.S. Data over Time," Center for Applied Research in the Apostolate, 2022.

Frey, Sylvia R., and Marian J. Morton. *New World, New Roles: A Documentary History of Women in Pre-Industrial America.* Contributions in Women's Studies, no. 65. New York: Greenwood Press, 1986.

"Full Report of Adam Marshall on Financial Condition of Province, 1820–1824." Maryland Province Archives, Maryland Province Archives of the Society of Jesus, Box 60, Folder 7, Booth Family Center for Special Collections, Georgetown University Library, Washington, DC.

"Georgetown Apologizes for 1838 Sale of More than 270 Enslaved, Dedicates Buildings." Georgetown University, April 18, 2017. https://www .georgetown.edu/news/georgetown-apologizes-for-1838-sale-of-272-slaves -dedicates-buildings/.

"Georgetown College." *United States Telegraph,* September 11, 1830.

"Georgetown College, District of Columbia." *United States Telegraph,* September 22, 1829.

Georgetown Slavery Archive, "Proslavery Oration by Rev. James Ryder, SJ, August 30, 1835." GSA. http://slaveryarchive.georgetown.edu/items /show/88.

Gerbner, Katharine. "Slavery in the Quaker World." *Friends Journal,* September 1, 2019, https://www.friendsjournal.org/slavery-in-the-quaker -world/.

Gleason, Philip. "From an Indefinite Homogeneity: Catholic Colleges in Antebellum America." *Catholic Historical Review* 94, no. 1 (January 2008): 45–74. https://doi.org/10.1353/cat.2008.0047.

Green, William. *Narrative of Events in the Life of William Green, (Formerly a Slave.) Written by Himself.* Springfield, IL: L. M. Guernsey, 1853. https:// docsouth.unc.edu/neh/greenw/greenw.html.

Grivno, Max L. *Gleanings of Freedom: Free and Slave Labor Along the Mason-Dixon Line, 1790–1860.* Urbana: University of Illinois Press, 2011.

A Guide to the History of Slavery in Maryland. Maryland State Archives, 2020.

Hair, P.E.H. "A Jesuit Document on African Enslavement." *Slavery & Abolition* 19, no. 3 (December 1, 1998): 118–27. https://doi.org/10.1080 /01440399808575258.

"Hanged, Slaves by Date, 1726–1775." Maryland State Archives, https://msa .maryland.gov/megafile/msa/speccol/sc2900/sc2908/000001/000819/pdf /chart28.pdf.

Hawkins, Lee, and Douglas Belkin. "For Georgetown, Jesuits and Slavery Descendants, Bid for Racial Healing Sours over Reparations." *Wall Street Journal,* March 25, 2022.

The Heights, Volume VI, Number 24–24 March 1925, Accessed December 22, 2021. https://newspapers.bc.edu/?a=d&d=bcheights19250324&.

Heitman, Francis B. *Historical Register and Dictionary of the United States Army, 1789–1903,* Vol. 1. Washington, DC: Government Printing Office, 1903.

Hennesey, James J. *American Catholics: A History of the Roman Catholic Community in the United States.* Oxford, UK: Oxford University Press, 1983.

"History and Traditions." Loyola University Maryland. https://www.loyola
.edu/about/history-traditions.

Hoffman, Ronald. *Princes of Ireland, Planters of Maryland: A Carroll Saga, 1500–1782.* Chapel Hill: University of North Carolina Press and the Omo-hundro Institute of Early American History and Culture, 2002.

Horton, Tom. "Woodstock Resident to Mark 100 Years." *Baltimore Sun,* August 4, 1972.

Hughes, Thomas. *History of the Society of Jesus in North America, Colonial and Federal.* Vol. 1: *1605–1838.* Cleveland: Burrows Brothers Company, 1908.

———. *History of the Society of Jesus in North America, Colonial and Federal.* Vol. 2: *1605–1838.* New York: Longmans, Green, 1910.

———. "History of the Society of Jesus in North America, Colonial and Federal Text." Vol. 3: "From 1773 till 1822." Unpublished. Maryland Province Archives of the Society of Jesus, Booth Family Center for Special Collections, Georgetown University Library, Washington, DC, n.d.

Hynson, Jerry M. *Free African-Americans of Maryland, 1832.* Westminster, MD: Heritage Books, 2007.

"John Quincy Adams: Gag Rule Controversy, Question of Non-reception, House of Representatives, Monday, January 9, 1837," Wake Forest University. https://users.wfu.edu/zulick/340/gagrule1.html.

"Johnson, Henry." US House of Representatives. https://history.house.gov /People/Listing/J/JOHNSON,-Henry-(J000137)/.

Johnson, Robert Underwood, and Clarence Clough Buel, eds. *Battles and Leaders of the Civil War: Being for the Most Part Contributions by Union and Confederate Officers.* Vol. 2. Thomas Yoseloff, 1956. https://ehistory.osu.edu /books/battles/vol2.

Johnson, Walter. *Soul by Soul: Life Inside the Antebellum Slave Market.* Cambridge, MA: Harvard University Press, 1999.

Judge, Robert K. "First Years of the Maryland Province." *Woodstock Letters* 88, no. 4 (November 1959): 376–406.

Kauffman, Christopher J. *Tradition and Transformation in Catholic Culture: The Priests of Saint Sulpice in the United States from 1791 to the Present.* New York: MacMillan Publishing, 1988.

Kendi, Ibram X. *Stamped from the Beginning: The Definitive History of Racist Ideas in America.* New York: Bold Type Books, 2016.

Kimmel, Ross. "Blacks Before the Law in Colonial Maryland," chap. 4. MA thesis, University of Maryland, 1974. https://msa.maryland.gov/msa /speccol/sc5300/sc5348/html/chap4.html.

King, Julia, Skylar A. Bauer, and Alex J. Flick. "The Politics of Landscape in Seventeenth-Century Maryland." *Maryland Historical Magazine* 3, no. 1 (Spring–Summer 2016): 6–41.

Kolchin, Peter. *American Slavery, 1619–1877.* New York: Hill and Wang, 2003.

Kulikoff, Allan. *Tobacco and Slaves: The Development of Southern Cultures in the Chesapeake, 1680–1800.* Chapel Hill: University of North Carolina Press, 1986.

Kuzniewski, Anthony J. "'Our American Champions': The First American Generation of American Jesuit Leaders After the Restoration of the Society." *Studies in the Spirituality of Jesus* 46, no. 1 (2014).

LaFarge, John. *The Manner Is Ordinary*. New York: Harcourt, 1954.

———. *The Manner Is Ordinary*. New York: Image Books, 1957.

Lapomarda, Vincent A. *The Jesuit Heritage in New England*. Worcester, Mass.: Holy Cross College, 1977.

Leon, Sharon M. "Enslaved People Owned by the Jesuits." Life and Labor Under Slavery: The Jesuit Plantation Project. http://jesuitplantationproject .org/s/jpp/item?item_set_id=11&sort_by=bio:birth&sort_order=desc.

———. "Jesuit Slaveholding." Life and Labor Under Slavery: The Jesuit Plantation Project, February 9, 2019. https://jesuitplantationproject.org/s/jpp /page/sj-slaveholding.

Lythgoe, Darrin, "Henry Darnell, 1645–1711," Early Colonial Settlers of Southern Maryland and Virginia's Northern Neck Counties. https://www .colonial-settlers-md-va.us/getperson.php?personID=I2149&tree=Tree1.

Mann, Alison T. "'Horrible Barbarity': The 1837 Murder Trial of Dorcas Allen, a Georgetown Slave." *Washington History* 27, no. 1 (Spring 2015): 3–14.

———. "Slavery Exacts an Impossible Price: John Quincy Adams and the Dorcas Allen Case, Washington, DC." PhD dissertation, University of New Hampshire, 2010.

Mannard, Joseph G. "'We Are Determined to Be White Ladies': Race, Identity and the Maryland Tradition in Antebellum Visitation Convents." *Maryland Historical Magazine* 109, no. 2 (Summer 2014): 133–57.

Marchand, Sidney A. *The Story of Ascension Parish, Louisiana*. J. E. Ortlieb, 1931.

Marine, William Matthew, and Louis Henry Dielman. *The British Invasion of Maryland, 1812–1815*. Wentworth Press, 2016.

Marks, Bayly Ellen. "Economics and Society in a Staple Plantation System: St. Marys County, Maryland, 1790–1840." PhD dissertation, University of Maryland, 1979.

Maryland Province Archives. "'The Power of Managers to Dispose Unruly Slaves,' May 24, 1803." Proceedings of the Corporation of Roman Catholic Clergymen, May 24, 1803, Box 24, Folder 1, Maryland Province Archives, Booth Family Center for Special Collections, Georgetown University. GSA, May 24, 1803. https://slaveryarchive.georgetown.edu/items/show /358.

"Maryland State Colonization Society." Legacy of Slavery in Maryland. http://slavery.msa.maryland.gov/html/casestudies/mscscountycs.html.

Masci, David, and Gregory A. Smith. "7 Facts About U.S. Catholics." Pew Research Center. https://www.pewresearch.org/fact-tank/2018/10/10/7 -facts-about-american-catholics/.

Masur, Kate. *Until Justice Be Done: America's First Civil Rights Movement, from the Revolution to Reconstruction*. New York: W. W. Norton, 2021.

Masur, Laura E. "A Spiritual Inheritance: Black Catholics in Southern Mary-land." *International Symposia on Jesuit Studies,* no. 2019, Symposium (March 1, 2021). https://doi.org/10.51238/ISJS.2019.10.

Maxwell, John Francis. *Slavery and the Catholic Church: The History of Catholic Teaching Concerning the Moral Legitimacy of the Institution of Slavery.* London: Barry Rose, 1975.

McClure, Olivia. "About 500 Descendants of Slaves Sold by Jesuit Priests Gather for Unique Reunion in Iberville Parish." *Advocate,* June 9, 2018. https://www.theadvocate.com/baton_rouge/news/article_45306f18-6a72-11e8-9f0c-8f0c93ceb080.html.

McGreevy, John T. *Catholicism: A Global History from the French Revolution to Pope Francis.* New York: W. W. Norton, 2022.

———. *Catholicism and American Freedom: A History.* New York: W. W. Norton, 2004.

McKenna, Horace B. "Colored Catholics in St. Mary's County." *Woodstock Letters* 79, no. 1 (1950): 55–78.

McPherson, James M. *Battle Cry of Freedom: The Civil War Era.* Oxford, UK: Oxford University Press, 2003.

McSherry, William, Andrew White, and N. C. Brooks. *A Relation of the Colony of the Lord Baron of Baltimore, in Maryland, Near Virginia: A Narrative of the Voyage to Maryland.* Force, Peter. Tracts, v. 4, no. 12. Washington, DC: W. Q. Force, 1846.

Mendelsohn, Joyce, and James E. Garrity. "History." Basilica of St. Patrick's Old Cathedral. https://oldcathedral.org/history.

Mintz, S., and McNeil, S. "The Growth of Political Factionalism and Sectionalism, Panic of 1819." Digital History. https://www.digitalhistory.uh.edu/disp_textbook.cfm?smtID=2&psid=3531.

Morrissey, Thomas J. *As One Sent: Peter Kenney SJ, 1779–1841: His Mission in Ireland and North America.* Blackrock, Co. Dublin: Four Courts Press, 1996.

The Mulledy/Healy Legacy Committee. "What We Know: Report to the President of the College of the Holy Cross." College of the Holy Cross, March 18, 2016. https://www.holycross.edu/sites/default/files/files/mulledy-healy/mulledycommitteereportfinal.pdf.

Murphy, Thomas. *Jesuit Slaveholding in Maryland, 1717–1838.* New York: Routledge, 2016.

Nalezyty, Susan. "The History of Enslaved People at Georgetown Visitation." *U.S. Catholic Historian* 37, no. 2 (2019): 23–48. https://doi.org/10.1353/cht.2019.0014.

Noonan, John T. "Development in Moral Doctrine." *Theological Studies* 54, no. 4 (December 1993): 662–77. https://doi.org/10.1177/004056399305400404.

Northup, Solomon. *Twelve Years a Slave.* New York: 37 Ink, 2013.

———. *Twelve Years a Slave: Narrative of Solomon Northup, a Citizen of New-York, Kidnapped in Washington City in 1841, and Rescued in 1853.* Electronic Edition. Chapel Hill: University of North Carolina at Chapel Hill, 1997.

O'Donnell, Catherine. "John Carroll and the Origins of an American Catholic Church, 1783–1815." *William and Mary Quarterly* 68, no. 1 (2011): 101. https://doi.org/10.5309/willmaryquar.68.1.0101.

"The Old Generation of Ascension." *Donaldsonville* [LA] *Chief,* August 19, 1882. https://www.newspapers.com/clip/31654037/the-old-generation-of-ascension-part-1/.

O'Malley, John W. *The First Jesuits.* Cambridge, MA: Harvard University Press, 1995.

Orique, David Thomas. *Bartolomé de Las Casas, OP: History, Philosophy, and Theology in the Age of European Expansion.* Leiden: Brill, 2018.

Otterbein, Miriam. "Born of Slave Parents, 100-Year-Old Woodstock Man Lauds Freedom." *Community Times,* August 10, 1972.

Papenfuse, Edward C. "A Biographical Dictionary of the Maryland Legislature 1635–1789." Vol. 426, p. 597. Maryland State Archives, https://msa.maryland.gov/megafile/msa/speccol/sc2900/sc2908/000001/000426/html/am426–879.html.

Papenfuse, Eric Robert. "From Redcompense to Revolution: Mahoney v. Ashton and the Transfiguration of Maryland Culture, 1791–1802." *Slavery & Abolition* 15, no. 3 (December 1994): 38–62. https://doi.org/10.1080/01440399408575138.

Parsons, J. Wilfrid. "Rev. Anthony Kohlmann, S.J. (1771–1824)." *Catholic Historical Review* 4, no. 1 (April 1918): 38–51.

"Pope Nicolas V and the Portuguese Slave Trade." Lowcountry Digital History Initiative. https://ldhi.library.cofc.edu/exhibits/show/african_laborers_for_a_new_emp/pope_nicolas_v_and_the_portugu.

Pope Paul III. "Sublimus Deus: On the Enslavement and Evangelization of Indians." 1537. Papal Encyclicals Online. https://www.papalencyclicals.net/paulo3/p3subli.htm.

The Portal to Jesuit Studies. https://jesuitportal.bc.edu/publications/symposia/2019symposium/symposia-masur/.

Pound, DaNean Olene. "Slave to the Ex-Slave Narratives." Master's thesis, Northwestern State University of Louisiana, 2005.

Power, Garrett. "Calvert Versus Carroll: The Quit-Rent Controversy Between Maryland's Founding Families." Digital Commons, March 30, 2005. https://digitalcommons.law.umaryland.edu/fac_pubs/44.

Radcliffe, Nancy. "St. Mary's County Slave Revolt of 1817: Possible Religious Connections," November 13, 1996.

Register, Woody, and Benjamin King. "A Research Summary on Slavery and Race at the University of the South and in the Community of Sewanee." Sewanee, the University of the South. https://new.sewanee.edu/roberson-project/learn-more/research-summary/.

Reid, Patricia A. "The Legal Construction of Whiteness and Citizenship in Maryland, 1780–1820." *Law, Culture and the Humanities* 15, no. 3 (October 2019): 656–83. https://doi.org/10.1177/1743872116652886.

"Rev. John Ashton (b. circa 1742–d. 1815)." Maryland State Archives, http://

msa.maryland.gov/megafile/msa/speccol/sc5400/sc5496/041700/041715
/html/041715bio.html.

Ridgeway, Michael A. "A Peculiar Business: Slave Trading in Alexandria,
Virginia, 1825–1861." MA thesis, Georgetown University, 1976.

Riffel, Judy. "Bibiana Mahoney Report." Georgetown Memory Project.

———. "Descendants of Jones, Arnold." GU272 Memory Project, American
Ancestors. https://gu272.americanancestors.org/family/jones.

———. "History of Marengo Plantation." Report, Georgetown Memory
Project.

———. "Union Soldiers among the GMP Ancestor and Descendants Database." Report, Georgetown Memory Project.

———. "The Mahoney Family." GU272 Memory Project, American Ancestors. https://gu272.americanancestors.org/family/mahoney.

Riffel, Judy, and Cellini, Richard. "Henry Johnson and the Founding of
Sewanee." Georgetown Memory Project, March 23, 2020.

"Riot Among the Negroes in St. Mary's." *Daily National Intelligencer,* April 18,
1817.

Rodrigue, John C. *Reconstruction in the Cane Fields: From Slavery to Free Labor
in Louisiana's Sugar Parishes, 1862–1880.* Baton Rouge: Louisiana State University Press, 2001.

Rothman, Adam. "The Jesuits and Slavery." *Journal of Jesuit Studies* 8, no. 1
(December 15, 2020): 1–10. https://doi.org/10.1163/22141332-0801P001.

———. " 'Nothing to Stay Here For': How Enslaved People Helped to Put
Slavery to Death in New Orleans." *Slate,* September 22, 2015. https://slate
.com/human-interest/2015/09/the-end-of-slavery-in-new-orleans.html.

Rothman, Joshua D. *The Ledger and the Chain: How Domestic Slave Traders
Shaped America.* New York: Basic Books, 2021.

Ruane, Michael E. "New Orleans Seethed Under Union Occupation." *Washington Post,* May 19, 2017.

Ruffner, Malissa. "Identification of St. Thomas Manor Priests as Slaveholders:
1830 Through 1860 Censuses." Baltimore, MD, 2016.

———. "St. Mary's County Plantation Census Analysis." Baltimore, MD,
August 24, 2016.

———. "Whitemarsh Plantation Census Analysis." Baltimore, Md, September 5, 2016.

Ryan, John J. *Historical Sketch of Loyola College, Baltimore, 1852–1902.* 1903.
http://archive.org/details/historicalsketchooryan.

Sacher, John M. *A Perfect War of Politics: Parties, Politicians, and Democracy in
Louisiana, 1824–1861.* Baton Rouge: Louisiana State University Press, 2003.

Samford, Patricia. "Mattapany-Sewall." Jefferson Patterson Park & Museum,
State Museum of Archaeology, 2016. https://apps.jefpat.maryland.gov
/mdunearth/SiteSummaries/Site18ST390.aspx.

Scammell, Geoffrey V. *The Imperial Age: European Overseas Expansion,
1500–1715.* New York: Routledge, 2003.

Schermerhorn, Calvin. *The Business of Slavery and the Rise of American Capitalism, 1815–1860.* New Haven, CT: Yale University Press, 2015.

————. "The Maritime United States Slave Trade, 1807–1850." *Journal of Social History* 47, no. 4 (Summer 2014).

Schmidt, Anna Marie. "The Political Career of Henry Johnson." MA thesis, Louisiana State University, 1935.

Schmidt, Kelly L. "'Without Slaves and Without Assassins': Antebellum Cincinnati, Transnational Jesuits, and the Challenges of Race and Slavery." *U.S. Catholic Historian* 39, no. 2 (2021): 1–26. https://doi.org/10.1353/cht.2021.0010.

Schroth, Raymond A. *The American Jesuits: A History.* New York: New York University Press, 2007.

"Searching for Truth in the Garden: Gonzaga's History with Slavery," Gonzaga College High School, 2019. https://www.gonzaga.org/about/history/slavery-research-project.

Seward, William Henry. *Life and Public Services of John Quincy Adams: Sixth President of the United States.* Miller, Orton & Mulligan, 1856.

Shea, John Gilmary. *Memorial of the First Century of Georgetown College, D.C.* New York: P. F. Collier, 1891.

"Sixteen Dollars Reward." *Maryland Gazette,* January 8, 1798. Maryland State Archives. https://msa.maryland.gov/megafile/msa/speccol/sc5400/sc5496/041700/041715/images/19980108mdg1.pdf.

Smith, H. C. *The Darnall, Darnell Family. Including Darneal, Darneille, Darnielle, Darnold, Dernall, Durnall, Durnell, and Names Variously Spelled, with Allied Families.* Vol. 1. Los Angeles: American Offset Printers, 1954.

Smyth, Patrick. *The Present State of the Catholic Mission, Conducted by the Ex-Jesuits in North America.* Dublin: P. Byrne, 1788.

Spalding, Thomas W. *The Premier See: A History of the Archdiocese of Baltimore, 1789–1989.* Baltimore, MD: Johns Hopkins University Press, 1989.

Spencer, Richard Henry. *Genealogical and Memorial Encyclopedia of the State of Maryland: A Record of the Achievements of Her People in the Making of a Commonwealth and the Founding of a Nation.* New York: American Historical Society, 1919.

Stroyer, Jacob. *My Life in the South.* Salem, NC: Salem Observer Book and Job Print, 1885.

Svrluga, Susan. "Descendants of Slaves Sold to Benefit Georgetown Call for a $1 Billion Foundation for Reconciliation." *Washington Post,* September 9, 2016. https://www.washingtonpost.com/news/grade-point/wp/2016/09/08/descendants-of-slaves-sold-by-georgetown-call-for-a-1-billion-foundation-for-reconciliation/.

Swarns, Rachel L. "272 Slaves Were Sold to Save Georgetown. What Does It Owe Their Descendants?" *New York Times,* April 16, 2016. https://www.nytimes.com/2016/04/17/us/georgetown-university-search-for-slave-descendants.html.

————. "A Catholic Order Pledged $100 Million to Atone for Taking Part in the Slave Trade. Some Descendants Want a New Deal." *New York Times,* April 17, 2021. https://www.nytimes.com/2021/04/17/us/catholic-church-jesuits-reparations.html.

————. "Catholic Order Pledges $100 Million to Atone for Slave Labor." *New York Times*, March 15, 2021. https://www.nytimes.com/2021/03/15 /us/jesuits-georgetown-reparations-slavery.html.

————. "Georgetown University Plans Steps to Atone for Slave Past." *New York Times*, September 1, 2016. https://www.nytimes.com/2016/09/02/us /slaves-georgetown-university.html.

————. "Intent on a Reckoning with Georgetown's Slavery-Stained Past." *New York Times*, July 11, 2016. https://www.nytimes.com/2016/07/11/us /intent-on-a-reckoning-with-georgetowns-slavery-stained-past.html.

————. "Is Georgetown's $400,000-a-Year Plan to Aid Slave Descendants Enough?" *New York Times*, October 30, 2019. https://www.nytimes.com /2019/10/30/us/georgetown-slavery-reparations.html.

————. "The Nuns Who Bought and Sold Human Beings." *New York Times*, August 2, 2019. https://www.nytimes.com/2019/08/02/opinion/sunday /nuns-slavery.html.

————. "The Seminary Flourished on Slave Labor. Now It's Planning to Pay Reparations." *New York Times*, September 12, 2019. https://www.nytimes .com/2019/09/12/us/virginia-seminary-reparations.html.

Swisher, Howard Llewellyn. *History of Hampshire County, West Virginia: From Its Earliest Settlement to the Present*. Morgantown, WV: A. B. Boughner, 1897.

Tanner, Lynette Ater, ed. *Chained to the Land: Voices from Cotton & Cane Plantations: From Interviews of Former Slaves*. Winston-Salem, NC: John F. Blair, 2014.

Thomas, William G. "Charles Mahoney v. John Ashton. Special Verdict from October 1797 Trial." O Say Can You See: Early Washington, D.C., Law & Family. https://earlywashingtondc.org/doc/oscys.mdcase.0008.048.

————. *A Question of Freedom: The Families Who Challenged Slavery from the Nation's Founding to the Civil War*. New Haven, CT: Yale University Press, 2020.

Toole, Sean. "Institutional Peculiarity: Jesuit Slave Trading in Maryland." MA thesis, Santa Clara University, 2015.

Ulshafer, Thomas R. "Slavery and the Early Sulpician Community in Maryland." *U.S. Catholic Historian* 37 (Summer 2019): 1–21.

Vlach, John Michael. "'Snug Li'l House with Flue and Oven': Nineteenth-Century Reforms in Plantation Slave Housing." *Perspectives in Vernacular Architecture* 5 (1995): 118–29. https://doi.org/10.2307/3514250.

Walsh, Francis Michael. "Resurrection: The Story of the St. Inigoes Mission, 1634–1994," 2016.

Warner, William W. *At Peace with Their Neighbors: Catholics and Catholicism in the National Capital, 1787–1860*. Washington, DC: Georgetown University Press, 1994.

"What We Have Learned: Missouri." Jesuit Conference of Canada and the U.S. https://www.jesuits.org/our-work/shmr/what-we-have-learned /missouri/.

Wheeler, Peter and Charles Lester Edwards. *Chains and Freedom: Or, The Life and Adventures of Peter Wheeler, a Colored Man Yet Living. A Slave in Chains, a Sailor on the Deep, and a Sinner at the Cross.* New York: E.S. Arnold & Co, 1839.

Wiggins, David K. "The Play of Slave Children in the Plantation Communities of the Old South, 1820–1860." *Journal of Sport History* 7, no. 2 (Summer 1980): 21–39.

Wilder, Craig Steven. "War and Priests; Catholic Colleges and Slavery in the Age of Revolution." In *Slavery's Capitalism: A New History of American Economic Development.* Edited by Sven Beckert and Seth Rothman, 227–42. Philadelphia: University of Pennsylvania Press, 2018.

Woodstock Letters 78, no. 1 (February 1950). https://jesuitonlinelibrary.bc.edu/?a=d&d=wlet19500201-01&.

Working Group on Slavery, Memory, and Reconciliation. *Report of the Working Group on Slavery, Memory, and Reconciliation to the President of Georgetown University.* Washington, DC: Georgetown University, 2016.

Works Progress Administration. *Slave Narratives: A Folk History of Slavery in the United States From Interviews with Former Slaves: Indiana Narratives.* Project Gutenberg EBook, 2004: https://www.gutenberg.org/files/13579/13579-8.txt.

Zanca, Kenneth J., ed. *American Catholics and Slavery, 1789–1866: An Anthology of Primary Documents.* Lanham, MD: University Press of America, 1994.

Zwinge, Joseph. "The Jesuit Farms in Maryland, Facts and Anecdotes." *Woodstock Letters* 39, no. 3 (1910): 374–82.

———. "The Jesuit Farms in Maryland, Facts and Anecdotes." *Woodstock Letters* 41, no. 2 (1912): 195–222.

———. "The Jesuit Farms in Maryland, Facts and Anecdotes." *Woodstock Letters* 42, no. 1. (1913): 1–13.

———. "The Jesuit Farms in Maryland, Facts and Anecdotes: The Negro Slaves." *Woodstock Letters* 41, no. 3 (1912): 276–91.

———. "The Jesuit Farms in Maryland, Facts and Anecdotes: The War of 1812." *Woodstock Letters* 42, no. 3 (1913): 336–52.

Index

About the Author

RACHEL L. SWARNS is a professor of journalism at New York University and a contributing writer for *The New York Times*. She is the author of *American Tapestry: The Story of the Black, White, and Multiracial Ancestors of Michelle Obama* and a co-author of *Unseen: Unpublished Black History from the New York Times Photo Archives*. Her work has been recognized and supported by the National Endowment for the Humanities, the Ford Foundation, the Biographers International Organization, the Leon Levy Center for Biography, the MacDowell artist residency program, and others.

rachelswarns.com
Facebook.com/rachel.l.swarns/
Twitter: @rachelswarns

About the Type

This book was set in Bembo, a typeface based on an old-style Roman face that was used for Cardinal Pietro Bembo's tract *De Aetna* in 1495. Bembo was cut by Francesco Griffo (1450–1518) in the early sixteenth century for Italian Renaissance printer and publisher Aldus Manutius (1449–1515). The Lanston Monotype Company of Philadelphia brought the well-proportioned letterforms of Bembo to the United States in the 1930s.